Visions of Glory

VISIONS *of* GLORY

An Anthology of Reflections

Compiled by William Sykes

 The Bible Reading Fellowship

Compilation and introductions
copyright © William Sykes 1995

The author asserts the moral right
to be identified as the author of this work

Published by
The Bible Reading Fellowship
Peter's Way
Sandy Lane West
Oxford OX4 5HG
ISBN 0 7459 2977 X
Albatross Books Pty Ltd
PO Box 320, Sutherland
NSW 2232, Australia
ISBN 0 7324 0902 0

First edition 1995

Acknowledgments

Unless otherwise stated, Scripture is taken from
The Revised Standard Version of the Bible,
copyright © 1946, 1952, 1971 by the Division of
Christian Education of the National Council of the
Churches of Christ in the USA.

Extracts are reproduced by permission of the
publishers, or, in some cases, by permission of
the holders of the rights of reproduction.

Extracts from the Authorized Bible (The King
James Bible) the rights in which are invested in
the Crown, are reproduced by permission of the
Crown's patentee, Cambridge University Press.

New English Bible © 1970 by permission of
Oxford and Cambridge University Presses.

Every effort has been made to trace and contact
copyright owners. If there are any inadvertent
omissions in the acknowledgments we apologize
to those concerned.

A catalogue record for this book is available
from the British Library

Printed in Great Britain by
J. W. Arrowsmith Ltd, Bristol

Contents

Preface	7	Grace	108	Pride	204
Introduction	11	Guidance	112		
				Reconciliation	208
Agnosticism	15	Heaven	117	Redemption	211
Atheism	18	Hell	121	Religion	214
		Holy Spirit	124	Renunciation	218
Baptism	22			Repentance	221
Belief	25	Image of God	129	Resurrection	224
Bible	28	Incarnation	133	Revelation	228
		Inner life	136		
Christian	33	Intercession	140	Salvation	233
Church	36			Service	237
Commitment	40	Jesus Christ	143	Sin	241
Conversion	43	Judgment	147	Sons of God	245
Creation	47			Soul	248
Cross	50	Kingdom of God	151	Suffering	252
		Knowledge	155		
Death	55			Temptation	257
Divinity	59	Life	159	Thanksgiving	260
Doubt	63	Light	162	Theology	263
Dying to self	66			Trinity	267
		Man	167	Trust	270
Eternal life	71	Meditation	171	Truth	274
Evil	74	Miracles	174		
Experience	78	Mystics and		Union	278
		mysticism	177		
Faith	83			Vocation	282
Fellowship	86	Obedience	182		
Finding God	90	Other faiths	185	The way	286
Forgiveness	94			Will	290
Fulfilment	97	Paradise	190	Wisdom	293
		Power	193	Worship	296
Glory	101	Prayer	196		
God	104	Presence	200	Index	300

Preface

A READER'S VIEW

Steve Sheppard teaches law in Michigan in the United States. He was at University College, Oxford, pursuing his D.Phil. from 1989 to 1992. He has written prefaces for *Visions of Hope* and *Visions of Love*. This is what he has now written about *Visions of Glory*...

The Oxford student may be the most cynical and sceptical animal to roam the earth. In the midst of a brooding mass of such creatures, Bill Sykes roams as something of a zookeeper, dispensing calm insight over a cup of coffee to a surprising number of them. This book is part of his remarkable success.

Bill Sykes has grappled with our demons—not the hoary Old Testament demons of Hollywood movies, but the mundane, modern demons that stalk our minds in the early hours with doubt and fear. This extraordinary book, and its two companion volumes, are a record of his struggles, taken from his readings across the spectrum of writings of saints and sinners, arrayed in topics for reflection. Each topic is introduced by our sturdy pilgrim, placing the idea into the world as he experienced it.

I met Bill when *Visions of Glory* was bound in massive notebooks, heaped behind the couch in his rooms in college. I and my confederates would meet for our ominously named 'reflection group' weekly during the academic term, and we would haul these tomes out to consider their themes. We were rarely prepared to admit how eagerly we sought these meetings. We were not easily focused on the role of 'belief', 'heaven' or 'hell' in our own lives, at least not in front of witnesses. We would much rather sort out the lives of everyone else. Eventually, someone would volunteer a topic from the index, and we would each nurse cups of Bill's tea whilst silently digesting the material from these pages for twenty minutes. With Bill's gentle prodding, the discussion would begin, the student on the hot seat inventing a quick lie to explain why the topic was chosen. The conversations that followed could be predictable, but at times they were a furnace of inspiration, driven by these readings and catalysed by Bill's insightful questions.

When I left Oxford a few years ago, with my doctoral thesis above me in its Damoclean way, I thought I had left the reflection group behind. I was, happily, wrong, and when *Visions of Love* was published, I found that it re-entered my life like an old friend. Last year, Bill released *Visions of Hope*, the second volume. I had given many copies of *Visions of Love* as gifts, and I was delighted to find that nearly every person who had read the first volume wanted the second as well. I'd also been asked by many people how to find the other books. (This was a problem in the States at first because of the book's British distribution.) I had a largish crate of *Visions of Hope* sent over, which turned out to be nowhere near enough for demand. Bill's project is splendid, and each book complements the others in a rather seductive way.

The best part of all this is that the books continue to animate those who read them. Even among my less speculative friends, *Visions* have sparked some wonderful insights.

Visions of Glory weaves the final threads of a rich tapestry, a journey by a surprisingly reverend priest across the ages of writings in search of his own understanding. I am certain that *Visions of Glory* will guide many, many more on the same pilgrimage.

HOW A SCHOOLMASTER USES AN ANTHOLOGY
OF REFLECTIONS

Robert Aldred is a housemaster at St Edward's School, a boys' boarding school in Oxford. A few years ago his wife, Alison, was the nurse at University College, and working closely in that capacity with the chaplain of the college, Bill Sykes. Through that contact Robert discovered Bill Sykes' first anthology, *Visions of Faith* (now out of print) and from the moment he read it he realized what an invaluable resource it was. He has been using it for various groups in the school ever since and I asked him how.

'I use it in just one way,' he told me. 'We have copies of the book for the boys. We had a set of about forty at one stage, but over the years they have diminished. It is a very stimulating book, and sometimes a boy will say "Can I borrow it?" And he will take it away for a while and then bring it back—but not always!

'What I do is to give them just one section of quotations to look at in one period, which usually lasts for forty minutes. They stay in the classroom and I ask them just to go through the quotations, to think about them, and to make notes. Then the following week they come back and we discuss them. I use the book two or three times a year, and I try to choose subjects which the boys themselves are interested in pursuing.

'Basically, I use the same method that Bill uses himself, in order to get people to think about whatever subject it is, and to meditate upon it. I actually use the word meditate, and I say to them, "To meditate means to chew it over and to thrash it through, to ask yourself whether you agree with it, and to ask yourself: *What is it actually saying? What does it mean by this phrase, and that phrase?*' I find that it raises the intellectual level of discussion to a much more serious one.

'Quite often a group will tend to treat things at the level where they are, which can be rather shallow. But I have found that this book forces them to go to a level which is more mature and more demanding, and there is a greater level of seriousness in the discussion. This year I have got four groups. Three of them are fine, but one is rather hard work, because of the level of input (or the lack of it) from the various members. There is a group within the group who are somewhat immature, and they tend to be flippant and a bit silly. But using Bill's book has forced them to be more thoughtful.

'It is enormously stimulating, and it provides a broad spectrum of types of writing. To give you an example, I wanted to do something with the sixth form on marriage and sexuality, and when I was looking through those sections I found this marvellous quotation from *The Prophet*, by Kahlil Gibran:

> But let there be spaces in your togetherness,
> and let the winds of heaven dance between you.

'Brilliant! First of all I found it strange to see that juxtaposed against the Christian view of marriage. But then I thought, "Well, there's nothing much wrong with that!" And it made me realize how good it was to read people who were writing from all backgrounds, and from all walks of life and all the Church traditions. It's an enlarging experience.

'It is interesting how the pupils invariably pick out that passage from *The Prophet*. And when we are looking at the theme of suffering they almost always pick out the passage said to have been written by a young cancer patient (and often known as 'Footprints'):

> One night a man had a dream. He dreamt he was walking along the beach with his Lord. Across the sky flashed scenes from his life. For each scene he noticed two sets of footprints in the sand, one belonging to him, the other to the Lord. When the last scene in his life flashed before him he looked back at the footprints on the sand. He noticed that many times along the path of his life there was only one set of footprints. He also noticed that it happened at the very lowest and saddest times of his life. This really bothered him, and he questioned the Lord about it. 'Lord, you said that, once I decided to follow you, you would walk with me all the way. But I've noticed that during the most difficult times in my life there is only one set of footprints. I don't understand why, in times when I needed you most, you would leave me.' The Lord replied, 'My precious child, I love you and would never leave you during your trials and sufferings; when you see only one set of footprints, it was then that I carried you.'

The Reverend Shelagh Brown
Bible Reading Fellowship

The story behind *Visions of Glory*
HOW IT CAME INTO BEING AND HOW TO USE IT

A priest who lost his faith

What happens when a priest thinks he has lost his faith? I was thirty years old, and faced with this situation saw three options: leave the Church; stay put in the Church and go through the motions; or stand my ground and fight. I had one thing on my side in making the choice—fresh memories from being a Gurkha officer. I had to fight.

Where he started the fight to find it

I started anew in the Book of Genesis. In the story of the creation of man, God is depicted as fashioning and shaping man in his own image. He breathed into man and man became a living being. I was fascinated by this simple story. I took it to mean that God breathed something of his own nature into man, giving a divine potential to life.

Then I turned to the Gospels and found this 'something of God in man' worked out in the man—Jesus Christ. He found the Father in the depths of himself. He tried to explain this to the disciples: 'Do you not believe that I am in the Father and the Father in me? . . . the Father who dwells in me does his works' (John 14:10). As I struggled with what these words meant, I began to understand Jesus as the image of the invisible God.

Starting to see the way of glory

This understanding brought me a new insight. Jesus discovered not only the presence of 'the Father' in himself, but also discovered that this presence is *glory*, not just as an abstraction, but for people individually: 'And the Word became flesh and dwelt among us, full of grace and truth; we have beheld his glory, glory as of the only Son from the Father' (John 1:14). Jesus spelt out the implications of this verse for us in a crucial passage recorded later on in St John's Gospel: 'The glory which thou hast given me I have to given to them, that they may be one even as we are one, I in them and thou in me, that they may become perfectly one' (17:22–23). The vision of glory was beginning to take shape.

I went back to the Epistles. Paul discovered that what Christ had experienced in his life, we can all experience in some measure. Some time after his conversion on the Damascus road, Paul wrote: 'It is no longer I who live, but Christ who lives in me . . .' (Galatians 2:20). 'In him the whole fullness of deity dwells bodily and you have come to fullness of life in him' (Colossians 2:9–10). I knew this meant much to me, that the whole power of the Trinity could be found in each of us: life, light, truth, joy—and glory! Paul outlines this insight in an important passage: 'That the God of our Lord Jesus Christ, the

Father of glory, may give you a spirit of wisdom and of revelation in the knowledge of him, having the eyes of your hearts enlightened, that you may know what is the hope to which he has called you, what are the riches of his glorious inheritance in the saints, and what is the immeasurable greatness of his power in us who believe, according to the working of his great might' (Ephesians 1:17–19). I held fast to this vision and thought of Christ's words: 'I came that they may have life, and have it abundantly' (John 10:10). But I still felt that I was missing some part of his vision for me.

Dust and divinity

Then something clicked into place: *that which was fashioned and shaped in the image and likeness of God was taken from the dust of the earth.* I saw then that in addition to being born with a 'divine' potential, we are still earthy and creaturely. This was no news to me, but now I saw that if either side was repressed or allowed too much sway the consequences would be negative and destructive.

But how could I make such a balance? I went back again to the Gospels. What do we find in the life of Christ? An integration of the divine and the earthy, the godly and the creaturely—'very God and very man'—a perfect combination of the divine and the human. i now began to understand why he was called 'the second Adam'. By his life, death and resurrection he had pioneered a way of integrating both sides of his nature, and so became the prototype of a new humanity. The vision of glory underlying this anthology finally made sense.

In many people over many years

Granted this vision of glory, I thought I might find evidence of it in the experience of men and women in the last 2,000 years. I started searching for signs of this vision in the thoughts and words of others. First, I sought it in the recorded experience of saints and theologians; secondly, from poets, novelists, playwrights, musicians and artists; thirdly, from philosophers, scientists, states- men, historians, politicians, economists and psychologists.

The material I found has been set out in seventy-six topics. These contain many aspects of glory, and their opposites—with some related topics.

How to grow in the vision

The aim of the anthology is to provide a means to grow in this vision of glory. This is done primarily through the practice of reflection, hence the subtitle, *An Anthology of Reflections.*

The *Concise Oxford Dictionary* defines 'reflection' as to 'go back in thought, meditate, or consult with oneself, remind oneself, or consider'. Reflection indicates a way of thinking with the mind, the imagination, intuition and feelings. It includes 'lateral thinking' and 'vertical thinking'—thinking which takes into account the spiritual dimension. A good description comes from the Collect for the Second Sunday in Advent (a prayer for the study of the Scriptures)... 'Grant that we may in such wise hear them, read, mark, learn and inwardly digest them.' Reflection can have such a devotional aspect, and merge into meditation and contemplation. I hope *Visions of Glory* can be used in many ways—as a book to dip into from time to time—as a bedside book—as a guide in time of need—as an aid to keeping a journal—as a personal book of devotion.

How to run a reflection group

As Chaplain and Fellow of an Oxford college, I have used the material for 'reflection groups'. These have been very popular, and in term-time at least thirty groups of up to five students meet each week.

I have been asked to describe in detail how these groups function. We meet for an hour a week at a mutually convenient time. We begin with a cup of tea, coffee or hot chocolate and briefly catch up on news. A list of topics is circulated and after two or three minutes a topic is chosen by consensus. Each topic consists of an introduction and some twenty quotations, two from the Old Testament, two from the New Testament, and the remaining sixteen from a wide variety of sources. Each person in the group is then given a copy of this material and the reflection group gets under way.

We then have about half an hour of silence. We look through the quotations, thinking them through, and working out what they mean to us individually. Some of our participants are not used to being quiet and find silence difficult at first, so I make available a clipboard, pen and paper. We have found that writing down thoughts and insights has eased this period of silence and been a useful way of developing ideas.

As convenor of the group, I use this half-hour period to go through the quotations in the same way as the others, but in addition to formulate some questions. These can be useful for stimulating discussion in the second half of the reflection group.

At the half-way stage, I ask if everyone has completed the material. I then ask, 'Was there any particular reason for choosing this topic?' Someone usually comes forward with a reason. My next question is: 'Did you find anything helpful?' The person who has chosen the topic responds, and then the other members of the group join in. Having reflected on the same material, conversation comes fairly easily. As convenor, my role is mainly to listen and make sure everyone has an opportunity to contribute. Sometimes the questions formulated by me earlier are a help; often they are not needed. The group ends promptly on the hour. (Time is precious in an eight-week term.)

How a reflection group begins

I usually start a new group with one person. Before long he or she usually suggests a person to join. Sometimes the addition is actually uninterested in religion but a good thinker. Sometimes it is someone committed to a particular creed, often not that of the first in the group. The two of them then invite a third member and so on. So the groups are based on trust and friendship, not orthodoxy. In the groups we have Roman Catholics, Methodists, members of the Church of England, the United Reformed Church, and the Christian Union, and the occasional Jew, Hindu, Muslim, Buddhist, atheist and agnostic.

Sometimes a group doesn't grow. Some people are shy, and are not ready for the group experience. Others want to go forward slowly. A few need individual attention. Some function quite happily in twos and threes. I reckon four or five is the best working number. Trust can still be maintained, and everyone can fully participate. Above this number, communication tends to break down.

I see *Visions of Glory* as a skeleton (or framework) of glory—and I leave it to the individual to put upon it (to clothe it with) his or her own flesh and blood.

Bill Sykes

AGNOSTICISM

Agnosticism—nothing is known, or likely to be known, of the existence of a God or of anything beyond material phenomena

In 1968, I went out to Nigeria for a six-month period to look after a church, whilst the regular priest came home to England on long leave. At that time, Nigeria was caught up in a bitter civil war, but the church I was looking after was just outside Ibadan, 300 miles from the war-front. Here there had been almost no fighting. Life went on much as usual in Ibadan, apart from shortages of food and materials.

I remember one evening being invited out to dinner at the home of a prominent member of the British Council who was also a member of our church. Sitting on my left at the dinner table was an expatriate who wasted no time in letting me know he was an agnostic. He went on to challenge everything I believed in. Whether God was knowable or not certainly came in for a severe battering. He ended up by saying he was only prepared to believe in things that he could see, feel and touch, and was rather scornful of my beliefs and convictions. I tried to hold my own but he came out of the encounter scoring heavily.

Imagine my surprise some eighteen years later to hear a knock on the door of my rooms in Oxford followed by the somewhat cautious entrance of my expatriate friend. To cut a long story short, the dinner had been a turning-point in his life and he was now a man of faith and had recently settled down in Oxford.

He takes away understanding from the chiefs of the people of the earth, and makes them wander in a pathless waste. They grope in the dark without light...

Job 12:24–25

For the hope of the ungodly is like dust that is blown away with the wind.

Wisdom of Solomon 4:14 (AV)

For he that is not against us is for us.

Mark 9:40

For as I passed along, and observed the objects of your worship, I found also an altar with this inscription, 'To an unknown god.'

Acts 17:23

Consciously, I was religious in the Christian sense, though always with this reservation: 'But it is not so certain as all that!'

C.G. Jung, *Memories, Dreams, Reflections*, William Collins Sons & Co., 1971, page 38

As one goes on, it is the things one doesn't believe and finds one doesn't have to believe which are as liberating as the things one does.

John Robinson, *Honest to God*, SCM Press, 1963, page 20

I do not see much difference between avowing that there is no God, and implying that nothing definite can for certain be known about Him.

John Henry Newman, *The Scope and Nature of University Education*, Longman, Green, Longman, and Roberts, 1859, page 46

All intelligent faith in God has behind it a background of humble agnosticism. The ultimate truth about the universe cannot be caught and cabined in our limited minds.

Harry Emerson Fosdick, *Dear Mr Brown*, William Collins Sons & Co., 1962, page 26

Many a humble agnostic, worshipping an unknown God, is nearer to the Kingdom of God than is a theologian confident in *his* theology . . .

Many an 'atheist' is rejecting false conceptions of God which he assumes to be Christian beliefs about Him; many an agnostic has a reverence for the unknown God which puts to shame the pride of a superficial dogmatist.

Frederic Greeves, *The Meaning of Sin*, Epworth Press, 1956, pages 178 and 183

With this virtual negation of God, the universe—to me—has lost its soul of loveliness. And when I think at times, as think at times I must, of the appalling contrast between the hallowed glory of that creed, which once was mine, and the lonely mystery of existence, as I now find it—at such times I shall ever feel it impossible to avoid the sharpest pang of which my nature is susceptible.

Professor Romanes, in C.L. Drawbridge, *Thoughts on Religion*, Robert Scott, 1914, conclusion

There is no doubt that modern scientific and technical progress can lead to a certain phenomenism or agnosticism; this happens when scientific methods of investigation, which of themselves are incapable of penetrating to the deepest nature of things, are unjustifiably taken as the supreme norm for arriving at truth. There is a further danger that in his excessive confidence in modern inventions man may think he is sufficient unto himself and give up the search for higher values.

Vatican Council II, in Austin Flannery, O.P., general editor, *The Conciliar and Post-conciliar Documents*, Fowler Wright Books, 1981, page 962

What can we know? Why is there anything at all? Why not nothing? Where does man come from and where does he go to? Why is the world as it is? What is the ultimate reason and meaning of all reality?

What ought we to do? Why do what we do? Why and to whom are we finally responsible? What deserves forthright contempt and what love? What is the point of loyalty and friendship, but also what is the point of suffering and sin? What really matters for man? What may we hope? Why are we here? What is it all about? What is there left for us: death, making everything pointless at the end? What will give us courage for life and what courage for death?

Immanuel Kant, in Hans Küng, *On Being a Christian*, translated by Edward Quinn, William Collins Sons & Co., 1977, page 75

The greatest problems in the field of history centre in the Person and Life of Christ. Who He was, what He was, how and why He came to be it, are questions that have not lost and will not lose their interest for us and for mankind. For the problems that centre in Jesus have this peculiarity: they are not individual, but general—concern not a person, but the world. How we are to judge Him is not simply a curious point for historical criticism, but a vital matter for religion. Jesus Christ is the most powerful spiritual force that ever operated for good on and in humanity. He is to-day what He has been for centuries—an object of reverence and love to the good, the cause of remorse and change, penitence and hope to the bad; of moral strength to the morally weak, of inspiration to the despondent, consolation to the desolate, and cheer to the dying. He has created the typical virtues and moral ambitions of civilized man; has been to the benevolent a motive to beneficence, to the selfish a living ideal that has steadied and raised, awed and guided youth, braced and ennobled manhood, mellowed and beautified age. In Him the Christian ages have seen the manifested God, the Eternal living in time, the Infinite within the limits of humanity; and their faith has glorified His sufferings into a sacrifice by the Creator for the creature, His death into an atonement for human sin. No other life has done such work, no other person been made to bear such transcendent and mysterious meanings. It is impossible to touch Jesus without touching millions of hearts now living or yet to live. He is, whatever else He may be, as a world's imperishable wonder, a world's everlasting problem, as a pre-eminent object of human faith, a pre-eminent subject of human thought.

A.M. Fairbairn, *Studies in the Life of Christ*, Hodder and Stoughton, 1881, page 2

Are there Two Kinds of Agnostic?

Yes, there are. There are those... who deny that God is knowable; but there are others who say that, while He may be knowable, He isn't known to them.

The distinction is important and deep. If you are an agnostic, you ought to be clear, first, what kind of agnostic you are. To say quite definitely that God can't be known is a bold affirmation. It seems tantamount to saying that 'what I don't know can't be known'. It appears to label the saints and seers and prophets of all ages (whose insights are among the treasures of our race) as sadly misguided men.

A little girl came home from school one day and announced triumphantly: 'I know all the tables; even twelve times.' Her grandpa said, with a twinkle in his eye. 'What is 13 times 13?' and the little girl answered with instant scorn: 'Don't be silly, Grandpa. There is no such thing.'

We can forgive finality in a little girl, but no rational man would claim that the limits of his knowledge were the limits of all knowledge, that because he didn't know a thing, nobody else did.

What about the other kind of agnostic—the man who admits that God *may* be knowable but isn't known to *him*?

To that man we can say only: 'How much time are you prepared to give to learn what God is like? Do you admit that the Creator (if He is there) has claims on you? If you would willingly give months and months to learn a foreign language, would you be willing to give as much time to learn about God?'

Frankly, this high quest is not just for scamped moments. God has said: 'You shall seek me, and find me, *when you search for me with all your heart*' (Jeremiah 29:13).

W.E. Sangster, *Give God a Chance*, Epworth Press, 1968, page 31

Isn't it Best to be Agnostic?

An agnostic is not an atheist. He doesn't say there isn't a God. He says, 'I don't know. Perhaps there is; perhaps there isn't. Who can tell?' Many agnostics feel strongly that their position is rational and humble and as far as they can go.

We recognize and respect this position. We have conceded that God cannot be proved by a scientific experiment, by mathematics, or by irresistible logic. We have shown that the only way to personal certainty is by an act of faith which the agnostic (even if he is a swimmer!) will not take.

Is there, then, no way forward? Must his loyalty to fixed ideas of how truth should be understood remain for ever a barrier to truth itself? Is he to be left saying: 'I have no personal experience of God, and the arguments for His existence break even. There is love in the world—but hate also. There is design in the world—but chaos too. *I don't know.* Beyond this no man of mental integrity can go!'

Can't he? Not one step further? Isn't it true that when an honest mind faces an even argument, and life itself presses for a decision, with no loss of integrity, a man should back the higher alternative, and his own sensitive conscience will approve him in what he does?

For those are the facts. When the road forks, a man can mark time all his life at the fork (which is what the agnostic does) or take one of the two ways. He can decide that this is a purposeless universe and 'build his house on the rock of unyielding despair' (as one traveller on this path describes it), or make the experiment of faith which *could* issue in the discovery of understanding, meaning, purpose, peace, joy. Is it so unscientific to experiment? Why not take the path which makes sense?

And—remember this—even Christians are agnostic about many things. They don't claim to have 'all the answers'.

W.E. Sangster, Give God a Chance, Epworth Press, 1968, page 30

ATHEISM

Atheism—disbelief in the existence of God; godlessness

At Bradford Cathedral, we used to run a group called 'CPV'—which stood for 'Christian Points of View'. On a Saturday morning in term-time, large numbers of teenagers from Bradford Grammar School—both boys and girls—would come to the Cathedral Hall at 7.00 a.m. for a Bible study. This was followed by breakfast and further discussion. In the holidays the format changed and a three-day conference was held. Sometimes the venue was a large country house in the Yorkshire Dales; alternatively we went to the Lake District for a change of scenery.

I remember on one occasion a heated conversation taking place. One of my colleagues was having a chat with a truculent member of the group. The young man claimed to be an atheist. 'The trouble with you Christians,' he exclaimed somewhat angrily, 'is that you all have shut minds.' Unperturbed by this accusation my colleague came back with the retort: 'This is also true of atheists, isn't it? Haven't you, too, got a shut mind? Isn't it time you opened up—otherwise you might miss the deepest and best things in life?'

I forget how the exchange ended. For me the Christian faith has been a great eye-opener, and the *Visions* series and the practice of reflection a way of opening up the mind and the spiritual dimension.

In the pride of his countenance the wicked does not seek him; all his thoughts are, 'There is no God.'

Psalm 10:4

The fool says in his heart, 'There is no God.'

Psalm 14:1

... they exchanged the truth about God for a lie and worshipped and served the creature rather than the Creator, who is blessed for ever!

Romans 1:25

But how are men to call upon him in whom they have not believed?

Romans 8:14

With the soul of an Atheist, he wrote down the godliest things.

Herman Melville, *Pierre*, The New American Library of World Literature, 1964, page 380

The wildest scorner of his Maker's laws
Finds in a sober moment time to pause.

William Cowper, 'Tirocinium', in *The Poetical Works of William Cowper*, Oxford University Press, 1950, page 243

It's an interesting view of atheism, as a sort of *crutch* for those who can't bear the reality of God.

Tom Stoppard, *Jumpers*, act II, Faber and Faber, 1972, page 69

An atheist may be simply one whose faith and love are concentrated on the impersonal aspects of God.

Simone Weil, in W.H. Auden, *A Certain World*, Faber and Faber, 1982, page 174

There is no strength in unbelief. Even the unbelief of what is false is no source of might. It is the truth shining from behind that gives the strength to disbelieve.

George MacDonald, *The Marquis of Lossie*, George Newnes, 1900, page 125

But God's trustiest lieutenants often lack official credentials. They may be professed atheists who are also men of honour and high public spirit.

George Bernard Shaw, 'Back to Methuselah', in *The Complete Prefaces of Bernard Shaw*, Paul Hamlyn, 1965, page 533

Human life demands hope, and the priest is a symbol of hope; there is always a moment when the religionist doubts, and there is also a moment when the atheist says, 'Who knows, perhaps.'

George Moore, *Evelyn Innes*, Bernhard Tauchnitz, 1898, volume 2, page 102

There are conscientious 'atheists' or 'agnostics' who are among the most moral people on earth, whose standards of public duty and private integrity may put many believers to shame.

F.R. Barry, *Secular and Supernatural*, SCM Press, 1969, page 56

If you are a Christian you do not have to believe that all the other religions are simply wrong all through. If you are an atheist you do have to believe that the main point in all the religions of the whole world is simply one huge mistake.

C.S. Lewis, *Mere Christianity*, William Collins Sons & Co., 1961, page 39

I hold to my old thesis that mankind nowadays largely not only lacks God, either having never known him or having shaken him off by its own decision—but its godlessness goes much deeper. Present day man has fallen into a pattern of life in which he is incapable of susceptibility to God. All efforts on behalf of the humanity of to-day and of the future must be directed to making it susceptible to God once more and thereby susceptible to religion.

Written by a priest in a Nazi prison

Atheism can be a very comfortable philosophy. It not only reduces the intensity of moral conflict, but it renders the mystery of pain and suffering less poignant. The problem remains, it is true, but we are relieved of the agonizing task of trying to harmonise the love of an all-powerful God with the evil in human nature and in history. And the atheist is in a position where he can nimbly side-step the charge of hypocrisy. If his creed is nil, he can go about accumulating credit for living better than his creed.

Murdo Ewen MacDonald, *The Call to Obey*, Hodder and Stoughton, 1963, page 13

Bishop John V. Taylor (of Winchester) is well aware that he is annoying them [atheists] when he insists: Quite a lot of their experiences, which they acknowledge to be real, are what I mean by God. If God is God he is likely to be the most common of human experiences: people keep bumping into Him all the time, but that is not what they call Him. I think the Church has helped to create a division by giving the impression that religious experience is an exceptional and spooky thing.

Gerald Priestland, *Priestland's Progress*, BBC Publications, 1982, page 47

I once made a journey round the world. I never once saw 'The Atheists' Home for Orphans' or 'The Agnostics' Crippleage', but everywhere I went I saw the Christian Church caring for the destitute and needy.

Don't misunderstand me! I know individual agnostics and atheists who are compassionate and generous, and no doubt they have their glad share in subscriptions to good causes. But the world's need is barely touched in that way. People must give *themselves*, and give themselves utterly, if the fringe of this vast need is to be touched.

W.E. Sangster, *Give God a Chance*, Epworth Press, 1968, page 87

Man has never been the same since God died.
He has taken it very hard. Why, you'd think it was only yesterday,
The way he takes it.
Not that he says much, but he laughs much louder than he used to,
And he can't bear to be left alone even for a minute, and he can't
Sit still.

Edna St Vincent Millay, *Conversations At Midnight*, Hamish Hamilton, 1937, page 94

The ideal, cheerful, sensuous, pagan life is not sick or sorry. No; yet its natural end is the sort of life which Pompeii and Herculaneum bring so vividly before us—a life which by no means in itself suggests the thought of horror and misery, which even in many ways, gratifies the senses and the understanding; but by the very intensity and unremittingness of its appeal to the senses and the understanding, by its stimulating a single side of us too absolutely, ends by fatiguing and revolting us; ends by leaving us with a sense of confinement, of oppression—with a desire for an utter change, for clouds, storms, effusion and relief.

Matthew Arnold, in Cyril Connolly, *The Unquiet Grave*, Hamish Hamilton, 1973, page 8

Of all the things which demonstrate the amazing order of the universe nothing demonstrates it so much as the movement of the world. Astronomers tell us that there are as many stars as there are grains of sand upon the seashore. If we may put it in human terms, think of the traffic problems of the heavens. And yet the heavenly bodies keep their appointed courses and travel their appointed way. An astronomer is able to forecast to the minute and to the inch when and where a certain planet will appear. An astronomer can tell us when and where an eclipse of the sun will happen hundreds of years from now, and he can tell us to the second how long it will last. It has been said that 'no astronomer can be an atheist'. When we look upwards we see God.

William Barclay, *The Gospel of John*, The Saint Andrew Press, 1965, volume 1, page 37

The form which the infidelity of England, especially, has taken, is one hitherto unheard of in human history. No nation ever before declared boldly, by print and word of mouth, that its religion was good for show, but 'would not work'...

I had no conception of the absolute darkness which has covered the national mind in this respect, until I began to come into collision with persons engaged in the study of economical and political questions. The entire naïvete and undisturbed imbecility with which I found them declare that the laws of the Devil were the only practical ones, and that the laws of God were merely a form of poetical language, passed all that I had ever before heard or read of mortal infidelity. I knew the fool had often said in his heart, there was *no* God; but to hear him say clearly out with his lips, 'There is a foolish God,' was something which my art studies had not prepared me for. The French had indeed, for a considerable time, hinted much of the meaning in the delicate and compassionate blasphemy of their phrase '*le bon Dieu*', but had never ventured to put it into more precise terms.

Now this form of unbelief in God is connected with, and necessarily productive of, a precisely equal unbelief in man.

John Ruskin, *Modern Painters*, George Allen & Sons, 1910, volume 5, page 377

Isn't Life Easier if you are an Atheist?

It is, in some ways. Rules are always awkward things to our selfish human nature and it is nice to believe that there aren't any absolute ones. Conscience is an annoying murmur inside any man of strong passions, who has a firm determination to get what he wants, so it is easier to brush the silly things aside if you can convince yourself that it is just the generalization of social custom and has no real authority.

There are other advantages in being an atheist, too. The problem of pain and suffering, which is a near nightmare to people who believe in a God of love, is no problem to him at all. The charge of hypocrisy (which is constantly levelled at Christians if they stumble in their high-way) can never be brought against him. Indeed, he can get an extra glow of virtue when he does a good turn, because he is under no supernatural constraint to live a life of love. He can say to his mates at work: 'Look at me. I believe in nothing, but I'm always doing good turns.' It is nice to remember, after all this, that many atheists are not like the people depicted above, but (benefiting often by the moral fruit of the religion they have discarded) they are kind, unselfish, humble people, and good colleagues in the fight against social evils.

But are there important losses to set down beside the 'gains' the atheist appears to enjoy? There are...

He must give up all hope of finding any deep meaning in life. If he himself loves beauty, truth, and goodness, his own love of them are inexplicable and their origin a complete mystery. Did matter alone produce beauty, truth, goodness... and his own deep care for them? All noble men, sacrificing themselves for their ideals, are an enigma; Jesus Christ (whom the atheist can classify only as a man) is the greatest enigma of all. When the atheist is grateful, he has no one to thank. He has no hope of re-union with his dear ones beyond the grave. He misses the companionship of God in this life (life's greatest treasure, as Christians think) and may be so firmly fixed on the path which leads to outer darkness that he will miss the best in the next life as well.

W.E. Sangster, *Give God a Chance*, Epworth Press, 1968, page 29

BAPTISM

*Baptism—religious rite of immersing (person) in, or sprinkling
with, water in sign of purification and (with Christians) of
admission to the Church, generally accompanied by name-giving*

Two things have helped me to understand baptism. The first is the practice of the early Church. The person to be baptized (let us say, a woman) would be led to the bank of a river. She would enter the waters, and be totally submerged. This was the outward and visible sign of leaving behind her former manner of life, and symbolized death to this by drowning. The inner and spiritual grace was cleansing and purification.

She would then be raised from the depths of the waters, symbolizing resurrection. The inner and spiritual grace was rebirth to newness of life—in the name of the Father, Son and Holy Spirit. She would then cross the river and be welcomed by a group of Christians who would help her to grow as a Christian from then onwards.

The second is the familiar Genesis story of the creation of man. At the beginning of a baptism service I usually draw attention to this story and mention the divine inbreathing. I point out the person to be baptized has already an enormous source of life in the depths of their being—something of the Father, Son and Holy Spirit, as well as qualities such as life, light, joy, truth and love. In this sacrament these are brought to birth, and godparents (suitably named) then have the task of nurturing and stimulating this divine life. Seen from these perspectives, what an important sacrament baptism is.

And thus you shall do to them, to cleanse them: sprinkle the water of expiation upon them.
Numbers 8:7

Wash me thoroughly from my iniquity, and cleanse me from my sin!
Psalm 51:2

I baptize you with water for repentance, but he who is coming after me is mightier than I, whose sandals I am not worthy to carry; he will baptize you with the Holy Spirit and with fire.
Matthew 3:11

He has put his seal upon us and given us his Spirit in our hearts as a guarantee.
2 Corinthians 1:22

To be baptised, then, is to be born according to Christ and to receive our very being and nature, having previously been nothing.
Nicholas Cabasilas, *The Life in Christ*, translated by Carmino J. deCatanzaro, St Vladimir's Seminary Press, 1974, page 66

Baptismal grace, the presence within us of the Holy Spirit—inalienable and personal to each one of us—is the foundation of all Christian life.
Vladimir Lossky, *The Mystical Theology of the Eastern Church*, James Clarke & Co., 1957, page 171

... the all-important matter was not how or when water was applied, but the reception of *Christ's real baptism*, an inner baptism, a baptism of spirit and power, by which the believing soul, the inner man, is clarified, strengthened, and made pure.

Rufus M. Jones, *Spiritual Reformers in the 16th and 17th Centuries*, Macmillan and Co., 1914, page 80

... our baptism in the Spirit is that aspect of our life in Christ, in which the Holy Spirit breaks through into our experience, so that we know ourselves to be empowered and gifted to be his witnesses, given a love and a power that do not come from ourselves, but which give us a new appreciation of what it means to belong to Christ and his Body, and new hope and resources to engage in the service to men to which we are called.

Thomas A. Smail, *Reflected Glory*, Hodder and Stoughton, 1975, page 145

Commonly, baptism was by total immersion, and that practice lent itself to a symbolism which sprinkling does not so readily lend itself to. When a man descended into the water, and the water closed over his head, it was like being buried in a grave. When he emerged from the water, it was like rising from the grave. Baptism was symbolically like dying and rising again. The man died to one kind of life and rose to another kind of life. He died to the old life of sin and rose to the new life of grace. He went down into the water a man of the world and rose a man in Christ.

William Barclay, *The Letter to the Romans*, The Saint Andrew Press, 1969, page 84

What the Christian sacrament of baptism purports to do is of the greatest importance for the psychic development of mankind. Baptism endows the human being with a unique soul. I do not mean, of course, the baptismal rite in itself as a magical act that is effective at one performance. I mean that the idea of baptism lifts a man out of his archaic identification with the world and changes him into a being who stands above it. The fact that mankind has risen to the level of this idea is baptism in the deepest sense, for it means the birth of spiritual man who transcends nature.

C.G. Jung, *Psychological Reflections*, selected and edited by Jolande Jacobi, Routledge & Kegan Paul, 1953, page 325

Christ's baptism is with power from above, and He cleanses from sin not with water but with the Holy Ghost and the burning fire of love. As soon as the spiritual man possesses 'the key of David,' and has entered upon 'the true Sabbath of his soul,' he holds lightly all forms and ceremonies which are outward and which can be gone through with in a mechanical fashion without creating the essential attitude of worship and of inner harmony with the will of God: 'When the Kingdom of God with its joy and love has come in us we do not much care for those things which can only happen outside us.'

Rufus M. Jones, *The Spiritual Reformers in the 16th and 17th Centuries*, Macmillan & Co., 1914, page 39

Sanctity may be defined as: 'a divine life, communicated and received'. This life is communicated from above, by God, by Christ. It is received by man, from the moment of his baptism. This sacrament confers the grace of adoption and thus sanctifies the soul; it brings to it, as it were, the dawn of the divine life, but this brightness is intended to increase steadily to the glory of a noon that will not fade. Baptismal or sanctifying grace implants in the soul a capacity to share in the very nature of God, by knowledge, by love, and by the possession of the divinity in an intuitive manner which is natural to God alone. This divine gift establishes in man a wonderful and supernatural participation in the divine life.

D. Columba Marmion, *Christ—the Ideal of the Priest*, Sands & Co., 1952, page 36

'The Son of God, the Eternal Word of the Father, the Glance and Brightness and Power of Eternal Light must become man and *be born in you*; otherwise you are in the dark stable and go about groping.' 'If thou art born of God, then within the circle of thy own life is the whole undivided Heart of God.' It is a transforming event by which one swings over from life in the outer to life in the inner world, from life in the dark world to life in the light world, and is born into the kingdom, or principle, which Christ revealed in His triumphant spiritual Life. The human spirit, by this innermost Birth, reaches the principle of Life by which Christ lived, and the gate into heaven is opened and paradise is in the soul.

Rufus M. Jones, *Spiritual Reformers in the 16th and 17th Centuries*, Macmillan and Co., 1914, page 196

It is owned on all hands that we are baptized into a renovation of some divine birth that we had lost. And that we may not be at a loss to know what that divine birth is, the form in baptism openly declares to us that it is to regain that first birth of Father, Son, and Holy Ghost in our souls, which at the first made us to be truly and really images of the nature of the Holy Trinity in unity. The form in baptism is but very imperfectly apprehended, till it is understood to have this great meaning in it. And it must be owned that the Scriptures tend wholly to guide us to this understanding of it. For since they teach us a birth of God, a birth of the Spirit, that we must obtain, and that baptism, the appointed sacrament of this new birth, is to be done into the name of the Father, Son, and Holy Ghost, can there be any doubt that this sacrament is to signify the renovation of the birth of the Holy Trinity in our souls?

William Law, in Stephen Hobhouse, editor, *Selected Mystical Writings of William Law*, Rockliff, 1948, page 12

May not God say to us what He once said by the voice of His prophet: 'I passed by thee and saw thee: and behold thy time was the time of lovers, and I spread my garment over thee and I entered into a covenant with thee and thou became mine' (Ezekiel 16:8). Yes, we have become His by Baptism, which is what St Paul means by the words: 'He called them,' called them to receive the seal of the Blessed Trinity. By baptism we were made, in St Peter's words (2 Peter 1:4), 'partakers of the divine nature' and received 'the principle by which we are grounded in Him'. Then 'He justified us', by His sacraments, by His direct touches when we were recollected in the depths of our soul. He has also 'justified us by faith' (Romans 5:1) and according to the measure of our faith in the redemption acquired for us by Jesus Christ. Lastly He wills 'to glorify us', and therefore, says St Paul, He has 'made us fit to share the light which saints inherit' (Colossians 1:12). But we shall be glorified in the measure in which we have been 'moulded into the image of His Son'.

Sister Elizabeth of the Trinity, *Spiritual Writings*, Geoffrey Chapman, 1962, page 147

God loves infinitely an infinite goodness; the Son loves it in the Father whence it comes, the Father loves it in the Son in whom he places it, and upon whom he pours it out: 'This is my Son, my only beloved, in whom I am well-pleased.'

The Father's unqualified delight, his outpouring of his Holy Spirit, comes down with Christ from heaven to earth...

When St. John came to write the story of Christ's baptism, he connected it with Jacob's dream of the ladder from heaven to earth, on which the angels of God ascended and descended (John 1:32, 51; Gen. 28:12). And certainly the Baptism has so many levels of meaning in it, that without ever going outside it we can run up as though by steps from earth to heaven and down again. At the height of it is the bliss of the Trinity above all worlds; in the midst is the sonship of Jesus to his Heavenly Father; at the foot of it (and here it touches us) is the baptism of any Christian...

We cannot be baptized without being baptized into his baptism; and the unity we have with him both in receiving baptism and afterwards in standing by it, brings down on us the very blessing and the very Spirit he received. In so far as we are in Christ, we are filled with Holy Ghost, and the Father's good pleasure rests upon us; infinite Love delights in us.

Austin Farrer, *The Triple Victory*, The Faith Press, 1965, page 32

BELIEF

Belief—trust or confidence (in); acceptance of the Christian theology; thing believed, religion, opinion, intuition

Mark Rutherford, in this section, encourages us to struggle earnestly to increase our beliefs. 'Every addition to these,' he writes, 'is an extension of life both in breadth and depth.' My belief started off as a belief in God the Creator. In my teens I went one stage further and found I could assent to a belief in the contents of a creed. In my early twenties belief focused mainly in the person of Jesus Christ and the Holy Spirit, and this was later fortified by the study of theology. At the age of thirty the system of belief I had worked out broke down and I had to start again. A real struggle followed, and as I have indicated elsewhere, I was greatly helped by an anthology compiled by Dorothy Berkley Phillips, *The Choice is Always Ours*. It was through reading this book that I came to a belief in 'the God within'—something of the Father, Son and Holy Spirit, as well as life, light, joy, truth and love. I struggled hard to see if I could justify this position from Scripture, and then began a quest in the writings of the last 2,000 years. The results are to be found in *Visions of Faith, Hope, Love* and *Glory*. What I like about this way of belief is that it does lead to an extension of life both in breadth and depth, and enables us to make maximum use of our mind, feelings, intuition, instinct and imagination. The anthologies act as a skeleton or framework of belief, but enable us to put our own flesh and blood on them through the practice of reflection, and thereby increase our belief.

Believe in the Lord your God, and you will be established; believe his prophets, and you will succeed.

2 Chronicles 20:20

Behold, he whose soul is not upright in him shall fail, but the righteous shall live by his faith.

Habakkuk 2:4

Have you believed because you have seen me? Blessed are those who have not seen and yet believe.

John 20:29

Without having seen him you love him; though you do not now see him you believe in him and rejoice with unutterable and exalted joy. As the outcome of your faith you obtain the salvation of your souls.

1 Peter 1:8–9

Belief makes the mind abundant.

W.B. Yeats, in Samuel H. Miller, The Great Realities, Longmans, Green and Co., 1956, page 112

You ought never to believe something that you dare not think over.

Helmut Thielicke, I Believe—The Christian's Creed, translated by John W. Doberstein and H. George Anderson, William Collins Sons & Co., 1969, page 123

He does not believe, that does not live according to his Belief.

Thomas Fuller, Gnomologia, Stearn Brock, 1773, page 71

When I believe, I am no longer a mere man, I am already a son of God.

Carlo Carretto, *Summoned by Love*, translated by Alan Neame, Darton, Longman & Todd, 1977, page 35

In the world of today the crisis of Christianity is essentially a crisis of belief.

F.R. Barry, *Secular and Supernatural*, SCM Press, 1969, page 36

He's a Blockhead who wants a proof of what he can't Perceive,
And he's a Fool who tries to make such a Blockhead believe.

William Blake, 'To Flaxman', in *Complete Writings*, edited by Geoffrey Keynes, Oxford University Press, 1974, page 540

But we ought to struggle earnestly to increase our beliefs. Every addition to these is an extension of life both in breadth and depth.

Mark Rutherford, *Last Pages From a Journal*, Oxford University Press, 1915, page 318

Belief's fire, once in us,
Makes of all else mere stuff to show itself:
We penetrate our life with such a glow
As fire lends wood and iron.

Robert Browning, 'Bishop Bloughram's Apology', in *The Poetical Works of Robert Browning*, Smith, Elder, & Co., 1897, volume 1, page 536

First I believe in the reality of God as the centre of human aspiration and history. What I believe about man, made in the image of God, derives first and foremost from what I believe about God.

David Sheppard, *Bias to the Poor*, Hodder and Stoughton, 1983, page 151

That all things are possible to him who *believes*, that they are less difficult to him who *hopes*, they are more easy to him who *loves*, and still more easy to him who perseveres in the practice of these three virtues.

Brother Lawrence, *The Practice of the Presence of God*, A.R. Mowbray & Co., 1977, page 19

I believe in Jesus Christ, in whom I get a picture of God within the limits of my comprehension. Upon Him rests the whole fabric of my life: He alone holds it together in form and purpose, and without Him it would disintegrate.

Hugh Redwood, *Residue of Days*, Hodder and Stoughton, 1958, page 20

Men believe in 'sagacity,' 'shrewdness,' which is the baptismal name for cunning. They believe in avarice, which is too often called 'laudable enterprise.' They believe in dealing with things as they find them with 'spirit,' by which they mean anger.

Henry Ward Beecher, *Proverbs from Plymouth Pulpit*, Charles Burnet & Co., 1887, page 98

I am confident that, if a single ray of light reaches a man from Christ, penetrates into his being and influences his way of living, he is further along the road towards true belief in Him than if he gave his unreflecting assent to a multitude of orthodox propositions which have no perceptible effect upon his conduct.

J.H. Oldham, *Life is Commitment*, SCM Press, 1953, page 70

There comes a time when we have to believe where we cannot prove, and to accept where we cannot understand. If, even in the darkest hour, we believe that somehow there is a purpose in life, and that somehow that purpose is love, then even the unbearable becomes bearable, and even in the darkness there is still a glimmer of light.

William Barclay, *The Gospel of John*, The Saint Andrew Press, 1965, volume 2, page 177

One thing, however, which the apologist must always have in mind is that the debate between belief and unbelief is by no means merely a debate between himself who believes and another who disbelieves. It is also in large part a debate within himself, who both believes and disbelieves, and who must ever continue to pray humbly, 'Lord, I believe; help thou mine unbelief'.

John Baillie, *Invitation to Pilgrimage*, Oxford University Press, 1942, page 18

As one who has put God to the test in peace and war, who has let himself go on Jesus, who has tried the way of love and the path of prayer, I am not the less definite here. I believe in God. I believe in the love of God. I believe in the trustworthiness of Jesus. I believe that He was the Authentic Word of the Father. I believed He lived, and died, and rose again. I believe in mercy. I believe in judgement. These are not opinions with me. These are convictions. By these I steer. Respecting this chart, I am confident of coming in safety to the haven under the hill.

W.E. Sangster, *These Things Abide*, Hodder and Stoughton, 1939, page 78

And so I accept God, and I accept him not only without reluctance, but, what's more, I accept his divine wisdom and purpose—which are completely beyond our comprehension. I believe in the underlying order and meaning of life. I believe in the eternal harmony into which we are all supposed to merge one day. I believe in the Word to which the universe is striving and which itself was 'with God' and which was God, and, well, so on and so forth, *ad infinitum.*

Fyodor Dostoyevsky, *The Brothers Karamazov*, translated by David Magarshack, Penguin Books, 1963, volume 1, page 275

Twelve Life Convictions

1. That there is a moral universe which always has the last word.
2. That the revelation of God to man is progressive, appearing in varying degrees among all races and culminating in the final and perfect revelation in Jesus Christ.
3. The deepest place of that revelation is the Cross.
4. The Kingdom of God is written not only into the Bible, but into the nature of reality and into us.
5. The Christian Way is the natural way to live.
6. The Kingdom of God is God's total answer to man's total need.
7. The way to meet unmerited suffering and injustice is not to bear them, but to use them.
8. That the Holy Spirit is the birthright of believers.
9. That the way to live is by grace and receptivity.
10. That Jesus Christ will have the last word in human events.
11. That love is the strongest force in the universe and will finally prevail.
12. That the Christian way works.

E. Stanley Jones, *Growing Spiritually*, Hodder and Stoughton, 1954, page 352

I am not attempting here to discuss the difficulties attaching to Christian belief. I know that they are real and manifold. I am only pointing out that those who have encountered Christ and made a wholehearted response to that encounter have found an answer to the problem of man and truth. They have been given a faith which they do not have to carry, but which carries them. It is the testimony of Christians that amid all the uncertainties of relativism they have discovered that to which they may surrender themselves in complete trust. They have encountered a reality which gives them confidence that the universe is trustworthy. What they have known and experienced of love is something that they believe will hold firm in all the stresses and tests of life and prove stronger than death itself.

That is one answer to the problem of man and truth. I do not myself know of any other answer in which my mind can rest.

But it is inherent in that answer, as I understand it, that the answer must vindicate itself in open and free discussion, that all formulations of the answer made by fallible men are necessarily defective and incomplete and are in constant need of correction and enrichment by the contribution of the experience of all serious seekers after truth.

J.H. Oldham, Life is Commitment, SCM Press, 1953, page 130

I recognise, of course, that this statement of belief is partly governed by the circumstance that I am old, and in at most a decade or so will be dead. In earlier years I should doubtless have expressed things differently. Now the prospect of death overshadows all others. I am like a man on a sea voyage nearing his destination. When I embarked I worried about having a cabin with a porthole, whether I should be asked to sit at the captain's table, who were the more attractive and important passengers. All such considerations become pointless when I shall so soon be disembarking.

As I do not believe that earthly life can bring any lasting satisfaction, the prospect of death holds no terrors. Those saints who pronounced themselves in love with death displayed, I consider, the best of sense; not a Freudian death-wish. The world that I shall soon be leaving seems more than ever beautiful; especially its remoter parts, grass and trees and sea and rivers and little streams and sloping hills, where the image of eternity is more clearly stamped than among streets and houses. Those I love I can love even more, since I have nothing to ask of them but their love; the passion to accumulate possessions, or to be noticed and important, is too evidently absurd to be any longer entertained.

A sense of how extraordinarily happy I have been, and of enormous gratitude to my creator, overwhelms me often. I believe with a passionate, unshakable conviction that in all circumstances and at all times life is a blessed gift; that the spirit which animates it is one of love, not hate or indifference, of light, not darkness, of creativity, not destruction, of order, not chaos; that, since all life—men, creatures, plants, as well as insensate matter—and all that is known about it, now and henceforth, have been benevolently, not malevolently, conceived, when the eyes see no more and the mind thinks no more, and this hand now writing is inert, whatever lies beyond will similarly be benevolently, not malevolently or indifferently, conceived. If it is nothing, then for nothingness I offer thanks; if another mode of existence, with this old worn-out husk of a body left behind, like a butterfly extricating itself from its chrysalis, and this floundering muddled mind, now at best seeing through a glass darkly, given a longer range and a new precision, then for that likewise I offer thanks.

Malcolm Muggeridge, Jesus Rediscovered, William Collins Sons & Co., 1982, page 57

BIBLE

Bible—the scriptures of the Old and New Testament, a copy of them,
a particular edition of them, authoritative text

Looking back over the early part of my life I can see several stages in my reading of the Bible. As a teenager I dipped into the Bible from time to time, but was never really a devotee. I flirted for a while with the Bible Reading Fellowship notes and found these helpful. In my early twenties I joined a beginner's group and was given some basic teaching on the Scriptures. This was followed up at theological college with a detailed study of the Bible involving biblical and literary criticism. About this time I came across the *Daily Study Bible* commentaries of William Barclay. The author was Professor of Divinity and Biblical Criticism at Glasgow University. Three things appeal to me in these New Testament commentaries. First, they are very readable. The author explains the meaning of certain Greek words in simple terms, and this sometimes alters radically our understanding of a passage. Secondly, he explains the environment and context in which words were spoken and this adds greatly to our insight. Thirdly, he makes the teaching of the New Testament relevant for us today, and thereby helps us in everyday life. I remember an undergraduate saying she would be eternally grateful to me for introducing her to the William Barclay commentaries.

Finally, I have found *A Theological Word Book of the Bible*, edited by Alan Richardson, a good scholarly companion to the William Barclay commentaries.

Man does not live by bread alone, but... by everything that proceeds out of the mouth of the Lord.

Deuteronomy 8:3

Thy word is a lamp to my feet and a light to my path.
Psalm 119:105

Heaven and earth will pass away, but my words will not pass away.
Mark 13:31

All scripture is inspired by God and profitable for teaching, for reproof, for correction, and for training in righteousness.

2 Timothy 3:16

That God pities and pardons, it is precious to know. But that He loves with special affection, and can take delight in us—this is overwhelming. Yet both the Old and New Testaments teach this.

Henry Ward Beecher, *Proverbs from Plymouth Pulpit*, Charles Burnet & Co., 1887, page 140

So we pick out a Text here, and there to make it serve our turn; whereas, if we take it all together, and consider'd what went before, and what followed after, we should find it meant no such thing.

John Selden, 'Bible, Scriptures', in *The Table Talk of John Selden*, Alex. Murray & Son, 1868, page 21

The point of reading the Bible is to relive that disclosure of God which the Bible story is depicting, and then to use it to stimulate the imagination to see his disclosure in the contemporary scene.

Frank Wright, *The Pastoral Nature of the Ministry*, SCM Press, 1980, page 18

I for my part love and cherish the Bible. My moral education I owed almost exclusively to it, and its stories, doctrines, symbols, parables—all had made a deep impression upon me and influenced me in one way or another.

Johann Wolfgang von Goethe, *Wisdom and Experience*, selected by Ludwig Curtius, translated and edited by Hermann J. Weigand, Routledge & Kegan Paul, 1949, page 65

... we must reject the assertion of neo-orthodox biblicism that the Bible is the '*only*' source. The biblical message cannot be understood and could not have been received had there been no preparation for it in human religion and culture.

Paul Tillich, *Systematic Theology*, James Nisbet & Co., 1953, volume 1, page 39

What a book the Holy Bible is! What a miracle and what strength is given with it to man! Just like a sculpture of the world and man and human characters, and everything is named there and everything is shown for ever and ever. And how many solved and revealed mysteries.

Fyodor Dostoyevsky, *The Brothers Karamazov*, translated by David Magarshack, Penguin Books, 1963, volume 1, page 343

Had the Bible been in clear straightforward language, had the ambiguities and contradictions been edited out and had the language been constantly modernized to accord with contemporary taste it would almost certainly have been, or have become, a work of lesser influence.

J.K. Galbraith, *Economics, Peace and Laughter*, essays edited by Andrea D. Williams, Andre Deutsch, 1971, page 34

... I perused the books of the Old and New Testaments—each book as a whole, and also as an integral part. And need I say that I have met every where more or less copious sources of truth, and power, and purifying impulses—that I have found words for my inmost thoughts, songs for my joy, utterances for my hidden griefs, and pleadings for my shame and my feebleness?

Samuel Taylor Coleridge, *Aids to Reflection and The Confessions of an Enquiring Spirit*, George Bell & Sons, 1884, page 294

There was something deep and disturbing in the lines. I thought they only moved me as poetry: and yet I also felt, obscurely enough, that there was something personal about them. God often talks to us directly in Scripture. That is, He plants the words full of actual graces as we read them and sudden undiscovered meanings are sown in our hearts, if we attend to them, reading with minds that are at prayer.

Thomas Merton, *Elected Silence*, Hollis and Carter, 1949, page 245

We need to approach our reading and study of the Bible with reverence, prayer, and the spirit of obedience. If we set ourselves to listen for the voice of God in our Bible reading we must be ready to obey what He tells us to do or to renounce. This attitude will not come of itself—often it will be very difficult—our minds are very individualistic, and we have an innate tendency to revolt. Only the determination to surrender to God at all costs will enable us to enter into that prayer and silent 'waiting' upon Him in which we shall come to know that: 'this is the way, walk ye in it.'

Olive Wyon, *On the Way*, SCM Press, 1958, page 113

Central to my own thinking about the authority of the Bible is the conviction that we can say nothing worthwhile about the Bible except by beginning with the Christian gospel that existed before there ever was a Bible and could survive if every Bible was destroyed. The centre of the gospel is not about knowledge, but about love: the love of God for a fallen world, and his will to restore it through Christ. About this gospel the Bible—in both

Testaments—provides us with all kinds of information, both historical and theological. By reading the Bible, studying it with all our critical powers, using it in worship, and being challenged by it as a literary text, we can come face to face with the gospel and respond to it with our whole lives. If that is not to accord authority to the Bible, I do not know what would be.

John Barton, *People of the Book: The Authority of the Bible in Christianity*, SPCK, 1988, page 89

Certainly the Bible always remains the foundation book of Christianity, precisely because it is genuine in itself and free from ideological prejudices. But for all this, regarded realistically, it has, so far as we are concerned, receded so far back in history from us that it is no longer possible for a religious book to be a florilegium of passages from scripture with a few words of commentary attached to each. Scripture is indeed too remote, historically speaking for *our* lives, and we must learn to recognise this realistically, and not to be full of pious enthusiasm as to use it exaggeratedly and without discretion. In all cases in which it is not scientific exegesis that is being aimed at the religious author should quietly spare the reader the long journey (whenever and wherever it is in fact long) from the letter of scripture to the reality signified by it. He should speak directly of this reality itself. And when it is always open to him, in appropriate cases, to say at the end of his investigation 'and this is already to be found in such-and-such a passage of scripture.'

Karl Rahner, S.J., *Theological Investigations*, volume 8, *Further Theology of the Spiritual Life*, translated by David Bourke, Darton, Longman & Todd, 1971, page 253

Christians are not those who believe in the Bible, but those who believe in Christ. It should by now be more than clear that I do not believe there is any practical way to Christ today that does not involve the Bible at some point on the road. I am quite sure the authenticity of our knowledge of and faith in Christ cannot be established unless we have the Bible, the earliest documents of the Christian religion, to act as a check and a source. Equally, the truth that the Bible can indeed become the Word of God, God's way of continuing to speak to the Church, when it is heard and read in faith, is for me beyond dispute. But all this is a million miles away from enthroning the Bible as the sole arbiter of what is Christian, in faith or practice; binding the Church to so called 'scriptural' doctrines; requiring other sources of knowledge to be rejected in the name of scriptural authority; and—the ultimate contradiction—forcing the Bible to say what we want to hear, because we cannot believe anything unless we think it is from the Bible that we are hearing it. This is to press a valuable metaphor—the Bible as God's Word, as though it were a literal definition of ultimate truth, and indeed the most important and central such definition in the Christian faith.

John Barton, *People of the Book: The Authority of the Bible in Christianity*, SPCK, 1988, page 83

The true and essential Word of God is the divine revelation in the soul of man. It is the *prius* of all Scripture and it is the key to the spiritual meaning of all Scripture.

    ... from its inherent nature, a written Scripture cannot be the final authority in religion: (a) It is outward, external, while the seat of religion is in the soul of man. (b) It is transitory and shifting, for language is always in process of change, and written words have different meanings to different ages and in different countries, while for a permanent religion there must be a living, eternal Word that fits all ages, lands, and conditions. (c) Scripture is full of mystery, contradiction, and paradox which only 'The Key of David'—the inner experience of the heart—can unlock. Scripture is the Manger, but, unless the Holy Spirit comes as the day star in the heart, the Wise man will not find the Christ. (d) Scripture at best brings only knowledge. It lacks the power to deliver from the sin which it describes. It cannot create the faith, the desire, the love, the will purpose which are necessary to win that which the Scriptures portray. No book—no amount of 'ink, paper, and letters'—can make a man good, since religion is not knowledge, but a way of living, a transformed life, and *that* involves an inward life-process, a resident creative power.

Rufus M. Jones, *Spiritual Reformers in the 16th and 17th Centuries*, Macmillan and Co., 1914, page 60

The Bible is a map, says Bunyan, to show us the way of life.

What does this mean? How can the Bible guide us on our journey through life? We are naturally suspicious of a 'magic' use of the Bible, such as opening the Bible at random and sticking a pin into the first text we see ... But Bunyan is right, although it is obvious that the Bible is much more than a map for our journey. Indeed, it is there that the Bible is absolutely essential for the spiritual life. If we are ignorant of it, and neglect to read and study it, the effect will be disastrous. Either our spiritual life will become very thin and our faith wavering and uncertain, or we may be easily led astray into enticing paths of thought which lead us off the true Way into by-paths which lead—nowhere.

The Bible is essential for the spiritual life for at least three reasons. First, because it contains the answers to those fundamental questions ... about the meaning of life, the meaning of man, the meaning of history, the riddle of the universe, and the reality of God. In the language of the present day all these are 'existential' questions, matters of life and death. The Bible does not give us ready-made answers, it is true, but the serious enquirer will surely find, if he seeks the right way.

Secondly, in spite of its diversity, the Bible is a unity, and its message is *one*. Until we realize this we may think that we 'know the Bible' because we know a few favourite passages which happen to appeal to us, but we have not found the clue to the whole. Now the Church—all down the ages—presents the Bible to us as the authentic revelation of the True God; it does so because *the whole Bible means one thing*: that God alone IS, and that He has sent His Son Jesus Christ, to be the Saviour, King and Judge of all mankind. That is why St Jerome says that 'to be ignorant of the Scriptures is to be ignorant of Christ'. In other words, apart from Christ, there is no Bible, no 'way of life', no Hope for mankind. For Jesus Christ is not only the centre of the message of the Bible. He is the centre of human history, the one Answer to our deepest longings—the Word made Flesh. And this 'Word' is Love Incarnate ...

Thirdly, it is a fact of experience that God speaks to men in and through the Bible. He has spoken to the world in a Person, and it is this Person, Jesus Christ, who is the 'Word of God'. This Book, however ... is the source of our knowledge of this Person, and it is in and through its pages that He makes Himself known to us. It is this quality which makes the Bible unique. All down the centuries the Bible has led men home to God, through Christ. For here revelation becomes personal. The Bible is not the story of man's search for God but of God's search for man. When we study the Bible in the light of its message of love, we see how God calls men, woos them, deals with them in their wanderings, trying by every means to bring them back to Himself, yet without once forcing them or infringing their self-respect, till at last in Christ He goes all lengths to reconcile them to Himself ...

Olive Wyon, *On the Way*, SCM Press, 1958, page 110

CHRISTIAN

Christian—an adherent of Christianity

I grew up thinking I was a Christian as I had been baptized as an infant. At the age of sixteen I was confirmed, and having reached the years of discretion took upon myself promises made on my behalf at baptism. In retrospect this was an assent to the contents of a creed rather than to a belief in a personal God. I became a regular communicant, but this practice was interrupted by National Service, and I lapsed to become a nominal Christian. Within a few weeks of arriving in Oxford I burnt my boats and made a commitment to the person of Jesus Christ. In the next few weeks and months this grew through the influence of the Holy Spirit. I now felt that in following Christ lay the very essence of being a Christian. Ordination beckoned me forward. I completed my law degree, and went on a university expedition to Nepal before going to theological college.

Six busy years passed by and I found myself in a crisis. Intuitively I felt something was radically wrong. It was at this stage I became Chaplain to University College, London, and discovered the book *The Choice is Always Ours*, by Dorothy Berkley Phillips. This brilliant anthology enabled me to find the 'God within'—that at the depths of our being we can discover something of the Father, Son and Holy Spirit, and divine attributes such as life, light, truth, joy and love, elsewhere described in this book. At last I had found what I was looking for, and what a relief. I now think of a Christian as a person who experiences something of the richness of divine life in the depths of his or her being and lives by it.

You are the salt of the earth.
Matthew 5:13

You are the light of the world . . . Let your light so shine before men, that they may see your good works and give glory to your Father who is in heaven.
Matthew 5:14, 16

Agrippa said to Paul, 'In a short time you think to make me a Christian!' And Paul said, 'Whether short or long, I would to God that not only you but also all who hear me this day might become such as I am.'
Acts 26:28–29

. . . yet if one suffers as a Christian, let him not be ashamed, but under that name let him glorify God.
1 Peter 4:16

It doesn't take much of a person to be a Christian, but it takes all there is of him—person and possessions.
E. Stanley Jones, *Growing Spiritually*, Hodder and Stoughton, 1954, page 188

The ultimate criterion of a person's Christian spirit is not theory but practice: not how he thinks of teachings, dogmas, interpretations, but how he acts in ordinary life.

Hans Küng, *On Being a Christian*, translated by Edward Quinn, William Collins Sons & Co., 1977, page 380

The life of every Christian on earth has in it much that is mysterious. It is aiming at an awful grandeur which has never been unveiled. God carries in His bosom the full ideal. We know it not.

Henry Ward Beecher, *Proverbs from Plymouth Pulpit*, Charles Burnet & Co., 1887, page 171

When the imitation of Christ does not mean to live a life like Christ, but to live your life authentically as Christ lived his, then there are many ways and forms in which a man can be a Christian.

Henri J.M. Nouwen, *The Wounded Healer*, Doubleday, 1979, page 99

... That simplicity which was usually found in the primitive Christians, who were (as most Anglers are) quiet men, and followers of peace; men that were so simply-wise, as not to sell their Consciences to buy riches.

Izaak Walton, *The Compleat Angler*, The Nonesuch Press, 1929, page 18

To live Christ is not to screw oneself up to great heights of moral endeavour and self-sacrifice. It is to accept, to accept what God says is possible for us. This is the achievement, the only achievement for a Christian, to become open to what God offers and what God can do.

Henry McKeating, *God and the Future*, SCM Press, 1974, page 58

Not only do I leave the door open for the Christian message, but I consider it of central importance for Western man. It needs, however, to be seen in a new light, in accordance with the changes wrought by the contemporary spirit. Otherwise, it stands apart from the times, and has no effect on man's wholeness.

C.G. Jung, *Memories, Dreams, Reflections*, William Collins Sons & Co., 1971, page 236

What originality Christianity admits! A man may be a Christian and yet lose nothing of that which is truly original in him. Nay, more, it provokes originality, just as the polishing of a pebble brings out the beauty and definiteness of its structure. I can call to mind people whom I knew forty or fifty years ago ... who had become *individual* through their religion.

Mark Rutherford, *Last Pages From a Journal*, Oxford University Press, 1915, page 266

The Christian man, however, even with his new 'nativity' and with his re-created spirit of love, differs in one respect from Christ. Christ is wholly heavenly, His Nature is woven throughout of spiritual and divine substance. There is no rent nor seam in it. Man, on the other hand, is double, and throughout his temporal period he remains double. By his new 'nativity' man can become inwardly spirit though he remains outwardly composed of flesh.

Rufus M. Jones, *Spiritual Reformers in the 16th and 17th Centuries*, Macmillan and Co., 1914, page 144

What distinguishes the Christian from the non-Christian? NOTHING. The Christian is no better or worse; he is no more virtuous than the others—in fact, he might even be less so. No more loving, giving or fraternal than anyone else—there are people who love more. There's only one difference: the Christian believes God loves him and that if he welcomes this love, it will be transmitted to the world through him, and on this love the world will be built.

Michel Quoist, *With Open Heart*, translated by Colette Copeland, Gill and Macmillan, 1983, page 193

To be a Christian . . . is to be in measure like Christ, and to be ready to be offered as He gave Himself to be offered. I do not say that we *are* perfect as Christ was, but I say rather that we are to seek the perfection which Christ never lost. Christ calls Himself the Light of the world, but He also tells His disciples that *they* too are the light of the world. All Christians in whom the Holy Ghost lives—that is all real Christians—are one with Christ in God and are like Christ. They will therefore have similar experiences, and what Christ did they will also do.

Rufus M. Jones, *Spiritual Reformers in the 16th and 17th Centuries*, Macmillan and Co., 1914, page 23

Christians are, or should be, the pioneers of the new humanity which God is bringing into being through Christ, for they are already experiencing in themselves the renewal which God intends for all his creation. Christ is not only 'the first born among a large family of brothers', but he is also in relation to mankind as a whole 'a second Adam'. In Christ, God made a new and fresh beginning and its success is assured by the victory which Christ, 'the second Adam', achieved over evil. Those who are inspired by his spirit and live in his way are the prototype of a new re-ordered humanity.

David Brown, *God's Tomorrow*, SCM Press, 1977, page 55

A Christian must be as a revolving circle, the central point fixed and immovable, whilst at the same time each point of the circumference performs its constant round. Thus, for the Christian, the central point is the still abiding in the presence of God, and with the outer man, with all the powers of body, soul, and spirit, must he ever be occupied in the work of God. But all that is good and divine that is found in our outward life is purely the effect of the supernatural power of God; therefore it is needful to abide quietly and fixedly in Christ, that this power may be manifested in us. The outer man should move as a door does that is fixed upon its hinge, but move in quietness and without violence, for the door might be wrenched from its hinge by the energy of nature.

Gerhard Tersteegen, in Frances Bevan, *Sketches of the Quiet in the Land*, John F. Shaw and Co., 1891, page 435

Consider the language in which Our Lord and His Apostles describe the gift—'If a man loves Me,' says Christ, 'he will keep My words, and My Father will love him, and We will come unto him, and make Our abode with him.' Again, in St. Paul's words 'Ye are the temple of the Living God; as God hath said, I will dwell in them and walk with them.' Again, 'know ye not that your body is the temple of the Holy Ghost, which is in you, which ye have of God, and ye are not your own?' And St. John, 'Whosoever shall confess that Jesus is the Son of God, God dwelleth in him and he in God.' Is it not plain, that such a doctrine as is here declared will exceedingly raise the Christian above himself, and without impairing, nay even while increasing his humility, will make him feel all things of earth as little, and of small interest or account, and will preserve him from the agitations of mind which they naturally occasion.

Christians are called upon to think little of the ordinary objects which men pursue, wealth, luxury, distinction, popularity, and power. It was this negligence about the world, which brought upon them in primitive times the reproach of being indolent.

Their heathen enemies spoke truly; indolent and indifferent were they about temporal matters. If the goods of this world came in their way, they were not bound to decline them nor would they forbid others in the religious use of them; but they thought them vanities, the toys of children, which serious men let drop. Nay, St. Paul betrays the same feeling as regards our temporal callings and states generally. After discoursing about them, suddenly he breaks off as if impatient of the multitude of words; 'But this I say, brethren,' he exclaims, 'the time is short.'

Hence, too, the troubles of life gradually affect the Christian less and less, as his view of his own real blessedness, under the Dispensation of the Spirit, grows upon him; and even though persecuted, to take an extreme case, he knows well that, through God's inward presence, he is greater than those who for the time have power over him, as Martyrs and Confessors have often shown.

And in like manner, he will be calm and collected under all circumstances; he will make light of injuries, and forget them from mere contempt of them. He will be undaunted, as fearing God more than man; he will be firm in faith and consistent, as 'seeing Him that is invisible'; not impatient, who has no self-will; not soon disappointed, who has no hopes; not anxious, who has no fears; nor dazzled, who has no ambitions; nor bribed, who has no desires.

And now, further, let it be observed, on the other hand, that all this greatness of mind which I have been describing, which in other religious systems degenerates into pride, is in the Gospel compatible, nay rather intimately connected with the deepest humility. If they do aught well, what have they which they have not received? and how know they but He, by whom their souls live, will withdraw that life, nay will to a certainty withdraw it, if they take that glory to themselves which is His?

... Our strength, and our holiness, our blessedness and our influence depart from us like a lamp that expires, or a weight that falls, as soon as we rest in them, and pride ourselves in them, instead of referring them to the Giver.

God in His mercy keep us from this sin! St. Paul shows us how we should feel about God's gift, and how to boast without pride, when he first says, 'I laboured more abundantly than they all'; and then adds 'yet not I, but the grace of God which was with me.'

Accordingly, the self-respect of the Christian is no personal and selfish feeling, but rather a principle of loyal devotion and reverence towards that Divine Master who condescends to visit him. He acts, not hastily, but under restraint and fearfully, as understanding that God's eye is over him, and God's hand upon him, and God's voice within him. He acts with the recollection that his Omniscient Guide is also his future Judge; and that while He moves him, He is also noting down in His book how he answers to His godly motions. He acts with a memory laden with past infirmity and sin, and a consciousness that he has much more to mourn over and repent of, in the years gone by, than to rejoice in. Yes, surely, he has many a secret wound to be healed; many a bruise to be tended; many a sore like Lazarus; many a chronic infirmity; many a bad omen of perils to come. It is one thing not to trust in the world; it is another thing not to trust in one's self.

John Henry Newman, 'On Christian Nobleness', in *A Lectionary of Christian Prose*, Longmans, Green and Co., 1941, page 57

CHURCH

Church—building for public Christian worship; body of all
Christians, organized Christian society, clergy or clerical profession

I was listening recently to a student from the United States on a summer school in Oxford. He was telling me that although he had a spiritual awareness he found organized religion boring. As far as I could tell he was being thoroughly honest and voicing what a large number of people felt, particularly the younger generation.

I remember trying to tackle this problem in my early twenties. Three of us got together and used to meet for an hour a week, trying to work out the aim and the function of the Church. We were greatly helped by Ernest Southcott's book *The Parish Comes Alive*. The author, a parish priest, recorded his experiences at Halton, Leeds. As I recall it, when he first went there he found the church services dull, boring and sterile. He felt the small congregation was going through the motions of worship with little inner conviction. He tackled this at two levels. Firstly, he formed a number of house churches which used to meet in the parish during the week. Secondly, the life generated by these house churches was fed into the corporate life of the church. As a result, the parish did indeed come alive.

The three of us were excited by this strategy. The eventual outcome was *Visions of Faith, Hope, Love* and *Glory*. These anthologies are designed for the individual and for house churches, to foster and nurture inner conviction. It is hoped they will bring new life to the Church as a whole.

I have built thee an exalted house, a place for thee to dwell in for ever.
2 Chronicles 6:2

Unless the Lord builds the house, those who build it labour in vain.
Psalm 127:1

They devoted themselves to the apostles' teaching and fellowship, to the breaking of bread and the prayers.
Acts 2:42

... strive to excel in building up the church.
1 Corinthians 14:12

The maintenance of powerful benevolence is more vital to the Christian church than dogmatic systems.
Henry Ward Beecher, *Proverbs from Plymouth Pulpit*, Charles Burnet & Co., 1887, page 109

... the church is itself a mystery which opens on to the 'ineffable riches of Christ,' which we must accept in their totality.
Leon Joseph Cardinal Suenens, *A New Pentecost?*, translated by Francis Martin, Darton, Longman & Todd, 1975, page 1

The Church has a right to edify itself by the gifts of all its members. Nothing is more striking than the latent and undeveloped power in the Church to-day.
Henry Ward Beecher, *Proverbs from Plymouth Pulpit*, Charles Burnet & Co., 1887, page 198

There must be vitality, elasticity, variety, and liberty in church life, or it will fail for the most part in the great ends for which it was established.
Henry Ward Beecher, *Proverbs from Plymouth Pulpit*, Charles Burnet & Co., 1887, page 200

A humiliated and defenceless church must go out into a hostile world to re-discover the God-man in the least of his brethren.
Paul Oestreicher, in Hans Jürgen Schultz, *Conversion to the World*, SCM Press, 1967, page 32

... it belongs to the very life of the people of God that it must accept again and again to have its life renewed by a new confrontation with its Lord and his holy will.
W.A. Visser 'T Hooft, *The Renewal of the Church*, SCM Press, 1956, page 23

The church exists to proclaim the good news of where true humanity is to be found and to exemplify in the midst of this present world what growth towards maturity in Christ means.
Daniel Jenkins, *Christian Maturity and the Theology of Success*, SCM Press, 1976, page 67

The true Church is... the communion and fellowship of spiritual persons—an invisible congregation, ever-enlarging with the process of the ages and with the expanding light of the Spirit.

Rufus M. Jones, *Spiritual Reformers in the 16th and 17th Centuries*, Macmillan and Co., 1914, page 38

Jesus never required membership of a church as a condition of entry into God's kingdom. The obedient acceptance of his message and the immediate and radical submission to God's will sufficed.

Hans Küng, *On Being a Christian*, translated by Edward Quinn, William Collins Sons & Co., 1977, page 285

A Church without hope has nothing to offer anyone. It is just a collection of demoralized individuals so concerned about their own survival that they haven't the freedom to offer society the Gospel in its power and comprehensiveness.

Colin Morris, *The Hammer of the Lord*, Epworth Press, 1973, page 10

The Church is most true to its own nature when it seeks nothing for itself, renounces power, humbly bears witness to the truth but makes no claim to be the *possessor* of truth, and is continually dying in order that it may live.

J.H. Oldham, *Life is Commitment*, SCM Press, 1953, page 95

The great problem of the Church (and therefore of its theologians) is to establish or re-establish some kind of vital contact with that enormous majority of human beings for whom the Christian faith is not so much unlikely as irrelevant and uninteresting.

H.E. Root, in A.R. Vidler, editor, *Soundings*, Cambridge at the University Press, 1962, page 6

The Church must take care that in trying to build a bridge across to the secularized modern world, it does not abandon the bridgehead on the Christian side and find itself left with nothing to communicate and nothing distinctively Christian to contribute.

F.R. Barry, *Secular and Supernatural*, SCM Press, 1969, page 33

It is not permissable to designate as 'unchurched' those who have become alienated from organized denominations and traditional creeds. In living among these groups for half a generation I learned how much of the latent Church there is within them.

Paul Tillich, *On the Boundary*, William Collins Sons & Co., 1967, page 67

Without contemplation and interior prayer the Church cannot fulfill her mission to transform and save mankind. Without contemplation, she will be reduced to being the servant of cynical and worldly powers, no matter how hard her faithful may protest that they are fighting for the Kingdom of God.

Thomas Merton, *Contemplative Prayer*, Darton, Longman & Todd, 1973, page 144

If we manage to be clever and busy about all else—contemporary problems and contemporary tasks, even the meeting of other great and real human needs, but are silent or ineffective about the mystery of the soul's communion with God, then the greatest riches offered to the Church are lost and its ultimate distinctiveness from all other associations has gone.

Norman Goodall, *The Local Church*, Hodder and Stoughton, 1966, page 28

The Church is people, fallible and sinful people, and if it is no better than any other human institution it is certainly no worse. It is nonsense to pretend that we could have our religion without it; and though it has fallen into grave error from time to time, I doubt if it has done as much harm as nationalism, materialism, colonialism, capitalism, communism, fascism, militarism and apathy.

Gerald Priestland, *Priestland's Progress*, BBC Publications, 1982, page 213

The persistence of poverty, together with inadequate provision in social care, makes its own demands on the Church. Some of the most basic explanations of the present situation lie in the area of public values and public policy. If the Church, as a company of people seeking to be loyal servants of the Gospel, is to respond truthfully and helpfully it needs to be an aware and understanding body. Both at the level of its national organisation and at the level of its congregational life, the Church... needs a deeper and more informed awareness of social need and public policy.

Faith in the City, Church House Publishing, 1985, page 278

Dedication to the Gospel must always lead to a new and living sense of brotherhood with all men. Yet our tired segments of the Church, burdened by the whole weight of their history, try to take men captive by shutting them off in a special compartment from the rest of mankind. All too often the churches are saddled with reactionary views, rooted in the past and limping along behind the times. We accept this state of affairs too readily, generally without admitting it to ourselves. We allow ourselves to be caught up in a Christian environment that we find congenial and in the process create a ghetto of like-minded people who are quite unmindful of the real world.

Roger Schutz, in Hans Jürgen Schultz, *Conversion to the World*, SCM Press, 1967, page 74

... we want a resurrection for the Church. Some despair of seeing this accomplished. That is faithlessness. Church history proves that there is in the Church an ever-present possibility of resurrection. The Church is in fact a great 'community of the resurrection'. In a mysterious but definite way, the Christians who are suffering with our Lord's suffering, dying with our Lord's death, and living with our Lord's life, *hold the world together*, as the famous passage in the Epistle to Diognetus says: 'the soul is enclosed in the body and yet itself holdeth the body together; so Christians are kept in the world as in a prison-house, and yet they themselves hold the world together'.

Eric Symes Abbott, *The Compassion of God and the Passion of Christ*, Geoffrey Bles, 1963, page 40

Within the strange, sprawling, quarrelling mass of the churches, within their stifling narrowness, their ignorance, their insensitivity, their stupidity, their fear of the senses and of truth, I perceive another Church, one which really is Christ at work in the world. To this Church men seem to be admitted as much as by a baptism of the heart as of the body, and they know more of intellectual charity, of vulnerability, of love, of joy, of peace, than most of the rest of us. They have learned to live with few defences and so conquered the isolation which torments us. They do not judge, especially morally; their own relationships make it possible for others to grow. It does not matter what their circumstances are, what their physical and mental limitations are. They really are free men, the prisoners who have been released and who in turn can release others.

Monica Furlong, *With Love to the Church*, Hodder and Stoughton, 1965, page 22

This church which Jesus founded has today become a stumbling block to almost anyone who is drawn to him. For the life of the church falls far below the level of the life of God's reign on earth as we see this bursting forth in the early Christian community. The New Testament church as it is reflected in the book called the Acts of the Apostles was (to use its own language) filled with the Holy Spirit. It was pervaded by the spirit of Jesus of Nazareth, now exalted as Christ and Lord (the Holy Spirit and the spirit of Jesus are identified at several points in the New Testament). It is true that there were quarrels and rifts and deep differences of opinion: but the force which eventually overcame these differences and preserved the essential unity of the Christian community was the spirit of the risen Lord working among his disciples.

John Hick, *Christianity at the Centre*, SCM Press, 1968, page 76

COMMITMENT

*Commitment—act of committing or being committed; dedication or
obligation to particular action or cause, etc.*

Three quotations specifically appeal to me in this section, because they seem to ring true to my own experience of commitment. This incidently took place shortly after I arrived in Oxford, when I took the step of becoming a committed Christian.

The first is that of John Keats. Metaphorically speaking I had leaped headlong into the sea, and had become better acquainted with the soundings, the quicksands and the rocks, than if I had stayed upon the green shore. From the step of commitment onwards I understood the Christian faith in a new way—from the inside. Christianity now began to make sense. I came to believe this transforming faith can only be understood from the inside, from a position of commitment.

The second is that of Clay Ford. Shortly after I had taken the step of commitment I became aware of something happening to me. It was as if Jesus Christ had stepped out of the Bible and in a mysterious way, beyond comprehension, had come into my life and made himself real to me. His 'presence' began to transform me. I became conscious of a whole new dimension of life, as a consequence of a commitment to a personal God.

The third is that of Rabindranath Tagore. This helped me to see the importance of our response to the 'King of all kings' here and now. Commitment leads to an experience of that more abundant life in the present moment, suggested in that story by that valuable grain of gold.

Take good care to observe the commandment and the law which Moses the servant of the Lord commanded you, to love the Lord your God, and to walk in all his ways, and to keep his commandments, and to cleave to him, and to serve him with all your heart and with all your soul.

Joshua 22:5

Commit your way to the Lord; trust in him, and he will act.

Psalm 37:5

Father, into thy hands I commit my spirit!

Luke 23:46

I appeal to you therefore, brethren, by the mercies of God, to present your bodies as a living sacrifice, holy and acceptable to God, which is your spiritual worship.

Romans 12:1

Why always 'not yet'? Do flowers in spring say 'Not yet'?

Norman Douglas, *An Almanac*, Chatto and Windus in association with Martin Secker & Warburg, 1945, page 59

The words he spoke, the deeds he performed, the demands he raised confronted people with a final decision. Jesus left no one neutral. He himself had become the great question.

Hans Küng, *On Being a Christian*, translated by Edward Quinn, William Collins Sons & Co., 1977, page 286

I say, the acknowledgement of God in Christ
Accepted by thy reason, solves for thee
All questions in the earth and out of it.

Robert Browning, 'A Death in the Desert', in *The Poetical Works of Robert Browning*, Oxford University Press, 1949, page 489

The most sovereign act of an independent person is to give the one thing he owns—himself. Then God gives the most precious thing He owns—Himself. Then we are filled with the Holy Spirit.

E. Stanley Jones, *Mastery*, Hodder and Stoughton, 1956, page 45

I leaped headlong into the Sea, and thereby have become better acquainted with the Soundings, the quicksands, & the rocks, than if I had stayed upon the green shore, and piped a silly pipe, and took tea & comfortable advice.

John Keats, 'To James Augustus Hessey, Friday 9 Oct. 1818', in Maurice Buxton Forman, editor, *The Letters of John Keats*, number 90, Oxford University Press, 1952, page 221

... the self is not lost when it is surrendered to Christ. It is lost in a higher will, redeemed from a self-centred will, and found again in obedience to that higher will. So it all ends in self-affirmation. The self is not cancelled—it is heightened.

E. Stanley Jones, *The Word became Flesh*, Hodder and Stoughton, 1964, page 343

The death by which we enter into life is not an escape from reality but a complete gift of ourselves which involves a total commitment to reality. It begins by renouncing the illusory reality which created things acquire when they are seen only in their relation to our own selfish interests.

Thomas Merton, *Thoughts in Solitude*, Burns & Oates, 1958, page 17

He [Jesus] provoked a final *decision*; but not a yes or no to a particular title, to a particular dignity, a particular office, or even to a particular dogma, rite or law. His message and community raised the question of the aim and purpose to which a man will ultimately direct his life. Jesus demanded a final decision for God's cause and man's.

Hans Küng, *On Being a Christian*, translated by Edward Quinn, William Collins Sons & Co., 1977, page 291

Either we must confess our blindness and seek the opening of our eyes; or else we must accept the light and walk by it. What we may not do, yet all strive to do, is to keep our eyes half open and live by half the light. That kind of sight holds us to our sin and our sin to us. But the only way of avoiding it is to look with eyes wide open upon ourselves and the world as the full light reveals it; but this is the surrender of faith, and pride resists it.

William Temple, *Readings in St. John's Gospel* (First and Second Series), Macmillan and Co., 1947, page 161

The one thing he [Jesus] seems to have condemned utterly was evasion of choice. The man in the parable who was afraid to risk his bag of gold and brought it back uninvested and uncommitted was flung out into the dark. To choose is to commit yourself. To commit yourself is to run the risk of failure, the risk of sin, the risk of betrayal. Jesus can deal with all those, for forgiveness is his metier. The only thing he can do nothing with is the refusal to be committed. Even Judas should do quickly whatever he chooses to do and be responsible.

John V. Taylor, *The Go-Between God*, SCM Press, 1973, page 98

There are some commitments that need a lifetime to be fulfilled. The commitment of baptism, which is simply the special Christian expression of the general commitment to become a truly human person along the way of transcendence; to be a loyal and reliable friend, in season and out of season; to be a good husband or wife, father or mother, to make a success of marriage and family; to be devoted to a vocation, whether it be that of priest or scientist or nurse or farmer; these all need a lifetime, and even at the end of a lifetime there is more to be done.

John Macquarrie, *In Search of Humanity*, SCM Press, 1982, page 157

Father Raymond tells the charming story of a little child whose mother was teaching him to pray. When he got to the part, 'Lord, I surrender everything to thee, everything I own,' he abruptly broke off and whispered to himself, 'except my baby rabbit.'

All of us have our baby rabbits. Sometimes it is an ugly thing, sometimes beautiful, sometimes large, sometimes small; but we are more attached to it than to anything else. But this is the thing that God asks of us and that he touches upon when we sincerely ask guidance of him. God does not, however, ask us to seek out our neighbour's little rabbits.

Paul Tournier, *Escape from Loneliness*, translated by John S. Gilmour, SCM Press, 1962, page 111

In absolute trust and complete reliance, the whole man with all the powers of his mind commits himself to the Christian message and to him whom it announces. It is simultaneously an act of knowing, willing and feeling, a trust which includes an acceptance of message and person as true.

Hence I do not simply believe various facts, truths, theories, dogmas: I do not believe this or that. Nor do I believe merely in a person's trustworthiness: I do not simply believe this man or that. But I venture quite confidently to commit myself to a message, a truth, a way of life, a hope, ultimately quite personally to someone: I believe 'in' God and in him whom God sent.

Hans Küng, *On Being a Christian*, translated by Edward Quinn, William Collins Son & Co., 1977, page 162

The terrible thing, the almost impossible thing is to hand over your whole self—all your wishes and precautions—to Christ. But it is far easier than what we are all trying to do instead. For what we are trying to do is to remain what we call 'ourselves,' to keep personal happiness as our great aim in life, and yet at the same time to be 'good'. We are all trying to let our mind and heart go their own way—centred on money or pleasure or ambition—and hoping, in spite of this, to behave honestly and chastely and humbly. And that is exactly what Christ warned us you could not do. As He said, a thistle cannot produce figs. If I am a field that contains nothing but grass-seed, I cannot produce wheat... If I want to produce wheat, the change must go deeper than the surface. I must be ploughed up and re-sown.

C.S. Lewis, *Mere Christianity*, William Collins Sons & Co., 1961, page 164

I had gone a-begging from door to door in the village path, when thy golden chariot appeared in the distance like a gorgeous dream and I wondered who was this King of all kings!... The chariot stopped where I stood. Thy glance fell on me and thou camest down with a smile. I felt that the luck of my life had come at last. Then of a sudden thou didst hold out thy right hand and say, 'What hast thou to give me?' Ah, what a kingly jest was it to open thy palm to a beggar to beg! I was confused and stood undecided, and then from my wallet I slowly took out the least little grain of corn and gave it thee.

But how great my surprise when at the day's end I emptied my bag on the floor to find a least little grain of gold among the poor heap. I bitterly wept and wished that I had had the heart to give thee my all.

Rabindranath Tagore, *Gitanjali*, Macmillan and Co., 1971, page 42

I read a book by Rudolf Bultmann, *Jesus and the Word*. He describes the teachings of Jesus. Jesus wasn't saying believe this, or do that: he was saying, 'Commit your life to me, give yourself to me, follow me. It's either-or, yes or no, paint or get off the ladder.'

Without realizing what was happening I committed my life to follow Jesus Christ. I did not know he was alive, that he had actually risen from death. That seemed ridiculous to me, a leg-end perhaps built up about him by well-meaning followers. But something happened when I committed my life to follow Jesus Christ. He made himself real to me. The Person of Jesus Christ stepped out of the Bible and into my life. His love engulfed me; the power of his presence transformed me. I became aware of a whole new dimension of life. I came to know a personal God, a God who is a loving Father. My life had meaning. It made sense now. I am a child of God, responsible to him and for every human being.

Clay Ford, *Jesus and the Street People*, Lutterworth Press, 1972, page 41

People today no longer want to make lifelong commitments. This is a serious failure. An adult is someone who can put a lot of thought into what he's doing, with or without outside help, and who is capable of making a definitive choice whether it is on an occupation or another person. Faithfulness is then the ability to stick with his choice, the will to fight for it, and turn any obstacles into positive elements on his chosen path.

Unfaithfulness is a disease afflicting both the individual and society. Society throws the individual into new experiences which are never brought to any conclusion. Unfaithfulness is to be put off by any obstacles; weakness is man's downfall. Constantly uprooted, he can never reach maturity and bear fruit.

Fidelity within marriage is the most profound of all because the root it takes in the love of each spouse cannot be pulled up. A married couple may grow apart but they can no longer 'unmarry'.

Michel Quoist, *With Open Heart*, translated by Colette Copeland, Gill and Macmillan, 1983, page 117

CONVERSION

Conversion—converting or being converted, especially in belief or religion; bringing over (to an opinion, party, faith, etc.); turning of sinners to God

I wonder if too much prominence has been given in Church circles to the sudden conversion of St Paul. A superficial reading of the biblical accounts suggest this profound change all took place in the space of a few moments on the road to Damascus. Some commentators, however, regard his conversion as the result of a long search. They even suggest he spent several years afterwards 'in Arabia' working out the implications of his conversion experience. I am sympathetic to this point of view.

My own experience was also of a fairly 'sudden' conversion experience whilst listening to a sermon. The preacher was the Bishop of Coventry, Cuthbert Bardsley, and the venue was St Aldate's Church in Oxford. I think this 'conversion' was the result of a long search. Early on I began working out the implications of my baptism. At the age of ten I joined a church choir, and was subjected to many sermons. I was confirmed in my teens and rebellion set in during my early twenties. It was at this time a friend persuaded me to go to St Aldate's. Much to my surprise I found myself crossing the Rubicon and becoming converted to Christianity.

Initially I expected everything to change overnight. This, of course, did not happen. Instead I have had the good fortune to consolidate my conversion experience over the years. I have been greatly helped to grow by reflection, and as you would expect, the practice continues. I now think the process of conversion is the work of a lifetime.

Let the wicked forsake his way, and the unrighteous man his thoughts; let him return to the Lord, that he may have mercy on him, and to our God, for he will abundantly pardon.
Isaiah 55:7

Cast away from you all the transgressions which you have committed against me, and get yourselves a new heart and a new spirit!
Ezekiel 18:31

Truly, I say to you, unless you turn and become like children, you will never enter the kingdom of heaven.
Matthew 18:3

Jesus answered him, 'Truly, truly, I say to you, unless one is born anew, he cannot see the kingdom of God.'
John 3:3

To be converted, to be regenerated, to receive grace, to experience religion, to gain an assurance, are so many phrases which denote the process, gradual or sudden, by which a self hitherto divided, and consciously wrong, inferior and unhappy, becomes unified and consciously right, superior and happy, in consequence of its firmer hold upon religious realities. This at least is what conversion signifies in general terms...
William James, *The Varieties of Religious Experience*, William Collins Sons & Co., 1974, page 194

There is only one influence that converts, and that is the example of a life which is shot through and through with the glory and strength of the spirit of Christ. The main task of the Church is to prove that it is itself interested above everything else in living a life as sacrificial, as honest, as straightforward and as charitable as was the life of its Founder. In a word, the Church cannot possibly be less righteous than a wholly converted Christian individual. It must show beyond any shadow of doubt that in its corporate capacity it is living true to the standards which are expected of men who could be called Christ-like.
H.R.L. Sheppard, *The Impatience of a Parson*, Hodder and Stoughton, 1927, page 114

Although the actual moment of a conversion often seems quite sudden and unexpected, yet we know from experience that such a fundamental occurence always has a long period of unconscious incubation. It is only when the preparation is complete, that is to say, when the individual is ready to be converted, that the new view breaks forth with great emotion. St. Paul had already been a Christian for a long time, only unconsciously; hence his fanatical resistance to the Christians, because fanaticism is only found in individuals who are compensating secret doubts. Therefore converts are always the worst fanatics.
C.G. Jung, *Psychological Reflections*, selected and edited by Jolande Jacobi, Routledge & Kegan Paul, 1953, page 318

God does not force us, and we are free to reject His advances, but His presence is always with us, and when we let His presence have its effect then there must come about in us that turning right round to Him which is conversion. Conversion, of course, is something that is going on all through our lives. It is the story of the complete conquest of the love of God, the conquest of our whole being, so that His love reigns in our minds and our whole mentality is the mentality of Christ: 'Let this mind be in you which was also in Christ Jesus.'

It is the conquest of our hearts, that this love may be in us which is also in Christ Jesus: the conquest of our wills, that this will may be in us which is also in Christ Jesus.

Father Andrew, S.D.C., *The Good Shepherd*, A.R. Mowbray & Co., 1949, page 17

I recall with deep sorrow the fact that, in our days, in the case of newly-converted souls, the necessity of advance and pressing forward in holiness of life, is not sufficiently insisted upon; whereas, the Scripture is so clear and full upon this subject. In the Scripture we find that holiness includes a real and actual cleansing from sin and pollution, in the renewing of the inner man, in a changing from glory to glory after the image of Him who created us, in conformity to Jesus Christ. Let us seek after all these things, praying earnestly, and withdrawing ourselves into the seclusion of the inner sanctuary of communion with God, who is so inexpressibly near to us, who desires, by the power of the resurrection of Christ, by the spirit of holiness, to sanctify us wholly, to work by us, to live and move in us.

Gerhard Tersteegen, in Frances Bevan, *Sketches of the Quiet in the Land*, John F. Shaw and Co., 1891, page 396

If it is a total misunderstanding of the Gospel to suppose that we are to seek our own satisfaction, our own perfection, and ignore the needs of the world, ignore the very purpose of the human life of Christ, it is also a total misunderstanding to suppose that we can work for the world, as Christians, and to become saints, without being identified with Christ. 'Unless the grain of wheat falling into the ground die, itself remaineth alone.' We must not wait until we are wholly transformed into Christ before attempting to share in His work in the world—if we did we should have little to offer Him, most of us, when we died. It is a logical, not a temporal, order ... But unless we try to make every thought and desire and action more and more completely identical with the mind and will of God, our work may remain our work instead of His, and then it will be of little value, and we may even commit the blasphemy of confusing end with means, and subordinating the love of God to the love of men.

Gerald Vann, *The Divine Pity*, William Collins Sons & Co., 1956, page 15

The key biblical words for conversion are *naham* and *shub* in Hebrew, and *metanoia* and *epistrophe* in Greek. If conversion means a radical turning, or a redirection of one's life, the first word in each pair, emphasizing repentance, specifies a turning *from* (sin), while the second indicates a turning *towards* (God). Emphasis on conversion as repentance for sin has probably kept Christians from thinking of Jesus as having experienced conversion, even though he did present himself to John for baptism. It has been the extraordinary experience of Paul on the road to Damascus, rather, that has dominated Christian thinking about conversion in the New Testament (especially accounts in Acts). Many contemporary theologians, however, realizing the full *religious* depth of conversion beyond the moral, recognize in Jesus's response to crises in his life and ministry a transformation of faith, a re-thinking of his relationship to the Father that defines the very essence of religious conversion.

Walter E. Conn, in Gordon S. Wakefield, editor, *A Dictionary of Christian Spirituality*, SCM Press, 1986, page 96

It is not a question of 'doing penance' externally, in sackcloth and ashes. It is not an intellectually determined or strongly emotional religious experience. It is a decisive change of will, an awareness changed from the roots upwards, a new basic attitude, a different scale of values. It is therefore a radical rethinking and re-turning on the part of the whole man, a completely new attitude to life.

Nevertheless, Jesus does not expect an acknowledgement of sin, a confession, from the person who wants to change his ways. He is not very interested in the latter's problematic past, which of course has to be abandoned. All that matters is the better future, this future which God promises and gives to man, to which the latter must turn irrevocably and unreservedly, without looking back, now that his hand is on the plow. Man can live on forgiveness. This is conversion based on that imperturbable, unshakable confidence in God and in his word which even in the Old Testament was known as *faith*. It involves a believing trust and a trustful faith.

Hans Küng, *On Being a Christian*, translated by Edward Quinn, William Collins Sons & Co., 1977, page 250

Jesus... did not demand and still less did he set in motion a politico-social revolution. What he did set going was a decidedly *non-violent revolution*: a revolution emerging from man's innermost and secret nature, from the personal centre, from the heart of man, into society. There was to be no continuing in the old ways, but a radical change in man's thinking and a conversion (Greek, *metanoia*), away from all forms of selfishness, toward God and his fellow men. The real alien powers, from which man had to be liberated, were not the hostile world powers but the forces of evil: hatred, injustice, dissension, violence, all human selfishness, and also suffering, sickness and death. There had to be therefore a changed awareness, a new way of thinking, a new scale of values. The evil that had to be overcome lay not only in the system, in the structures, but in man. Inner freedom had to be established and this would lead to freedom from external powers. Society had to be transformed through the transformation of the individual.

Hans Küng, *On Being a Christian*, translated by Edward Quinn, William Collins Sons & Co., 1977, page 191

This whole work of conversion, of transformation, of 'lasting change,' must have its origin in something within ourselves. We cannot turn from baubles and 'toys' and 'our desire for that which is high in the world' until a Light from some source plainly shows us an eternal reality for which we may 'highly adventure tryal.' There is... only one place where such a guiding Light could arise, and that is within the soul itself, as an inward and immediate knowledge: ''Tis not far to seek. We direct thee to within thyself. Though oughtest to turn into, to mind and have regard unto, that which is within thee, to wit, the Light of Truth, the true Light which enlighteneth every man that cometh into the world. Here 'tis that thou must be and not without thee. Here thou shalt find a Principle certain and infallible, through which increasing and going on into, thou mayest at length arrive unto a happy condition... And if thou happenest to be one of those that would know all things before thou dost begin... know this, Thou dost therein just as those that would learn to read without knowing the Letters. He that will not adventure till he be fully satisfied, shall never begin, much less finish his own salvation. We say then, that we exhort every one to turn unto the Light that's in him.'

Rufus M. Jones, *Spiritual Reformers in the 16th and 17th Centuries*, Macmillan and Co., 1914, page 129

But sometimes the step is a distinct and vivid experience. Then we get the strange facts of conversion: when through some object or event—perhaps quite small object or event—in the external world, another world and its overwhelming attraction and demand is realised. An old and limited state of consciousness is suddenly, even violently, broken up and another takes its place. It was the voice of a child saying 'Take, read!' which at last made St. Augustine cross the frontier on which he had been lingering, and turned a brilliant and selfish young professor into one of the giants of the Christian Church; and a voice which seemed to him to come from the Crucifix, which literally made the young St. Francis, unsettled and unsatisfied, another man than he was before. It was while St. Ignatius sat by a stream and watched the running water, and while the strange old cobbler Jacob Boehme was looking at a pewter dish, that there was shown to each of them the mystery of the Nature of God. It was the sudden sight of a picture at a crucial moment of her life which revealed to St. Catherine of Genoa the beauty of Holiness, and by contrast her own horribleness; and made her for the rest of her life the friend and servant of the unseen Love. All these were various glimpses of one living Perfection; and woke up the love and desire for that living perfection, latent in every human creature, which is the same thing as the love of God, and the substance of a spiritual life. A spring is touched, a Reality always there discloses itself in its awe-inspiring majesty and intimate nearness, and becomes the ruling fact of existence; continually presenting its standards, and demanding a costly response.

Evelyn Underhill, *The Spiritual Life*, Harper & Row, 1936, page 53

CREATION

Creation—all that has been made; the bringing into being of the world

I was invited to spend a few weeks in Kenya with some close friends. Our base was their home in Nairobi, but from there we visited several game parks, had a memorable holiday by the sea at Malindi, and went on a mini-expedition to Lake Rudolf (now Lake Turkana). The climax was the climb on Mount Kenya. We began our ascent walking up a marsh about a mile long. Once we left the tree-line behind we made good progress and soon found ourselves in the Teleki valley. Here we had some excellent views and were impressed with the scenery, especially giant groundsel. We spent a restless night in the Teleki hut, already feeling the affects of altitude. Next day we moved into rock and snow as the three peaks, Nelion, Batian and Lenana, came into view. We struggled up to Top Hut, where we spent a bitterly cold night.

Early next morning we were spellbound by the dawn. Below us at 10,000 feet was a vast sea of cloud. Two hundred miles away we could see Mount Kilimanjaro peeping out of the clouds. The sun was shining brightly with a glorious array of colours. The whole scene profoundly affected me. Some words of St Paul came to mind: 'Ever since the creation of the world his invisible nature, namely, his eternal power and deity, has been clearly perceived in the things that have been made.' These in turn reminded me of Wordsworth: 'and I have felt a presence that disturbs me with the joy of elevated thoughts; a sense sublime of something far more deeply interfused.' Our climb on Mount Kenya still strengthens my belief in the Creator and his Creation.

In the beginning God created the heavens and the earth. The earth was without form and void, and darkness was upon the face of the deep; and the Spirit of God was moving over the face of the waters.

Genesis 1:1–2

For thou didst form my inward parts, thou didst knit me together in my mother's womb. I praise thee, for thou art fearful and wonderful. Wonderful are thy works! Thou knowest me right well.

Psalm 139:13–14

Ever since the creation of the world his invisible nature, namely, his eternal power and deity, has been clearly perceived in the things that have been made.

Romans 1:20

He is the image of the invisible God, the first-born of all creation; for in him all things were created, in heaven and on earth, visible and invisible, whether thrones or dominions or principalities or authorities—all things were created through him and for him. He is before all things, and in him all things hold together.

Colossians 1:15–17

The mystery of Creation is the mystery of that which goes on to-day and is continuous.

Mark Rutherford, *Last Pages From a Journal*, Oxford University Press, 1915, page 314

In order to create there must be a dynamic force, and what force is more potent than love?

Igor Stravinsky, *An Autobiography*, Calder & Boyars, 1975, page 81

He is no sound judge in any department of human endeavour who fails to identify himself with the creator's point of view, however repugnant it may be to his own.

Norman Douglas, *An Almanac*, Chatto and Windus in association with Martin Secker & Warburg, 1945, page 66

Creation should not be presented as a past event but as continuous activity for God is to be presented as the creator of all the stirrings in the human mind as well as of the shifting clouds and the song of the birds.

R.E.C. Browne, *The Ministry of the Word*, SCM Press, 1958, page 110

There is grandeur in this view of life, with its several powers, having been originally breathed by the Creator into a few forms or into one; and that, while this planet has gone circling on according to the fixed law of gravity, from so simple a beginning endless forms most beautiful and most wonderful have been and are being evolved.

Charles Darwin, *The Origin of Species*, A.L. Burt, 1900, page 505

We have got to realize the littleness of creation and to see it for the nothing that it is before we can love and possess God who is uncreated. This is the reason why we have no ease of heart or soul, for we are seeking our rest in trivial things which cannot satisfy, and not seeking to know God, almighty, all-wise, all-good. He is true rest.

Julian of Norwich, *Revelations of Divine Love*, translated by Clifton Wolters, Penguin Books, 1976, page 68

This world is an unfinished work which Man can only make something of as he makes something of himself. Ask for bread and God doesn't drop a loaf in your lap but sprinkles a few seeds in your hands. Demand maturity and God offers only the power of procreation— what you do with the embryo is up to you. Cry for peace and he will grant you the capacity for sacrifice. Yearn for the Promised Land and he will point first to the desert and then to your feet and tell you to get walking!

Colin Morris, *The Hammer of the Lord*, Epworth Press, 1973, page 69

The visible and invisible creation, in all its degrees and stages, is the outgoing and unfolding of God, who in His Essence and Godhead is one, indivisible and incomprehensible. But as He is essentially and eternally Good, He *expresses* Himself in revelation, and goes out of Unity into differentiation and multiplicity; but the entire spiritual movement of the universe is back again toward the fundamental Unity, for Divine Unity is both the Alpha and the Omega of the deeper inner world.

Rufus M. Jones, *Spiritual Reformers in the 16th and 17th Centuries*, Macmillan and Co., 1914, page 40

I have seen
A curious child, who dwelt upon a tract
Of inward ground, applying to his ear
The convolutions of a smooth-lipped shell;
To which, in silence hushed, his very soul
Listened intensely; and his countenance soon
Brightened with joy; for from within were heard
Murmurings, whereby the monitor expressed
Mysterious union with its native sea.
Even such a shell the universe itself
Is to the ear of Faith; and there are times,
I doubt not, when to you it doth impart
Authentic tidings of invisible things;
Of ebb and flow, and ever-during power;
And central peace, subsisting at the heart
Of endless agitation.

William Wordsworth, 'The Excursion', iv. 1133, in E. de Selincourt and Helen Darbishire, editors, *The Poetical Works of William Wordsworth*, Oxford at the Clarendon Press, 1959, page 145

It was always a basic Greek thought that where there is order there must be a mind. When we look at the world we see an amazing order. The planets keep to their appointed courses. The tides observe their appointed times. Seed time and harvest, summer and winter, day and night come in their appointed order. Clearly there is order in nature, and, therefore, equally clearly there must be a mind behind it all. Further, that mind must be greater than any human mind because it achieves results that the human mind can never achieve. No man can make day into night, or night into day; no man can make a seed that will have in it the power of growth; no man can make a living thing. Therefore the mind in nature is far above the human mind in man. If then in the world there is order, there must be mind; and if in that order there are things which are beyond the mind of man to do, then the mind behind the order of nature must be a mind above and beyond the mind of man—and straightway we have reached God. To look outwards upon the world is to come face to face with the God who made the world.

William Barclay, *The Gospel of John*, The Saint Andrew Press, 1965, volume 1, page 36

When we contemplate the physical creation, we see an unimaginable complex, organized on many planes one above another; atomic, molecular, cellular; vegetable, animal, social. And the marvel of it is that at every level the constituent elements run themselves, and, by their mutual interaction, run the world. God not only makes the world, he makes it make itself; or rather, he causes its innumerable constituents to make it. And this in spite of the fact that the constituents are not for the most part intelligent. They cannot enter into the creative purposes they serve. They cannot see beyond the tip of their noses, they have, indeed, no noses not to see beyond, nor any eyes with which to fail in the attempt. All they can do is blind away at being themselves, and fulfil the repetitive pattern of their existence. When you contemplate this amazing structure, do you wonder that it should be full of flaws, breaks, accidents, collisions and disasters? Will you not be more inclined to wonder why chaos does not triumph; how higher forms of organization should ever arise, or, having arisen, maintain and perpetuate themselves? . . .

Though a thousand species have perished with the mammoth and the dodo, and though all species, perhaps, must perish at the last, it is a sort of miracle that the species there are should have established themselves. And how have they established themselves? Science studies the pattern, but theology assigns the cause: that imperceptible persuasion exercised by creative Will on the chaos of natural forces, setting a bias on the positive and achieving the creatures.

Austin Farrer, *Saving Belief*, Hodder and Stoughton, 1967, page 51

The story in Genesis about God's creation is not a literal piece of history or science, but a marvellous parable of how the world depends utterly upon God, and how he made the world in its many stages or phases.

But of course the discoveries of modern science—geology, biology and the rest—have shown us more and more of what these marvellous successive stages in the process of divine creation are: the existence of inorganic matter, then the emergence of life, primitive animals, mammals, animals in which intelligence and consciousness appear. Then, at some undefinable point in the series, there comes man, man so marvellous—but perhaps man is not more marvellous than the marvel of what emerged at every single stage of the process.

But this is the drama of divine creation: the Spirit of God working in the world with man as climax, suggesting that the whole process is in order that man may emerge in his glory and his potentialities.

And what is there in this creative process about man that makes him so utterly different from the phenomena which have preceded him? There are lots of ways in which that might be analysed or described, but the Bible says, 'God created man in his own image, after his own likeness'.

The wonderful thing about man is that he is describable as being in God's own image. Not that God and man are identical in all respects—far from it. God remains the Creator, and we always remain creatures, utterly dependent upon him. Yet there is a true affinity between God and man. Man has powers of memory, thought, consciousness, purpose, appreciation of beauty, appreciation of truth, moral distinction between right and wrong, and a rare potentiality of freedom. Above all he has the possibility of really knowing God, and having fellowship with God.

Michael Ramsey, *Through the Year with Michael Ramsey*, edited by Margaret Duggan, Hodder and Stoughton, 1975, page 46

CROSS

Cross—stake (usually with traverse bar) used by the ancients for crucifixion, especially that on which Christ was crucified; Christian religion; trial, affliction, annoyance

I wonder if we place too much emphasis on the historical cross of Christ, and not enough on taking up our cross daily and following Christ.

I am fond of Jesus' teaching, that unless a grain of wheat falls into the earth and dies, it remains alone; but if it dies it bears much fruit. This parable contains a vital truth for understanding one of the mysteries of the cross.

The grain of wheat, of course, does not wholly die when sown. The outer case perishes, but this lets in the nutrients of the soil, stimulating growth from the centre. Roots grow downward and the stem grows upwards seeking sun, warmth and rain. Growth continues until the grain is ripe—and plentiful. Apply this parable now to the human scene. We have already read about the Genesis story of the creation of man. God fashions and shapes man in his own image and likeness and breathes into man something of his own nature. We remember that which was fashioned in the image and likeness of God was taken from the dust of the earth so that man is earthy and creaturely as well as having a divine potential.

Sadly we have tended to centre ourselves on the earthy and creaturely. What is needed is a death to the primacy of the earthy and creaturely and a new birth so that we centre ourselves on the divine in the depths of our being. This is what I mean by taking up our cross daily and following Christ. It is a very painful process, but in it lies the secret of life.

... he who does not take his cross and follow me is not worthy of me. He who finds his life will lose it, and he who loses his life for my sake will find it.

Matthew 10:38–39

This was why the Jews sought all the more to kill him, because he not only broke the sabbath but also called God his own Father, making himself equal with God.

John 5:18

We know that our old self was crucified with him so that the sinful body might be destroyed, and we might no longer be enslaved to sin.

Romans 6:6

I have been crucified with Christ; it is no longer I who live, but Christ who lives in me; and the life I now live in the flesh I live by faith in the Son of God, who loved me and gave himself for me.

Galatians 2:20

The cross preceded the resurrection; but the resurrection has not abolished the cross. Suffering, sin, betrayal, cruelty of every kind, continued to exist after the crucifixion and they continue still. This is the failure of the cross...
God made failure an instrument of victory.

Una Kroll, *Lament for a Lost Enemy*, SPCK, 1977, page 126

It henceforth becomes our *business* to find Christ's life and Christ's death in us, to see that all His deeds are done in us. Christ's will must become our will, Christ's peace our peace, and then we may know 'the eternal Sabbath,' and keep 'quiet, even if the whole fabric of heaven and earth crack and mountains tumble down.'

Rufus M. Jones, *Spiritual Reformers in the 16th and 17th Centuries*, Macmillan and Co., 1914, page 250

The Christ of God was not then first crucified when the Jews brought him to the Cross; but Adam and Eve were his first real Murderers; for the Death which happened to them, in the Day that they did eat of the earthly Tree, was the Death of the Christ of God, or the Divine Life in their Souls. For Christ had never come into the World as a Second Adam to redeem it, had he not been originally the Life and Perfection, and Glory of the First Adam.

William Law, in Sidney Spencer, editor, *The Spirit of Prayer and the Spirit of Love*, James Clarke & Co., 1969, page 167

... the showdown came at Gethsemene and Golgotha. When guilt, suffering, and death began their painful encirclement, he could have broken out, he could have been spared all that humiliation by a wave of his hand. But, although it was possible for him to do it, that hand never moved. Instead, he let himself fall, living and dying, into the hands of his Father. He loved, literally until it killed him. For that reason, and for that alone, we have the unbelievable chance to count on God's loving us, knowing us, remaining true to us, and never abandoning us.

Helmut Thielicke, *I Believe: The Christian's Creed*, translated by John W. Doberstein and H. George Anderson, William Collins Sons & Co., 1969, page 84

In the death of Jesus, God is saying to us, 'I love you like that. I love you enough to see my Son suffer and die for you. I love you enough to bear the Cross on my heart, if only it will win you to myself.' The Cross is the proof that there is no length to which the love of God will refuse to go, in order to win men's hearts. The Cross is the medium of reconciliation because the Cross is the final proof of the love of God; and a love like that demands an answering love. If the Cross will not waken love and wonder in men's hearts, nothing will.

William Barclay, *Letters to Philippians, Colossians and Thessalonians*, The Saint Andrew Press, 1971, page 147

We have to learn that hard lesson, that Jesus did not win a victory in spite of the Cross, but that the Cross was the victory. We are inclined to think of the Resurrection and the Ascension as the victory, but they are only the crowning of our Lord's triumph. The Cross itself is the victory. It was really as a prophet that our Prime Minister spoke when he said: 'This is England's greatest hour.' It was not an hour of the waving of flags and joyful congratulations. It was an hour of standing alone for the things of the spirit, for liberty and justice and the integrity of life, unarmed and facing fearful odds, trusting only to the truth and integrity of God.

Father Andrew, S.D.C., *The Seven Signs of Christ*, A.R. Mowbray & Co., 1944, page 60

How Christ's death takes away thy sins thou wilt never know on earth—perhaps not in heaven. It is a mystery which thou must believe and adore. But *why* He died thou canst see at the first glance, if thou hast a human heart and will look at what God means thee to look at—Christ upon His Cross. He died because He was *Love*—love itself, love boundless, unconquerable, unchangeable—love which inhabits eternity, and therefore could not be hardened or foiled by any sin or rebellion of man, but must love men still—must go out to seek and save them, must dare, suffer any misery, shame, death itself, for their sake—just because it is absolute and perfect Love which inhabits eternity.

Charles Kingsley, *Daily Thoughts*, Macmillan and Co., 1884, page 83

He was like some terrible moral huntsman digging mankind out of the snug burrows in which they had lived hitherto. In the white blaze of this kingdom of his there was to be no property, no privilege, no pride and precedence; no motive indeed and no reward but love. Is it any wonder that men were dazzled and blinded and cried out against him? Even his disciples cried out when he would not spare them the light. Is it any wonder that the priests realized that between this man and themselves there was no choice but that he or priest-craft should perish? Is it any wonder that the Roman soldiers, confronted and amazed by something soaring over their comprehension and threatening all their disciplines, should take refuge in wild laughter, and crown him with thorns and robe in purple and make a mock Caesar of him? For to take him seriously was to enter a strange and alarming life, to abandon habits, to control instincts and impulses, to essay an incredible happiness...

Is it any wonder that to this day this Galilean is too much for our small hearts?

H.G. Wells, *The Outline of History*, Cassell and Company, 1923, page 274

'My God, my God, why hast thou forsaken me?' This is not a 'hymn of trust' as some have held, oversimplifying the test in the light of later verses of the Psalm. But neither is it a 'cry of despair' as others have thought as a result of disregarding the fact that it *is* an appeal to God. It is a death not simply accepted in patience, but endured screaming to God: God remains the final support in death, a support however which is incomprehensible to the one who is abandoned unsupported to suffering.

Here is the peculiarity of this death. Jesus died *not merely*—and this is toned down in Luke and John—*forsaken by men, but absolutely forsaken by God.* And it is only here that the most profound depth of this death finds expression: that which distinguishes this death from the 'beautiful death'—so often compared with it—of Socrates, who had been charged with atheism and corrupting youth, or of some Stoic sage. Jesus was utterly abandoned to suffering. There is no mention in the Gospels of serenity, inward freedom, superiority, grandeur of soul. This was not a humane death, coming gently by hemlock poisoning, after seventy years, in ripeness and repose. It was a death coming all too soon, breaking off everything, totally degrading, in scarcely endurable misery and torment. A death not characterized by lofty resignation, but by absolute and unparalleled abandonment. And yet, for this very reason: is there a death which has shaken but perhaps also exalted mankind in its long history more than death so infinitely human-inhuman in the immensity of its suffering?

Hans Küng, *On Being a Christian*, translated by Edward Quinn, William Collins Sons & Co., 1977, page 341

How seriously do I believe that Christ died for me? For *me.* How has the consciousness of this revelation formed my life?

Is the thought always before me as a guiding principle? Clearly it should be if I regard myself as a Christian. Of course, I claim to believe this, but if I really do, can it be said that the way I lead my daily life reflects this awareness? That Christ died for me gives me tremendous worth.

I am, as it is, infinitely valuable; I have been redeemed by an infinite sacrifice. Do I see myself as someone of consequence? I should, since, for me, God sent the only begotten Son. Well, if I am, in such a sense, the centre of a universe, am I acting in a fit manner? We might be aware that petty behaviour is *not* what is called for. Rather, action befitting one for whom Christ died. For example, should a person who so received the attentions from God the Creator be a gossip? Or a chronic complainer? Am I particularly quick and eager to blame others when the chance arises? Do I really believe in the dignity of my own life? Goethe wrote that good manners have their basis in heaven. Are my manners reflective of this? There is a tremendous responsibility put on me as one who has 'benefitted' from the crucifixion. How have I accepted this? By cheating in little business deals? By admiring athletes who break the rules and don't get caught? By encouraging others to hedge on certain regulations? Do I use language befitting one for whom Christ died? Am I anxious to make snap judgments about other persons? Do I, in fact, reflect enough on what it means that Jesus made me the great gift of himself? That has got to be a humbling thought when realized. Yet it is possible that most who call themselves followers of Christ fail to fully deal with this concept. If we did, most of us would change our lives radically. What does it really mean in my life? Christ died for *me?*

Harry James Cargas, *Encountering Myself*, SPCK, 1978, page 6

What the Cross means

(a) *Sacrifice* is used of Jesus' death to show that it was costly and involved death.

(b) *Reconciliation* is used to show that man is no longer estranged from God.

(c) *Justification* is used to show that we have been all 'put in the right' with God (i.e. accepted).

(d) *Ransom* is used to show that his death was costly and that it brings liberation.

(e) *Triumph* is used because by his death Jesus passes beyond the powers of evil, and so triumphed over them.

What the Cross Is Not

(a) The angry Father appeasing his wrath by taking it out of his loving Son. Such a viewpoint betrays a sub-Christian idea of God. God may be angry at sins, but he always loves the sinner. His feelings are not swayed by the punishment of anyone.

(b) The Son standing in my place to take the punishment that I ought to have. Such a view is immoral. In any case no one person could suffer the whole world's punishments. And even if he could, this would mean that everyone could go on sinning without any fear of punishment.

What the Cross Is

(a) God does for us what we cannot do for ourselves. God in action shows his love for everyone by the death of his Son on behalf of us (not 'instead of us') as our representative. By so doing he takes away our guilt.

(b) God, by accepting on the Cross the worst that human beings can do to him, draws the sting of our resentments against him, and removes our basic fears and insecurities.

We have been accepted. We can accept ourselves. We can begin to return God's love to him, and to hand it on to our neighbours. We are no longer estranged from God, but reconciled to him and to our fellows.

The basic Christian symbol is not the crucifix but the *empty* cross because Jesus triumphed over death by his resurrection. The resurrection does not add to the victory of the cross, but it does publicly placard it for all who are willing to see.

Hugh Montefiore, *Confirmation Notebook*, Fifth Edition, SPCK, 1985, page 21

DEATH

Death—dying, end of life, ceasing to be, annihilation,
want of spiritual life

I remember a teacher at primary school telling us time was valuable. 'Every minute of your life is precious,' she said. 'One day you will die, so never waste time. Make the most of your life, and then you will be happy.' She had such a determined look in her eyes I took these words to heart and have lived by them ever since.

Teenage years were very full as a consequence. I had also taken on board some advice from my parents that you only get out of life what you are prepared to put into it. Later I was helped by a motto: 'I am going to out-live, out-love, out-laugh everyone else.'

I was still not satisfied. Something vital was missing. A book by Ralph Waldo Trine, *In Tune with the Infinite*, opened my eyes to the spiritual dimension. In Cuthbert Bardsley, the Bishop of Coventry, I was confronted by a man living in the power of the Spirit, and this encouraged me to take a step of faith and commitment. Through prayer, reflection and meditation I began to discover a new quality and value of life. From time to time I was given brief moments of what experts in the spiritual life call 'eternal life'. In them I experienced such feelings of joy, ecstasy, freedom, harmony, wholeness and wonder, the fear of death was transcended. When I die, I hope to enter more fully a dimension I have already experienced. The emphasis, however, is living fully in the present moment, in what has been called *the eternal now*. Death is then seen as a culmination, not an annihilation.

In the sweat of your face you shall eat bread till you return to the ground, for out of it you were taken; you are dust, and to dust you shall return.

Genesis 3:19

Let me die the death of the righteous.

Numbers 23:10

In my Father's house are many rooms; if it were not so, would I have told you that I go to prepare a place for you? And when I go and prepare a place for you, I will come again and will take you to myself, that where I am you may be also.

John 14:2-3

For we brought nothing into the world, and we cannot take anything out of the world.

1 Timothy 6:7

Death helps us to see what is worth trusting and loving and what is a waste of time.

J. Neville Ward, *Five for Sorrow, Ten for Joy*, Epworth Press, 1971, page 83

Death, with the might of his sunbeam,
Touches the flesh and the soul awakes.

Robert Browning, 'The Flight of the Duchess', in *The Poetical Works of Robert Browning*, Oxford University Press, 1949, page 347

In the nineteenth century the problem was that *God is dead*; in the twentieth century the problem is that *man is dead*.

Erich Fromm, *The Sane Society*, Routledge & Kegan Paul, 1979, page 360

People who love life and love giving to it and receiving from it do not find themselves particularly perturbed about death.

J. Neville Ward, *Friday Afternoon*, Epworth Press, 1982, page 131

Walking with God . . . means walking through death. It means living with death behind one rather than ahead of one.

John S. Dunne, *The Reasons of the Heart*, SCM Press, 1978, page 61

Death's stamp gives value to the coin of life; making it possible to buy with life what is truly precious.

Rabindranath Tagore, 'Stray Birds', xcix, in *Collected Poems and Plays of Rabindranath Tagore*, Macmillan and Co., 1936, page 299

The distance that the dead have gone
Does not at first appear—
Their coming back seems possible
For many an ardent year.

Emily Dickinson, in Thomas H. Johnson, editor, *The Complete Poems of Emily Dickinson*, Faber and Faber, 1977, number 1742, page 706

I have a feeling that there probably is some fellowship and communion of like-minded people beyond death, which can begin here—and that our jealous and exclusive friendships and alliances rather hinder it. But it is all a very big subject!

A.C. Benson, *Extracts from the Letters of Dr. A.C. Benson to M.E.A.*, Jarrold Publishing, 1927, page 22

It makes it possible for us to rest in the certainty that the end of life on earth is not the end of life; that the haunting fragility of things has a meaning, that love is given for eternity, that no accident in these dimensions of time and space can prevent the accomplishment of the ends for which men and women with minds and hearts have come into existence.

Norman Goodall, *The Local Church*, Hodder and Stoughton, 1966, page 18

People who believe that death is part of God's purpose, one of the forms of his caring, can take their time over life. There being a message of beginning or deepening in every ending, their sufferings are worth working through with considerable care. They are not going to miss or lose anything that matters. And there is never any reason for ceasing to love, even for loving less, since every moment, every experience, brings God with it and the possibility of deeper communion with life.

J. Neville Ward, *Friday Afternoon*, Epworth Press, 1982, page 103

It was not physical life and physical death of which Jesus was thinking. He meant that, for the man who fully accepted Him, there was no such thing as death. Death had lost its finality. The man who enters into fellowship with Jesus has entered into a fellowship which is independent of time. The man who accepts Jesus has entered into a relationship with God which neither time nor eternity can sever. Such a man goes, not from life to death, but from life to life. Death is only the introduction to the nearer presence of God.

William Barclay, *The Gospel of John*, The Saint Andrew Press, 1965, volume 2, page 38

I don't think we *can* know what is coming after death. It seems to me outside our *range*; just as there are certainly endless notes, both above and below what we can hear, and endless colours beyond what we can *see*. And I'm sure too there is a good and right reason for our not knowing it—it may be to produce a certain frame of mind; it may be that we can't see what may be happening all about us at every minute; it may be that we couldn't bear to go on living if we *did* know, and we may be being bribed to live for the sake of experience.

A.C. Benson, *Extracts from the Letters of Dr. A.C. Benson to M.E.A.*, Jarrold Publishing, 1927, page 31

What is death? When life is withdrawn from the material body, the material envelope in which it mysteriously dwells, we say that that is death. But science teaches us very clearly that matter cannot be destroyed: it can only be redistributed. Even when anything is burnt, it is not destroyed but merely reduced to its ultimate elements. If matter cannot be destroyed, it would be unreasonable to think that spirit can be destroyed.

In our incarnate state in this life we have a material body which subserves the purposes of our self-expression here. We can trust God, who has given to us a material body for this stage of our eternal life, to provide us with a spiritual body to subserve the purposes of our self-expression in that higher stage to which we believe that at death we pass.

Father Andrew, S.D.C., *Meditations for Every Day*, A.R. Mowbray & Co., 1941, page 9

The death of someone we love is always shattering. To love is to carry another within oneself, to keep a special place in one's heart for him or her. This spiritual space is nourished by a physical presence; death, then, tears out a part of our own heart. Those who deny the suffering of death have never truly loved; they live in a spiritual illusion.

To celebrate death, then, is not to deny this laceration and the grief it involves, it is to give space to live it, to speak about it, and even to sing of it. It is to give mutual support, looking the reality in the face and placing all in the Heart of God in deep trust. Jesus did not come to abolish suffering and death, but he showed us the way to live them both fruitfully. We must penetrate the mystery of suffering by surrender and sacrifice.

Jean Vanier, *Man and Woman He Made Them*, Darton, Longman & Todd, 1985, page 149

Death is nothing at all . . . I have only slipped away into the next room. I am I and you are you. Whatever we were to each other that we are still. Call me by my old familiar name, speak to me in the easy way which you always used. Put no difference in your tone; wear no forced air of solemnity or sorrow. Laugh as we always laughed at the little jokes we enjoyed together. Play, smile, think of me, pray for me. Let my name be ever the household word that it always was. Let it be spoken without effort, without the ghost of a shadow on it. Life means all that it ever meant. It is the same as it ever was; there is absolutely unbroken continuity. Why should I be out of mind because I am out of sight? I am just waiting for you for an interval, somewhere very near, just around the corner. All is well.

Henry Scott Holland, source not traced

Death surrenders us totally to God; it makes us enter into him; we must, in return, surrender ourselves to death with absolute love and self-abandonment—since, when death comes, all we can do is to surrender ourselves completely to the domination and guidance of God . . . I feel that there'd be something to say about the joy (the healthy joy) of death, about its harmony in life, about the intimate connexion (and at the same time the barrier) between the world of the dead and the world of the living, about the unity of both in one and the same cosmos. Death has been treated too much as a subject for melancholy reflexion, or as an occasion for self-discipline, or as a rather hazy theological entity . . . What we have to do is to see it in its true context, see it as an active reality, as one more phase, in a world and a 'becoming' that are those of our own experience.

Pierre Teilhard de Chardin, *The Making of a Mind*, William Collins Sons & Co., 1965, page 145

Death is the meaning of life. It is the goal toward which all our acts tend, consciously or unconsciously. Seen thus, death is a fulfillment in the ultimate sense. Death is the extreme point in self-culture. Every person is called upon to create the self to the fullest degree. It is at death that the process of my own self-creation will end. My purpose is to see that, whenever it is that death occurs, I am as fully prepared for it as I can be. This implies a worthiness to die. Do I deserve to die, in a certain sense? It is a holy death for which I ought to be preparing. Will it be? Perhaps the most difficult aspect of death for those of us in a materialistically oriented society is the truth that *death is alone*. It happens to me, by myself, naked before God. There will be no excuses for what I did or, perhaps more importantly, for what I failed to do. I'll not be able to point to everyone else who didn't act either and use that as an excuse. The call to Christianity is a call to the heroic life. Anything less is just that, less. With how much less are we going to be satisfied? Again there will be no excuses... Only absolute truth is allowed then. Death is thus the real meaning of life. In that very important sense, each of us must be a philosopher, a kind of self-philosopher wherein what we learn that is meaningful we apply to our own self-creation. The French Essayist Montaigne wrote that 'to philosophize is to learn to die.' Ancient Rome's Cicero said that 'to study philosophy is nothing but to prepare one's self to die.' The true philosopher, noted Socrates, 'is always pursuing death and dying.'

Harry James Cargas, *Encountering Myself*, SPCK, 1978, page 38

We would ask now of Death.
And he said:
You would know the secret of death.
But how shall you find it unless you seek it in the heart of life?
The owl whose night-bound eyes are blind unto the day cannot unveil the mystery of light.
If you would indeed behold the spirit of death, open your heart wide unto the body of life.
For life and death are one, even as the river and the sea are one.

In the depth of your hopes and desires lies your silent knowledge of the beyond;
And like seeds dreaming beneath the snow your heart dreams of spring.
Trust the dreams, for in them is hidden the gate to eternity.
Your fear of death is but the trembling of the shepherd when he stands before the king whose hand is to be laid upon him in honour.
Is the shepherd not joyful beneath his trembling, that he shall wear the mark of the king?
Yet is he not more mindful of his trembling?

For what is it to die but to stand naked in the wind and to melt into the sun?
And what is it to cease breathing but to free the breath from its restless tides, that it may rise and expand and seek God unencumbered?

Only when you drink from the river of silence shall you indeed sing.
And when you have reached the mountain top, then you shall begin to climb.
And when the earth shall claim your limbs, then shall you truly dance.

Kahlil Gibran, *The Prophet*, William Heinemann, 1923, page 93

DIVINITY

Divinity—theology; being divine, Godhood

At school we had a lesson a week of divinity. In this allotted time the Chaplain taught us about the Bible, focusing our attention mainly on the Gospels and Epistles. Most of us found the divinity lesson dull and boring, a time for catching up on sleep. We eagerly awaited a respite in the summer. The Chaplain was obsessed with cricket so in some divinity lessons we were allowed an illicit listen to Test matches. This was far more interesting than learning about St Paul's missionary journeys. As a result I used to come bottom in the divinity exam and registered a 'disappointing' in my school report.

I had left both school and theological college behind before discovering divinity is really about the art of becoming divine. At the end of my curacy I was conscious of spiritual bankruptcy and was determined to do something about it. The turning-point came with the discovery of the book *The Choice is Always Ours*, edited by Dorothy Berkley Phillips. This book is about ways and means of becoming divine and contains what I discovered to be the essence of divinity. New ways were opened up. I began to search for spiritual insights recorded during the last 2,000 years in the writings of saints, poets, novelists, playwrights, artists, musicians, philosophers, scientists, historians, statesmen and psychologists. These have been sorted out into some kind of order. The result is *Visions of Faith, Hope, Love* and *Glory*, and a simple technique, reflection, as a means of becoming divine. Happy the person to whom this becomes a living reality.

'This very thing that you have spoken I will do; for you have found favour in my sight, and I know you by name.' Moses said, 'I pray thee, show me thy glory.' And he said, 'I will make all my goodness pass before you, and will proclaim before you my name "The Lord" . . . But,' he said, 'you cannot see my face; for man shall not see me and live.'

Exodus 33:17–20

Can you find out the deep things of God? Can you find out the limit of the Almighty?

Job 11:7

His divine power has granted to us all things that pertain to life and godliness, through the knowledge of him who called us to his own glory and excellence, by which he has granted to us his precious and very great promises, that through these you may escape from the corruption that is in the world because of passion, and become partakers of the divine nature. For this very reason make every effort to supplement your faith with virtue, and virtue with knowledge, and knowledge with self-control, and self-control with steadfastness, and steadfastness with godliness, and godliness with brotherly affection, and brotherly affection with love.

2 Peter 1:3–7

We know that we are of God.

1 John 5:19

The essential truth . . . is that man is under an absolute mandate to express divinity in his own nature and in his whole life.

F. Ernest Johnson, *The Social Gospel Re-examined*, James Clarke & Co., 1942, page 50

He is divinely favoured who may trace a silver vein in all the affairs of life, see sparkles of light in the gloomiest scenes, and absolute radiance in those which are bright.

Henry Ward Beecher, *Proverbs from Plymouth Pulpit*, Charles Burnet & Co., 1887, page 116

This is the life of gods, and of godlike and blessed among men, liberation from the alien that besets us here, a life taking no pleasure in the things of earth, the passing of solitary to solitary.

Plotinus, *The Enneads*, VI, ix, translated by Stephen MacKenna, Faber and Faber, 1956, page 625

And in the peasants' world there is no room for reason, religion, and history. There is no room for religion, because to them everything participates in divinity, everything is actually, not merely symbolically, divine.

Carlo Levi, *Christ Stopped at Eboli*, translated by Frances Frenaye, Cassell and Company, 1948, page 116

I take possession of man's mind and deed.
I care not what the sects may brawl.
I sit as God holding no form of creed,
But contemplating all.

Alfred, Lord Tennyson, 'The Palace of Art', in *The Works of Alfred Lord Tennyson*, Macmillan and Co., 1898, page 47

The soul may rise through all earthly influences into such a susceptible spiritual condition that the throb and impulse of the Divine nature shall fall upon our souls and give us an abiding state of wisdom, of peace, of rest, and of joy in the Holy Ghost.

Henry Ward Beecher, *Proverbs from Plymouth Pulpit*, Charles Burnet & Co., 1887, page 155

Divinity is essentially the first of the professions, because it is necessary for all at all times; law and physic are only necessary for some at some times. I speak of them, of course, not in their abstract existence, but in their applicability to man.

Samuel Taylor Coleridge, *The Table Talk and Omniana of Samuel Taylor Coleridge*, Oxford University Press, 1917, page 216

To the poet, to the philosopher, to the saint, all things are friendly and sacred, all events profitable, all days holy, all men divine. For the eye is fastened on the life, and slights the circumstance. Every chemical substance, every plant, every animal in its growth, teaches the unity of cause, the variety of appearance.

Ralph Waldo Emerson, 'Essay on History', in *The Works of Ralph Waldo Emerson*, George Bell & Sons, 1960, volume 1, *Essays* and *Representative Men*, page 6

... it takes a divine man to exhibit anything divine, Socrates, Alfred, Columbus, Wordsworth, or any other brave preferrer of the still voice within to the roar of the populace—a thing very easy to speak and very hard to do for twenty-four hours. The rest are men potentially, not actually, now only pupas or tadpoles—say rather quarries of souls, heroes that shall be, seeds of gods.

Ralph Waldo Emerson, *Journals*, Constable & Co., 1910, volume 3, page 14

... the new in art is always formed out of the old. The Genius of the Hour always sets his ineffaceable seal on the work and gives it an inexpressible charm for the imagination. As far as the spiritual character of the period overpowers the artist and finds expression in his work, so far it will always retain a certain grandeur, and will represent to future beholders the Unknown, the Inevitable, the Divine.

Ralph Waldo Emerson, *Emerson's Essays, First Series: Art*, Thomas Y. Crowell Company, 1926, page 247

'All divinity is love, or wonder,' John Donne wrote in one of his poems. No phrase could better express the intense religious life of the group of spiritual poets in England who interpreted in beautiful, often immortal, form this religion of the spirit, this glowing consciousness that the world and all its fulness is God's and that eternity is set within the soul of man, who never is himself until he finds his Life in God.

Rufus M. Jones, *Spiritual Reformers in the 16th and 17th Centuries*, Macmillan and Co., 1914, page 322

I think it might be said not (with Voltaire) that we invent our gods, but that we carry them with us and inside us.

Cutting across the differences in doctrines between the great world religions—of Moses and Jesus, of Lao-tzu and Buddha, of Confucius and Mohammed—there remains the truth that God is what man finds that is divine in himself. God is the best way man can behave in the ordinary occasions of life, and the farthest point to which man can stretch himself.

Max Lerner, *The Unfinished Country*, Simon and Schuster, 1959, page 724

For I have seen my sons most unlike Gods.
Divine ye were created, and divine
In sad demeanour, solemn, undisturbed,
Unruffled, like high Gods, ye lived and ruled.
Now I behold in you fear, hope, and wrath;
Actions of rage and passion—even as
I see them, on the mortal world beneath,
In men who die. This is the grief, O son
Sad sign of ruin, sudden dismay and fall!

John Keats, 'Hyperion', I. 329, in Miriam Allott, editor, *The Poems of John Keats*, Longman, 1986, page 414

There is but one thing needful—to possess God. All our senses, all our powers of mind and soul, all our external resources, are so many ways of approaching the Divinity, so many modes of tasting and of adoring God. We must learn to detach ourselves from all that is capable of being lost, to bind ourselves absolutely only to what is absolute and eternal, and to enjoy the rest as a loan... To adore, to understand, to receive, to feel, to give, to act: there is my law, my duty, my happiness, my heaven. Let come what will—even death. Only be at peace with self, live in the presence of God, in communion with Him, and leave the guidance of existence to those universal powers against whom thou canst do nothing!

Henri Frédéric Amiel, *Amiel's Journal*, translated by Mrs Humphry Ward, Macmillan and Co., 1918, page 1

Man, according to the Bible, is 'made in the image and likeness of God' (cf. Gen. 1:26), and the Fathers commonly distinguish between these two words. The image refers to man's reason and freedom, that which distinguishes him from the animals and makes him kin to God, while 'likeness' refers to 'assimilation to God through virtues' (St John of Damascus). It is possible for man to become like God, to become deified, to become god by grace.

... it should be noted that deification does not mean absorption into God, since the deified creature remains itself and distinct. It is the whole human being, body and soul, who is transfigured in the Spirit into the likeness of the divine nature, and deification is the goal of every Christian, to be reached by the faithful following of Christ in the common life of his body the church.

Symeon Lash, in Alan Richardson and John Bowden, editors, *A New Dictionary of Christian Theology*, SCM Press, 1985, page 147

The only biblical text which seems to bear directly on deification is II Peter 1:4, where the destiny of Christian believers is described as becoming 'partakers of the divine nature.'

However other passages (such as Rom. 2:7; II Tim. 1:10) speak of Christians being endowed with the divine property of 'incorruption'—freedom from the tendency of the finite world to disorder and disintegration. There is an unmistakable borrowing here from the vocabulary of Hellenistic religiosity; and it is not confined only to the later parts of the New Testament.

At the same time, however, early Christianity was developing a doctrine of incorporation into Christ through the indwelling of 'Spirit': what distinguishes Christians is their right to relate to God as Father, in the way that Jesus did (Rom. 8). And this can also be expressed in terms of Father and Son 'making their home' in the believer (John 14:23). Thus the Christian is taken into a relation of unlimited intimacy with God; and for the Johannine tradition, this relation exists as an eternal reality in God's life, because the Word is in relation to God (*pros ton theon*) from the beginning (John 1:1), and the Son shares the Father's glory before the world is made (John 17:5). The 'glory' and 'eternal life' given to the believer consist precisely in sharing this relationship.

Thus there are two strands making up the classical patristic view of deification. One, the more obviously available convention in the religious language of the day, thinks primarily in terms of a communication of divine attributes, the other in terms of participating in an intra-divine relationship.

Rowan Williams, in Gordon S. Wakefield, editor, *A Dictionary of Christian Spirituality*, SCM Press, 1986, page 106

To seek our divinity merely in books and writings, is to seek the living among the dead: we do but in vain seek God many times in these, where His truth too often is not so much enshrined as entombed. No; seek for God within thine own soul; He is best discerned, as Plotinus phraseth it—by an 'intellectual touch' of Him . . .

That is not the best and truest knowledge of God which is wrought out by the labour and sweat of the brain, but that which is kindled within us by a heavenly warmth in our hearts. As, in the natural body, it is the heart that sends up good blood and warm spirits into the head, whereby it is best enabled to perform its several functions; so that which enables us to know and understand aright in the things of God, must be a living principle of holiness within us. When the tree of knowledge is not planted by the tree of life, and sucks not up sap from thence, it may as well be fruitful with evil as with good, and bring forth bitter fruit as well as sweet. If we would indeed have knowledge thrive and flourish, we must water the tender plants of it with holiness. When Zoroaster's scholars asked him what they should do to get winged souls, such as might soar aloft in the bright beams of divine truth, he bids them bathe themselves in the waters of life: they asking what they were, he tells them, the four cardinal virtues, which are the four rivers of paradise . . .

There is a knowing of 'the truth as it is in Jesus'—as it is in a Christ-like nature, as it is in that sweet, mild, humble, and loving spirit of Jesus, which spreads itself, like a morning sun, upon the souls of good men, full of light and life. It profits little to know Christ Himself after the flesh; but He gives His spirit to good men, that searcheth the deep things of God. There is an inward beauty, life, and loveliness in divine truth, which cannot be known but then when it is digested into life and practice . . .

Divine truth is better understood, as it unfolds itself in the purity of men's heart and lives, than in all those subtle niceties into which curious wits may lay it forth. And therefore our Saviour, who is the great master of it, would not, while He was here on earth, draw it up into any system or body, nor would His disciples after Him; He would not lay it out to us in any canons or articles of belief, not being indeed so careful to stock and enrich the world with opinions and notions as with true piety, and a Godlike pattern of purity, as the best way to thrive in all spiritual understanding. His main scope was to promote a holy life, as the best and most compendious way to a right belief. He hangs all true acquaintance with divinity upon doing God's will: 'If any man will do His will, he shall know of the doctrine, whether it be of God.' This is that alone which will make us, as St. Peter tells us, 'that we shall not be barren nor unfruitful in the knowledge of our Lord and Saviour.'

John Smith, *Select Discourses*, Cambridge at the University Press, 1859, page 3

DOUBT

Doubt—feeling of uncertainty about something, undecided state of mind; inclination to disbelieve; uncertain state of things; lack of full proof or clear indication

Shortly after becoming a committed Christian, I joined a beginners group, and went through a course of basic instruction on the Bible. In the weeks that followed I was encouraged not to doubt, as doubt showed a lack of faith. This was probably good advice in that situation. I was a newcomer to the faith and needed time and space to establish new roots. In retrospect, I realized I had repressed my doubts. Two years later they came to the surface with a vengeance, demanding to be faced.

I set aside my fears and confronted my doubts. I began to ask some fundamental questions about the nature of the faith and set about finding my own answers. To my surprise I discovered doubt had provoked me to think. Before long, uncertainties were transformed into valuable sources of revelation and greater understanding. Faith received an impetus.

Life moved on. I was ordained, and the next four years were heavily committed to the active life. There was no time to doubt or to engage in creative thought. I had to keep my head above water and concentrate on the immediate tasks in hand. Again, in retrospect, I realized I had repressed my doubts, but for different reasons. Nature swiftly moved in and took revenge. I went through a very dry and arid period, in which my old faith broke down. I confronted my doubts again at the start of a new job. What a revelation followed this enquiry. Doubt once again turned out to be an invaluable workman.

Your words have upheld him who was stumbling, and you have made firm the feeble knees. But now it has come to you, and you are impatient.

Job 4:4–5

But Zion said, 'The Lord has forsaken me, my Lord has forgotten me.' Can a woman forget her sucking child, that she should have no compassion on the son of her womb?

Isaiah 49:14–15

Let us hold fast the confession of our hope without wavering.

Hebrews 10:23

He who doubts is like a wave of the sea that is driven and tossed by the wind. For that person must not suppose that a double-minded man, unstable in all his ways, will receive anything from the Lord.

James 1:6–8

Honest doubt is suspended judgment.

A.R. Orage, *On Love*, The Janus Press, 1957, page 60

All fanaticism is a strategy to prevent doubt from becoming conscious.

H.A. Williams, C.R., *True Wilderness*, William Collins Sons & Co., 1983, page 49

If we are sensible, we will not doubt God, we will doubt our world and we will doubt ourselves.

Agnes Sanford, *The Healing Light*, Arthur James, 1949, page 52

The sum of all is—yes, my doubt is great,
My faith's still greater, then my faith's enough.

Robert Browning, 'Bishop Blougram's Apology', in *The Poetical Works of Robert Browning*, Smith, Elder, & Co., 1897, volume 1, page 538

To doubt is to live, to struggle, to struggle for life and to live by struggle... A faith which does not continue to doubt is a dead faith.

Miguel de Unamuno, *The Agony of Christianity*, Payson & Clarke, 1928, page 27

When we say: 'Yes, I doubt, but I do believe in God's love more than I trust my own doubts,' it becomes possible for God to act.

Anthony Bloom, *The Essence of Prayer*, Darton, Longman & Todd, 1989, page 69

I refused to allow myself to accept any of it in my heart, because I was afraid of a headlong fall, but I was hanging in suspense which was more likely to be fatal than a fall.

St Augustine of Hippo, *Confessions*, translated by R.S. Pine-Coffin, Penguin Books, 1964, page 116

Our doubts are traitors,
And make us lose the good we oft might win,
By fearing to attempt.

William Shakespeare, *Measure for Measure*, I. v. 78

There are the shadows of doubts and uncertainties. Sometimes the way ahead is far from being clear. Sometimes we feel like people groping among the shadows with nothing firm to cling to.

William Barclay, *The Gospel of John*, The Saint Andrew Press, 1965, volume 2, page 151

Enthusiasm for the universe, in knowing as well as in creating, also answers the question of doubt and meaning. Doubt is the necessary tool of knowledge. And meaninglessness is no threat so long as enthusiasm for the universe and for man as its centre is alive.

Paul Tillich, *The Courage To Be*, James Nisbet & Co., 1952, page 115

Religious doubts: mediocrity. The description that others have given me of their doubts has always bored and embarrassed me. Such doubts are born of a diffident mind that thinks one can lose sight of God as soon as one ceases looking in the direction of Mecca.

André Gide, *The Journals of André Gide*, 1894, translated by Justin O'Brien, Secker & Warburg, 1947, page 41

A man was meant to be doubtful about himself, but undoubting about the truth; this has been exactly reversed. Nowadays the part of a man that a man does assert is exactly the part he ought not to assert—himself. The part he doubts is exactly the part he ought not to doubt—the Divine Reason.

G.K. Chesterton, *Orthodoxy*, The Bodley Head, 1935, page 53

But this is an age not of faith, but of cathartic doubt, and unless everything can, potentially at least, be questioned, then there is a kind of betrayal of the spirit of the times. It seems possible that doubt *is* our search for meaning, and that whatever refuses this painful path has cut itself off from our search for life.

Monica Furlong, *The End of our Exploring*, Hodder and Stoughton, 1973, page 16

If we depend on thought, we have to doubt the world, doubt our being, doubt the future, and end our life in doubt. But since we must either react on our environment or be destroyed by it, the force of the life within drives us irresistibly to faith. There are spiritual impulses which refuse to be set aside at the bidding of logic. No one can live on negation.

Sir Sarvepalli Radhakrishnan, *Indian Philosophy*, George Allen & Unwin, 1926, volume 2, page 516

Doubt is the vestibule which *all* must pass, before they can enter into the temple of wisdom; therefore, when we are in doubt, and puzzle out the truth by our own exertions, we have gained a something that will stay with us, and which will serve us again. But if, to avoid the trouble of the search, we avail ourselves of the superior information of a friend, such knowledge will not remain with us; we have not bought, but borrowed it.

Charles Caleb Colton, *Lacon*, William Tegg, 1866, page 75

You say that you have doubts about the goodness of God. Where do those doubts come from? They are born in the very nature that God has created. He gave you the power of doubt as much as He gave you the power of faith. The doubt you feel may very well be the protest of the divine life in you against the injustice and the pain of the world. Your doubt may very well be God's way of enlisting you on His side in His fight, with His own weapons of sacrifice and love, against that same pain and injustice that has occasioned your doubt. If the world owes most to people's faiths, it owes much to the doubts of men who have questioned those faiths and by their questioning purified them.

Father Andrew, S.D.C., *The Adventure of Faith*, A.R. Mowbray & Co., 1933, page 57

We shall counsel the doubtful by listening to them attentively, lovingly, and prayerfully and then speaking to them the truth of God, firmly, gently, and with love.

We shall sustain the tempted by our prayer, penance, and understanding love and when opportunity offers also by enlightening and encouraging words.

We shall befriend the friendless and comfort the sick and sorrowful by our real love and personal concern for them, identifying ourselves with them in their pain and sorrow and by praying with them for God's healing and comfort and by encouraging them to offer their sufferings to the Lord for the salvation of the whole world.

Mother Teresa, *Jesus, the Word to be Spoken*, compiled by Brother Angelo Devananda, William Collins Sons & Co., 1990, page 112

A command performance,
A unique appearance,
Especially for Thomas,
Even though 'the doubter is like a heaving sea ruffled by the wind',
Even though 'a man of that kind must not expect the Lord to give him anything; he is double-minded, and never can keep a steady course'.
A private showing for the doubter *par excellence*.
'Unless I see the mark of the nails on his hands, unless I put my finger into the place where the nails were, and my hand into his side, I will not believe.'
No matter how literally or otherwise we take the passage,
The point is this:
A man full of doubts and disbelief after the death of his leader saw a sign that was sufficient proof for him to say 'my Lord and my God'.

Thomas was a lucky man, Lord, to have an experience that unseated the uncertainties from his mind.

No such luck for many of us now,

For we are those 'who never saw' you, 'and yet have found faith'.

Enable us to work through our doubts to faith in you.

Enable me to pray,

'My Lord and my God'.

Rex Chapman, *A Glimpse of God*, SCM Press, 1973, page 15

... it is in a man's *individual* existence that doubt especially assails him. It is not for nothing that we are enjoined by Scripture not to neglect the assembly of the saints (Heb. 10:25). Within the gathered group there is less room for doubt, and certainties are reinforced; but, though 'no man is an ilande, intire of itself', neither does he escape the solitude that makes up a significant part of his day any more than he can escape the inevitable solitude of his own subjectivity. Personal religion is a constant encounter and engagement with doubt, and as one's awareness of limitation increases with knowledge so too does doubt. The more we know of God the stronger and more subtle the attack from doubt. In the Genesis story there is a clear illustration of the way doubt can indeed be the temptation that Newman described; for the fall springs from that doubt of God's purpose which the serpent succeeds in creating. Just as in social existence any doubt which is not the product of neurosis is overcome by the social exchange of friendship, so can religious doubt be overcome in personal religion. The 'meaning of prayer' is precisely that we can be so schooled by this communication with God that God's communication with us reveals us those things which had been doubted.

J. Heywood Thomas, in Alastair V. Campbell, editor, *A Dictionary of Pastoral Care*, SPCK, 1987, page 76

DYING TO SELF

Dying to self—a dying to the supremacy of the ego in order to live for God

At University College, London, we used to take a group of students away for a weekend to stay at a farmhouse cottage in Sussex. The name of this cottage was Micklepage, and it was situated midway between two villages, Nuthurst and Maplehurst. Five features in particular appealed to the students: low ceilings, wooden beams, a kitchen with an Aga cooker, a blazing log fire in the sitting room, and an atmosphere of peace.

I remember a group discussing this topic—dying to self. 'It is all very well for you,' one of the students retorted, 'you are in your thirties, and have had a chance to develop a self. We haven't had a chance to develop a self yet, so how can we die to it?'

I took his point. It made me think over my experience since being a student. I had gone up to university with two aims, to get a golf blue and as good a degree as I could. After the step of faith I realized these aims were selfish. The first was an ego-trip, and the second was preparatory to qualifying as a solicitor, which would mean status, money, wife and family, comfort and security—all selfish aims. In the next few years I began to discover something of the riches of 'God within' and my priorities were turned upside down. Dying to self came to mean death to the ego and instead living according to the dictates of the 'God within'. To the outsider this looks ridiculous, but to the adherent it is the gateway to that more abundant life Christ came to bring.

I will not offer burnt offerings to the Lord my God which cost me nothing.

2 Samuel 24:24

For thou hast no delight in sacrifice; were I to give a burnt offering, thou wouldst not be pleased. The sacrifice acceptable to God is a broken spirit; a broken and contrite heart, O God, thou wilt not despise.

Psalm 51:16–17

And every one who has left houses or brothers or sisters or father or mother or children or lands, for my name's sake, will receive a hundredfold, and inherit eternal life.

Matthew 19:29

If any man would come after me, let him deny himself and take up his cross daily and follow me. For whoever would save his life will lose it; and whoever loses his life for my sake, he will save it. For what does it profit a man if he gains the whole world and loses or forfeits himself?

Luke 9:23–25

Fast and pray,
That so perchance the vision may be seen
By thee and those, and all the world be heal'd.

Alfred, Lord Tennyson, 'The Holy Grail', in *The Works of Alfred Lord Tennyson*, Macmillan and Co., 1898, page 420

Let us acquiesce. Let us take our bloated nothingness out of the path of the divine circuits. Let us unlearn our wisdom of the world. Let us lie low in the Lord's power, and learn that truth alone makes rich and great.

Ralph Waldo Emerson, 'Spiritual Laws', in *The Works of Ralph Waldo Emerson*, George Bell & Sons, 1906, volume 1, *Essays* and *Representative Men*, page 87

It is the triumph over one's own nature that means full victory; for when a man has himself under control so that every desire submits to reason and reason submits to me, then he is really victorious over self, and is master of the world.

Thomas à Kempis, *The Imitation of Christ*, translated by Betty I. Knott, William Collins Sons & Co., 1979, page 196

... Christianity heightens as well as deepens the human as well as the divine affections. I am happy, for the less hope, the more faith ... God knows what is best for us; we do not. Continued resignation, at last I begin to find, is the secret of continual strength. 'Daily *dying*,' as Boehmen interprets it, is the path of daily *living* ...

Charles Kingsley, *Daily Thoughts*, Macmillan and Co., 1884, page 217

Are you willing to be sponged out, erased, cancelled, made nothing?
Are you willing to be made nothing, dipped into oblivion?
If not, you will never really change. The phoenix renews her youth only when she is burnt,
burnt alive, burnt down to hot and flocculent ash.
Then the small stirring of a new small bub in the nest with strands of down like floating ash
Shows that she is renewing her youth like the eagle, immortal bird.

D.H. Lawrence, *The Complete Poems of D.H. Lawrence*, edited by Vivian de Sola Pinto and Warren Roberts, William Heinemann, 1967, volume 2, page 728

Releasing and being released is like dying, like willingly dying. It is like going through the letting go of everyone and everything that one is called upon to go through on one's deathbed. There is great aloneness then too: I am dying while others, even those closest to me, go on living. There can be great darkness and coldness also, expecting others to take away that final aloneness, feeling bitter and abandoned when they inevitably fail. Going through all this in the midst of life... means going through death before one dies, going through at least the letting-go that death imposes.

John S. Dunne, *The Reasons of the Heart*, SCM Press, 1978, page 61

We have only to think of what this world would have lost if there had been no men who were not prepared to forget their personal safety, to forget security, to forget selfish gain and selfish advancement. The world owes everything to people who recklessly spent their strength and gave themselves to God and to others. No doubt we will exist longer if we take things easily, if we avoid all strain, if we sit at the fire and husband life, if we look after ourselves as a hypochondriac looks after his health. No doubt we will *exist* longer—but we will never *live* at all.

William Barclay, *The Gospel of John*, The Saint Andrew Press, 1965, volume 2, page 144

Thus when our Lord says, 'Except a man hateth his father and mother, yea, and his own life, he cannot be my disciple,' it is because our best tempers are yet carnal and full of the imperfections of our fallen nature. The doctrine is just and good; not as if father and mother were to be hated, but that love, which an unregenerate person or natural man has towards them, is to be hated as being a blind self-love, full of all the weakness and partiality with which fallen man loves, honours, esteems, and cleaves to himself. This love, born from corrupt flesh and blood and polluted with self, is to be hated and on such a motive as Christ has loved us.

William Law, in Stephen Hobhouse, editor, *Selected Mystical Writings of William Law*, Rockliff, 1948, page 95

Generally, the older we are the deeper is the rut in which we live. This is perhaps why Jesus said that the kingdom of heaven is open to little children and that to enter it we must become like them. For they are still universally receptive and do not have to break out of enclosed worlds of meaning in order to respond to the divine reality. But we adults have lost the innocent openness of the child. And to meet Jesus of Nazareth would be for us such a profoundly disturbing experience precisely because it would threaten the existence that we have made for ourselves. We should realize that here is someone who is going to undermine our world, the world of meaning of which we are the centre. We should even find ourselves threatened with a kind of death, the death of our present selves...

John Hick, *Christianity at the Centre*, Macmillan and Co., 1968, page 20

What is 'spirit'? (for Christ is spirit, his religion that of the spirit). Spirit is: to live as though dead (dead to the world).

This way of life is so entirely foreign to man that to him it is quite literally worse than death.

Very carefully introduced for an hour or so in the distance of the imagination, natural man can bear it, it even pleases him. But if it is brought nearer him, so near that it becomes, in all seriousness, something required of him: the natural instinct of self-protection rises up so powerfully in him that a regular uproar follows, as with drink... And in that condition, in which he is beside himself, he demands the death of the man of spirit, or rushes upon him to put him to death.

Søren Kierkegaard, in Alexander Dru, editor, *The Journals of Kierkegaard*, Harper & Row, 1959, page 254

'When the Son of Man cometh, shall he find faith on the earth?' Luke 18:8.

If he were to come at this moment, would he find it in us? Where is our faith? What are the proofs of it? Do we believe that this life is only a short passage to a better? Do we believe that we must suffer with Jesus before we can reign with him? Do we look upon the world as a vain show, and death as the entrance into true happiness? Do we live by faith? Does it animate us? Do we enjoy the eternal truths that it presents to us? Do we feed our souls with them, as we nourish our bodies with healthful aliment? Do we accustom ourselves to view everything with the eye of faith? Alas! instead of living by faith, we extinguish it in our souls. How can we truly believe what we profess to believe, and act as we act?

May we not fear, lest the kingdom of heaven be taken from us, and given to others who will bring forth more fruit? This kingdom of heaven is faith, when it dwells and reigns in the heart. Blessed are the eyes that see this kingdom; flesh and blood have not seen it; earthly wisdom is blind to it. To realise its glories, we must be born again, and to do this we must die to self.

François de la M. Fénelon, 'Mrs Follen', in *Selections from the Writings of Fénelon*, Edward T. Whitfield, 1850, page 222

When, however, God destroys the false self with its false securities, He does so to make room for the true self to grow. There will probably be a time-lag between our awareness of the destruction and our awareness of what is growing, but the growth in fact begins at the very moment of demolition; or rather, the dying of this or that aspect of the false self is always a sign that we are ready to receive from God what we truly are. And the more we receive from God what we truly are, the more content shall we be for the ramshackle empire of our isolated ego to collapse. Of course it doesn't happen in a day. It is a long, costly—and glorious—process.

The self we truly are, the self which flows directly from God's continuous creative act, is a self alive with an inexpressibly rich quality of life because it is totally open (and hence totally vulnerable) to its own inner dispositions (none of which it disavows), to other people, to the truth wherever it may lead, to the created world in its profusion and variety sometimes threatening and sometimes succouring us, to pleasure—and to affliction. And in all these things it finds the God who is Joy. It is a self that knows in the deepest places of its being that nothing can separate it from the love of God, and that His love, spread abroad and, so to speak, solidified in His world, is Joy unspeakable and full of glory. It is a self that confronts the recurrent 'in spite of' of human living (in spite of my misfortune or illness or of Betty's death) and swallows up this 'in spite of' with the triumphant 'how much more' of God's self-giving love. For God makes of a loss that is real and devastating the means of an increased apprehension of Himself, which is our only ultimate gain—though that is a truth that it takes years or a life-time to realize.

H.A. Williams, C.R., *The Joy of God*, Mitchell Beazley Publishers, 1980, page 65

We must... try to discover the Divine attributes and the Divine Character by first finding out what our own deepest nature implies. If God is to speak to us it must be in terms of our nature. Before undertaking to fathom with the plummet of logic the unsoundable mystery of foreknowledge, let us see what we can know through a return to the real nature of man as he is, and especially to the real nature of the new Adam who is Christ, the Son of God. Man, as both Scripture and his own inner self testify, is made *in the image of God*, is dowered with freedom to determine his own destiny, may go upward into light, or downward into darkness. Man thus made, when put on trial, *failed*, followed lower instincts instead of higher, and experienced the awful penalty of sin, namely its cumulative power, the tendency of sin to beget sin, and to make higher choices even more difficult. Christ, however, the new Adam, has *succeeded*. He has completely revealed the way of obedience, the way in which spirit conquers flesh. He is the new kind of Person who lives from above and who exhibits the cumulative power of goodness. His victory, which was won by His own free choice, inspires all men who see it with faith and hope in man's spiritual possibilities... He sees in Him the Heart and Character of God, the certainty of Divine love and forgiveness, and the way of life for all who desire to be spiritually saved, which means, for him, the formation of a new inward self, a purified nature, a morally transformed man, a will which no longer loves or wills sin. 'Christ alone,' he says, 'can heal the malady of the soul, but He can heal it.' 'There is,' he says again, 'no other way of salvation for any man than the way of self-denial. He must put off his old man and put on Christ—however much blood and sweat the struggle may cost.' Man, he insists, is always wrong when he represents God as angry. Christ showed that God needed no appeasing, but rather that man needed to be brought back to God by the drawing of Love, and be reconciled to Him.

Rufus M. Jones, *Spiritual Reformers in the 16th and 17th Centuries*, Macmillan and Co., 1914, page 99

ETERNAL LIFE

*Eternal life—existing always, without end or usually beginning; a
quality and value of life; endless life after death; being eternal*

Two writers who feature in *Visions of Glory* have given me an insight into the meaning of eternal life. The first is William Barclay, who wrote that eternal life is the life of God, and to have eternal life is to share in the life of God. The second is George Appleton. According to him Jesus did not promise simply life after death, but a quality of life now. He promised us eternal life, the sharing of God's life, participation in his own risen life. This is a quality of life, the kind of life Jesus had, human life permeated by the grace and love of God, and so invulnerable to physical death. He concluded that if we have this life within us now, we shall not worry about our last migration into the spiritual world, for we shall know a good deal about it already.

I have found both these insights helpful in understanding my limited experience of eternal life. I recall hearing a piece of music and feeling as if another dimension of life was opening up for me. I remember standing in front of a work of art and being transported with delight into what seemed to be another world. Sometimes a poem has triggered off all sorts of exciting harmonious feelings. The practice of reflection has been full of such openings. My experience of eternal life, limited as it is, is best summed up by the account written by Johannes Anker-Larsen at the end of this section.

The eternal God is your dwelling place, and underneath are the everlasting arms.
Deuteronomy 33:27

But the steadfast love of the Lord is from everlasting to everlasting upon those who fear him, and his righteousness to children's children.
Psalm 103:17

But whoever drinks of the water that I shall give him will never thirst; the water that I shall give him will become in him a spring of water welling up to eternal life.
John 4:14

This is eternal life, that they know thee the only true God, and Jesus Christ whom thou hast sent.
John 17:3

Time is eternity; and we live in eternity now.
Herman Melville, *Mardi*, The New American Library of World Literature, 1964, page 516

The truest end of life is to know the life that never ends.
William Penn, *Fruits of Solitude*, A.W. Bennett, 1863, page 60

The noise of the moment scoffs at the music of the Eternal.
Rabindranath Tagore, 'Stray Birds', xcvi, in *Collected Poems and Plays of Rabindranath Tagore*, Macmillan and Co., 1936, page 299

If there is a God and a future life, then there is truth and goodness; and man's highest happiness consists in striving to attain them.

Leo Tolstoy, *War and Peace*, translated by Rosemary Edmonds, Penguin Books, 1969, volume 1, page 455

The real business of life... is to 'piece this life with the life of Heaven, to see it as one with all Eternity, a part of it, a life within it.'

Rufus M. Jones, *Spiritual Reformers in the 16th and 17th Centuries*, Macmillan and Co., 1914, page 335

But all things abided eternally as they were in their proper places. Eternity was manifest in the Light of the Day, and something infinite behind everything appeared.

Thomas Traherne, *Centuries*, The Faith Press, 1969, page 110

Any one who feels the full significance of what is involved in knowing the *truth* has a coercive feeling that Eternity has been set within us, that our finite life is deeply rooted in the all-pervading Infinite.

Rufus M. Jones, *Spiritual Reformers in the 16th and 17th Centuries*, Macmillan and Co., 1914, page xxxiv

The One remains, the many change and pass;
Heaven's light forever shines, Earth's shadows fly;
Life, like a dome of many-coloured glass,
Stains the white radiance of Eternity...

Percy Bysshe Shelley, *Adonais*, lii. 460, in *The Complete Poetical Works of Percy Bysshe Shelley*, Oxford University Press, 1935, page 110

Eternal life is not a gift as something out of the hand of God, like a sceptre, or like a coronet. It is a gift as education is; something wrought patiently and long in a man. It is a gift as the sunlight is to the flowers—an influence which enters into them and fashions them.

Henry Ward Beecher, *Proverbs from Plymouth Pulpit*, Charles Burnet & Co., 1887, page 168

... so shalt thou see and hear
The lovely shapes and sounds intelligible
Of that eternal language, which thy God
Utters, who from eternity doth teach
Himself in all, and all things in himself.

Samuel Taylor Coleridge, 'Frost at Midnight', in *The Complete Poetical Works of Samuel Taylor Coleridge*, Oxford at the Clarendon Press, 1981, volume 1, page 242

... Eternity is not an endless addition of 'times'—a weak infinite series of durations, but rather a Reality in which all true realities abide, and which retains in a present *now* all beginnings and all endings. Eternity is just the real world for which we were made and which we enter through the door of love.

Rufus M. Jones, *Spiritual Reformers in the 16th and 17th Centuries*, Macmillan and Co., 1914, page 335

Now there are some things we all know, but we don't take'm out and look at'm very often. We all know that *something* is eternal. And it ain't houses and it ain't names, and it ain't earth, and it ain't even the stars ... everybody knows in their bones that *something* is eternal, and that something has to do with human beings. All the greatest people ever lived have been telling us that for five thousand years, and yet you'd be surprised how people are always losing hold of it. There's something way down deep that's eternal about every human being.

Thornton Wilder, *Our Town*, act III, Longmans, Green and Co., 1964, page 93

We have defined the 'eternal' as what is perfect and unchanging; the life of the blessed must be perfect in the sense that it is all of one quality—and that the highest and holiest; it is unchanging in the sense that nothing is lost and nothing gained, for all is at the same level. On the other hand, the blessed are not the same as God, nor are they the same as one another; therefore outside (so to speak) the perfection of each there is an ocean of perfection that can be the object of their experience. God is unchanging, because there is nothing outside Himself; the blessed, while firm in the unity of their inner perfection, may have constant enrichment *from outside*—if I may again use what is only a metaphor.

Frank Herbert Brabant, *Time and Eternity in Christian Thought*, Longmans, Green and Co., 1937, page 221

Eternally, and for ever, in heaven, says St John, Christ says and is and does what prophets prophesied of Him that He would say and be and do. 'I am the Root and Offspring of David, the bright Morning Star. And let him that is athirst, come: and whosoever will, let him take the Water of Life freely.' For ever Christ calls to every anxious soul, every afflicted soul, to every man who is ashamed of himself, and angry with himself, and longs to live a gentler, nobler, purer, truer, and more useful life, 'Come, and live for ever the eternal life of righteousness, holiness, and peace, and joy in the Holy Spirit, which is the one true and only salvation bought for us by the precious blood of Christ our Lord.'

Charles Kingsley, *Daily Thoughts*, Macmillan and Co., 1884, page 11

'Eternal life'—or, what in these writings is the same thing, 'life'—comes through the reception of the Spirit, in a birth from above. 'That which is born of the flesh is flesh, and that which is born of the Spirit is Spirit.' When the Spirit comes as the initiator of this abundant life, then we 'know that we abide in Him and He in us, because He hath given us of His Spirit,' and it becomes possible for the Spirit-led person to be guided 'into all the truth,' to 'love even as He loved,' and to 'overcome the world.' Here, again, the human race is divided into those who have 'received of the Spirit,' and those who have not so received; those who are 'born from above' and those who have had only a natural birth; the twice born and the once-born; those who are 'of the Spirit,' *i.e.* spiritual, and those who are 'of this world,' *i.e.* empirical.

Rufus M. Jones, *Spiritual Reformers in the 16th and 17th Centuries*, Macmillan and Co., 1914, page xii

Now let us take the idea of *eternal life*. It is far better to speak of *eternal* life than to speak of *everlasting* life. The main idea behind eternal life is not simply that of duration. It is quite clear that a life which went on for ever could just as easily be hell as heaven. The idea behind eternal life is the idea of a certain quality, a certain kind of life. What kind of life? There is only one person who can properly be described by this adjective eternal (*aionios*) and that one person is God. Eternal life is the kind of life that God lives; it is God's life. To enter into eternal life is to enter into possession of that kind of life which is the life of God. It is to be lifted up above merely human, temporary, passing, transient things, into that joy and peace which belong only to God. And clearly, a man can only enter into this close communion and fellowship with God when he renders to God that love, that reverence, that devotion, that obedience which truly bring him into fellowship with God.

William Barclay, *The Gospel of John*, The Saint Andrew Press, 1965, volume 1, page 118

Now I come to that which is the most difficult to explain—the meeting with Eternity.

While I was still on my way, I noticed how Time and Space had loosened my handcuffs. Yearnings and painful longings were diminished, whether it be toward places or people whom I had become attached. Not that my feelings had grown cold, but I could no longer feel *separation* with the old force. There is a condition in which it ceases to exist.

Every object which we know has been christened by Time and Space. Every name means limitation, every word is an expression for something in distinction to something else. In the everlasting Now there is neither Space nor Time, neither limitation nor distinction. Even the language of the gods would be inadequate to describe it, and the 'language of Heaven' cannot be spoken or written; it is *lived*. Tongue and pen can tell lies, the language of Heaven is the life of true reality in man and imparts itself directly from soul to soul, with those who are wholly and really living in truth. Words cannot describe the wordless, and I am no artist in handling words, even within the realm of words.

But now I will try to express myself on the subject as plainly and simply as I can. I select a summer day's meeting between Time and Eternity and describe it in as far as it can be described.

I had been sitting in the garden working and had just finished. That afternoon I was to go to Copenhagen, but it was still an hour and a half before the departure of the train. The weather was beautiful, the air clear and pure. I lighted a cigar and sat down in one of the easy-chairs in front of the house. It was still and peaceful—around me and within me. Too good, in fact, to allow one to think much about anything. I just sat there. Then it began to come, that infinite tenderness, which is purer and deeper than that of lovers, or of a father toward his child. It was in me, but it also came to me, as the air came to my lungs. As usual, the breathing became sober and reverent, became, as it were, incorporeal; I inhaled the tenderness. Needless to say the cigar went out. I did not cast it away like a sin, I simply had no use for it.

This deep tenderness which I felt, first within myself and then even stronger around and above me, extended further and further—it became all-present. I saw it, and it developed into knowing, into knowing all, at the same time it became power, omnipotence, and drew me into the eternal Now.

That was my first actual meeting with Reality; because such is the real life: a Now which *is* and a Now which *happens.* There is no beginning and no end. I cannot say any more about this Now. I sat in my garden, but there was no place in the world where I was not.

During the whole time my consciousness was clear and sober. I sat in the garden and acknowledged it with a smile. There was something to smile over, for time and space, characteristics of the Now which happens were so to speak 'outside.' But what is the Now which happens? It is continuously active creation with all its birth throes. I saw time and space as instruments or functions of this creation. They come into existence with it and in the course of it, and with it they come to an end. The Newly Created stands in the Now and discards these tools. The freedom, the real *Being* begins.

Johannes Anker-Larsen, from *With the Door Open*, in Anne Freemantle, editor, *The Protestant Mystics*, The New American Library, 1965, page 253

EVIL

Evil—morally bad, wicked; harmful, tending to harm; evil thing,
wickedness

My favourite phrase in this section comes from Etty Hillesum—'the rottenness of others is in us too.' This fits in with the now familiar Genesis story of the creation of man. In this story God fashions and shapes man (man and woman) in his own image and likeness and breathes something of his own nature into man. Man then becomes a living being, with an enormous source of divine life in the depths of his being. There is a second truth in this story, crucially important for our understanding of the nature of evil: That which is fashioned and shaped in the image and likeness of God is taken from the dust of the earth. This means although man has a divine potential, he is also earthy and creaturely, having within him all the instincts and passions of the animals.

I do not wish to denigrate the earthy and the creaturely. This is a valuable part of our nature. If we look at the Gospels we can see the perfect integration and combination of the divine and the earthy and creaturely in the life of our Lord. Hence he was described as 'very God and very Man'. The result was a whole full-blooded life, freed from the power of evil.

I found my life dominated by the earthy and creaturely. Thanks to Etty Hillesum, I could no longer project my evil on to others. Evil within myself had been accepted and transformed by God's grace. A rough integration has been worked out between the divine and the earthy and creaturely. I now find the power of evil not quite so strong, but myself more alive.

Fret not yourself because of the wicked, be not envious of wrongdoers! For they will soon fade like the grass, and wither like the green herb.

Psalm 37:1–2

Wash yourselves; make yourselves clean; remove the evil of your doings from before my eyes; cease to do evil, learn to do good; seek justice, correct oppression; defend the fatherless, plead for the widow.

Isaiah 1:16–17

Do not be overcome by evil but overcome evil with good.

Romans 12:21

Let no evil talk come out of your mouths, but only such as is good for edifying, as fits the occasion, that it may impart grace to those who hear.

Ephesians 4:29

Ill deeds is doubled with an evil word.

William Shakespeare, *The Comedy of Errors*, III. ii. 20

Society is knee-deep with men who have no other function in life than to destroy their fellow-men.

Henry Ward Beecher, *Proverbs from Plymouth Pulpit*, Charles Burnet & Co., 1887, page 188

God laid no foundation of Wickedness, in the principles of His creation; it is an unnatural Super-structure of our own, *without* a foundation.

Benjamin Whichcote, *Moral and Religious Aphorisms*, viii. 158, Elkin Mathews & Marrot, 1930, page 85

Evil is eternal in the sight of God unless checked and cured; sin, like a poisonous weed, resows itself and becomes eternal by reproduction.

Henry Ward Beecher, *Proverbs from Plymouth Pulpit*, Charles Burnet & Co., 1887, page 188

However difficult the idea of a power of evil may be theologically or philosophically, it is one which experience understands only too well.

William Barclay, *The Letters to the Corinthians*, The Saint Andrew Press, 1988, page 196

If I did not believe in a special Providence, in a perpetual education of men by evil as well as good, by small things as well as great, I would believe nothing.

Charles Kingsley, *Daily Thoughts*, Macmillan and Co., 1884, page 209

The little respect paid to chastity in the male world is, I am persuaded, the grand source of many of the physical and moral evils that torment mankind, as well as of the vices and follies that degrade and destroy women.

Mary Wollstonecraft, in Miriam Brody Kramnick, editor, *Vindication of the Rights of Woman*, Penguin Books, 1978, page 282

But 'tis strange:
And oftentimes, to win us to our harm,
The instruments of darkness tell us truths;
Win us with honest trifles, to betray's
In deepest consequence.

William Shakespeare, *Macbeth*, I. iii. 122

For nought so vile that on the earth doth live,
But to the earth some special good doth give;
Nor aught so good, but, strain'd from that fair use,
Revolts from true birth, stumbling on abuse.

William Shakespeare, *Romeo and Juliet*, II. iii. 17

Whatever may be the meaning of the process of the world, however disheartening some steps in its evolution may be, they are necessary and without them, perhaps, some evil could not thoroughly have been worked out.

Mark Rutherford, *More Pages From a Journal*, Oxford University Press, 1910, page 219

For whenever we speak of the Adam, and disobedience, and of the old man, of self-seeking, self-will, and self-serving, of the I, the Me, and the Mine, nature, falsehood, the Devil, sin; it is all one and the same thing. These are all contrary to God, and remain without God.

Theologia Germanica, translated by Susanna Winkworth, Stuart & Watkins, 1966, page 112

Past civilisations have been destroyed by barbarians from without, but we are doing the job ourselves. We breed our own barbarians at the public expense, and our writers and newsmen faithfully chronicle their moral rottenness and hold it up for admiration.

Elizabeth Manners, *The Vulnerable Generation*, Cassell and Company, 1971, page 190

'The rottenness of others is in us too,' I continued to preach at him. 'I see no other solution, I really see no other solution than to turn inwards and to root out all rottenness there. I no longer believe that we can change anything in the world until we have first changed ourselves.'

Etty Hillesum, *A Diary, 1941–43*, translated by Arnold J. Pomerans, Jonathan Cape, 1983, page 71

When evil men plot, good men must plan. When evil men burn and bomb, good men must build and bind. When evil men shout ugly words of hatred, good men must commit themselves to the glories of love. Where evil men would seek to perpetuate an unjust status quo, good men must seek to bring into being a real order of justice.

Martin Luther King, *The Words of Martin Luther King*, selected by Coretta Scott King, William Collins Sons & Co., 1986, page 51

The good . . . is that which furthers growth, integration, transcendence, and renewal. Evil, by contrast, is that which brings about disintegration and de-building, arrests growth, creates a permanent unbalance, dissipates energy, degrades life, baffles and frustrates the spirit, and prevents the emergence of the divine.

Lewis Mumford, *The Conduct of Life*, Secker & Warburg, 1952, page 168

The result of this junction of finite and infinite in us is that a Christian life is bound to be a strenuous contest: 'you must expect to fight a great battle.' 'You are ... bidden to fight with your own selves, with your own desires, with your own affections, with your own reason, with your own will; and therefore if you will find your enemies, never look without. If you will find out the Devil and what he is and what his nature is, look within you. *There* you may see him in his colours, in his nature, in his power, in his effects and in his working.'

Rufus M. Jones, *Spiritual Reformers in the 16th and 17th Centuries*, Macmillan and Co., 1914, page 249

God permits evil. His Son submitted to it on the cross, and by so doing he was victorious over its power to harm him. The origin of evil remains a mystery. But without the possibility of evil we would not choose the good. Christians believe that Christ has delivered them from falling under the power of evil. We mature and grow in character by refusing the evil and choosing the good. God leaves us free to choose, because he wants us to grow into his own perfect freedom. This freedom of choice, however, involves the possibility of people perpetrating great evil.

Hugh Montefiore, *Confirmation Notebook*, Fifth Edition, SPCK, 1985, page 7

... the Bible is never in any doubt that there is a power of evil in this world. The Bible is not a speculative book, and it does not discuss the origin of that power of evil, but it knows that it is there. Quite certainly this petition of the Lord's Prayer should be translated not, 'Deliver us from evil,' but, 'Deliver us from the Evil One.' The Bible does not think of evil as an abstract principle or force, but as an active, personal power in opposition to God ...

So the Bible wastes no time in speculation about the origin of evil. It equips man to fight the battle against the evil, which is unquestionably there.

William Barclay, *The Gospel of Matthew*, The Saint Andrew Press, 1965, volume 1, page 226

Our Lord in the great Parable of the Judgement said nothing about the love of God at all: He simply talked of the love of people. What we have to learn is what love really is. If we love another person, we love that person's good, and could not possibly stand in the way of his true development. To live for another at your own expense is love ....

Four things come out of the parable. (1) The orgin of evil is a mystery. 'While men slept, an enemy came and sowed tares.' He is an enemy of God whose will is a selfish will. In this world or any world if a human will, or a spirit will, lives and works for self at the expense of others, that will becomes God's enemy, and the result of the sowing is a crop of weeds. (2) This evil principle must cause perplexity and distress to the servants of the Lord. (3) The Lord permits the tares and the thorns to go on growing, but He Himself more than any other was wounded by the thorns. (4) Good and evil go on side by side for a time, but ultimately there must be a separation. The wheat must be drawn out, the evil must be exposed.

Father Andrew, S.D.C., *The Romance of Redemption*, A.R. Mowbray & Co., 1954, page 20

I understand at last what Jesus meant when he said, 'Ye have heard that it was said, An eye for an eye, and a tooth for a tooth; but I say unto you, Resist not evil.' Jesus says, 'It has been instilled into you, you have become accustomed to account it a good and reasonable thing, that you should withstand evil by force, and pluck out an eye for an eye, that you should not establish courts of law, police officers, and soldiers, and that you should fight against your enemies; but I say unto you, Do no violence, take no part in violence, do evil to no one, not even to those whom you call your enemies.'

I understand now that in laying down the proposition of non-resistance to evil, Jesus not only points out its immediate result to every man, but that in opposition to the principles prevailing from the time of Moses to his own, accepted by the Roman Law, and still existing in the codes of the different nations, he also lays down this rule of non-resistance (which, according to his teaching, should be the binding principle of our social life), to free humanity from the evil wrought by itself. He says to mankind, 'You think that your laws correct evil; they only increase it. There is one only way of extirpating evil—to return good to all men without distinction. You have tried your principle for thousands of years; try now mine, which is its reverse.'

Leo Tolstoy, What I Believe ('My Religion'), C.W. Daniel, 1922, page 41

EXPERIENCE

Experience—personal observation of or involvement with fact,
event, etc.; knowledge or skill based on this; event that affects one

When Harry Williams was Dean of Trinity College, Cambridge, he is reputed to have said he would never preach anything he himself had not personally experienced. I remember being challenged by this statement. Up to that point my preaching had been based on the Bible and on doctrines emanating from the Gospels. Early on in life, religious experience had been a valuable ingredient in my faith. This had somehow been set aside at theological college. Here the emphasis was mainly biblical, doctrinal and theological. The hurdle of exams had to be surmounted as a condition for ordination. In the parish, frenzied activity was the order of the day. At the end of four years I was in desperate need of a different outlook.

My tattered faith broke down to give way to a faith based on religious experience—my own and others. This led to the evolution of *Visions of Faith, Hope, Love* and *Glory*. I remember a young woman coming to see me in desperate straits. We turned to a section in this anthology. After a few minutes she suddenly brightened up. She had caught sight of a passage written by Harry Williams, and joyfully exclaimed: 'Gosh, this man has put in to words exactly what I feel. That's wonderful.' This was a turning-point for her. Someone else's experience matched her own and struck a helpful chord.

Religious experience has been crucial for me. The end product is an inner conviction of mind, heart and soul, which is at one with our deepest intuitions and instincts.

I have learned by divination that the Lord has blessed me because of you.

Genesis 30:27

I have acquired great wisdom... and my mind has had great experience of wisdom and knowledge.

Ecclesiastes 1:16

Yet he is not far from each one of us, for 'In him we live and move and have our being.'

Acts 17:27

... we rejoice in our sufferings, knowing that suffering produces endurance, and endurance produces character, and character produces hope, and hope does not disappoint us, because God's love has been poured into our hearts through the Holy Spirit which has been given us.

Romans 5:3–5

Never, 'for the sake of peace and quiet', deny your own experience or convictions.

Dag Hammarskjöld, Markings, translated by W.H. Auden and Leif Sjoberg, with a foreword by W.H. Auden,
Faber and Faber, 1964, page 85

Experience is by industry achiev'd
And perfected by the swift course of time.

William Shakespeare, *Two Gentlemen of Verona*, I. iii. 22

So much of the Gospel as has been reproduced in a living form in Christian people's experience is what the world needs more than almost anything else.

Henry Ward Beecher, *Proverbs from Plymouth Pulpit*, Charles Burnet & Co., 1887, page 173

All authentic religion originates with mystical experience, be it the experience of Jesus, of the Buddha, or Mohammed, of the seers and prophets of the *Upanishads*.

William Johnston, *The Inner Eye of Love*, William Collins Sons & Co., 1978, page 81

The notes of religious experience that ring out of the soul are notes gladder than marriage-bells. Religion is real if it is experimental. Religion is glorious, and experimental religion is the most glorious of all.

Henry Ward Beecher, *Proverbs from Plymouth Pulpit*, Charles Burnet & Co., 1887, page 163

His emphasis is always . . . upon the native divine possibilities of the soul, upon the fact of a spiritual environment in immediate correspondence and co-operation with the soul, and upon the necessity of personal and inward experience as the key to every gate of life.

Rufus M. Jones, *Spiritual Reformers in the 16th and 17th Centuries*, Macmillan and Co., 1914, page 190

'Tis greatly wise to talk with our past hours;
And ask them, what report they bore to Heaven;
And how they might have borne more welcome news.
Their answers form what men Experience call;
If Wisdom's friend, her best; if not, worst foe.

Edward Young, *Night Thoughts*, ii. 376, in *The Complete Works of Edward Young*, William Tegg and Co., 1854, volume 1, page 23

He who receives Christ *experiences* something, but he hardly notices it. The wonder of the new life, the joy of forgiveness, and the liberation from fear keep him looking constantly to this figure from whom streams of living water flow into his life, reclaiming the desert of his lost heart and working the miracle of a new beginning.

Helmut Thielicke, *I Believe: The Christian's Creed*, translated by John W. Doberstein and H. George Anderson, William Collins Sons & Co., 1969, page 11

A creed is always the result and fruit of many minds and many centuries, purified from all the oddities, shortcomings, and flaws of individual experience. But for all that, the individual experience, with its very poverty, is immediate life, it is the warm red blood pulsating today. It is more convincing to a seeker after truth than the best tradition.

C.G. Jung, *Psychological Reflections*, selected and edited by Jolande Jacobi, Routledge & Kegan Paul, 1953, page 322

If religion is essentially of the inner life, it follows that it can be truly grasped only from within. But beyond a doubt, this can be better done by one in whose own inward consciousness an experience of religion plays a part. There is but too much danger that the other (the non-believer) will talk of religion as a blind man might of colours, or one totally devoid of ear, of a beautiful musical composition.

William Schmidt, *The Origin and Growth of Religion*, translated by H.J. Rose, Methuen & Co., 1931, page 6

. . . the first experience of the blossoming forth of the world of sense in my life seemed to put me in touch with genuine, original nature, whereas everything that presented itself to the senses at a later date had something of the air of a copy about it that, while approaching the original, nevertheless lacked the freshness of its spirit and meaning.

Johann Wolfgang von Goethe, *Wisdom and Experience*, selected by Ludwig Curtius, translated and edited by Hermann J. Weigand, Routledge & Kegan Paul, 1949, page 108

It is one thing to be told that Jesus is the Saviour of the World, and to accept that truth with the intellect. It is another thing to sing, both with heart and mind: 'Rock of Ages, cleft for *me*', and really to believe it. It is one thing to be told that the Bible has authority because it is divinely inspired, and another thing to feel one's heart leap out and grasp its truth.

Leslie Weatherhead, *The Christian Agnostic*, Hodder and Stoughton, 1965, page 29

... strain every nerve in every possible way to know and experience yourself as you really are. It will not be long, I suspect, before you have a real knowledge and experience of God as he is. Not as he is in himself, of course, for that is impossible to any save God; and not as you will in Heaven, both in body and soul. But as much as is now possible for a humble soul in a mortal body to know and experience him... and as much as he will permit.

The Cloud of Unknowing, translated by Clifton Wolters, Penguin Books, 1971, page 71

Out of the chaos of human experience an individual is now and then lifted to the peak of spiritual consciousness. As man develops, and his intelligence slowly unfolds, these individual peaks are more frequently seen; but they are never precisely alike. Each one is a light-bringer; but the light is so infinitely varied by the medium through which it is transmitted that it is sometimes difficult to perceive its Divine source.

Helen Keller, *My Religion*, Hodder and Stoughton, 1927, page 79

Are 'revelation' and 'experience' different ways of speaking about the same reality, one stressing the divine pole and the other the human? If so, how do the experiences of contemporary Christians relate to those recorded in scripture? If not, what is the relationship between faith and experience, in the Bible and today? In either case, can contemporary experience ever do more than confirm scripture? Such questions clamour for refinement and elucidation but they point to a crucial issue for Christian faith and practice, past and present.

Graham Slater, in Gordon S. Wakefield, editor, *A Dictionary of Christian Spirituality*, SCM Press, 1986, page 141

Science has never discovered any 'God', epistemological criticism proves the impossibility of knowing God, but the psyche comes forward with the assertion of the experience of God. God is a psychic fact of immediate experience, otherwise there would never have been any talk of God. The fact is valid in itself, requiring no non-psychological proof and inaccessible to any form of non-psychological criticism. It can be the most immediate and hence the most real of experiences, which can be neither ridiculed nor disproved. Only people with a poorly developed sense of fact, or who are obstinately superstitious, could deny this truth.

C.G. Jung, *The Collected Works of C.G. Jung*, volume 8, *The Structure and Dynamics of the Psyche*, translated by R.F.C. Hull, Routledge & Kegan Paul, 1969, page 328

The difficulty about religious experience is not to get it, but to recognize it when it comes. It is always coming our way. We are like Jacob, who slept all night on the bare earth and knew not till the morning broke that he was in the house of God and before the gate of heaven. We are liable to go wrong at that point, thinking of religious experience as a thing yet to be attained, while all the time it is in the deep and silent places of our lives... Religious experience is not an exceptional thing reserved for privileged souls, nor exceptional even in the sense that it occurs only at the rare moments of life. *It is the normal experience of the plain man, grasped in its entirety and deeply felt.*

L.P. Jacks, *Elemental Religion*, Williams & Norgate, 1934, page 48

Here is the thing to grasp! Difficult as the idea may be for a plain man to believe, the indwelling of Christ in the human heart is a glorious reality, enjoyed (in varying degrees) by millions, and not impossible to any human soul. It may sound mystic, occult and impractical. But it is real, homely and 'day-to-day.' It is for *all* men and women, in all walks of life: for cabinet ministers and cabinet makers; ambassadors and bus-drivers; journalists and junior clerks. You can run a business on it, and run a home. It is *not* 'airy-fairy.' ... It is the open secret of the Christian message and leads to the finest experience this earth affords.

W.E. Sangster, *The Secret of the Radiant Life*, Hodder & Stoughton, 1957, page 31

Religious experience is absolute. It is indisputable. You can only say that you have never had such an experience, and your opponent will say: 'Sorry, I have.' And there your discussion will come to an end. No matter what the world thinks about religious experience, the one who has it possesses the great treasure of a thing that has provided him with a source of life, meaning and beauty and that has given him a new splendour, to the world and to mankind. He has *pistis* and peace. Where is the criterium by which you could say that such a life is not legitimate, that such experience is not valid and thus such *pistis* is mere illusion? Is there, as a matter of fact, any better truth about ultimate things than the one that helps you to live?

C.G. Jung, *Psychology and Religion*, Yale University Press, 1960, page 113

But the very characteristics of mystical religion which give it its self-evidence and power at the same time mark limits to its scope and range. It is and must be primarily and essentially first-hand experience, and yet it is an experience that is by no means universal. It is not, so far as we can see from the facts at hand, an experience which attaches to the very nature of consciousness as such, or indeed one which is bound to occur even when the human subject strains forward all the energies of his will for the adventure, or when by strict obedience to the highest laws of life known to him he *waits* for the high visitation. Some aspect is involved over which the will has no control. Some other factor is implied besides the passion and the purity of the seeking soul. The experience 'comes,' as an inrush, as an emergence from the deeper levels of the inner life, but the glad recipient does not know how he secured the prize or how to repeat the experience, or how to tell his friend the way to these 'master moments' of blessedness.

Rufus M. Jones, *Spiritual Reformers in the 16th and 17th Centuries*, Macmillan and Co., 1914, page xxii

Experience dispenses with proof; proof rests upon, and can rest upon nothing else than experiences, which speak for themselves. Is beauty ever in need of demonstration? Or is goodness? Religion, like poetry, music and painting, requires an organ of vision. You may have a mathematical genius like Newton, or a musical genius like Bach, or a religious genius like St. Francis, or a poetic genius like Virgil, or a genius for action like Napoleon. You may also without genius have an appreciation of such things. The discovery of poetry is man's discovery, the discovery of music is man's discovery. The discovery of religion and morals are his discoveries. *Est Deus in nobis.* There is no other revelation than the revelation of his own soul. And what is the implication of these discoveries? That in your soul itself resides a divine principle of which these are the fruits. Like music and poetry, religion provides its own justification, like them is witness to its own worth.

W. Macneile Dixon, *The Human Situation*, Edward Arnold & Co., 1937, page 275

So many Christians are like deaf people at a concert. They study the programme carefully, believe every statement made in it, speak respectfully of the quality of the music, but only really hear a phrase now and again. So they have no notion at all of the mighty symphony which fills the universe, to which our lives are destined to make their tiny contribution, and which is the self-expression of the Eternal God.

Yet there are plenty of things in our normal experience, which imply the existence of that world, that music, that life. If, for instance, we consider the fact of prayer, the almost universal impulse to seek and appeal to a power beyond ourselves, and notice the heights to which it can rise in those who give themselves to it with courage and love—the power it exerts, the heroic vocations and costly sacrifices which it supports, the transformations of character which it effects—it is a sufficiently mysterious characteristic, of man. So, too, all who are sensitive to beauty know the almost agonising sense of revelation its sudden impact brings—the abrupt disclosure of the mountain summit, the wild cherry-tree in blossom, the crowning moment of a great concerto, witnessing to another beauty beyond sense. And again, any mature person looking back on their own past life, will be forced to recognise factors in that life, which cannot be attributed to heredity, environment, opportunity, personal initiative or mere chance. The contact which proved decisive, the path unexpectedly opened, the other path closed, the thing we felt compelled to say, the letter we felt compelled to write. It is as if a hidden directive power, personal, living, free, were working through circumstances and often against our intention or desire; pressing us in a certain direction, and moulding us to a certain design.

All this, of course, is quite inexplicable from the materialistic standpoint. If it is true, it implies that beneath the surface of life, which generally contents us, there are unsuspected deeps and great spiritual forces which condition and control our small lives. Some people are, or become, sensitive to the pressure of these forces. The rest of us easily ignore the evidence for this whole realm of experience, just because it is all so hidden and interior; and we are so busy responding to obvious and outward things. But no psychology which fails to take account of it can claim to be complete. When we take it seriously, it surely suggests that we are essentially spiritual as well as natural creatures; and that therefore life in all its fulness, the life which shall develop and use all our capacities and fulfil all our possibilities, must involve correspondence not only with our visible and ever-changing, but also with our invisible and unchanging environment: the Spirit of all spirits, God, in whom we live and move and have our being.

Evelyn Underhill, *The Spiritual Life*, Harper & Row, 1936, page 18

FAITH

Faith—strong belief, especially in the Christian faith; things believed; loyalty, trustworthiness

My faith had a small beginning, but over the years has grown. Perhaps this is why I am so fond of our Lord's parable of faith as a grain of mustard seed. I once saw a grain of mustard seed, so small it was scarcely visible to the naked eye. Yet I knew that this microscopic seed had the capacity to grow into a large bush, out of all proportion to its original size. Such has been the unfolding of my faith.

The small beginning was something simple and ordinary: my godmother taking me to a church at Christmas to see the baby Jesus in a crib. This was the start of my faith. In my teens I grew towards some sort of commitment which required a step of faith in my early twenties—mainly to the person of Jesus Christ and the Holy Spirit. This was followed up by Bible reading and prayer, and the study of theology. A big breakthrough came with *The Choice is Always Ours*, leading to a fresh understanding of the Genesis story of the creation of man. A consequence was the discovery of 'the God within'— something of the Father, Son and Holy Spirit in the depths of my being, as well as other divine attributes such as life, light, truth, joy, grace and love, experienced in the practice of reflection. The object of faith was no longer just a transcendent God, high and lifted up, or the Jesus of history, both difficult to believe in, but also a divine presence within, close, near and loving. Thanks be to God for his unspeakable gift.

And Abram... believed the Lord; and he reckoned it to him as righteousness.
Genesis 15:3, 6

And though they have not seen me with bodily eyes, yet in spirit they believe the thing that I say.
2 Esdras 1:37 (AV)

For we walk by faith, not by sight.
2 Corinthians 5:7

Now faith is the assurance of things hoped for, the conviction of things not seen.
Hebrews 11:1

We live in an age which asks for faith, pure faith, naked faith, mystical faith.
William Johnston, *The Inner Eye of Love*, William Collins Sons & Co., 1978, page 85

To abandon religion for science is merely to fly from one region of faith to another.
Giles and Melville Harcourt, *Short Prayers for the Long Day*, William Collins Sons & Co., 1978, page 18

The life of faith is a continually renewed victory over doubt, a continually renewed grasp of meaning in the midst of meaninglessness.
Lesslie Newbigin, *Honest Religion for Secular Man*, SCM Press, 1966, page 98

Faith in Christ was not primarily a matter of doctrinal or intellectual belief, but a way of life, a following, an allegiance.

Said of Edward Wilson, in George Seaver, *Edward Wilson of the Antarctic,* John Murray, 1935, page 104

... Faith is not belief in static propositions or the mental assent to information about God, but a dynamic, daily renewed practice of fellowship with God.

W.B.J. Martin, *Five Minutes to Twelve,* William Collins Sons & Co., 1957, page 98

Faith is in essence that boldness or heroic daring of the soul against all the darkness and adversity of the world to lay claim to certain things that all the facts of life deny.

Samuel H. Miller, *The Great Realities,* Longmans, Green and Co., 1956, page 126

Like all human knowledge, the knowledge of faith is also fragmentary. Only when faith remains aware of this does it remain free from arrogance, intolerance and false zeal.

Hans Küng, *On Being a Christian,* translated by Edward Quinn, William Collins Sons & Co., 1977, page 159

To have faith is to meet the world with the conviction that in spite of all its ambiguities and its downright evils, there can be discerned in it the reality of love and a ground of hope.

John Macquarrie, *Paths in Spirituality,* SCM Press, 1972, page 33

Proofs are the last thing looked for by a truly religious mind which feels the imaginative fitness of its faith and knows instinctively that, in such a matter, imaginative fitness is all that can be required.

George Santayana, *Interpretations of Poetry and Religion,* Charles Scribner's Sons, 1916, page 95

How do we stand in respect of our use of the watch-tower of Faith? Are we so busy on the ground floor that we take it for granted, and seldom go upstairs? It is true that those stairs are dark and steep; but if we never make the effort, never ascend to the soul's summit, we remain something less than human.

Evelyn Underhill, in John Stobbart, editor, *The Wisdom of Evelyn Underhill,* A.R. Mowbray & Co., 1951, page 18

And the proper response to revelation is rightly said to be faith, faith being not an intellectual assent to general truths, but the decisive commitment of the whole person in active obedience to, and quiet trust in, the divine will apprehended as rightfully sovereign and utterly trustworthy at one and the same time.

H.H. Farmer, *The World and God,* James Nisbet & Co., 1936, page 88

They say that Abraham is a great example of faith. I sometimes wonder. It says that 'he went out not knowing...' I sometimes fancy that he had left faith far behind; that he was way away out on the edge of things, where only a sliver of hope sustains. When we can join him out there on that edge, in hope sacrificing hope—only then may we see light, and be satisfied.

Henry McKeating, *God and the Future,* SCM Press, 1974, page 84

Faith claims a certain 'knowledge' of God, and therewith of the nature of the world and human destiny. But by its very nature as trust in a God transcending finitude, it requires an admission of much that is unknown and unknowable. In the New Testament, faith is contrasted with 'sight' which is reserved for eternity (II Cor. 5:7). In Christian tradition, faith therefore combines a certitude with an equal acknowledgement of mystery.

Keith Clements, in Alan Richardson and John Bowden, editors, *A New Dictionary of Christian Theology,* SCM Press, 1985, page 208

... it is only by living completely in this world that one learns to believe... This is what I mean by worldliness—taking life in one's stride, with all its duties and problems, its successes and failures, its experiences and helplessness. It is in such a life that we throw ourselves utterly into the arms of God and participate in his sufferings in the world and watch with Christ in Gethsemene. That is faith, that is *metanoia*, and that is what makes a man and a Christian.

Dietrich Bonhoeffer, *Letters and Papers from Prison*, William Collins Sons & Co., 1963, page 125

Faith today is difficult. This is an indisputable sign of our times. The collapse of cultures has stripped it bare, the death of civilization has filled it with sorrow. I would say that today we discover God more easily in His negative. Normally we do not hear His melody when He whispers, but when He is silent, then we build.

Another reason why man feels alone is because the Churches have been taken by surprise and gripped by panic and they often think that the way to save themselves is by looking to the past instead of marching towards the newness of God with the trust of children.

Carlo Carretto, *The Desert in the City*, translated by Barbara Wall, William Collins Sons & Co., 1983, page 88

Faith gives a face as of heaven to the whole earth, and by it our hearts are ravished and transported to converse in heaven. Faith is the light of time: alone it attains truth without seeing it; it touches what it does not feel, it beholds this world as if it were not there, seeing something quite different to what appears on the surface. Faith is the key to the treasury, the key of the abyss of divine wisdom, the key of the science of God. It is faith that gives the lie to all creation, it is by faith that God reveals and manifests himself in all things. It is faith that divinizes things, which lifts the veil and reveals to us eternal truths.

Jean-Pierre de Caussade, S.J., *Self-Abandonment to Divine Providence*, translated by Algar Thorold, William Collins Sons & Co., 1972, page 51

'Faith ... is not historical knowledge for a man to make articles of it and to depend on them, but faith in one spirit with God, it is the activity of God; it is free, but only for the right and for pure Love, in which it draws the breath of its power and strength. It is, finally, itself the substance.' Faith is, thus, not knowledge, it is not believing facts of history, it is not accepting metaphysical dogma. It is, as he is never weary of saying, 'strong earnestness of spirit,' the earnest will to live in the inward and eternal, passionate hunger and thirst for God, and finally the *act* of receiving Christ into the soul as a present power and spirit to live by. 'I must die,' he wrote, 'with my outward man (the man of self-centred will) in Christ's death and arise and live anew in Him. Therefore I live now by the will of faith in the spirit of Christ and receive Christ with His humanity into my will ... He became that which I am, and now He has made me that which He is!'

Rufus M. Jones, *Spiritual Reformers in the 16th and 17th Centuries*, Macmillan and Co., 1914, page 195

Faith—which for every prophet of human redemption is the key that unlocks all doors of the soul—is ... the supreme moral force by which man turns God's revelations of Himself into spiritual victories and into personal conquests of character. It is never something forensic, something magical. It is, as little, mere belief of historical facts and events. It is, on the contrary, a moral power that moves mountains of difficulty, works miracles of transformation, and enables the person who has it to participate in the life of God. It is a passionate leap ('*elan*') of the soul of the creature toward the Creator; it is a way of renewing strength in Him and of becoming a participator in His divine nature. It is a return of the soul to its source. It is a *persistent will*, which multiplies one's strength a hundredfold, makes Pentecost possible again, and enables us to achieve the goal which the vision of our heart sees. The only obstacle to this all conquering faith is selfishness, the only mortal enemy is self-will.

Rufus M. Jones, *Spiritual Reformers in the 16th and 17th Centuries*, Macmillan and Co., 1914, page 100

'Then Jesus answered and said unto her, "O woman, great is thy faith; be it unto thee even as thou wilt."' (Matt. 15:28)

You remember the story from which the words are taken. Jesus has travelled outside of the regions of the Jews, and there has come to him a Canaanitish woman asking Him to cure her poor afflicted daughter. He has hesitated and remonstrated, but at last she overcomes Him with her urgency, and He yields to her, saying, 'O woman, great is thy faith; be it unto thee even as thou wilt.' It would be possible to give reasons, which no doubt would be true ones, for Christ's reluctance. But I cannot but think that the truest and simplest way to look at this beautiful story, is to consider it as a record of the spiritual necessities of Jesus. The idea which seems to me to be in it is this, that Jesus gave the woman what she wanted just as soon as it was possible for Him to give it; and that, just as soon as it was possible for Him to give it, in some true sense He had to give it, it was impossible for Him to refuse it any longer. He was not holding it, as it were, behind His back, watching her face to see when was the best moment to give it to her. He was telling her of a genuine impossibility when He said, 'I am not sent but unto the lost sheep of the house of Israel.' He could not give her what she wanted then; but when by her belief in Him she had crossed the line and become spiritually one of His people, then the impossibility was removed, and we may even say, I think, that He could not help helping her.

Phillips Brooks, *Sermons Preached in English Churches*, Macmillan and Co., 1883, pages 157, 158–59

I am utterly convinced of the truth of Christian faith. Like most of my contemporaries, I have known doubt and questioning, certainly I have been forced to face the problems which that faith presents to us. I have been obliged to engage in a great deal of re-construction, re-thinking, re-statement, in order to maintain what I take to be the abiding elements in that faith. But that the basic reality of the world is the driving energy of a personalized and personalizing love, supremely and definitively manifested for us men in a fellow Man: to this I must return again and again as all that makes life worth living. So it is too with other aspects of the historical Christian tradition. Question as I must, feel doubts as I do, puzzle as I may, there is something there which is *true*—true not only in my own experience but true because it provides an explanation of what is going on in the world, despite the evil, pain, anguish, violence, and wickedness which I cannot deny. One's whole life is centred in that *something* and one feels impelled to help others to see that there is a glory there as well as a truth, in terms of which (in Clement of Alexandria's lovely phrase) 'our sunsets become a sunrise.' I may be mistaken about it all, life is a risk and I cannot claim absolute knowledge which would relieve me from the supreme venture of faith. But I do not think myself mistaken; and in my best moments, few as they are, I am profoundly certain that I am not. Yet I am equally sure that only if, as, and when that abiding Christian *something* is in touch with men as they are, can it provide for them what it has provided for me—an anchor in my life's quest. That is why I am sure that re-conception is required.

Norman Pittenger, *The Christian Situation Today*, Epworth Press, 1969, page 44

FELLOWSHIP

Fellowship—friendly association with others; companionship, brotherhood

In this topic there is a short quotation by J. Neville Ward. I remember reading his book *The Use of Praying* over twenty years ago, and noticed his remarks about Christian fellowship. I felt a certain sympathy with his observation that much local church 'togetherness' is a waste of time.

Two phrases from hymns have enabled me to understand the nature of fellowship. The first is from the hymn 'Christ, whose glory fills the skies'. In the third verse there is the line—'Fill me, radiancy divine.' This fits in well with our underlying vision, and the practice of reflection. The request to be filled with radiancy divine can happen quite naturally—the God within can come alive and permeate our inner being. I have already emphasized the vast potential of the divine in the depths of ourselves. The second is from the rousing hymn, 'For all thy saints who from their labours rest'. A line of the fourth verse has the phrase 'fellowship divine'. If we have been filled with 'radiancy divine' we shall then have something in common with others of enormous importance, a fellowship in which the divine predominates. What a difference this would make if realized. Church life would be transformed overnight.

Although we have this section specifically on fellowship, *Visions of Glory* as a whole contains material designed to stimulate fellowship and enrich our friendly associations with others, our companionship (literally those with whom we break bread), and our brotherhood.

And I will make my abode among you, and my soul shall not abhor you. And I will walk among you, and will be your God, and you shall be my people.

Leviticus 26:11–12

I am a companion of all who fear thee, of those who keep thy precepts.

Psalm 119:63

So if there is any encouragement in Christ, any incentive of love, any participation in the Spirit, any affection and sympathy, complete my joy by being of the same mind, having the same love, being in full accord and of one mind.

Philippians 2:1–2

And let us consider how to stir up one another to love and good works, not neglecting to meet together, as is the habit of some, but encouraging one another.

Hebrews 10:24–25

For there is a fellowship more quiet even than solitude, and which, rightly understood, is solitude made perfect.

Robert Louis Stevenson, *Travels With a Donkey*, Chatto and Windus, 1909, page 122

In 'fellowship,' the recognition of other people's hopes and desires and designs, lies a great source of strength; and that kind of co-operation seems to be the new spirit which is affecting the world.

A.C. Benson, *Extracts from the Letters of Dr. A.C. Benson to M.E.A.*, Jarrold Publishing, 1927, page 8

A New Testament expression, *koinonia* may be translated as 'fellowship,' 'communion,' 'participation,' or even 'community.' The basic idea is that of sharing. The Christian life is a shared life, shared with God through Christ, and with the other members of the body of Christ, the community of the Spirit.

John Macquarrie, in James F. Childress and John Macquarrie, editors, *A New Dictionary of Christian Ethics*, SCM Press, 1986, page 340

Think of Christ as a very Gracious and Understanding Person quite near to you. Talk to Him now in your mind. Is it a foolish thing to do? The best people of all the ages have talked to God in their mind. You can only know Him personally by personal fellowship and that means (as it would mean with *any* person) by conversation. Speak to Him . . . and listen!

W.E. Sangster, *The Secret of Radiant Life*, Hodder and Stoughton, 1957, page 44

The only fellowship that is the fellowship of the Spirit is that in which Christians are gathered together in worship (once a week, on Sunday, is enough), in study of the Bible or Christian faith, or in service to the community. Life is much too short, and too serious, for the cultivation of Christian fellowship for the sake of Christian fellowship. Indeed much of local church 'togetherness' is a waste of time.

J. Neville Ward, *The Use of Praying,* Epworth Press, 1967, page 60

The fulness of the Christian life cannot be known except in fellowship—fellowship with God and fellowship with one another. Moreover, the purposes of God in this world require a social organism by which to express themselves. Far as the Church has fallen below the intention of her divine Founder, she is still His best instrument in this world for doing His will.

W.E. Sangster, *Give God a Chance,* Epworth Press, 1968, page 84

One of the intriguing mysteries of nature is a flock of wild geese flying in a V-shaped formation. When a group of aerodynamic engineers studied this phenomenon, they made an interesting discovery. 'As the geese fly in a V-shaped formation, the flapping of the wings of each bird gives an uplift to the one before and the one behind him, and he in turn receives an uplift from them. This lift creates approximately 70 per cent more forward thrust, so that as a group the geese fly further than they can individually. If one goose slips out of formation and tries to fly on his own, he gives and receives nothing.'

Anon.

Let us become conscious of ourselves as a fellowship pledged to God and to one another to stand and contend for international and social justice; to set little store by our possessions and much by our responsibilities; to seek, in worship, at once the under-standing of our task and the quality by which we may perform it; to make use of the service appointed by our Lord as the symbol of our social life and the means of our personal dedication; and daily to commit ourselves, our country and all mankind to God in the prayer our Lord has taught us.

William Temple, *The Hope of a New World,* SCM Press, 1940, page 71

It is the potentiality of knowing the Creator of the infinite universe and having fellowship with him that is man's marvel, though of course when we speak of man's fellowship with God, we remember that it is not a fellowship of equals, but a fellowship deeply shot through with awe and dependence.

The nearer we get to God in real intimate fellowship as the very friend of God, the more we are humbled by this awe and dependence, abasing ourselves in the very start of our friendship with him, and we do what the Bible calls, 'give glory to God'.

The end of this intimacy between man and God—man made in God's image—is nothing less than heaven. Heaven is the crown and consummation of man's rightful destiny as created in the image of God.

Michael Ramsey, *Through the Year with Michael Ramsey,* edited by Margaret Duggan, Hodder and Stoughton, 1975, page 47

The earthly workshop of the Holy Spirit, the place where the glory of Christ is reflected, is the corporate community of Christians. Not the individual 'I' but the corporate 'we' are being changed into Christ's likeness. What the Spirit does personally in each, has its full significance only in relation to what he is doing corporately. The appointed witness to Christ risen and ascended is his Body, the Church, of which individuals are the members, the building into which individuals are to be built together as living stones. The Holy Spirit makes us witnesses by joining and co-ordinating us together in a shared life of strong relationships and ordered ministries of various gifts.

To be called to Christ is by definition to be called to fellowship with those who are called with us. It was so in Galilee, it was so at Pentecost and it is so now. The Holy Spirit, as well as reflecting the character and the power of Christ in Christians, is also concerned with the creation of *koinonia*, the fellowship of a shared life, which will bind them together in one Body, subordinated to the Head and ordered in love with one another.

Thomas A. Smail, Reflected Glory, Hodder and Stoughton, 1975, page 128

It is in fellowship that life, through all its vast hierarchy of being, from lowest to highest, has its significance. The very first step in the process of living in a germinating seed is always a breach of self-centred isolation. The potential life which lay dormant within it, when once the quickening influences have reached it—the moisture and the warmth—exhibits itself always in an endeavour to enter into vital relations with what the scientific man calls so suitably its environment. The tiny thing swells, breaks from its limiting husk, strikes down into mother-earth its fine filaments, and shoots upwards to enter into harmonious relations with the great sun, the air, the light, the dew, the rain. Let some wanton hand tear that clump of sweet violets from its nestling-place in the hedgerow and fling it out into the way. In a few hours you pick it up and say it is dead. What did it die of? The answer is plain, and most significant. It died because that fellowship was ruptured which is at once the equivalent and interpretation of Life. It lived by communion; it dies when the communion is broken. Just so ... do human souls live; and so likewise do they dwindle and die. From the lowest forms of life up to that mystery supreme which meets us, hidden in excess of light, in the doctrine of the Trinity, as an expression such as we may receive of the life of the ever-blessed God—everywhere it is revealed that Fellowship is Life ... In this all-inclusive Fellowship with Christ will be found the heart of a Religion which, while it gives due place to creeds and politics and ritual, must find its throbbing life in none of these, but in a perfected Communion with God and with one another.

William Medley, Christ the Truth, Macmillan and Co., 1900, pages 193, 238

The Incarnation revealed and fulfilled the relations which already existed between the Son of God and mankind. From the beginning, Christ had entered into fellowship with us. When we sinned, He remained in fellowship with us still. He was in partnership with us; the miseries of the race were His, His by His own choice, and He endured them all. It 'behoved' the eternal Son of God to share the fortunes of God's earthly children. He not only became man, but submitted to all the sufferings and humiliations of our earthly condition. He endured the pains which are common to man and to inferior races. He was tried by hunger, thirst, and weariness, and physical torture. He endured the sharper agonies, the deeper sorrows, which are man's special and separate inheritance, as the result of His revolt against God. He was tempted by the Devil; He was suspected, hated, slandered. His friends were not always faithful; one of them betrayed Him. The most appalling woe—the woe which we might have thought could never have come on the Son of God, and which to many of us seems incredible—fell upon Him: in the mysterious darkness of His last hours, He cried, 'My God, My God, why hast Thou forsaken Me?' That sorrow broke His heart, and He died. He clung to us through death, and so He saved us. Through His blood we have remission of sins; in His resurrection we rise to the eternal life of God. There is solidarity between the human race and Christ. His fellowship with us is real; our fellowship with Him is not less real. That relationship between the Eternal Son of God and us which made it possible for Him to share our weakness and the desolation which was the result of our sin, also makes it possible for us to share His work in this world and His glory in the next. His fellowship with us is the foundation of our fellowship with Him.

R.W. Dale, Fellowship with Christ, Hodder and Stoughton, 1891, page 7

FINDING GOD

Finding God—the search, discovery and coming to a personal knowledge of God

I suppose I didn't really find God until I was in my early thirties. The penny finally dropped on reading *The Choice is Always Ours*. Whilst making a careful study of this book I suddenly found God where I least expected to find him—in the depths of myself.

Up to that point there had been a number of foreshadowings. As a child I was conscious of a sense of awe and wonder in nature, partly a consequence of being brought up in a large house with a spacious garden, full of trees and flowers. In my teens, my parents introduced me to the Yorkshire Dales, the Lake District and Scotland. This fostered a love of the countryside, leading later to a love of the mountains of the Himalayas and the Alps. Surely there must be a power behind nature—a God perhaps. Music also set me off on a search to find God. Aged ten I joined Huddersfield Parish Church Choir, and developed a love of church music. I was also extremely fortunate in a number of people I met in my teens. Two schoolmasters, in particular, pointed me in the direction where I might find God. Several books aided me in my search. The first was *In Tune with the Infinite* by R.W. Trine, and the second, *Margaret* by James Davidson Ross. As mentioned elsewhere, things took off in my early twenties in which the person of Jesus Christ, the Bible and an awareness of the Holy Spirit were paramount. Even so, a vital element was still missing. Later I realized I was always trying to find God outside myself. *The Choice is Always Ours* enabled me to look within. Here I found God in all his fulness.

Oh, that I knew where I might find him, that I might come even to his seat!

Job 23:3

For he will be found of them that tempt him not; and sheweth himself unto such as do not distrust him.

Wisdom of Solomon 1:2 (AV)

Seek, and you will find.

Matthew 7:7

For whoever would draw near to God must believe that he exists and that he rewards those who seek him.

Hebrews 11:6

None of the formal arguments for the existence of God really convince. The proof lies in hints and dreams which are not expressible by human language.

Mark Rutherford, *Last Pages From a Journal*, Oxford University Press, 1915, page 274

I found Him in the shining of the stars,
I marked Him in the flowering of His fields
But in His ways with men I find Him not.

Alfred, Lord Tennyson, 'The Passing of Arthur', in *The Works of Alfred Lord Tennyson*, Macmillan and Co., 1898, page 467

There is only one 'place' to look for God and that is in one's own soul, there is only one 'region' in which to find heaven or hell, and that is in the nature and character of the person's own desire and will.

Rufus M. Jones, *Spiritual Reformers in the 16th and 17th Centuries*, Macmillan and Co., 1914, page 187

Here and there, among rich and poor, there are those whose heart and flesh, whose conscience and whose intellect, cry out for the *Living* God, and will know no peace till they have found Him. For till then they can find no explanation of the three great human questions—Where am I? Whither am I going? What must I do?

Charles Kingsley, *Daily Thoughts*, Macmillan and Co., 1884, page 7

To discover God is not to discover an idea but to discover oneself. It is to awake to that part of one's existence which has been hidden from sight and which one has refused to recognise. The discovery may be very painful; it is like going through a kind of death. But it is the one thing which makes life worth living.

Bede Griffiths, O.S.B., *The Golden String*, The Harvill Press, 1954, page 12

The French religious writer Père Jean de Caussade insisted, in one of his discussions of Christian prayer, that we are to find God 'in the sacrament of the present moment'. That is, we are to find him when we are confronted with the demands of life, given the opportunity to make our response to those demands, and enabled to labour responsibly for God in the place where we are.

Norman Pittenger, *The Christian Situation Today*, Epworth Press, 1969, page 116

The longer one travels toward the city he seeks the nearer and nearer he comes to the goal of his journey; exactly so is it with the soul that is seeking God. If he will travel away from himself and away from the world and seek only God as the precious pearl of his soul, he will come steadily nearer to God, until he becomes one spirit with God the Spirit; but let him not be afraid of mountains and valleys on the way, and let him not give up because he is tired and weary, *for he who seeks finds.*

Rufus M. Jones, *Spiritual Reformers in the 16th and 17th Centuries*, Macmillan and Co., 1914, page 52

As in Palestine, so everywhere, Christ—not only Christ after the flesh, but after the Spirit—is a crucified Christ. Only those can open the Sealed Book—can penetrate the divine Revelation—who bear the mark of the Cross on their forehead, who have eaten the flesh and drunk the blood of the suffering and crucified Christ, who have discovered that the Word of God is eternally a Word of the Cross. God is nearest to us when He seems farthest away. He was nearest to Christ when He was crying: 'My God, why hast thou forsaken me?' So, too, now he who is nearest to the cross is nearest to God, and where the flesh is being crucified and the end of all outward things is reached, *there God is found.*

Rufus M. Jones, *Spiritual Reformers in the 16th and 17th Centuries*, Macmillan and Co., 1914, page 62

... How did I come to Him? He alone knows. I groped for Him and could not find Him. I prayed to Him unknown and He did not answer ... Then, one day, He was there again.... It should be an occasion, I knew. One should be able to say: 'This was the time, the place, the manner of it. This was my conversion to religion. A good man spoke to me and I became good. I saw creation in the face of a child and I believed.' It was not like that at all. He was there. I knew He was there, and that He made me and that He still loved me. There were no words to record, no stones scored with a fiery finger, no thunders on Tabor. I have a Father and He knew me and the world was a house He had built for me ... I never understood till this moment the meaning of the words 'The gift of faith'.

Morris West, *The Devil's Advocate*, Heinemann/Octopus, 1977, page 168

We must look *inwards.* Where did we get the power to think, to reason and to know? Where did we get our knowledge of right and wrong? Why does even the most uncontrolled and evil-ridden man know in his heart of hearts when he is doing a wrong thing?

Kant said long ago that two things convinced him of the existence of God—the starry heavens above him and the moral law within him. We neither gave ourselves life, nor did we give ourselves the reason which guides and directs life. It must have come from some power outside ourselves. Where do remorse and regret and the sense of guilt come from? Why can we never do what we like and be at peace? When we look inwards we find what Marcus Aurelius called 'the god within,' and what Seneca called 'the holy spirit which sits within our souls.' No man can explain himself apart from God.

William Barclay, *The Gospel of John*, The Saint Andrew Press, 1965, volume 1, page 37

Many persons, Christians and non-Christians, whose thought has been influenced by a particular philosophy and by modern scientific attitudes, profess themselves no longer able to admit the concept of God as presented by the Church. Any facet of the human personality that has been projected upon this concept, must, they feel, be stripped away. They go so far as to speak of idols. Others even maintain that we can neither say anything nor can we know anything about God. Now in so far as this demand to clarify and advance in the knowledge of God is legitimate and possible, it must be recognized that the contemplatives who have been able to translate their experiences of the divine into human language, give us the loftiest and the purest possible concept of God. To appreciate this, we have only to read the greatest among them—Saint John of the Cross, for example. It is not that we are unable to know God with the intelligence—we cannot adequately express the mystery, which is a different thing. The language of the mystics cannot, of course, match that of science or reason. Yet, in a world craving for evidence from real life, it will remain one of the means through which our contemporaries can find God.

René Voillaume, *The Need for Contemplation*, translated by Elizabeth Hamilton, Darton, Longman & Todd, 1972, page 57

And if we cannot find God in your house and mine, upon the roadside or the margin of the sea; in the bursting seed or opening flower; in the day-duty and the night musing; in the genial laugh and the secret grief; in the procession of life, ever entering afresh, and solemnly passing by and dropping off; I do not think we should discern him any more on the grass of Eden, or beneath the moonlight of Gethsemene. Depend upon it, it is not the want of greater miracles, but of the soul to perceive such as are allowed us still, that makes us push all the sanctities into the far spaces we cannot reach. The devout feel that wherever God's hand is, *there* is miracle: and it is simply indevoutness which imagines that only where miracle is, can there be the real hand of God. The customs of heaven ought surely to be more sacred in our eyes than its anomalies; the dear old ways, of which the Most High is never tired, than the strange things which he does not love well enough ever to repeat. And he who will but discern beneath the sun, as he rises any morning, the supporting finger of the Almighty, may recover the sweet and reverent surprise with which Adam gazed on the first dawn in Paradise.

It is no outward change, no shifting in time or place, but only the loving meditation of the pure in heart, that can re-awaken the Eternal from the sleep within our souls; that can render him a reality again, and vindicate for him once more his ancient Name of 'THE LIVING GOD.'

James Martineau, *Endeavours after the Christian Life, Discourses*, Longmans, Green, Reader, and Dyer, 1876, page 352

I can meet God in the depths of my being, my real self. It's true. That's where he is, that's where he moves, that's where the source springs forth. I must go beyond my different faces—they're just a screen, in the way.

I'm thirsty. I'm invited to drink. I hear the call, the voice, but I have difficulty finding the way to the source.

First, I must allow silence to enter me, then I must listen. Don't force it.

I'm always surprised to find it so near. It's the path on the other side of the bush, but I don't see it. I imagine it's miles away. I'm dying of thirst not knowing that the source is right there. It's madness!

I wanted to look at the countryside; instead I was invited to go indoors. I shut my eyes, and immediately I saw that He was infinitely more beautiful than any countryside.

Experiencing God. An indescribable embrace, dazzling, breathtaking. A certainty, a sureness that wipes out months and years of searching, thinking, doubts and discussion. Oh yes, you can reason on the subject of God, but 'knowing' him (being born to him) is a different matter altogether!

I need to write down these moments of life—real life, not the superficial daily spectacle that passes for life. I'm trembling. I fear that words may turn out to be obstacles.

A few minutes, and I'm drunk with light. I don't know anything any more. I just feel very peaceful.

Michel Quoist, *With Open Heart*, translated by Colette Copeland, Gill and Macmillan, 1983, page 180

'How long shall I go on saying "tomorrow, tomorrow"? Why not now? Why not make an end of my ugly sins at this moment?'

I was asking myself these questions, weeping all the while with the most bitter sorrow in my heart, when all at once I heard the sing-song voice of a child in the nearby house. Whether it was the voice of a boy or a girl I cannot say, but again and again it repeated the refrain 'Take it and read, take it and read'. At this I looked up, thinking hard whether there was any kind of game in which children used to chant words like these, but I could not remember ever hearing them before. I stemmed my flood of tears and stood up, telling myself that this could only be a divine command to open my book of Scripture and read the first passage on which my eyes should fall ...

So I hurried back to the place ... where I had put down the book containing Paul's Epistles. I seized it and opened it, and in silence I read the first passage on which my eyes fell: *Not in revelling and drunkenness, not in lust and wantonness, not in quarrels and rivalries. Rather, arm yourselves with the Lord Jesus Christ; spend no more thought on nature and nature's appetites.* I had no wish to read more and no need to do so. For in an instant, as I came to the end of the sentence, it was as though the light of confidence flooded into my heart and all the darkness of doubt was dispelled.

St Augustine of Hippo, *Confessions*, translated by R.S. Pine-Coffin, Penguin Books, 1964, page 177

'Behold, I stand at the door and knock' (Rev. 3:20). Why does He not come in? Is not this Divine Spirit omnipotent? Has He not power to enter where He will, to breathe where He chooses, to blow where He listeth? Why, then, does He stand without, knocking at the door of a frail human heart? Could He not break down that door in a moment, in the twinkling of an eye, and annihilate that opposing barrier which disputes His claim to universal empire? Yes, but in so doing He would annihilate also the man. What makes me a man is just my power to open the door. If I had no power to open or to forbear opening I would not be responsible. The Divine Spirit might then, indeed, do with me what He will, but I would not be worth His possession. I would be simply as the unconscious stars which He fills with light, as the blind winds which He directs on their way. But if the stars and the winds had been enough He would never have said, 'Let us make man.' He made me because He meant me to be more than a star, more than a breath of heaven. He meant me to respond to Himself, to open on His knocking at the door. He could have no joy in breaking down the door, in taking the kingdom of my heart by violence; there would be no response in that, no answer of a heart to His heart, no acceptance of a will by His Will. Therefore, He prefers to stand without till I open, to knock till I hear, to speak till I respond. He would not have my being to be lost in His, for His being is love, and love demands love.

Whether Thou comest to me in sunshine or in rain, I would take Thee into my heart joyfully. Thou art Thyself more than the sunshine, Thou art Thyself compensation for the rain; it is Thee and not Thy gifts I crave; knock and I shall open unto Thee.

George Matheson, *Moments on the Mount*, James Nisbet & Co., 1884, page 144

FORGIVENESS

Forgiveness—act of forgiving; state of being forgiven

Shortly after being ordained, as part of my ongoing training, I was required to attend a series of four one-hour lectures on the doctrine of the atonement. These lectures were about forgiveness; the act of forgiving and the state of being forgiven as defined above. The lectures turned out to be brilliant. The lecturer spoke for an hour without notes and was meticulous in his delivery. At the end of the series I was still not satisfied so stayed behind and asked the lecturer a simple question: 'How do we know our sins have been forgiven by Christ's death on the cross?' The lecturer paused for a moment and replied: 'We don't actually know how it happened. At the end of the day we rely on Christ's words on the cross—"Father, forgive them, for they know not what they do." We take Christ at his word and it is then that we experience forgiveness.' I rather liked that answer. There was an honest ring about it. Later we were required to write an essay on these lectures. I was tired of essays, having had to write one a week for the last five years. The prospect of yet another essay reduced me to a state of despair. Imagine my delight on receiving the essay question: 'How do we know our sins have been forgiven by Christ's death on the cross?' I sent off the short answer. Later I received a stiff letter from the Archdeacon: 'To sum up the doctrine of the atonement in 72 words seems to me to show a lack of serious intent. You either write this essay out in full or you go to the Bishop.' I wrote the essay out in full. The point, however, was taken—no more essays. Forgiveness had won the day.

But thou art a God ready to forgive, gracious and merciful, slow to anger and abounding in steadfast love.

Nehemiah 9:17

For as the heavens are high above the earth, so great is his steadfast love toward those who fear him.

Psalm 103:11

For if you forgive men their trespasses, your heavenly Father also will forgive you; but if you do not forgive men their trespasses, neither will your Father forgive your trespasses.

Matthew 6:14–15

Father, forgive them; for they know not what they do.

Luke 23:34

Do you have the courage to forgive?

Anon.

The Glory of Christianity is To Conquer by Forgiveness.

William Blake, *Jerusalem*, in Geoffrey Keynes, editor, *Complete Writings*, Oxford University Press, 1974, plate 52, page 683

Forgiveness is not an occasional act; it is a permanent attitude.

Martin Luther King, *The Words of Martin Luther King*, selected by Coretta Scott King, William Collins Sons & Co., 1986, page 23

But forgiveness needs to be accepted as well as offered, if it is to be complete.

C.S. Lewis, *The Problem of Pain*, The Centenary Press, 1941, page 110

How often could things be remedied by a word. How often is it left unspoken.

Norman Douglas, *An Almanac*, Chatto and Windus in association with Martin Secker & Warburg, 1945, page 74

There is so much for us all to forgive that we shall never get it done without putting in a lot of practice.

J. Neville Ward, *Five for Sorrow, Ten for Joy*, Epworth Press, 1971, page 53

Let us no more contend, nor blame
Each other, blam'd enough elsewhere, but strive
In offices of Love, how we may light'n
Each others burden in our share of woe.

John Milton, *Paradise Lost*, x. 958, in H.C. Beeching, editor, *The Poetical Works of John Milton*, Oxford at the Clarendon Press, 1900

We must develop and maintain the capacity to forgive. He who is devoid of the power to forgive is devoid of the power to love. There is some good in the worst of us and some evil in the best of us. When we discover this, we are less prone to hate our enemies.

Martin Luther King, *The Words of Martin Luther King*, selected by Coretta Scott King, William Collins Sons & Co., 1986, page 23

Forgiveness, my prison experience had taught me, was not mere religious sentimentality; it was as fundamental a law of the human spirit as the law of gravity. If one broke the law of gravity one broke one's neck; if one broke this law of forgiveness one inflicted a mortal wound on one's spirit and became once again a member of the chain-gang of mere cause and effect from which life has laboured so long and painfully to escape.

Laurens van der Post, *The Night of the New Moon*, The Hogarth Press, 1970, page 154

To have been forgiven oneself is the greatest possible impulse towards forgiving others, and the will to forgive others is the test of having effectively received God's forgiveness.

The true Christian is essentially the 'forgiven person'. It is this characteristic which helps him to be humble towards God, and to serve his fellows without becoming self-assertive or aggressive while he does so.

Lord, take my heart from me, for I cannot give it to thee.

Keep it for thyself, for I cannot keep it for thee. And save me in spite of myself.

Michael Ramsey, *Through the Year with Michael Ramsey*, edited by Margaret Duggan, Hodder and Stoughton, 1975, page 136

We normally hide our past, even from ourselves. It is painful to dredge up those broken relationships, hurts and unhealed feelings of guilt; indeed, this inability to have our past as part of our present is what we mean by guilt. The broken relationships of the past continue to dominate our present moments, since we must do everything in our power to conceal from ourselves and others the true extent of our inadequacy and unworthiness. To have one's past, to be able to accept and appropriate that past as a meaningful part of the present, to allow that past to be really past and not the unconscious ruler of the present: this is what it means to be forgiven, to be justified.

Gibson Winter, *The New Creation as Metropolis*, Macmillan and Co., 1963, page 70

As long as we refuse to accept that we are a mixture of light and darkness, of positive qualities and failings, of love and hate, of altruism and egocentricity, of maturity and immaturity, we will continue to divide the world into enemies—the 'baddies'—and friends—the 'goodies'. We will go on throwing up barriers within and around ourselves and spreading prejudice.

When we accept that we have weaknesses and flaws, but that we can still grow towards interior freedom and truer love, then we can accept the weaknesses and flaws of others, who can still grow towards the freedom of love; we can look at all men and women with realism and love. We are all mortal and fragile. But we have a hope; because it is possible to grow.

Jean Vanier, *Community and Growth*, Darton, Longman & Todd, 1991, page 35

When he tells me, 'Your sins are forgiven,' he erases everything that I have not coped with in my life, in all that I have behind me. It no longer belongs to me. Then at once the moment arrives when I can say, 'Now I may begin my journey anew, for the One over whom death has no power has made himself known to me. He who will change my lowly body to be like his glorious body has taken me by the hand.' Now I can enjoy the present moment of my life in calmness and composure. I no longer have to feel burdened by what is past: the false starts I have made, the things which I owed and for which I became guilty, everything that I didn't carry through on, and everything that I still haven't mastered. There is One who waved it all away with a commanding sweep of his hand. He tells me, 'Nothing can separate you from me. I have taken this burden of yours upon *my* shoulders. I have suffered *with* you and *for* you in this way, and for precisely this reason you are dear to me and I love you.'

Helmut Thielicke, *I Believe: The Christian's Creed*, translated by John W. Doberstein and H. George Anderson, William Collins Sons & Co., 1969, page 140

What occurs when I forgive another person? It does not mean . . . that I can 'forget' what he did to me. I just can't do that. No, when I forgive another, I myself step into the breach and say to myself, 'The same thing that made the other person mean, hateful, and guilty towards me is in my heart as well. Ultimately we are two of a kind.' If I tell my neighbour, 'I forgive you,' and I say it from the bottom of my heart, then, in a manner of speaking, I take over the burden of his guilt and place it on my own heart just as though it were mine. Then I don't tell him, 'Oh well, it wasn't so bad, I don't take it seriously.' No, indeed, forgiveness isn't that light a matter. Rather, I say, 'Yes, what you did to me was very wrong; it was even shocking. But I know from looking at myself how fickle and wicked the human heart is. Therefore I could do exactly what you did. It's coiled up in *me* too. So I'll suffer through it with you. I'll put myself in your place. I'll share your burden.' When I forgive another person, I share the burden of his guilt. I become his brother and his sister, a burden-bearer at his side.

Helmut Thielicke, *I Believe: The Christian's Creed*, translated by John W. Doberstein, and H. George Anderson, William Collins Sons & Co., 1969, page 116

When Jesus prayed 'Father, forgive them, they do not know what they are doing' he lifted up to God the whole tangled and unfathomable pattern of human ignorance and fear and injury and retaliation in which he was so hideously caught.

He stated his faith again that it was all within that fatherly love whose purpose is to make a kingdom of forgiveness and reconciliation.

We have beautiful and important anticipations of that great forgiveness here and now, whenever one human being forgives another or is forgiven by man, woman or God. But there is a vast area of the unforgiven and the apparently unforgivable in this world. There are people who do not yet want forgiveness and die not wanting it. There are those who are incapable of forgiving, like the brutalized child who is so damaged that he grows into an inadequate or psychopathic adult; he cannot understand what forgiving means, and no one can forgive on his behalf. There are some situations of fantastic horror, like the Nazi attempt to exterminate the Jews, that seem to go beyond anything we can attribute to any known person or persons. And there may be a dark infinity of distress reaching out from some of our own smallest wrongdoings. No one can scour the world for all those who have been injured or will yet be injured by his cruelties and failures and make amends to them all. The fact is that the word of full forgiveness cannot be heard by anyone in this world. If this world is all there is it cannot be heard at all.

However, it is Christian faith that ultimately, beyond history, it will be heard by all. In the world of time the immeasurable wrongness of life must remain incomprehensible.

Jesus finally referred this greatest mystery to God's purpose to transform all life in the fulfilment of his heavenly kingdom. That kingdom comes as men come to see God as forgiving love, always present, always overcoming evil with good ... As anxiety loosens they become free to give. The spirit of man in freedom is by a marvellous necessity a giver and lover. As the Bible ends, in a bewildering dazzle of images and symbols for that which all its packed religion discerns ahead of us, there is a recurring image of a final gift which is an unending love, the gift of praise to him who will at last be seen to have done all things well.

J. Neville Ward, *Friday Afternoon*, Epworth Press, 1982, page 28

FULFILMENT

Fulfilment—develop fully one's gifts and character

The key to understanding this topic lies in some words of Etty Hillesum—'I thank You for the sense of fulfilment I sometimes have; that fulfilment is after all nothing but being filled with You.' This fits in exactly with the vision behind this book. As a consequence of the Genesis story of the creation of man and the life of Christ, we are able to find something of this divine life in the depths of our being. This is difficult to communicate in words. Concepts such as Father, Son, Holy Spirit, life, light, truth, joy and love have a hollow ring about them for some people. Other terms, goodness, grace, glory, beauty, power, wisdom, and understanding, equally applicable, might be more helpful. This is one reason why these topics are to be found in *Visions of Faith, Hope, Love* and *Glory*. Seen from this perspective the parables of the pearl of great price, the treasure buried in a field, and faith as a grain of mustard seed begin to make sense as they never did before. The parable of the gift of talents is particularly appropriate to 'fulfilment'.

How then do we develop fully our gifts and character and feel a sense of fulfilment? I have found the practice of reflection helpful—thinking over the insights of the Bible, and the recorded experience of a wide variety of people down the ages. This draws to the surface something of that rich resource of divine life in the depths of our being, and enables us to live more fully. As an aid to reflection I keep a journal and, like the character in the parable of the talents, try to live this new life to the full. The outcome is a sense of fulfilment from time to time.

He died in a good old age, full of days, riches, and honour.
1 Chronicles 29:28

For he satisfies him who is thirsty, and the hungry he fills with good things.
Psalm 107:9

For this reason I bow my knees before the Father, from whom every family in heaven and on earth is named, that according to the riches of his glory he may grant you to be strengthened with might through his Spirit in the inner man, and that Christ may dwell in your hearts through faith; that you, being rooted and grounded in love, may have power to comprehend with all the saints what is the breadth and length and height and depth, and to know the love of Christ which surpasses knowledge, that you may be filled with all the fulness of God.

Ephesians 3:14–19

See that you fulfil the ministry which you have received in the Lord.
Colossians 4:17

Thou crossest desert lands of barren years to reach the moment of fulfilment.
Rabindranath Tagore, 'Stray Birds', ccciii, in *Collected Poems and Plays of Rabindranath Tagore*, Macmillan and Co., 1936, page 326

When we rejoice in our fullness, then we can part with our fruits with joy.
Rabindranath Tagore, 'Stray Birds', clix, in *Collected Poems and Plays of Rabindranath Tagore*, Macmillan and Co., 1936, page 307

It is by losing himself in the objective, in inquiry, creation, and craft, that a man becomes something.
Paul Goodman, *The Community of Scholars*, Random House, 1962, page 175

We must make the choices that enable us to fulfil the deepest capacities of our real selves.
Thomas Merton, *No Man Is an Island*, Burns & Oates, 1974, page 20

The truth is that all of us attain the greatest success and happiness possible in this life whenever we use our native capacities to their fullest extent.
Smiley Blanton, M.D., *Love or Perish*, The World's Work (1913), 1957, page 132

To me there is something completely and satisfyingly restful
in that stretch of sea and sand, sea and sand and sky—
complete peace, complete fulfillment.
Anne Morrow Lindbergh, *Bring Me a Unicorn*, A Helen and Kurt Wolff Book, 1972, page 38

Nothing is unthinkable, nothing impossible to the balanced person, provided it arises out of the needs of life and is dedicated to life's further developments.
Lewis Mumford, *The Conduct of Life*, Secker & Warburg, 1952, page 291

God is good, and He wishes a fulfilment for beings in the universe that they also may enjoy bliss and become Sons—that they may enter into the psychology of the Being who created the World.
A.R. Orage, *On Love*, The Janus Press, 1957, page 54

I think people ought to fulfil sacredly their desires. And this means fulfilling the deepest desire, which is a desire to live unhampered by things which are extraneous, a desire for pure relationships and living truth.
D.H. Lawrence, Letter to Catherine Caswell, 16 July 1916, in George J. Zytaruk and James T. Boulton, editors, *The Letters of D.H. Lawrence*, Cambridge University Press, 1981, volume 2, *1913-16*, page 633

The social, friendly, honest man,
Whate'er he be,
'Tis he, fulfils great Nature's plan,
And none but *he*.

Robert Burns, 'Second Epistle to John Lapraik', in James Kinsley, editor, *The Poems and Songs of Robert Burns*, Oxford at the Clarendon Press, 1968, volume 1, page 92

In order to reach the deepest levels of relationship to God one has to put imagination to work and start upon the daring venture of seeking a God who is loving beyond any experience we have and fulfilling in a way that few of us have ever dreamed of.

Morton T. Kelsey, *The Other Side of Silence*, SPCK, 1977, page 61

The greatness of the work of the fulfiller, as compared with the work of the destroyer, is indicated by the faculties and qualities which it requires. Destruction calls for nothing but hatred and vigour. Fulfilment calls for sympathy, intelligence, patience and hope.

Phillips Brooks, *Twenty Sermons*, Macmillan and Co., 1897, page 216

To be capable of giving and receiving mature love is as sound a criterion as we have for the fulfilled personality. But by that very token it is a goal gained only in proportion to how much one has fulfilled the prior condition of becoming a person in one's own right.

Rollo May, *Man's Search for Himself*, Souvenir Press, 1975, page 238

Oh God, I thank You for having created me as I am. I thank You for the sense of fulfilment I sometimes have; that fulfilment is after all nothing but being filled with You. I promise You to strive my whole life long for beauty and harmony and also humility and true love, whispers of which I hear inside me during my best moments.

Etty Hillesum, *A Diary, 1941–43*, translated by Arnold J. Pomerans, Jonathan Cape, 1983, page 61

We and God have business with each other; and in opening ourselves to his influence our deepest destiny is fulfilled.

The universe, at those parts of which our personal being constitutes, takes a turn genuinely for the worse or for the better in proportion as each one of us fulfills or evades God's demands.

William James, *The Varieties of Religious Experience*, William Collins Sons & Co., 1974, page 491

In every case of seeming need we learn to turn within to the Christ, the Invisible Presence, realising that Its function is to give us abundant life. It, drawing upon the Father, fulfils us with everything necessary. Just as a law of Nature draws into the tree from the surrounding earth all that is necessary for the tree's development, so does the Christ draw into us, from the Godhead, all that is necessary for *our* fulfilment.

Joel S. Goldsmith, *Living the Infinite Way*, George Allen & Unwin, 1954, page 113

We think of the enormous sacrifices of these early Christians; but what struck themselves was the immensity of their inheritance in Christ. Take that one phrase, surely the most daring that the mind of man ever conceived, 'We are the heirs of God.' That is what they felt about it, that not God Himself could have a life fuller than theirs, and that even He would share all that He had with them! . . .

And yet here are we whimpering about the steepness of the way, the soreness of the self-denial, the heaviness of the cross . . . giving those outside the utterly grotesque impression that religion is a gloomy kind of thing, a dim monastic twilight where we sit and shiver miserably, out of the sunshine that God made for us, and meant us to enjoy; all a doing what nobody would naturally choose, a refraining from what every one would naturally take.

A.J. Gossip, *From the Edge of the Crowd*, T. & T. Clark, 1924, page 8

There are so few people who become what they have it in them to be. It may be through lethargy and laziness, it may be through timidity and cowardice, it may be through lack of discipline and self-indulgence, it may be through the involvement in second-bests and byways. The world is full of people who have never realised the possibilities which are in them. We need not think of the task which God has in store for us in terms of some great act or achievement of which all men will know. It may be to fit a child for life; it may be at some crucial moment to speak that word and exert that influence which will stop someone ruining life; it may be to do some quite small job superlatively well; it may be something which will touch the lives of many by our hands, our voices or our minds. The fact remains that God is preparing us by all the experiences of life for *something*; and the fact remains that there are so many who refuse the task when it comes, and who never realise that they are refusing it.

William Barclay, *The Gospel of John*, The Saint Andrew Press, 1965, volume 1, page 40

There is no other way to growth and fulfillment than the most perfect unfolding of one's essence. 'Be thyself' is the ideal law, at least for a young man; there is no other way to truth and development.

This way is made difficult by many moral and other obstacles. The world would rather see us adapted and weak than independent, and for every man who is individualized beyond the average, this is a source of lifelong struggle. Each man must decide for himself, according to his own resources and his own needs, how far to submit to conventions or to defy them. When he throws the conventions, the demands of family, state, collectivity to the winds, it must be in full awareness that he is doing so at his own peril. There is no objective way of measuring the amount of danger a man is capable of taking on himself. Every excess, every overstepping of one's own measure must be paid for; no man can go too far in independence or in adaptation with impunity.

Hermann Hesse, in Volker Michels, *Reflections*, translated by Ralph Manheim, Jonathan Cape, 1977, page 64

We must have the courage to cast off the old symbols, the old traditions: at least, put them aside, like a plant in growing surpasses its crowning leaves with higher leaves and buds. There is something beyond the past. The past is no justification. Unless from us the future takes place, we are death only. That is why I am not a conscientious objector. The great Christian tenet must be surpassed, there must be something new: neither the war, nor the turning the other cheek.

What we want is the fulfilment of our desires, down to the deepest and most spiritual desire. The body is immediate, the spirit is beyond: first the leaves and the flower: but the plant is the integral whole: therefore *every* desire, to the very deepest. And I shall find my deepest desire to be a wish for pure, unadulterated relationship with the universe, for truth in being...

It is this establishing of pure relationships which makes heaven, wherein we are immortal, like the angels, and mortal, like men, both. And the way to immortality is in the fulfilment of desire...

God works in me (if I use the term God) as my desire. He gives me the understanding to discriminate... between greater and lesser desire.

D.H. Lawrence, in Harry T. Moore, editor, *The Collected Letters of D.H. Lawrence*, William Heinemann, 1965, volume 1, page 466

GLORY

Glory—exalted renown, honourable fame; resplendent majesty,
beauty, or magnificence, imagined unearthly beauty; state of
exaltation, prosperity etc.; circle of light round head or figure of
deity or saint, aureole, halo

In my early teens I remember seeing the film *Theirs is the Glory*. I was spellbound by the account of the First Airborne Division in their attempt to capture a vital bridge across the Rhine at Arnhem in 1944. The surprise attack was thwarted, and at best, only partially successful. Casualties were heavy, and yet the display of courage in this hard-fought battle was for me an introduction to glory. I was then encouraged to read Paul Brickhill's book *Reach for the Sky*, the life-story of Douglas Bader, the famous RAF pilot. As a young airman he lost both his legs in a flying accident, yet went on to become an ace fighter pilot with numerous enemy aircraft to his credit. He was later shot down and captured, and sent to Colditz. I found an aura of glory in this book. Later on I had my sporting heroes and heroines. There was glory to be found in their achievements, yet all too often they turned out to be fallible human beings, and their glory faded. I started looking for glory in a different direction, and eventually found it in the lives of the saints. They in turn directed me to Jesus Christ, to the glory of his transfiguration. Ultimately I came to see the real source of glory is to be found in the depths of ourselves. In the words of Scripture we are to become partakers of the glory that is to be revealed. In other words we are to become the glory we perceive. One way this can be done is by reflection.

The heavens are telling the glory of God; and the firmament proclaims his handiwork.

Psalm 19:1

Let not the wise man glory in his wisdom, let not the mighty man glory in his might, let not the rich man glory in his riches; but let him who glories glory in this, that he understands and knows me, that I am the Lord who practise steadfast love, justice, and righteousness in the earth; for in these things I delight, says the Lord.

Jeremiah 9:23–24

And the Word became flesh and dwelt among us, full of grace and truth; we have beheld his glory, glory as of the only Son from the Father.

John 1:14

The glory which thou hast given me I have given to them, that they may be one even as we are one, I in them and thou in me, that they may become perfectly one.

John 17:22–23

God! glory in His goodness.

Henry Ward Beecher, *Proverbs from Plymouth Pulpit*, Charles Burnet & Co., 1887, page 141

By faith we know His existence; in glory we shall know His nature.

Blaise Pascal, *Pensées*, translated by W.F. Trotter, Random House, 1941, page 80

To live and work for the glory of God cannot remain an idea about which we think once in a while. It must become an interior, unceasing doxology.

Henri J.M. Nouwen, *The Way of the Heart*, Darton, Longman & Todd, 1981, page 86

There is the supreme truth that the glory of God lies in His compassion, and that God never so fully reveals His glory as when He reveals His pity.

William Barclay, *The Gospel of John*, The Saint Andrew Press, 1965, volume 2, page 46

God does all for his *own* glory, by communicating good out of himself; *not* by looking for anything from his creatures; our duty is not for His sake: our duty is our perfection and happiness.

Benjamin Whichcote, *Moral and Religious Aphorisms*, iv. 321, Elkin, Mathews & Marrot, 1930

The glory of love is its unaccountability: it is not something rendered proportionately—such and such an excellence, so much regard for it—but is rather a divine overflow.

Mark Rutherford, *Last Pages From a Journal*, Oxford University Press, 1915, page 263

Sound, sound the clarion, fill the fife!
To all the sensual world proclaim,
One crowded hour of glorious life
Is worth an age without a name.

Anon., in Sir Walter Scott, *Old Mortality*, Oxford University Press, 1912, page 316

Every energetic person wants something they can count as 'glory.' There are those who get it—film stars, famous athletes, military commanders, and even some few politicians, but they are a small minority, and the rest are left to day dreams.

Bertrand Russell, *Authority and the Individual*, Unwin Paperbacks, 1977, page 21

It is to God that all glory must be referred. This glory is the end of the Divine work... If God adopts us as His children; if He realises this adoption through the grace of which the plenitude is in His Son Jesus, if He wills to make us partakers in Christ's eternal inheritance, it is for the exaltation of His glory.

D. Columba Marmion, *Christ the Life of the Soul*, Sands & Co., 1922, page 24

Now, it was necessary that man should be in the first instance created; and having been created, should receive growth; and having received growth, should be strengthened; and having been strengthened, should abound; and having abounded, should recover from the disease of sin; and having recovered, should be glorified; and being glorified, should see his Lord.

Irenaeus, *Against Heresies*, iv. 38:1–3, quoted in John Macquarrie, *In Search Of Humanity*, SCM Press, 1982, page 33

I believe God gives a glory to every period of life. I believe that the people who are wise—the people who live with Him—learn now to take the glory from each succeeding age. If you ask those people—those who have really learned the secret—at any stage of their life, 'What is the most glorious period of their life?' they will always say: 'Now! Now!'

W.E. Sangster, *Westminster Sermons*, Epworth Press, 1961, volume 2, *At Fast and Festival*, page 20

To God be the glory. Think how Jesus lived, prayed, worked, suffered, all to the *greater* glory of God. He sought always the Father's glory. His pure ambition was the glory of God and the Kingdom of God. Pre-eminently Jesus could have said: 'to thee, O Father, be the glory for ever and ever: Amen.' 'I seek not mine own glory, but the glory of him that sent me.' All was done to the Father's greater glory.

Eric Symes Abbott, *The Compassion of God and the Passion of Christ*, Geoffrey Bles, 1963, page 92

But the glory of God in everything is not going to shine out like a gentle nimbus around the commonplace. To discover it will be more like suddenly catching sight of the volcanic inferno beneath our earth's familiar crust. Horrors! So *that* is our milieu! The Holy Spirit is totally primordial. He is the elemental force beyond all other forces, and to call it, correctly, the force of love is not to temper its intensity but to increase fearfully our estimate of love's fervour.

John V. Taylor, *The Go-Between God*, SCM Press, 1973, page 45

According to the literal meaning, something more divine than the manifestation that happened in the tabernacle and the temple was brought into effect in the face of Moses, who consorted with the divine nature. According to the spiritual meaning, those things which are known clearly about God and which are beheld by a mind made worthy by exceeding purity, are said to be the glory of God which is seen. So the mind, purified and passing beyond everything material, so that it perfects its contemplation of God, is made divine in what it contemplates.

Origen, in Andrew Louth, *The Origins of the Christian Mystical Tradition*, Clarendon Press, Oxford, 1981, page 73

It is not given to any one person to reflect more than a little of God's glory. Each individual Christian can be nothing more than one in a circle of many mirrors set round a great central light. Each has its own glint of brightness, the reflection that is appropriate from that angle and in that situation, but it takes all the mirrors in right relationship to one another to reflect the brightness of the light from every angle. So the complete glory of Christ can be exhibited only in the complete Body of his people, as the Spirit reflects him, personally but not individualistically, deeply but not privately in the life that they share. The adequate mirror of Christ's glory can only be the whole Church of God.

Thomas A. Smail, *Reflected Glory*, Hodder and Stoughton, 1975, page 28

The masterpiece of visible creation, the image of God, man is the last and the supreme link in the chain of terrestrial beings, the term of the work of creation. Possessing a material body and a spiritual soul, he touches both the visible and the invisible world. Bearing in his body the likeness of inferior beings, bearing in his soul the likeness of God himself, he is placed between creation and the Creator as the meeting-place of matter and spirit, the link between heaven and earth ...

But why has God created me?—All things were made for God, therefore, I, too, am made for Him, solely for Him. He is alone my essential end, my total end; He is the entire reason of my existence, the sole purpose of my life. I have no other *raison d'être* than His glory. I only exist to procure this one good for Him ...

God's glory is the whole purpose of my life, it is my all, the whole of me; for if I do not procure it, I have no more *raison d'être*, I am good for nothing, and am nothing.

Joseph Tissot, *The Interior Life*, Burns, Oates & Washbourne, 1913, page 11

The Hebrew and Greek words translated 'glory' are frequently used by the writers in the Old Testament and New Testament to tell of the revealed character of God and of the response of his people in worship and in action. No words indeed are more suggestive of the range and character of Christian spirituality than the words glory and glorify. The Hebrew word *kabod* comes from a root meaning 'weight', and it is used of the power or riches of a man. Applied to God, it tells of his power and character, not least his majesty, transcendence and sovereignty. Besides the idea of weight the idea of light is sometimes linked with the word, and it tells thus of God's dazzling radiance in himself and in his manifestation in the world. The word had also a distinctive use for the divine presence in the cloud seen by the Israelites in the tabernacle in the wilderness. It seems significant that the word used for God himself in his transcendental aspects is also used for a particular sign of his presence amongst the people. It is part of the theme of glory that the glory of God evokes the human response both of acts of worship and praise and of living in accord with God's purpose. In both these ways God's people are called to 'glorify' him or to 'give glory' to him . . .

It is the Christian belief that man exists in order to glorify God with the glory of heaven as his goal. This response includes both adoration, with its awe and dependence and participation as men and women come to share in the glory and are thereby glorified. The participation, however, never blurs the line of distinction between adorer and Adored, redeemed and Redeemer, creature and Creator.

Michael Ramsey, in Gordon S. Wakefield, editor, *A Dictionary of Christian Spirituality*, SCM Press, 1986, page 175

The reason for the crucial importance of the Easter mystery is, of course, the fact that by His Resurrection Christ lives in us. And by living in us, He manifests Himself in the love by which we love one another. For this love is the love by which He loves us and by which He Himself is loved by the Father. The whole purpose of His Mission among us is that the love of the Father for the Son be made known in our unity and that men may see that God is love.

This shows us how vitally important it is for Christians to understand something of the central mystery of their faith, and to build their lives not only upon a hope of avoiding sin, of carrying out the 'practices of their religion,' of dying on the right side of the law, but above all upon a knowledge of God and His love. If our Christianity is merely a set of exterior practices camouflaging a life of compromise with the weakness and hypocrisy of the world, we fail in our mission to manifest the hidden nature of God to men in our own lives. We fail to let people know, by the spirituality and purity and strength of our own lives, that God is love, and that He loves them all as He loves His own Son, and that He wants all men to recover their true identity as His sons.

'And the glory that thou hast given me, I have given to them that they may be one even as we are one; I in them and thou in me; that they may be perfected in unity, and that the world may know that thou hast sent me, and that thou hast loved them even as thou hast loved me.'

Thomas Merton, *The New Man*, Burns & Oates, 1961, page 138

GOD

God—Supreme Being, Creator and Ruler of the universe, often the Lord God, Almighty God, God the Father, Son, Holy Ghost, Persons of the Trinity

I think I have always had an intuitive awareness of God. As a child I did believe in a supreme being, the creator and ruler of the universe. I was most acutely aware of this whilst gardening or out at play in the woods and fields near home. For some reason, which I have never completely fathomed, I joined a church choir at the age of ten. What lay behind this was a feel for the numinous in church music, whether singing or merely listening. At university I went through a phase where I came to believe all we can know about God is to be found in the person of Jesus Christ. Three books, *A Year of Grace, From Darkness to Light* (both by Victor Gollancz) and *The Choice is Always Ours* by Dorothy Berkley Phillips, revealed to me something of the breadth and length, and height and depth of God to be seen in Christ. In him I was able to discern something of the Father, something of the Holy Spirit, and as mentioned elsewhere, something of life, light, truth, joy and love, etc. These books directed my gaze beyond the historical Jesus, to the experiences of God enjoyed by many people down the ages. I found this helpful and reassuring. From there I was encouraged to look within—for the presence of God in my own soul. Suddenly the penny dropped. The wealth I found is beyond description. *Visions of Faith, Hope, Love* and *Glory* are attempts to round up something of this richness of God, but to know God we have to experience him in ourselves. Some form of contemplation is crucial.

God said to Moses, 'I am who I am.'

Exodus 3:14

Be still, and know that I am God.

Psalm 46:10

'Behold, a virgin shall conceive and bear a son, and his name shall be called Emmanuel' (which means, God with us).

Matthew 1:23

And I heard a loud voice from the throne saying, 'Behold, the dwelling place of God is with men. He will dwell with them, and they shall be his people, and God himself will be with them.'

Revelation 21:3

[God is] ... someone present in the quick of being ... in existence as it exists, in the fibre, in the pulse of the world.

Dennis Potter, 'The Other Side of The Dark', a Lent talk, Radio 4, March 1978, in *Blessings*, Mary Craig, Hodder and Stoughton, 1979, page 121

Our best conceptions, our truest ideals, our highest moods—even these interpret God but imperfectly to us. We see through a glass darkly.

Henry Ward Beecher, *Proverbs from Plymouth Pulpit*, Charles Burnet & Co., 1887, page 142

True Religion never finds it self out of the Infinite Sphere of Divinity and wherever it finds Beauty, Harmony, Goodness, Love, Ingenuity, Wisdom, Holiness, Justice, and the like, it is ready to say: *Here is God.*

Rufus M. Jones, *Spiritual Reformers in the 16th and 17th Centuries*, Macmillan and Co., 1914, page 315

... there is still a way in which God can be called 'transcendent.' It is not that God is beyond all human experience. It is, rather, that the experience is inexhaustible, that further insight is always possible.

John S. Dunne, *The Reasons of the Heart*, SCM Press, 1978, page 24

Thou mastering me
God! giver of breath and bread;
World's strand, sway of the sea;
Lord of living and dead.

Gerard Manley Hopkins, 'The Wreck of the *Deutschland*', in W.H. Gardner and N.H. MacKenzie, editors, *The Poems of Gerard Manley Hopkins*, fourth edition, revised and enlarged, Oxford University Press, 1980, page 51

I should like to speak of God not on the borders of life but at its centre, not in weakness but in strength, not, therefore, in man's suffering and death but in his life and prosperity . . . God is the beyond in the midst of life.

Dietrich Bonhoeffer, *Letters and Papers from Prison*, William Collins Sons & Co., 1963, page 93

. . . to say that God is Love is to say that God is the living, active, dynamic, ceaselessly desiring reality who will not let go until he has won the free response of his creation—and won this response, not by the employment of methods other than love, but by the indefatigable quality of his loving.

Norman Pittenger, *Christology Reconsidered*, SCM Press, 1970, page 21

. . . an inner flooding of the life with a consciousness of God, a rational apprehension of the soul's inherent relation to the Divine, and a transforming discovery of the meaning of life through the revelation in Christ, which sets all one's being athrob with love and wonder.

Rufus M. Jones, *Spiritual Reformers in the 16th and 17th Centuries*, Macmillan and Co., 1914, page 323

We know that God is everywhere; but certainly we feel His presence most when His works are on the grandest scale spread before us; and it is in the unclouded night-sky, where His worlds wheel their silent course, that we read clearest His infinitude, His omnipotence, His omnipresence.

Charlotte Brontë, *Jane Eyre*, Oxford at the Clarendon Press, 1969, page 414

What are the gods, then, what are the gods?
The gods are nameless and imageless
yet looking in a great full time-tree of summer
I suddenly saw deep into the eyes of god:
it is enough.

D.H. Lawrence, 'What Are The Gods?', in Vivian de Sola Pinto and Warren Roberts, editors, *The Complete Poems of D.H. Lawrence*, William Heinemann, 1967, volume 2, page 650

There is something in men which compels them instinctively to rebel against an irrational universe and which will not allow them to conceive of a Divine Being except as One who is the sum total, and much more, of everything they, in their highest moments, feel to be most beautiful and good and true.

F.C. Happold, *Mysticism*, Penguin Books, 1981, page 65

What can I say to you, my God? . . . Shall I say: Creator, Sustainer, Pardoner, Near One, Distant One, Incomprehensible One, God both of flowers and stars, God of the gentle wind and of terrible battles, Wisdom, Power, Loyalty, and Truthfulness, Eternity and Infinity, you the All-Merciful, you the Just One, you Love itself?

Hugo Rahner and Karl Rahner, *Prayers for Meditation*, Herder and Herder, 1966, page 12

His divinity is understood as the power of the future making our present appear in a new light. The future is God's: which means that, wherever the individual human being goes, in life or death, God is there. In whatever direction mankind as a whole evolves, rising or declining, God is there. He is there as the first and last reality.

Hans Küng, *On Being a Christian*, translated by Edward Quinn, William Collins Sons & Co., 1977, page 224

We can never know God by seeking to grasp and to manipulate him, but only by letting him grasp us. We know him not by taking him into our possession (which is absurd) but by letting ourselves be possessed by him, by becoming open to his infinite being which is within us and above us and around us.

John Macquarrie, *Paths in Spirituality*, SCM Press, 1972, page 55

As yet, no race has been discovered without some word for what is not-visible, not-finite, not-human, for something super human and divine... To my mind the historical proof of the existence of God, which is supplied to us by the history of the religions of the world, has never been refuted, and cannot be refuted.

F. Max Muller, Anthroprodigal Religion, Longmans, Green, and Co., 1892, page 90

I think I want a more familiar God whom I can turn to at any minute of the day without fear, rather than a Being who must be approached with extra special language on one's knees, or by priests in splendid vestments... It is everything not only to reverence Him but to love Him, and to feel that you know Him so well that you can even enjoy fun with Him.

Edward Wilson, in George Seaver, Edward Wilson of the Antarctic, John Murray, 1935, page 120

We have first of all to say that God is infinitely above the world He creates, that He is fully Himself without it; in other words that He is transcendent. As the creator we have to say that He is behind His creation holding it up, continuously keeping it in being. But we have also to say that He is within His creation, filling every part of it.

H.A. Williams, C.R., The Joy of God, Mitchell Beazley Publishers, 1980, page 25

In this world is God. Man is able to see God, not in the intellectual process, but in the feeling of value, whose purest form is love. There is a genuine recognition of value only in love. In love man soars to the vision of the eternal and highest value of the holy, God. He embraces the all in himself, he is able to embrace God himself in passionate gazing. That is the 'totality of life' which the totality of values discloses and comprehends in itself.

Dietrich Bonhoeffer, No Rusty Swords, William Collins Sons & Co., 1970, page 49

Who or What God is I do not pretend to know. I have encountered in my travels so many different conceptions of Him, ranging from those of the simplest Christian faith, such as the Karen Baptists of Burma, to devout animists and pagans from Nigeria to the Pacific Islands. But that there *is* a God is doubted by few people; and it does not worry me that many of those few are among those whose intelligence is rated most highly.

Nor am I worried that we know so little about God; nor by the question so often asked, as though it were the end to all argument: 'If there *is* a God, why does he allow so much suffering, and sorrow, and pain?'

It seems to me an impertinence, a piece of arrogance, that at this earthly stage of our development, we should expect to know all the answers. It so happens that I no longer own a dog, but I have owned several in my time. Each knew the area around my house: in fact, they knew it in far more detail than I did; but the world that they knew was confined to a few miles; they were not equipped, nor did they aspire, to know more. And as for pain: what parent is there among us who has not had to inflict pain upon a beloved child, without being able to explain that in the long run it is for his or her own good? It may still be a minor thing, like a mere jab against diphtheria; but I am still haunted by the memory of abandoning my three-year-old son, who was protesting deafeningly and with tears at being left in a hospital to have his tonsils out. How could I explain to him why we were doing it to him? I am satisfied to believe that one day we will understand all this: even such things as early and unexpected and seemingly undeserved bereavement.

This brings us on to the question of whether or not there is what we call—for want of a better phrase—'an after-life'.

I believe with complete confidence that there is; and in this belief I have never wavered, whether in peace or war. I have already confessed that I make no pretence to knowing Who or What God is; but I am sure that we all owe our existence to something much higher than a passing moment of sexual ecstasy between our parents. I find it impossible to believe that creatures so complex as every one of us is could have been called into being for such a short span as is granted even to those who have the doubtful privilege of living longest. I can no more imagine Death as being final than I can imagine Space ending in a brick wall, or in a sort of celestial knacker's yard.

Nor can I accept the Buddhist idea of Nirvana, where we are all absorbed into one perfected anonymous personality. I believe—and again, this is a belief in which I have never wavered—that we will be reunited with those whom we have loved, and with those who have loved us: as individuals whom we will recognize, and who will recognize us: in happiness, perfected and made whole.

When I was a boy at school, a singularly silly woman was cross-examining my headmaster about the curriculum. She wanted to know why her son was not being taught such things as book-keeping, accountancy, business practices, and the like. He endured her for a while in patience; until at last she asked him point-blank: 'In a word, Dr. Alington, what *are* you educating my son for?' And he replied: 'In a word, Madam, for Death.'

There was more in that reply than mere wit. Paradoxically, the one thing that is certain in this Life is Death. If we think that, when it comes, it will clang down before us like a portcullis, or down upon us like a guillotine, then indeed, as St Paul said, 'then is our faith vain'. But it is not only 'wishful thinking' that makes me reject this. All my reasoning compels me to believe that a 'creature'—in the literal sense of that word—so complicated as I am cannot be snuffed out like a candle. Immortality may seem unlikely; but to me anything less is not only unlikely; it is incredible. Each evening from my home in the hills 300 feet above the village of Ballantrae, I see the sun setting beyond the long peninsula of Kintyre, knowing that it will rise again behind me next morning over the hill of Beneraird. Every autumn as the days grow shorter, I know that spring will come again with all its welcome signs: the whaups bubbling away on the hill, the lambs cavorting, and the larches bursting out. These are signs of the faith which is instinctive in all of us; and so is the birth of every new baby.

These 'intimations of immortality', in Wordsworth's felicitous phrase, reassure us with their rhythm and their constancy, and fortify our sure and certain hope of even better things.

Lord Ballantrae, from a sermon preached in St Salvator's Chapel, St Andrew's University, October 1979

GRACE

Grace—unmerited favour of God, divine regenerating, inspiring and strengthening influence, condition (also state of grace) of being so influenced; divinely given talent

When I was working in Nigeria I went to visit one of our church members who had recently been admitted to hospital. David was a young man in his early twenties who had suddenly been afflicted with a rare disease. I had been warned beforehand not to be shocked on first seeing him. This was good advice. His face was wasting away and he was badly disfigured. Apparently there had only been twenty-five such reported cases of this disease in Nigeria and seventeen of them had been treated successfully in this hospital.

We talked for some time and the visit ended with the laying on of hands and prayer. I went again the following week and found David cheerful though his condition was unchanged. Again the visit ended with the laying on of hands and prayer. This procedure was repeated regularly during the following weeks, and we were somewhat perplexed there was no improvement in his condition. At last a change was observed for the better. The doctors apparently had stopped the treatment a few days previously. David's comment: 'Only when the official treatment ended was the grace of God given a chance to act and healing began to take place.'

I have frequently witnessed the grace of God in action, often in times of great need. My favourite words on grace are those of Christ. 'My grace is sufficient for you for my power is made perfect in weakness.' Sometimes I have been sorely tested, but so far his grace has been sufficient.

The Lord make his face to shine upon you, and be gracious to you.

Numbers 6:25

... the Lord waits to be gracious to you; therefore he exalts himself to show mercy to you.

Isaiah 30:18

And from his fulness have we all received, grace upon grace.

John 1:16

But by the grace of God I am what I am, and his grace toward me was not in vain. On the contrary, I worked harder than any of them, though it was not I, but the grace of God which is with me.

1 Corinthians 15:10

...God gives us grace, but leaves it to us to become new creatures.

Anthony Bloom, *The Essence of Prayer*, Darton, Longman & Todd, 1989, page 25

The greater the perfection to which a soul aspires, the more dependent it is upon divine grace.

Brother Lawrence, *The Practice of the Presence of God*, introduction by Dorothy Day, Burns & Oates, 1977, page 51

Christian graces are natural faculties which have blossomed under the influence of divine love.

Henry Ward Beecher, *Proverbs from Plymouth Pulpit*, Charles Burnet & Co., 1887, page 176

Grace was in all her steps, Heav'n in her Eye,
In every gesture dignitie and love.

John Milton, *Paradise Lost*, viii. 488, in H.C. Beeching, editor, *The Poetical Works of John Milton*, Oxford at the Clarendon Press, 1900

... he discovered the central significance of the new birth through a creative work of Grace within.

Rufus M. Jones, *Spiritual Reformers in the 16th and 17th Centuries*, Macmillan and Co., 1914, page 154

And when grace comes and your soul is penetrated by the spirit, you shouldn't pray or exert yourself, but remain passive.

John Osborne, *Luther*, II. ii, Faber and Faber, 1961, page 56

The chief characteristic of the new people of God gathered together by Jesus is their awareness of the boundlessness of God's grace.

Joachim Jeremias, *New Testament Theology*, SCM Press, 1971, volume 1, page 178

... it clearly seems that man by grace is made like unto God, and a partaker in His divinity, and that without grace he is like unto the brute beasts.

Blaise Pascal, *Pensées*, translated by W.F. Trotter, Random House, 1941, page 145

That the Inward man by the Light of Grace, through possession and practice of a holy life, is to be acknowledged and live in us.

Rufus M. Jones, *Spiritual Reformers in the 16th and 17th Centuries*, Macmillan and Co., 1914, page 148

It is not only through the qualities of native strength that God can work. Quite equally and more conspicuously He can make our weakness the opportunity of His grace.

William Temple, *Readings in St. John's Gospel*, First and Second Series, Macmillan and Co., 1947, page 29

Do you know that sentence from a prayer—'Give us grace to bear both our joys and our sorrows lightly'? It is so perfectly true and brave and sensible, and is often in my mind.

A.C. Benson, *Extracts from the Letters of Dr. A.C. Benson to M.E.A.*, Jarrold Publishing, 1927, page 60

God's designs, God's good pleasure, the will of God, the action of God and his grace are all one and the same thing in life. They are God working in the soul to make it like himself.

Jean-Pierre de Caussade, S.J., *Self-Abandonment to Divine Providence*, translated by Algar Thorold, William Collins Sons & Co., 1972, page 37

Grace strikes us when we are in great pain and restlessness. It strikes us when we walk through the dark valley of a meaningless and empty life. It strikes us when we feel that our separation is deeper than usual.

Paul Tillich, *The Shaking of the Foundations*, Penguin Books, 1962, page 163

Grace, *charis*, in its Greek religious usage means 'divine gift' or 'favour.' Thus a 'grace' was a quality or power usually bestowed by the gods, a quality that could be exhibited by a mortal. The English word 'graceful' reflects this meaning.

Daniel D. Williams, in James F. Childress and John Macquarrie, editors, *A New Dictionary of Christian Ethics*, SCM Press, 1986, page 254

By 'grace' we do not mean some magical power of God forcibly intervening in the events of history or in the inner life of man. We mean rather a humble presence. Grace is God's presence and solidarity with his creatures in their strivings. God is not a distant figure presiding in the skies, but one who stands with his creation, to strengthen and encourage whatever is affirmative in it.

John Macquarrie, *The Humility of God*, SCM Press, 1978, page 9

The historical term 'grace' has a rich meaning... despite the fact that for many people the word has been so much identified with deteriorated forms of the 'grace of God' that it is useless. One speaks of the graceful flight of a bird, the grace of a child's movements, the graciousness of the generous person. Grace is something 'given,' a new harmony which emerges; and it always 'inclines the heart to wonder.'

Rollo May, *Man's Search For Himself*, Souvenir Press, 1975, page 213

The word translates the New Testament term *charis*, which refers to God's graciousness towards mankind... it is the transformation (as the Greek Fathers boldly said, the deification, *theosis*) of human life... It consists of God giving himself to men, so that they can know him and love him, so entering into a relationship with him which totally exceeds the relationship of creature to Creator, and is therefore totally undeserved.

E.J. Yarnold, in Alan Richardson and John Bowden, editors, *A New Dictionary of Christian Theology*, SCM Press, 1985, page 244

There are two main ideas in the word grace. The first is the idea of *sheer beauty*. The Greek word *charis* means grace in the theological sense; but it always means beauty and charm;

and even when it is theologically used the idea of charm is never far away from it. If the Christian life has grace in it it must be a lovely thing. Far too often goodness exists without charm, and charm without goodness. It is when goodness and charm unite that the work of grace is seen. The second idea is the idea of *sheer undeserved generosity*. The idea is that of a gift which a man never deserved and could never earn, and which is given to him in the generous goodness and love of the heart of God. It is a word which has in it all the love of God.

William Barclay, *The Letter to the Galatians and Ephesians*, The Saint Andrew Press, 1958, page 8

Why speak of the God of Nature and the God of grace as two antithetical terms? The Bible never in a single instance makes the distinction, and surely if God be the eternal and unchangeable One, and if all the universe bears the impress of His signet, we have no right, in the present infantile state of science, to put arbitrary limits of our own to the revelation which He may have thought good to make of Himself in Nature. Nay, rather, let us believe that if our eyes were opened we should fulfil the requirement of genius and see the universal in the particular by seeing God's whole likeness, His whole glory, reflected as in a mirror in the meanest flower, and that nothing but the dullness of our single souls prevents them from seeing day and night in all things the Lord Jesus Christ fulfilling His own saying, 'My Father worketh hitherto, and I work.'

Charles Kingsley, *Daily Thoughts*, Macmillan and Co., 1884, page 105

From Him (Christ) we have received grace upon grace. Literally the Greek means *grace instead of grace*. What does that strange phrase mean?... The different ages and the different situations in life demand a different kind of grace. We need one grace in the days of prosperity and another in the days of adversity. We need one grace in the sunlit days of youth and another when the shadows of age begin to lengthen upon life. The Church needs one grace in the days of persecution and another when the days of acceptance have come. We need one grace when we feel that we are on the top of things and another when we are depressed and discouraged and near to despair. We need one grace to bear our own burdens and another to bear one another's burdens. We need one grace when we are sure of things and another when there seems nothing certain left in the world. The grace of God is never a static but always a dynamic thing. It never fails to meet the situation. One need invades life and one grace comes with it. That need passes and another need assaults us and with the other need another grace comes. All through life we are constantly receiving grace instead of grace.

William Barclay, *The Gospel of John*, The Saint Andrew Press, 1965, volume 1, page 53

Cheap grace is the deadly enemy of our Church. We are fighting to-day for costly grace.

Cheap grace means grace sold on the market like cheapjack's wares. The sacraments, the forgiveness of sin, and the consolations of religion are thrown away at cut prices... Cheap grace is the preaching of forgiveness without requiring repentance, baptism without Church discipline, Communion without confession, absolution without contrition. Cheap grace is grace without discipleship, grace without the Cross, grace without Jesus Christ, living and incarnate.

Costly grace is the treasure hidden in the field; for the sake of it a man will gladly go and sell all that he has. It is the pearl of great price to buy which the merchant will sell all his goods. It is the kingly rule of Christ, for whose sake a man will pluck out the eye which causes him to stumble, it is the call of Jesus Christ at which the disciple leaves his nets and follows him.

Costly grace is the gospel which must be *sought* again and again, the gift which must be *asked* for, the door at which a man must *knock*. Such grace is *costly* because it calls us to follow, and it is *grace* because it calls us to follow *Jesus Christ*. It is costly because it costs a man his life, and it is grace because it gives a man the only true life.

Dietrich Bonhoeffer, *The Cost of Discipleship*, translated by R.H. Fuller, SCM Press, 1956, page 37

The supreme instance of the revelation of the Universal through the particular, of the invisible through the visible, the Divine through the human, is seen in Christ. It was precisely such an event as might have been expected, for 'the Divine Bounty and Fulness has always been manifesting Itself to the sights of men.' Those who have lived by inward insight have perpetually found themselves 'hanging upon the arms of Immortal Goodness.' At length, in this One Life the Divine Goodness blossomed into perfect flower and revealed its Nature to men. In Him divinity and humanity are absolutely united in one Person. In Christ we have a clear manifestation of God and in Him, too, 'we may see with open face what human nature can attain to.' This stupendous event, however, was no 'gracious contrivance,' no scheme to restore lapsed men in order that God might have 'a Quire of Souls to sing Hallelujahs to Him'; it was just 'the overflowing fountain and efflux of Almighty Love bestowing itself upon men and crowning Itself by communicating Itself.' The Christ who is thus divine Grace become visible and vocal is also at the same time the irresistible attraction, 'strongly and forcibly moving the souls of men into a conjunction with Divine Goodness,' which is what Smith always meant by the great word, *Faith*. It is something in the hearts of men which by experience 'feels the mighty insinuations of Divine Goodness'; complies with it; perpetually rises into co-operation with it, and attains its true 'life and vivacity' by partaking of it. Christ is thus... the centre, of both Grace and Faith.

Rufus M. Jones, *Spiritual Reformers in the 16th and 17th Centuries*, Macmillan and Co., 1914, page 316

GUIDANCE

Guidance—guiding, being guided, advice on problems

I was greatly helped on guidance by Edward Wilson, the doctor on Scott's expedition to the Antarctic. In George Seaver's book, *Edward Wilson of the Antarctic*, the biographer describes how Wilson kept a journal. His practice was to go through the Gospels over a period of years. Often the meaning was obvious, but when this was not so, he would work out his own interpretations and record these in his 'spiritual diary'. Over the years he was conscious of being guided.

This practice appealed to me so I started keeping a journal. Following Edward Wilson, I began with the Gospels, and later moved on to other material. In the end I decided to compile my own material to foster guidance, hence *Visions of Glory*. What evolved was a listening form of prayer out of which came guidance. The rationale is that if God is within us, he might want to guide us in our perplexities. The first step is to be silent in his presence. The next step is to look carefully at the material and listen. I find I can best do this with a pen in my hand, recording what is presented to me in the journal. I find this practice makes use of the whole of my inner being, mind, feelings (instinct, intuition), imagination and experience, as well as being open to God's direct guidance.

One of our postgraduates described how she had been guided in this way. She had a problem and went to one of the *Visions* anthologies. She turned to the section most closely related to her problem and in silence looked through the material. There was no direct solution, but on reflecting she found her own answer. This form of guidance often happens in reflection groups, too.

Make me to know thy ways, O Lord; teach me thy paths. Lead me in thy truth, and teach me.

Psalm 25:4–5

I will put my law within them, and I will write it upon their hearts; and I will be their God, and they shall be my people.

Jeremiah 31:33

When they deliver you up, do not be anxious how you are to speak or what you are to say; for what you are to say will be given to you in that hour; for it is not you who speak, but the Spirit of your Father speaking through you.

Matthew 10:19–20

If you love me, you will keep my commandments. And I will pray the Father, and he will give you another Counsellor, to be with you for ever, even the Spirit of truth, whom the world cannot receive, because it neither sees him nor knows him; you know him, for he dwells with you, and will be in you.

John 14:15–17

Let me think that there is one among those stars that guides my life through the dark unknown.

Rabindranath Tagore, 'Stray Birds', cxlii, in *Collected Poems and Plays of Rabindranath Tagore*, Macmillan and Co., 1936, page 305

...We are not meant to live solely by intellectual convictions, we are meant more and more to open ourselves to the Spirit.

Basil Hume, O.S.B., *Searching for God*, Hodder and Stoughton, 1977, page 54

There is a spirit that works within us, and develops a power in us that teaches us how to accomplish what we will, and guides us by its inspiration to successful results.

Henry Ward Beecher, *Proverbs from Plymouth Pulpit*, Charles Burnet & Co., 1887, page 154

Guidance does not end when calamity begins. In every situation He meets us and out of every situation He can lead us to a greener pasture and a sphere of wider use.

W.E. Sangster, *God Does Guide Us*, Hodder and Stoughton, 1934, page 144

I don't think some decisions are made by the reasoning faculties, but by some instinct. One *knows* what one can do and what one cannot do, when the time arrives.

A.C. Benson, *Extracts from the Letters of Dr. A.C. Benson to M.E.A.*, Jarrold Publishing, 1927, page 7

God is not a Person of caprice. If we can venture at all on belief in His detailed guidance, we can believe also that the conditions of our life are known to Him, and that He will direct us in such circumstances as we find ourselves.

W.E. Sangster, *God Does Guide Us*, Hodder and Stoughton, 1934, page 190

And I will place within them as a guide
My umpire *Conscience*, whom if they will hear,
Light after light well us'd they shall attain,
And to the end persisting, safe arrive.

John Milton, *Paradise Lost*, iii. 194, in *The Works of John Milton*, Columbia University Press, 1931, volume 2, part 1, page 84

We do not need to be very old to look back on life and see that things that we thought were disasters worked out to our good; things that we thought were disappointments worked out to greater blessings. We can look back, and we can see a guiding and a directing hand in it and through it all.

William Barclay, *The Letter to the Romans*, The Saint Andrew Press, 1969, page 117

If I am to learn to want what God wants, the way to do it is not to disown the inmost desires of my heart, but rather deliberately to spread them out before God—to face with all the honesty I can achieve the real truth about my desires, to wrestle with the sham of professing desires which are not really mine, and *then* to pray.

John Burnaby, in A.R. Vidler, editor, *Soundings*, Cambridge at the University Press, 1962, page 235

Over and over again it will happen that if a man, having thought out such a problem to the best of his ability, will then lay the whole matter in the hands of God, and genuinely desire that God's Will shall be done in his life and not his own, he will become perfectly clear what that will is. Over and over again that happens.

William Temple, *Christian Faith and Life*, SCM Press, 1963, page 57

It is the chief object of prayer and of a seclusion of heart from outward things, that we should be brought to attend to the guidance of this tender Guide, and be wholly in His power, and according to His will. No human plans or forms can help in this matter—they only hinder. The soul must be as the clay—formless and passive in the hand of the potter. This Hand of love forms us according to His own heart.

Gerhard Tersteegen, in Frances Bevan, *Sketches of the Quiet in the Land*, John F. Shaw and Co., 1891, page 390

I have nothing to say at the finish except that if one wants a permanent rock in life and goes deep enough for it, it is difficult for historical events to shake it. There are times when we can never meet the future with sufficient elasticity of mind, especially if we are locked in the contemporary systems of thought. We can do worse than remember a principle which both gives us a firm Rock and leaves us the maximum elasticity for our minds: the principle: Hold to Christ, and for the rest be totally uncommitted.

Herbert Butterfield, *Christianity and History*, George Bell & Sons, 1949, page 145

All that is in the Scriptures has come out of man's experience and therefore can now be grasped by us. All that was in Adam lies in the ground and depth of any man. When the Apostle John wrote that there is an unction which teacheth all things and leadeth into all truth, he did not confine this possibility to apostles, but intended to include all men in the class of those who may be anointed, and all who know 'what is in man' realize that it is possible to attain to this inward and apostolic guidance.

Rufus M. Jones, *Spiritual Reformers in the 16th and 17th Centuries*, Macmillan and Co., 1914, page 214

The link between prayer and guidance also does not consist simply in God's response to man's requests to be shown the right way. Too often the 'Veni Creator' or prayer for guidance with which we like to open our religious conferences and committees scarcely rises to the level of harmless magic or a breaking of the Christian's colours. The night of prayer which preceded Jesus's selection of the twelve apostles was focussed, we must surely believe, upon the kingdom and the power and the glory of God rather than on any short-list of candidates. It was communion and submission and adoration, renewing and clarifying the human body and mind and soul of Christ, which led, quite incidentally, to that sure knowledge of the next step he had to take in doing his Father's will.

This is how it was at the first determinative communication at the start.

John V. Taylor, *The Go-Between God*, SCM Press, 1973, page 231

As fast as the life comes under the sway of the 'kingdom of conscience' and a solid moral character is formed, the inner guidance of the Word of God becomes more certain and reliable. Only the good person has a sure and unerring perception of the truth, just as only the scientist sees the laws of the world, and as only the musician perceives the harmony of sounds. Not only must all spiritual experience be subject to the moral test, it must further be tested by the Light of God in other men and in history, and by the *spirit of Scripture*, which is the noblest permanent fruit of the Eternal Word. Every person must *prove* the authority of his religion. He must have his heart conquered and his mind taken captive and his will directed by his truth so that he would be ready to face a thousand deaths for it, and he must, through his truth and insight, come into spiritual unity and co-operation with all who form the invisible Church.

Rufus M. Jones, *Spiritual Reformers in the 16th and 17th Centuries*, Macmillan and Co., 1914, page 58

If we are to grow in love and to become more fully men and women of peace, we need a guide. All alone we shall quickly become discouraged, fall away, and seek the more trodden path. Without a guide it is difficult to recognize the fruits of the presence of God in our lives.

When we touch a point of pain, we will panic and run away. We need a wise and loving guide, a follower of Jesus ... who will remind us of the call of Jesus and how he has been present in our lives, gently guiding us at all times; who will remind us that we are loved and called to walk with Jesus on the road of pain and compassion in resurrection.

Such a guide will not tell us what to do, but will listen and discern with us, our way in the Will of the Father. The guide will be able to put a name to what we are living. The guide will hold us in prayer, lovingly, calling the Spirit upon us, confirming us in our call, challenging us too and calling us to be true in all things ...

The one who is guide can show us also the gift of the forgiveness of Jesus ... who can carry all our sins and weaknesses, and to whom, as a gentle instrument of God's mercy, we can open our hearts ...

Jean Vanier, *The Broken Body*, Darton, Longman & Todd, 1988, page 119

Sometimes the person seeking the guidance of God has to put up with the fact that it may be God's will, perhaps for reasons known only to him, that this trusting Christian should be in uncertainty. Often the sense of certainty comes as we approach the time when action is necessary. Before that point we simply have to wait in faith.

God's guidance is not an interruption of the normal flow of life, a special occasion. It is with us all the time because his presence is with us all the time. His present guidance is generally clear.

We can generally know now what he wants us to do *now*. We cannot always know now what he will want us to do in the future. If we are thinking out a problem and light does not come, it is right to regard that as present guidance. Having done all the thinking we fruitfully can about the matter, we have clearly to endure the obscurity of the situation, and we had better leave the perplexing issue and give ourselves to the immediate duty or pleasure that is in front of us. There is always something God wants us to do *now*. It must always be one thing. It must always be something that we can do.

We should not assume that, because we believe in the guidance of the Spirit and have prayed and thought about the problem, the decision we finally come to will be the most prudent we could have reached and must be successful. God is wisdom and truth. We perceive this wisdom and truth imperfectly. Our conscience may be ill-informed and immature. The decision to which our minds finally come may be the wrong one. We may not always know what is the will of God in the sense of that which he wants done in this particular situation, but it is always God's will that we do that which in an attitude of prayer and extensive thought and faith we believe to be the best course. And when we have done that we can say that we have done God's will. But we say it in faith and humility, already asking for forgiveness, because we know that somewhere in it all there will be failure on our part—and leaving the issue to that fatherly providence which eternally directs and redirects the movement of life, and can, without invading their freedom, make the mistaken insights of men serve his purpose as long as they love him and want his will to prevail.

Our prayer for the guidance of the Spirit does not expect that the situation will be changed into some form more in accordance with our wishes or our strength. It is a means of expressing our Christian outlook, providing words for our deepest intention, and can be seen as the Holy Spirit bringing to our remembrance the things of Christ. One of the 'things of Christ' is the conviction that though life continually eludes calculation and manipulation there is always something for love to do. As we dwell on this we find ourselves defining the situation in new terms, some of our original wishes concerning it are seen to be quite irrelevant and it becomes clear that there is in fact a way forward and a grace to be relied on.

J. Neville Ward, *Five for Sorrow, Ten for Joy*, Epworth Press, 1971, page 117

HEAVEN

*Heaven—place believed to be the abode of God and of the righteous
after death; place or state of supreme bliss, delightful*

We still tend to think of heaven primarily as a place where God dwells which we might enter when our life ends on earth. A part of this hope is we shall meet up with our loved ones who have gone before. I prefer to follow the experience of Elizabeth of Dijon who regarded heaven as a place or state of supreme bliss, here and now. In her biography by Hans Urs von Balthasar, she is recorded as having said: 'How good is the presence of God! Right in the depths, in the heaven of my soul, I find him, for he never abandons me. God in me and I in him—that is my whole life.'

I remember experiencing heaven in this way whilst reading Ralph Waldo Trine's book *In Tune with the Infinite*. For a few precious moments I felt a great sense of peace and harmony, a wonderful feeling of unity and wholeness. As in the definition above, this was that state of supreme bliss and it was delightful. Spurred on by this experience, I came across the book *The Choice is Always Ours* and discovered something of the divine in the depths of my being. I have described elsewhere the attributes of God to be found within our souls. Traditionally this is something of the Father, Son and Holy Spirit. Others would describe divine attributes in terms such as light, life, truth, joy and love, and some would extend this to music, art and poetry. Reflection on the contents of *Visions of Glory* can help us to experience something of the delights of heaven in the present moment.

To you it was shown, that you might know that the Lord is God; there is no other besides him. Out of heaven he let you hear his voice.
Deuteronomy 4:35–36

God is in heaven, and you upon earth.
Ecclesiastes 5:2

Blessed are the poor in spirit, for theirs is the kingdom of heaven.
Matthew 5:3

Not every one who says to me, 'Lord, Lord,' shall enter the kingdom of heaven, but he who does the will of my Father who is in heaven.
Matthew 7:21

Each of us has Heaven and Hell in him.
Oscar Wilde, *The Picture of Dorian Gray*, Chivers Press, 1979, page 261

Heaven is always in the New Testament the sphere of eternity, the spiritual sphere.
Father Andrew, S.D.C., *The Pattern Prayer*, A.R. Mowbray & Co., 1942, page 60

... to ask where Heaven is, is to demand where the Presence of God is, or where we have the glory of that happy vision.

Sir Thomas Browne, *Religio Medici*, i. 49, in Geoffrey Keynes, editor, *The Works of Sir Thomas Browne*, Faber and Faber, 1964, volume 1, page 60

Heaven is not a space overhead to which we lift our eyes; it is the background of our existence, the all-encompassing lordship of God within which we stand.

Helmut Thielicke, *I Believe: The Christian's Creed*, translated by John W. Doberstein and H. George Anderson, William Collins Sons & Co., 1969, page 193

... for Heav'n
Is as the Book of God before thee set,
Wherein to read his wondrous Works.

John Milton, *Paradise Lost*, vii. 66, in Helen Darbishire, editor, *The Poetical Works of John Milton*, Oxford at the Clarendon Press, 1952, volume 1, page 166

It is nowadays correct to say that we do not regard heaven as some local place beyond the sky; we regard heaven as a state of blessedness when we will be forever with God, and inseparably with God.

William Barclay, *The Acts of the Apostles*, The Saint Andrew Press, 1953, page 6

That is man's destiny in heaven—to be like 'Christ': not Christ limited, as he was on earth, to the confines of time and flesh, but Christ risen, the great, free, timeless Christ of Easter morning.

David Winter, *Hereafter*, Hodder and Stoughton and Christian Book Promotion Trust, 1972, page 82

Heaven and hell—the spiritual world—are they merely invisible places in the space which may become visible hereafter? or are they not rather the moral world of right and wrong? Love and righteousness—is not that the heaven itself wherein God dwells? Hatred and sin—is not that hell itself, wherein dwells all that is opposed to God?

Charles Kingsley, *Daily Thoughts*, Macmillan and Co., 1884, page 109

The only 'road to heaven' is the earth itself. Every step I take on earth leads me to heaven: the steps I take today, on this earth where I live, surrounded by people, in my own community and my environment.

No road exists in my imagination or good ideas. My road is the earth and only my feet can take me anywhere.

Michel Quoist, *With Open Heart*, translated by Colette Copeland, Gill and Macmillan, 1983, page 137

In that prayer which they had straight from the lips of the Light of the world, and which He apparently thought sufficient prayer for them, there is not anything about going to another world; only something of another government coming into this; or rather, not another, but the only government—that government which will constitute it a world indeed. New heavens and new earth.

John Ruskin, *Modern Painters*, George Allen & Sons, 1910, volume 5, page 386

The heaven of faith is not the heaven of the astronauts, even though the astronauts themselves expressed it that way when they recited in outer space the biblical account of creation. The heaven of faith is the hidden invisible-incomprehensible sphere of God which no journey into space ever reaches. It is not a place, but a mode of being: not one beyond earth's confines, but bringing all to perfection in God and giving a share in the reign of God.

Hans Küng, *On Being a Christian*, translated by Edward Quinn, William Collins Sons & Co., 1977, page 352

The 'next world'—'the world beyond' is just *this* world, as it is in each one of us, with its essential spirit and nature and character clearly revealed and fulfilled. God creates and maintains no hell of everlasting torture; He builds and supports no heaven of endless glory. They are both formed out of the soul's own substance as it turns toward light or darkness, toward love or hate—in short, as 'it keeps house,'... with the eternal nature of things.

Rufus M. Jones, *Spiritual Reformers in the 16th and 17th Centuries*, Macmillan and Co., 1914, page 187

... there is a more functional interpretation of this idea of heaven which places it, not in a period after death, but in the midst of life itself... It is in such moments that life seems irradiated in every direction: moments detached from all preparatory activity or further result, moments so intensely good in themselves, so complete, so all-satisfying that neither further emergence nor transcendence, is needed, since they are present in the experience itself. These are the moments when art seems poignantly to encompass all of life's possibilities, or, by the same token, when life reveals the significance of art... To be alert to seize such moments of high insight, unconditioned action, and perfect fulfilment is one of the main lessons in life.

Lewis Mumford, *The Conduct of Life*, Secker & Warburg, 1952, page 169

To picture heaven is as idle as it would be for a mole to imagine what it would be like to be a seagull. Compare heaven with this present life and the best you can do is compare plastic flowers with real ones, the old-fashioned magic lantern with cinemascope, shadows with substance. Even to think of it as joy without regret, as love without jealousy, as service without misunderstanding, as peace without boredom, as rest without restlessness, does not get us far. These are only negative concepts, taking the flair out of such goods as we have been able to experience in life. It is like imagining a watch which will never go fast or slow and will tell the time without having to be wound up. It is like the drunkard thinking of drink without the consequences.

Hubert van Zeller, *Leave Your Life Alone*, Sheed and Ward, 1973, page 125

Since man is in the divine image, and the love of God for each and every member of the human race is infinite, the goal is heaven, which is the perfect fellowship of God's human creatures with himself in glory.

In heaven God's creatures perfectly reflect God's goodness in their selfless service of him and of one another, and enjoy the vision of him and the inexhaustible adventure of knowing, serving and seeing one whose goodness and beauty are perfect.

Heaven is everlasting, and it is the fulfilment of man's meaning as created in the divine image, and of God's infinite love for each and all. Thus heaven gives perspective to man's present existence, and man's life in this world is but a brief prelude to the goal for which he was created.

Michael Ramsey, *Through the Year with Michael Ramsey*, edited by Margaret Duggan, Hodder and Stoughton, 1975, page 143

Heaven and Hell were no longer thought of as terminal places, where the saved were everlastingly rewarded and the lost forever punished. Heaven and Hell were for them inward conditions, states of the soul, the normal gravitation of the Spirit toward its chosen centre. Heaven and Hell cease, therefore, to be eschatological in the true sense of the word; they become present realities, tendencies of life, ways of reacting toward the things of deepest import. Heaven, whether here or in any other world, is the condition of complete adjustment to the holy will of God; it is joy in the prevalence of His goodness; peace through harmonious correspondence with His purposes; the formation of a spirit of love, the creation of an inward nature that loves what God loves and enjoys what He enjoys.

Rufus M. Jones, *Spiritual Reformers in the 16th and 17th Centuries*, Macmillan and Co., 1914, page xlviii

Christ is my Saviour. He is my life. He is everything to me in heaven and earth. Once while travelling in a sandy region I was tired and thirsty. Standing on the top of a mound I looked for water. The sight of a lake at a distance brought joy to me, for now I hoped to quench my thirst. I walked toward it for a long time, but I could never reach it. Afterwards I found out that it was a mirage, only a mere appearance of water caused by the refracted rays of the sun. In reality there was none. In a like manner I was moving about the world in search of the water of life. The things of this world—wealth, position, honour and luxury—looked like a lake by drinking of whose waters I hoped to quench my spiritual thirst. But I could never find a drop of water to quench my thirst of the heart. I was dying of thirst. When my spiritual eyes were opened I saw the rivers of living water flowing from His pierced side. I drank of it and was satisfied. Thirst was no more. Ever since I have always drunk of that water of life, and have never been athirst in the sandy desert of this world. My heart is full of praise. His presence gives me a Peace which passeth all understanding, no matter in what circumstances I am placed. Amidst persecution I have found peace, joy and happiness. Nothing can take away the joy I have found in my Saviour. In home He was there. In prison He was there. In Him the prison was transformed into Heaven, and the cross into a source of blessing. To follow Him and bear His cross is so sweet and precious that, if I find no cross to bear in Heaven, I plead before Him to send me as His missionary, if need be to Hell, so that there at least I may have the opportunity to bear His cross. His presence will change even Hell into Heaven.

Now I have no desire for wealth, position and honour. Nor do I desire even Heaven. But I need Him who has made my heart Heaven. His infinite love has expelled the love of all other things. Many Christians cannot realise His precious, life-giving presence, because for them Christ lives in their heads or in their Bibles, not in their hearts. Only when a man gives his heart shall he find Him. The heart is the throne for the King of Kings. The capital of Heaven is the heart where that King reigns.

Sadhu Sundar Singh, in B.H. Streeter and A.J. Appasamy, *The Sadhu*, Macmillan and Co., 1921, page 50

Heaven and Hell

1. No one knows exactly what will happen to a person after death. All blueprints are guesswork.

2. No one knows how personality can survive death. Our character seems bound up with our glands, brain, etc. Yet there is evidence of survival. It is the witness of Christians that 'Jesus lives'. The Christian doctrine of 'resurrection' points to the continuance of the whole personality, not just a part of it.

3. Even in this life we catch a glimpse of God's love and we can exult in life; but our faith in life after death is grounded in (a) God's love for us, (b) our acknowledgement of our incomplete development. God has more in store for us.

4. We are not just individuals. Personality needs relationship to exist. Therefore what happens after death is not just a question for individuals, but for people as a whole.

5. The final destiny of human existence is to share the life of God. This involves ability to respond to his love.

6. In this world we are so to develop and deepen our characters that we may be more self-aware and responsive and sensitive to God.

7. Since we are people of this world, the Christian is very concerned with material circumstances as the soil out of which the flower of human character must grow.

8. Heaven describes the state of eternal and full response to God's love; hell describes a state of eternal inability to respond to love.

9. Pictures of the Last Judgement given in the New Testament should not obscure the fact, also given in the New Testament, that we pass judgement on ourselves.

10. Thus heaven is not a reward to the good, or hell a punishment for the bad. God always acts lovingly and gives us that state of being for which our character has fitted us.

11. It seems improbable that anyone's sole chance of development lies in this life. Yet this life is the only one we know.

12. Purgatory stands for the truths (a) that on our deathbed we are not yet ready to be fully responsive to God's love, (b) that self-awareness is often painful, (c) that God continues to love us and to lead us towards himself after death.

13. We cannot know the details of our future or final destiny. But we do know it cannot be dull to be closer to the Fount of all Being, the Source of all Love, and the Creator of all things.

Hugh Montefiore, *Confirmation Notebook*, Fifth Edition, SPCK, 1985, page 41

HELL

Hell—abode of the dead; abode of condemned spirits;
place, state of wickedness or misery

As with heaven, we tend to think of hell primarily as a place or state we might enter when our life ends on earth. I prefer to take seriously some words of Sir Thomas Browne, written many years ago. In his book *Religio Medici* he wrote, 'The heart of man is the place the devil dwells in; I feel sometimes a hell within myself.'

In the Genesis story of the creation of man, God fashions and shapes man in his own image and likeness and breathes something of his own nature into man so that man becomes a living being. When we accept this we centre ourselves on God and experience something of heaven in the here and now. On the other hand there is another vital truth in this story, extremely important for understanding our present condition; namely, that which was fashioned and shaped in the image and likeness was taken from the dust of the earth, so that as well as our having a divine (or heavenly) potential, we are at one and the same time earthy and creaturely, having within ourselves all the passions and instincts of the animals.

We no longer believe man to be made in the image and likeness of God so we centre ourselves on ourselves—on the earthy and creaturely. Features of society today are loneliness, depression, anxiety, guilt, cynicism, apathy, self-despising, frustration, self-pity and a sense of emptiness and isolation. For many people Sir Thomas Browne's words are all too true. We do feel a hell within ourselves. What we need is a shift of centre, opening up new sources of life.

I give thanks to thee, O Lord my God, with my whole heart, and I will glorify thy name for ever. For great is thy steadfast love toward me; thou hast delivered my soul from the depths of Sheol.

Psalm 86:12–13

For behold, the day comes, burning like an oven, when all the arrogant and all evildoers will be stubble; the day that comes shall burn them up, says the Lord of hosts, so that it will leave them neither root nor branch.

Malachi 4:1

But I say to you that every one who is angry with his brother shall be liable to judgment; whoever insults his brother shall be liable to the council, and whoever says, 'You fool!' shall be liable to the hell of fire.

Matthew 5:22

And do not fear those who kill the body but cannot kill the soul; rather fear him who can destroy both soul and body in hell.

Matthew 10:28

My self am Hell.

John Milton, *Paradise Lost*, iv. 75, in H.C. Beeching, editor, *The Poetical Works of John Milton*, Oxford at the Clarendon Press, 1900, page 248

There are materials enough in every man's mind to make a hell there.

Henry Ward Beecher, *Proverbs from Plymouth Pulpit*, Charles Burnet & Co., 1887, page 30

Long is the way
And hard, that out of Hell leads up to light.

John Milton, *Paradise Lost*, ii. 433, in *The Works of John Milton*, Columbia University Press, 1931, volume 2, part 1, page 53

A belief in hell and the knowledge that every ambition is doomed to frustration at the hands of a skeleton have never prevented the majority of human beings from behaving as though death were no more than an unfounded rumour and survival a thing beyond the bounds of possibility.

Aldous Huxley, *Themes and Variations*, Chatto and Windus, 1950, page 164

What is there in this world worth having without religion? Do you not feel that true religion, even in its most imperfect stage, is not merely an escape from hell after death but the only *real state* for a man—the only position to live in this world—the only frame of mind which will give anything like happiness here. I cannot help feeling at moments—if there were *no Christ*, everything, even the very flowers and insects, and every beautiful object, would be hell *now*—dark, blank, hopeless.

Charles Kingsley, *Daily Thoughts*, Macmillan and Co., 1884, page 265

Hell, here or elsewhere, is a disordered life, out of adjustment with the universal will of God; it is concentration upon self and self-ends; the contraction of love; the shrinking of inward resources; the formation of a spirit of hate, the creation of an inward nature that hates what God loves. Hell is the inner condition inherently attaching to the kind of life that displays and exhibits the spirit and attitude which must be overcome before God with His purposes of goodness can be ultimately triumphant and all in all.

Rufus M. Jones, *Spiritual Reformers in the 16th and 17th Centuries*, Macmillan and Co., 1914, page xlviii

HELL is a city much like London—
A populous and a smoky city;
There are all sorts of people undone,
And there is little or no fun done;
Small justice shown, and still less pity.

Lawyers—judges—old hobnobbers
Are there—bailiffs—chancellors—
Bishops—great and little robbers—
Rhymesters—pamphleteers—stock-jobbers—
Men of glory in the wars.

Percy Bysshe Shelley, 'Hell', lines 1–5, 41–45, in *The Complete Works of Percy Bysshe Shelley*, Ernest Benn, 1927, volume 3, *Poems, Peter Bell the Third*, Part the Third, page 267

There is no wrath that stands between God and us, but what is awakened in the dark fire of our own fallen nature; and to quench this wrath, and not His own, God gave His only begotten Son to be made man. God has no more wrath in Himself now than He had before the creation, when He had only Himself to love... And it was solely to quench this wrath, awakened in the human soul, that the blood of the Son of God was necessary, because nothing but a life and birth, derived from Him into the human soul, could change this darkened root of a self-tormenting fire into an amiable image of the Holy Trinity as it was at first created.

William Law, in Stephen Hobhouse, editor, *Selected Mystical Writings of William Law*, Rockliff, 1948, page 16

I thanke God, and with joy I mention it, I was never afraid of Hell, nor ever grew pale at the description of that place; I have so fixed my contemplations on Heaven, that I have almost forgot the Idea of Hell, and am afraid rather to lose the joyes of the one than endure the misery of the other; to be deprived of them is a perfect hell, & needs me thinkes no addition to compleate our afflictions; that terrible terme hath never detained me from sin, nor do I owe any good action to the name thereof: I feare God, yet am not afraid of him, his mercies make me ashamed of my sins, before his judgements afraid thereof.

Sir Thomas Browne, *Religio Medici*, i. 52, in Geoffrey Keynes, editor, *The Works of Sir Thomas Browne*, Faber and Faber, 1964, volume 1, page 63

To love at all is to be vulnerable. Love anything, and your heart will certainly be wrung and possibly be broken. If you want to make sure of keeping it intact, you must give your heart to no one, not even to an animal. Wrap it carefully round with hobbies and little luxuries; avoid all entanglements; lock it up safe in the casket or coffin of your selfishness. But in that casket—safe, dark, motionless, airless—it will change. It will not be broken; it will become unbreakable, impenetrable, irredeemable. The alternative to tragedy, or at least to the risk of tragedy, is damnation. The only place outside Heaven where you can be perfectly safe from all the dangers and perturbations of love is Hell.

C.S. Lewis, *The Four Loves*, William Collins Sons & Co., 1981, page 111

We must make a hell for ourselves, if we cannot find a heaven. Yes, a hell! the simple language is the best... What glimpse of daylight can we discern in the trackless abyss?

'He *descended into Hell.*' Mighty words! which I do not pretend that I can penetrate, or reduce under any forms of the intellect. If I could, I think they would be of little worth to me. But I accept them as news that there is no corner of God's universe over which His love has not brooded, none over which the Son of God and the Son of Man has not asserted His dominion. I claim a right to tell this news to every peasant and beggar of the land. I may bid him rejoice, and give thanks, and sing merry songs to the God who made him, because there is nothing created which his Lord and Master has not redeemed, of which He is not the King; I may bid him fear nothing around him or beneath him where he trusts in Him.

F.D. Maurice, *Theological Essays*, James Clarke & Co., 1957, page 123

I am thinking, 'What is hell?' And I am reasoning thus: 'The suffering that comes from the consciousness that one is no longer able to love.' Once, in the infinitude of existence, which cannot be measured by time or space, it was given to some spiritual being, on its appearance on earth, the ability to say: 'I am and I love.' Once, only once, was there given him a moment of active *living* love, and for that earthly life was given him, and with it times and seasons. And what happened? That happy being rejected the priceless gift, prized it not, loved it not, looked scornfully upon it and remained indifferent to it. Such a one, having left the earth, sees Abraham's bosom and talks with Abraham, as it is told in the parable of the rich man and Lazarus, and contemplates heaven, and can go up to the Lord, but what torments him so much is that he will go up to God without ever having loved and come in contact with those who love and whose love he has scorned. For he sees clearly and says to himself, 'Now I have the knowledge and though I yearn to love, there will be no great deed, no sacrifice in my love, for my earthly life is over, and Abraham will not come even with a drop of living water (that is to say, again with the gift of former active earthly life) to cool the fire of the yearning for spiritual love which burns in me now, having scorned it on earth; there is no more life and there is no more time! Though I would gladly give my life for others, I can do it no more, for the life I could have sacrificed for love is over and now there is a gulf between that life and this existence.' Men speak of material hell fire: I do not go into that mystery and I dread it, but I think that even if there were material fire, they would be genuinely glad of it, for I fancy that in material agony the much more terrible spiritual agony would be forgotten, even though for a moment. And, indeed, it is quite impossible to take that spiritual agony away from them, for it is not outside but within them. And even if it were possible to take it away, I cannot help thinking that their unhappiness would be more bitter because of it. For though the righteous ones in heaven, contemplating their torments, would have forgiven them, and called them to heaven in their infinite love, by doing so they would have multiplied their torments, for they would arouse in them still more strongly the fiery yearning for responsive, active, and grateful love, which is no longer possible. In the timidity of my heart, however, I cannot help thinking that the very consciousness of this impossibility would at last serve to alleviate their suffering, for by accepting the love of the righteous without the possibility of repaying it, by this submissiveness and the effect of this humility, they will at last acquire a certain semblance of that active love which they scorned in life, and a sort of activity which is similar to it... I am sorry, my friends and brothers, that I cannot express it more clearly...

Oh, there are some who remain proud and fierce even in hell, in spite of their certain knowledge and contemplation of irrefutable truth; there are some fearsome ones who have joined Satan and his proud spirit entirely. For those hell is voluntary and they cannot have enough of it; they are martyrs of their own free will. For they have damned themselves, having damned God and life. They feed upon their wicked pride, like a starving man in the desert sucking his own blood from his body. They will never be satisfied and they reject forgiveness, and curse God who calls them. They cannot behold the living God without hatred and demand that there should be no God of life, that God should destroy himself and all his creation. And they will burn eternally in the fire of their wrath and yearn for death and non-existence. But they will not obtain death...

Fyodor Dostoyevsky, *The Brothers Karamazov*, translated by David Magarshack, Penguin Books, 1963, volume 1, page 379

HOLY SPIRIT

Holy Spirit—third Person of the Trinity, God as spiritually acting, sevenfold gift of the Spirit: counsel, wisdom, understanding, knowledge, fear (awe, reverence), might (power) and the spirit of the Lord

In my last year as an undergraduate I was trying to work out what to do in life. A friend had given me a book for a birthday present, *Margaret* by James Davidson Ross. I remember reading this book on a train journey from the West Country to London. Margaret was a teenage girl. She was smitten with cancer. The way she faced up to her ordeal, dying at such a young age, convinced me of the reality of the Holy Spirit. In her short life there was ample evidence of God spiritually alive and active. My feelings at the time were summed up by the words of Goethe in this section: 'The spirit, alive and gifted, focusing with practical intent on the most immediate concerns, is the finest thing on earth.' The way ahead opened up. I wanted to dedicate myself to the finest things on earth, to the work of the Holy Spirit. Much to my surprise I soon found myself heading in the direction of ordination.

The next few years were taken up in training and completing my first appointment. An important insight then came to me. I came to see the 'divine inbreathing' of the Genesis story of the creation of man was fully worked out in the life of Christ. Moreover, at the end of his earthly life he 'breathed on' the disciples (reminiscent of Genesis) and said, 'Receive the Holy Spirit.' With the outward manifestation of the coming of the Holy Spirit at Pentecost, Christ's work was complete. The gifts of the Spirit are open to all and our spiritual heritage infinite—like the pearl of great price.

And the Spirit of the Lord shall rest upon him, the spirit of wisdom and understanding, the spirit of counsel and might, the spirit of knowledge and the fear of the Lord.

Isaiah 11:2

I will put my Spirit within you, and you shall live.

Ezekiel 37:14

And when he had said this, he breathed on them, and said to them, 'Receive the Holy Spirit.'

John 20:22

There appeared to them tongues as of fire, distributed and resting on each one of them. And they were all filled with the Holy Spirit and began to speak in other tongues, as the Spirit gave them utterance.

Acts 2:3–4

We lack the light touch in spiritual matters.

Norman Douglas, *An Almanac*, Chatto and Windus in association with Martin Secker & Warburg, 1945, page 70

The simple fact is that the world is too busy to give the Holy Spirit a chance to enter in.

William Barclay, *The Gospel of John*, The Saint Andrew Press, 1965, volume 2, page 195

The spirit, alive and gifted, focusing with practical intent on the most immediate concerns, is the finest thing on earth.

Johann Wolfgang von Goethe, *Wisdom and Experience*, selected by Ludwig Curtius, translated and edited by Hermann J. Weigand, Routledge & Kegan Paul, 1949, page 215

The Divine Spirit works along the line of a man's own thinking power, along the channel of a man's own motive power, and wakes up in the man that which was in him.

Henry Ward Beecher, *Proverbs from Plymouth Pulpit*, Charles Burnet & Co., 1887, page 152

He was an ideal pastor and true shepherd of his flock—loving them and being beloved by them. His ministry was fresh and vital, and made his hearers *feel* the presence and power of the Spirit of God.

Rufus M. Jones, *Spiritual Reformers in the 16th and 17th Centuries*, Macmillan and Co., 1914, page 139

... the Church's real business is the nurture of men and women in life's final meaning, the provision—the mediation—of resources for living in the power and grace and serenity (serenity amidst toil and sacrifice) of the Holy Spirit of God.

Norman Goodall, *The Local Church*, Hodder and Stoughton, 1966, page 33

Spirit is no less real than matter, and the spiritual values of truth, goodness, and beauty no mere creations of finite minds, but abiding characteristics of that reality in the apprehension of which all minds capable of apprehending it find their satisfaction.

C.C.J. Webb, *Religious Experience*, Oxford University Press, 1945, page 35

The true goal of the spiritual life is such a oneness with God that He is in us and we in Him, so that the inner joy and power take our outer life captive and draw us away from the world and its 'pictures' and make it a heartfelt delight to do all His commandments and to suffer anything for Him.

Rufus M. Jones, *Spiritual Reformers in the 16th and 17th Centuries*, Macmillan and Co., 1914, page 43

... spirituality is the basis and foundation of human life... It must underlie everything. To put it briefly, man is a spiritual being, and the proper work of his mind is to interpret the world according to his higher nature, and to conquer the material aspects of the world so as to bring them into subjection to the spirit.

Robert Bridges, *The Spirit of Man*, Longmans, Green and Co., 1973, page 1

The spiritual realities of life cannot be settled by laboriously piling up texts of Scripture, by subtle theological dialectic, or by learned exegesis of sacred words. If these spiritual realities are to become real and effective to us, it must be through the direct relation of the human spirit with the divine Spirit—the inward spiritual Word of God. 'He who will see the truth must have God for eyes.'

Rufus M. Jones, *Spiritual Reformers in the 16th and 17th Centuries*, Macmillan and Co., 1914, page 74

The Holy Ghost is... the manifest Energy of God in the world. He is, moreover, the indwelling Strengthener who enables man to live righteously in God's sight; the Guide who leads us into truth; the Revealer of the truths of God; the Consoler in our distresses; the Encourager in our tribulations. Our Lord in His promise of the special coming of the Spirit stresses His personal and loving attributes.

Carroll E. Simcox, *Living the Creed*, Dacre Press / A. and C. Black, 1954, page 116

True religion... is a reception and assimilation of the Life of God within the soul of man which is predisposed by its fundamental nature to the influx and formative influence of the Spirit of God, who is the environing Life and inner atmosphere of all human spirits; '*Spiritual Life comes from God's breath within us and from the formation of Christ within the soul.*'

Rufus M. Jones, *Spiritual Reformers in the 16th and 17th Centuries*, Macmillan and Co., 1914, page 310

Think of the Holy Spirit as a Person having a will of His own, who breatheth whither He listeth, and cannot be confined to any feelings or rules of yours or of any man's, but may meet you in the Sacraments or out of the Sacraments, even as He will, and has methods of comforting and educating you of which you will never dream; One whose will is the same as the will of the Father and of the Son, even a good will.

Charles Kingsley, *Daily Thoughts*, Macmillan and Co., 1884, page 146

No person will ever reach a stage of earthly life in which the spur of the flesh is eradicated, and so no person can be infallibly certain that he is beyond sin, but when Christ is inwardly united to the soul and His Spirit dwells in us and reigns in us and we are risen in soul, spirit, and mind with Him, then we no longer live after the flesh, or according to its thrust and push, but share His life and partake of the conquering power of His Spirit.

Rufus M. Jones, *Spiritual Reformers in the 16th and 17th Centuries*, Macmillan and Co., 1914, page 217

A spiritual religion of the full and complete type will, I believe, have inward, mystical depth, it will keep vitalized and intensified with its experiences of divine supplies, and of union and unification with an environing Spirit, but it must at the same time soundly supplement its more or less capricious and subjective, and always fragmentary, mystical insights with the steady and unwavering testimony of Reason, and no less with the immense objective illustration of History.

Rufus M. Jones, *Spiritual Reformers in the 16th and 17th Centuries*, Macmillan and Co., 1914, page xxix

The Holy Spirit carries on the work of the Saviour. While he assists the Church in the preaching of the gospel of Jesus Christ, he writes his own gospel, and he writes it in the hearts of the faithful. All the actions, all the moments of the saints, make up the gospel of the Holy Spirit. Their souls are the paper, their sufferings and their actions are the ink. The Holy Spirit, with his own action for pen, writes a living gospel, but it will not be readable until the day of glory when it will be taken out of the printing press of this life and published.

Jean-Pierre de Caussade, S.J., *Self-Abandonment to Divine Providence*, translated by Algar Thorold, William Collins Sons & Co., 1972, page 61

Spirituality of life is an achievement as well as a gift. It is not a mere negation, a sentimental attitude that ignores and eludes all the just claims of the great realities of human existence, but it is intellectual and moral energy raised to the highest degree; it is an absolute persistence in well-doing; it is justice and gentleness; it is consideration and good judgment and discriminating appreciation and love.

Spirituality of life is, indeed, life raised to the highest power.

Lilian Whiting, *Lilies of Eternal Peace*, Gay and Hancock, 1908, page 26

The Holy Spirit is the true counsellor. He shows us what is to come and also gives us the strength to face the difficulties that lie ahead of us. Indeed He is both the strength and the giver, for only under His inspiration can we surmount the present impasse and be lifted on to a new plane of endeavour in which fresh possibilities provide an outlet for a new way of approach. We cannot rise to the full stature of a person until the Spirit is manifestly working in us. We cannot be of any assistance to anyone else until we are led by that divine Spirit.

Martin Israel, *The Spirit of Counsel*, Hodder and Stoughton, 1983, page 14

We come down from these heights to consider what this complete self-giving to the Spirit can mean in our own quite ordinary lives. St. John of the Cross says that every quality or virtue which that Spirit really produces in men's souls has three distinguishing characters... Tranquillity, Gentleness, Strength. All our action—and now we are thinking specially of action—must be peaceful, gentle and strong. That suggests, doesn't it, an immense depth, and an invulnerable steadiness as the soul's abiding temper; a depth and a steadiness which come from the fact that our small action is now part of the total action of God, whose Spirit, as another saint has said, 'Works always in tranquillity.' Fuss and feverishness, anxiety, intensity, intolerance, instability, pessimism and wobble, and every kind of hurry and worry—these even on the highest levels, are signs of the self-made and self-acting soul; the spiritual parvenu. The saints are never like that. They share the quiet and noble qualities of the great family to which they belong; the family of the Sons of God.

If, then, we desire a simple test of the quality of our spiritual life, a consideration of the tranquillity, gentleness and strength with which we deal with the circumstances of our outward life will serve us better than anything that is based on the loftiness of our religious notions, or fervour of our religious feelings. It is a test that can be applied anywhere and at any time. Tranquillity, gentleness and strength, carrying us through the changes of weather, the ups and downs of the route, the varied surface of the road; the inequalities of family life, emotional and professional disappointments, the sudden intervention of bad fortune or bad health, the rising and falling of our religious temperature. This is the threefold imprint of the Spirit on the souls surrendered to His great action.

Evelyn Underhill, *The Spiritual Life*, Harper & Row, 1936, page 102

The Spirit of God works deeply within us. He lifts up our consciousness from its natural attachment to ourself and our concerns to an atmosphere of infinite love that lies deeper in us than even the core of our own being. In other words, the Holy Spirit raises us far beyond the limitations of our own understanding so that we may deeply drink of the knowledge of God. Human knowledge bases its trust on the discoveries of science, and is the fruit of living experience throughout the ages of mortal endeavour. Divine knowledge flows to the receptive human soul in the practice of contemplative prayer, so that a completely new perspective is given to all that the mind had previously accepted as final truth. The understanding that comes from God is true wisdom; unlike the knowledge that is the fruits of human endeavour, it is broad, expansive, all embracing and of transfiguring intensity. The knowledge that proceeds from man is discursive and analytical, and works best in categories of thought. It sees barriers rather than synthesis; it creates division, and exults when it has put everything into place. It likes to assume a dominant role, putting everything else into subjection to its own power.

But, in faith, there is one source alone of all knowledge, and that is God Himself. Were it not for the ceaseless activity of the Holy Spirit in the lives of men, their minds would fail to respond to the challenge of existence, and no fresh truth about the human condition would come to light and be the basis of a new understanding of the world and its workings. The Spirit of God never leaves us without His witness; He drives us on with a divine discontent that is the motivating force of all human creativity, whether artistic, scientific, philosophical or theological. The Spirit of God will never cease to grapple with the hard inertia of the human soul, longing above all else for indolent composure, until a new thing is born of its travail, until the virgin consciousness deep in the soul has conceived a greater truth and brought it into the light of common knowledge after a painful period of gestation. So the Spirit of God raises, by slow steps of disclosure, the purely human mind of spiritual illumination, bringing the separated soul into communion with all creation. This is the supreme gift of God to man; it determines the human spiritual nature and defines man's journey to completion, to a full participation in the divine reality.

Martin Israel, *The Spirit of Counsel*, Hodder and Stoughton, 1983, page 9

IMAGE OF GOD

*Image of God—man's original nature, made in the image and
likeness of God, fully worked out in the life of Christ*

In our first Old Testament verse we read 'the Lord God formed man of dust from the
ground, and breathed into his nostrils the breath of life; and man became a living
being.' Something of the consequences can be seen in the life of Bezalel the son of Uri,
son of Hur, of the tribe of Judah. Of him the Lord said: 'I have filled him with the Spirit of
God, with ability and intelligence, with knowledge and all craftsmanship.' Sadly his life
was the exception rather than the rule. Most people went their own way, with disastrous
consequences.

In the fulness of time our Lord was born. In the course of his life he worked out what
was meant by him being made in the image and likeness of God. He found the Father in
the depths of his being, the Holy Spirit, and divine attributes—life, light, truth, joy, love
and so on. He was the pioneer and the prototype of a new way of life, now opened up to
all who were prepared to follow him (that is, to live this way of life). St Paul recognized
him to be the image of the invisible God, and followed him. As a consequence his life was
radically changed and enriched. He went out to share this good news to the then known
world.

We also are made in the image and likeness of God. We have in the depths of our
being an enormous source of divine life. Baptism, with its emphasis on rebirth, can
catalyse or trigger off something of the richness of this divine life latent within us. This
can be nurtured and fostered by the practice of reflection on the contents of *Visions of
Glory*.

Then the Lord God formed man of dust from the ground, and breathed into his nostrils the
breath of life; and man became a living being.

Genesis 2:7

I have filled him with the Spirit of God, with ability and intelligence, with knowledge and all
craftsmanship.

Exodus 31:3

But we all, with open face beholding as in a glass the glory of the Lord, are changed unto
the same image from glory to glory, even as by the Spirit of the Lord.

2 Corinthians 3:18 (AV)

He is the image of the invisible God, the first-born of all creation.

Colossians 1:15

You never know yourself till you know more than your body. The Image of God is not
seated in the features of your face, but in the lineaments of your Soul.

Thomas Traherne, *Centuries*, The Faith Press, 1969, page 9

The God-image in man was not destroyed by the Fall but was only damaged and corrupted ('deformed'), and can be restored through God's grace.

C.G. Jung, *The Collected Works of C.G. Jung*, translated by R.F.C. Hull, Routledge & Kegan Paul, 1959, volume 9, part 2, *Aion*, page 39

... 'moulded into the image of his Son' (Romans 8:29). Let us gaze upon this adorable Image, remain always with His radiance, that He may impress Himself upon us. Then let us do everything in the same disposition as our Holy Master.

Sister Elizabeth of the Trinity, *Spiritual Writings*, Geoffrey Chapman, 1962, page 147

... they all proclaimed that deep in the central nature of man—an inalienable part of Reason—there was a Light, a Word, an Image of God, something permanent, reliable, universal, and unsundered from God himself. They all knew that man is vastly more than 'mere man.'

Rufus M. Jones, *Spiritual Reformers in the 16th and 17th Centuries*, Macmillan and Co., 1914, page xxx

The greatest of painters only once painted a mysteriously divine child; he couldn't have told how he did it, and we can't tell why we feel it to be divine. I think there are stores laid up in our human nature that our understandings can make no complete inventory of.

George Eliot, *Mill on the Floss*, Virtue & Co., 1908, volume 2, page 58

... 'Honour all men.' Every man should be honoured as God's image, in the sense in which Novalis says—that we touch Heaven when we lay our hand on a human body!... The old Homeric Greeks, I think, felt that, and acted up to it, more than any nation. The Patriarchs too seem to have had the same feeling...

Charles Kingsley, *Daily Thoughts*, Macmillan and Co., 1884, page 229

'Let us make man in OUR image.' Such is man's height and depth and breadth and mystery. He has not come from one principle or distinction of the Divine Nature, but out of all principles. Man is the image of the whole Deity. There is in him a sanctuary, for the Father, and for the Son, and for the Holy Ghost. 'We will make our abode with him.'

John Pulsford, *Quiet Hours*, James Nisbet & Co., 1857, page 75

The image of God in man is the conformity of the human soul, understanding, spirit, mind, will, and all internal and external bodily and spiritual powers with God and the Holy Trinity and with all divine qualities, virtues, wills, and characteristics. This is indicated in the decision of the Holy Trinity: Let us make man in our image after our likeness; and let him have dominion over the fish of the sea, and over the birds of the air, and over the cattle, and over all the earth (Gen. 1:26).

Johann Arndt, *True Christianity*, translated by Peter Erb, SPCK, 1979, page 29

How do we detect this spark within us? I imagine that it is different in each person, which would not be surprising since every person is unique. I think it has something to do with a longing deep down within us. We long to know and possess the good, or the good that we see in a great number of persons and objects which fall within our experience. In the end we discover that the pursuit of truth and goodness leads us to long for truth and goodness in their absolute form. This absolute truth and this absolute goodness we call God.

Basil Hume, O.S.B., *To Be a Pilgrim*, St Paul Publications, 1984, page 66

'Then God said, "Let us make man in our image, after our likeness; and let them have dominion..." So God created man in his own image, in the image of God he created him;

male and female he created them' (Gen. 1:26f; cf. 5:1 and 9:6; see also 1 Cor. 11:7 and James 3:9). The New Testament also views Christ as the image of the invisible God (2 Cor. 4:4; Col. 1:15), reflecting God's glory (Heb. 1:3), and the Christian as renewed in God's image by God's regenerative power through the Holy Spirit (2 Cor. 3:18). In theological anthropology, so important to Christian moral theology and ethics, the image of God has been central in debates about what was present before, what was lost in, and what remains after the Fall.

James F. Childress, in James F. Childress and John Macquarrie, editors, *A New Dictionary of Christian Ethics*, SCM Press, 1986, page 292

There is surely a peece of Divinity in us, something that was before the Elements, and owes no homage unto the Sun. Nature tels me I am the Image of God as well as Scripture; he that understands not thus much, hath not his introduction or first lesson, and is yet to begin the Alphabet of man. Let me not injure the felicity of others if I say I am as happy as any. (I have that in me that can convert poverty into riches, transforme adversity into prosperity. I am more invulnerable than Achilles. Fortune hath not one place to hit me... In briefe, I am content, and what should providence adde more? Surely this is it wee call Happinesse, and this doe I enjoy, with this I am happy in a dreame, and as content to enjoy a happinesse in a fancie as others in a more apparent truth and reality.)

Sir Thomas Browne, *Religio Medici*, 2. 11, in Geoffrey Keynes, editor, *The Works of Sir Thomas Browne*, Faber & Faber, 1964, page 87

Hardly ever, now, has a human face
the baffling light or the strange still gleam of the gods within it, upon it.
Even from the face of the children, now,
that spangled glisten is gone, that at-oneness without afterthought,
and they are bridled with cunning, and bitted
with knowledge of things that shall never be admitted,
even the fact of birth: even little children.
Holbein and Titian and Tintoret could never paint faces, now:
because those faces were windows to the strange horizons, even Henry VIII;
whereas faces now are only human grimaces,
with eyes like interiors of stuffy rooms, furnished.

D.H. Lawrence, 'The Human Face', in Vivian de Sola Pinto and Warren Roberts, editors, *The Complete Poems of D.H. Lawrence*, William Heinemann, 1967, volume 2, page 656

The difference between man and woman is a radical and fundamental one which permeates the depths of their consciousness and affects all human behaviour. It is at the beginnings of life itself. In Genesis 1:27 is said 'male and female he created them'. He wished that they be one, that they be 'one body' (Genesis 2:24).

Man and woman are complementary in their bodies and their psychology. They each discover their being in relation to God who created them; each in the image of God, they are called to become like God. Such is their fundamental ultimate goal in the universe.

However, they are also in the image of God in their union and their unity of love. Each one is with and for the other. Each one discovers his or her self in relationship to the other.

Jean Vanier, *Man and Woman He Made Them*, Darton, Longman & Todd, 1985, page 49

... the soul has never lost the divine Image, the pearl of supreme price, the original element which is God Himself in the soul. We are all, in the deepest centre of our being, like Adam, possessed of a substantial essence, not of earth, not of time and space, not of the shadow but of the eternal, spiritual, and heavenly type. It may become overlaid with the rubbish of earth, it may long lie buried in the field of the human heart, it may remain concealed, like the grain of radium in a mass of dark pitchblende, and be forgotten, but we have only to return home within ourselves to find the God who has never been sundered from us and who could not leave us without Himself. We do not need to cross the sea to find Him, we do not need to climb the heavens to reach Him—the Word is nigh thee, the Image is in thy heart, turn home and thou shalt find Him.

Rufus M. Jones, *Spiritual Reformers in the 16th and 17th Centuries*, Macmillan and Co., 1914, page 54

If we take Adam as a type of the natural man, and ask in whose image he was created, we are told that it was in God's image. Man alone has mind, intelligence, reason, and a nature destined to be enobled through the Incarnation. But the Divine Image has been defaced by sin.

If a portrait is spoilt, it can really only be restored by the artist who painted it. Human nature, the image of God, has been marred by sin, and the lost vision of humanity can only be restored by the Great Artist Himself. In the mystery of the Incarnation human nature has been re-drawn according to the perfect conception in the mind of God. That has been done once for all, and the beauty of that presentment can never be lost.

Always before the gaze of God is that fair Image manifest and set against all caricatures and shameful distortions which have been produced by men.

The image and superscription upon a coin can no longer be seen if it is soiled. But when it has been cleaned both reappear. The soul smirched by sin may lose all sign of the Image in which it was made, but the cleansing of a real repentance will bring out again the true lineaments of a child of God.

When coins become defaced, they have to be re-minted. In the fire of the Sacred Passion the coin of human nature was re-minted, and the superscription of divine possession shone out upon it perfectly clearly. The agony of the passion of any life may be the re-minting of a coin for God's treasury.

Father Andrew, S.D.C., *Meditations for Every Day*, A.R. Mowbray & Co., 1941, page 352

I am *made* in the image and likeness of God but whether or not I maintain that image effectively, whether I develop it, depends on me. I reflect God most by participating in the ongoing creation. One of the most significant descriptions of God is 'Creator.' That ought to be one of the important denotations of persons, too. Not 'creator' in the restrictive sense of sculptor, composer, author, wood-worker, and the like, but in an even more fulfilling and participatory way—creator on the fully human level. How creative are we in our approach to human relations? Are we creative in problem solving, homemaking, job delineation? If I am content to go along with the way it's always been done, to be led in all things, if I take the easy approach to existence, I'm lazy, I'm uncreative. I am in a very real way already dead. People are different from animals. People can make, can create, can participate in effecting the direction and speed of growth toward omega that the world will take. What a profound vocation each therefore has. And what a remarkable failure when we miss with our lives. Parents are called upon to be creative daily, hourly, with their children. Spouses who care do the same with each other. Such also is the ideal teacher–pupil relationship and that of neighbours and nations as well. So the woman or man who suppresses imagination only cripples. Political propaganda and all advertising are geared toward such mental paralyzing. Those of us who only think in clichés—the lazy way that is, through somebody else's words/ideas—do not respect ourselves enough to wish to work at development. Because, of course, the ultimate subject of creativeness, as well as the initial subject, is the self. If I sincerely work at continually recreating the self, I cannot help but recreate the universe. I am its centre and when I shift, the entire world does. And, conscious of this, I can significantly help to renew the face of the earth.

Harry James Cargas, *Encountering Myself*, SPCK, 1978, page 4

INCARNATION

Incarnation—embodiment in flesh, especially in human form;
living type (of quality); the incarnation of God in Christ

Christmas is the time of the year when we celebrate the incarnation—the birth of God in Jesus Christ. In the famous carol service from King's College, Cambridge, we hear the prophecies leading up to the birth in the stable, the visit of the shepherds and wise men, and the prologue of St John's Gospel, with its mystery of the incarnation. The nine lessons are interspersed with nine carols, beautifully sung, and now the service is broadcast to many countries overseas. Christmas is a time of great joy. We give and receive gifts, we send and receive numerous Christmas cards, and we feast on turkey and Christmas pudding.

A few years ago I discovered there is another 'birth' to celebrate at Christmas. Quite by accident I came across a piece of doggerel by Angelus Silesius which goes as follows:

Christ could be born a thousand times in Galilee—
But all in vain until he is born in me.

Discovering this simple verse led to a deeper understanding of Christmas and the mystery of the incarnation. The words of the carol 'O Little Town of Bethlehem' took on new meaning: 'How silently, how silently, the wondrous gift is giv'n! So God imparts to human hearts the blessings of his heav'n. No ear may hear his coming; But in this world of sin, Where meek hearts will receive him, still the dear Christ enters in.' There is a line in the last verse even more explicit: 'Be born in us today.' How important the incarnation is, both historically and today.

All things have been delivered to me by my Father.
Matthew 11:27

In the beginning was the Word, and the Word was with God, and the Word was God ... And the Word became flesh and dwelt among us, full of grace and truth.
John 1:1, 14

No one has ever seen God; the only Son, who is in the bosom of the Father, he has made him known.
John 1:18

If a man loves me, he will keep my word, and my Father will love him, and we will come to him and make our home with him.
John 14:23

God became man to turn creatures into sons: not simply to produce better men of the old kind but to produce a new kind of man.
C.S. Lewis, *Mere Christianity*, William Collins Sons & Co., 1961, page 179

Everyone has, inside himself ... what shall I call it? A piece of good news! Everyone is ... a very great, very important character!
Ugo Betti, *The Burnt Flower-Bed*, Act II, in *Three Plays by Ugo Betti*, translated by Henry Read, Victor Gollancz, 1956, page 151

God so united Himself to us and us to Him, that the descent of God to the human level was at the same time the ascent of man to the divine level.

St Leo, in F.C. Happold, *Religious Faith and Twentieth-Century Man*, Darton, Longman & Todd, 1980, page 145

In the *Incarnation* of Christ, we understand, *God* in conjunction with humane Nature: and this strengthens our Faith, that humane Nature *may* be conjoined to God eternally.

Benjamin Whichcote, *Moral and Religious Aphorisms*, iv. 306, Elkin Mathews & Marrot, 1930, page 37

God incarnated himself in Jesus Christ. Many people spend their time denying his incarnation. They search the sky and miss him right here on earth, where he is to be found in their daily lives.

Michel Quoist, *With Open Heart*, translated by Colette Copeland, Gill and Macmillan, 1983, page 147

Prayer then is the interiorizing of the Incarnation. The Word is to become enfleshed in me. Bethlehem is here. So Christmas Day is to become all days, and the adoration of Emmanuel, God with us, must be a daily and continuous event.

Kenneth Leech, *True Prayer*, Sheldon Press, 1980, page 13

He it is... that is born each instant in our hearts: for this unending birth, this everlasting beginning, without end, this everlasting, perfect newness of God begotten of Himself, issuing from Himself or altering His one-ness, this is the life that is in us.

Thomas Merton, *Elected Silence*, Hollis and Carter, 1949, page 361

The real difficulty which prevents people from believing in the Virgin Birth is not want of evidence, but belief in a 'closed universe', and the impossibility of miracles. But he who believes this, cannot believe in the Incarnation, and therefore cannot be a Christian at all.

C.B. Moss, *The Christian Faith*, SPCK, 1944, page 115

The soul of a monk is a Bethlehem where Christ comes to be born—in the sense that Christ is born where His likeness is re-formed by grace, and where His Divinity lives, in a special manner, with His Father and His Holy Spirit, by charity, in this 'new incarnation,' this 'other Christ.'

Thomas Merton, *Elected Silence*, Hollis and Carter, 1949, page 332

Now Jesus, who is born as a child in us, advances in wisdom and age and grace, in different ways in the hearts of those who receive Him. He is not the same in everyone, but only according to the measure of those in whom He dwells, adapting Himself to the capacity of each one who receive Him. To some He comes as a babe, to others as one advancing, to others in full maturity...

Gregory of Nyssa, in Andrew Louth, *The Origins of the Christian Mystical Tradition*, Clarendon Press, Oxford, 1981, page 95

But this Divine life which is in Christ Jesus is to overflow from Him upon us, upon the whole human race. This is a wonderful revelation which fills us with joy.

The Divine Sonship which is in Christ by nature, and makes Him God's own and only Son, is to be extended to us by grace, so that in the thought of God, Christ is the first-born of many brethren, who are by grace what He is by nature, sons of God.

D. Columba Marmion, *Christ the Life of the Soul*, Sands & Co., 1922, page 19

By virtue of the Creation and still more, of the Incarnation, *nothing* here below is *profane* for those who know how to see. On the contrary, everything is sacred to the men who can distinguish that portion of chosen being which is subject to Christ's drawing power in the process of consummation. Try, with God's help, to perceive the connection—even physical and natural—which binds your labour with the building of the Kingdom of Heaven...

May the time come when men, having awakened to a sense of the close bond linking all the movements of this world in the single, all-embracing work of the Incarnation, shall be unable to give themselves to any one of their tasks without illuminating it with the clear vision that their work—however elementary it may be—is received and put to good use by a Centre of the universe... To experience the attraction of God, to be sensible of the beauty, the consistency and the final unity of being, is the highest and at the same time the most complete of our 'passivities of growth'.

Pierre Teilhard de Chardin, *Le Milieu Divin*, William Collins Sons & Co., 1960, page 38

It makes a vast difference whether we can think of one historical life and character as the fullest and completest revelation of God, the word of God made flesh; or whether we have to piece together (as it were) our knowledge of God and His will from what may strike us as highest and best in many different lives, in many varied and partially discordant teachings. It was better for the world that God should be revealed to it through the life and teachings of one human being—interpreted, developed, applied to the needs of successive ages by the working of His Spirit in the Society of His followers—rather than by means of a gradual, diffused, and progressive revelation in many men and many societies. And that is why, we believe, God actually did reveal Himself in that way. 'The Word became flesh, and dwelt among us.' 'God who at sundry times and in divers manners spake in time past unto the fathers by the prophets, hath in these last days spoken unto us by His Son.' Christ Himself is 'the Way, the Truth and the Life.' 'In Him was life, and the life was' and is 'the light of men.'

Sane historical enquiry is... more and more confirming the old view that it was the historical Christ who made Christianity, not the Christian Church which has thrown back into the past a Christ of its own creation.

What Christianity teaches about the relation of Christ to God the Father no other religion... has even ventured to claim for its founders. Even to the Buddhist there are many Buddhas: to the Christian there is but one Christ. There have been many Sons of God; only one is in a supreme, a unique sense the Son, the word made flesh, God of God, God revealed in a human soul and a human life.

So the Church has taught. And I think, our own consciences and our own experience will confirm its teaching.

Certainly the Church has learned much about God and human life from other teachers; certainly Christianity, as it is, has been enriched and enlarged by much moral and spiritual truth that originally came from other sources; certainly the revelation of God and his mind and will for man is in a sense not complete yet. 'When He, the Spirit of truth shall come, he will guide you into all truth.' But surely most of us on reflection will feel that there is no other historical person whom we could with the least naturalness think of as being God manifest in the flesh, whom we could feel it natural, reasonable, right, to think of and feel towards as God—incarnate in a human soul—to take as our example, leader, guide—to make the captain of our salvation. In any case, our highest knowledge of God must be derived from our knowledge of what Humanity is, at its highest. In any case, we can only think of God at all by thinking of Him after the analogy of human nature at this best. But thoughts of God are apt to be vague and indefinite if we merely think of Him as more or less incarnate in many men. They are apt to become unworthy thoughts if we do not constantly bear in mind the difference between God and human nature as it is in average men, or even in any one man short of the highest. It is scarcely possible to exaggerate the religious advantage which we derive from being able to look at one historical personality as Him in whose character we can see God fully revealed, from having a single leader whom we can follow unreservedly... It makes and it will ever make a vast difference to the spiritual life of humanity that it has been able to discover in the one historical personality of Jesus an adequate embodiment of that ideal, and therefore one in whom the revelation of God can be regarded as supreme, eternal, in a sense final.

I believe it makes a great difference to the spiritual life of each one of us, whether we are or are not using to the full this great gift of a personal Revealer, Leader, Saviour, whether our own personal religious life does or does not take the form of a personal following, obeying, imitating a personal Christ as the supreme Revealer of a Personal God.

Hastings Rashdall, 'If Christ has not been born,' in *A Lectionary of Christian Prose*, Longmans, Green and Co., 1941, page 90

INNER LIFE

Inner life—interior, internal, man's soul or mind, spirit

I remember a conversation with a retired don. She was telling me about one of her undergraduates. She had set her an essay for her very first tutorial on the Roman Empire. The young lady arrived at the appointed hour and read out her essay. Factually, it was well nigh perfect. 'Now,' said the tutor, 'you have done an excellent job in presenting the facts to me, but tell me, what do you yourself think about the question?' A long period of silence followed. However, in that tutorial a crucial step forward had been taken. The undergraduate began to think for herself, and she never looked back. The elderly don continued, 'I have always made a distinction between academic knowledge and personal knowledge.' Both are important. By personal knowledge I mean self-knowledge, the truths we live by, and ultimately what we hold to be sacred. A good tutor should foster personal knowledge, for we are involved in an education of the whole person. Today though, this is difficult and great care is needed. Is this where the college chaplain comes in? I explained to her my reflection groups with their emphasis on personal knowledge, and she brightened up at this point. 'You are involved, are you not, in that old-style form of education coming from the Latin word *educere*.' The emphasis here is on leading out, drawing out, nurturing that 'inner life' in people, enabling them to become whole people. I do wish more of our education system was concerned with this. Nowadays the acquisition of academic knowledge is paramount.

Can we find such a man as this, in whom is the Spirit of God?
Genesis 41:38

I have heard of you that the spirit of the holy gods is in you, and that light and understanding and excellent wisdom are found in you.
Daniel 5:14

For I delight in the law of God, in my inmost self.
Romans 7:22

But the fruit of the Spirit is love, joy, peace, patience, kindness, goodness, faithfulness, gentleness, self-control; against such there is no law.
Galatians 5:22

The man who has no inner life is the slave of his surroundings.
Henri Frédéric Amiel, *Amiel's Journal*, translated by Mrs Humphry Ward, Macmillan and Co., 1918, page 114

It is wonderful how a time away, especially abroad, changes all one's views of life from within.

A.C. Benson, *Extracts from the Letters of Dr. A.C. Benson to M.E.A.*, Jarrold Publishing, 1927, page 67

... the inner life is the only means whereby we may oppose a profitable resistance to circumstance.

Henri Frédéric Amiel, *Amiel's Journal*, translated by Mrs Humphry Ward, Macmillan and Co., 1918, page 114

We carry to men the same faculties that are active in us, and excite in them the same feelings. Irritability produces irritation. Pride excites pride and the resistance of pride; mirth arouses mirth; anger, anger.

Henry Ward Beecher, *Proverbs from Plymouth Pulpit*, Charles Burnet & Co., 1887, page 30

... he turned more and more, as time went on, toward interior religion, the cultivation of an inner sanctuary, the deepening of the mystical roots of his life, and the perfection of a religion of inner and spiritual life.

Rufus M. Jones, *Spiritual Reformers in the 16th and 17th Centuries*, Macmillan and Co., 1914, page 97

There is in most of us a lyric germ or nucleus which deserves respect; it bids a man ponder, or create; and in this dim corner of himself he can take refuge and find consolations which the society of his fellow-creatures does not provide.

Norman Douglas, *An Almanac*, Chatto and Windus in association with Martin Secker & Warburg, 1945, page 59

A spiritual life is simply a life in which all that we do comes from the centre, where we are anchored in God: a life soaked through and through by a sense of His reality and claim, and self-given to the great movement of His will.

Evelyn Underhill, in John Stobbart, editor, *The Wisdom of Evelyn Underhill*, A.R. Mowbray & Co., 1951, page 8

He, within,
Took measure of his soul, and knew its strength,
And by that silent knowledge, day by day,
Was calmed, ennobled, comforted, sustained.

Matthew Arnold, 'Mycerinus', line 108, in *The Poems of Matthew Arnold*, Longmans, Green and Co., 1965, page 31

The 'Depth of God within the Soul,' the Inner Light, is the precious Pearl, the never-failing Comfort, the Panacea for all diseases, the sure Antidote even against death itself, the unfailing Guide and Way of all Wisdom.

Rufus M. Jones, *Spiritual Reformers in the 16th and 17th Centuries*, Macmillan and Co., 1914, page 219

Part of the discipline of the Christian's spiritual life is designed to bring the insights and the inspiration of the inner life to bear on his conduct in the outer life, in his relations with his fellows and his responsibilities towards his family and his country.

Christopher Bryant, S.S.J.E., *Jung and the Christian Way*, Darton, Longman & Todd, 1983, page 103

How greatly should we rejoice that God indwells our soul! Even more that our soul dwells in God! Our created soul is to be God's dwelling-place: and the soul's dwelling-place is to be God, who is uncreated. It is a great thing to know in our heart that God, our Maker, indwells our soul. Even greater is it to know that our soul, our created soul, dwells in the substance of God. Of that substance, God, are we what we are!

Julian of Norwich, *Revelations of Divine Love*, translated by Clifton Wolters, Penguin Books, 1976, page 157

'It takes the endowment of a robust constitution to practice introspection without morbidity.' To look into oneself soundly without undermining oneself; to venture into the unexplored deep not with illusion and make-believe, but with a pure gaze, is a rare gift. But then, too, the results of such exploration for the world and for science constitute a rare good fortune.

Johann Wolfgang von Goethe, *Wisdom and Experience*, selected by Ludwig Curtius, translated and edited by Hermann J. Weigand, Routledge & Kegan Paul, 1949, page 205

... but after his new experience, when he 'came to know himself,' and to 'know Jesus Christ and the Scriptures *experimentally* rather than grammatically, literally or academically,' he came to esteem lightly 'notions and speculation,' 'letter-learning' and 'University knowledge,' and he '*centred his spirit* on union and communion with God' and turned his supreme interest from 'forms, externals and generals' to the cultivation of 'the inner man,' and to 'acting more than talking.'

Rufus M. Jones, *Spiritual Reformers in the 16th and 17th Centuries*, Macmillan and Co., 1914, page 240

The empirical Christian Church shares many features in common with other forms of human organization, but it is distinguished from all of them by its inner principle of existence. Its outward form has varied considerably from age to age and from place to place, but its constant factor has been that of inward faith in God which... has persisted from the earliest days of its life. It is this enduring inward faith which makes the world-wide Church of the twentieth century continuous not only with the Church of the Apostles but also with the people-Church of the ancient Hebrew nation.

Alan Richardson, *Christian Apologetics*, SCM Press, 1947, page 89

I have nothing to give to another; but I have the duty to open him to his own life, to allow him to be himself—infinitely richer and more beautiful than he could ever be if I tried to enrich and shape him only from the outside. All is *within* him because the source lies in his heart of hearts. But so many obstacles prevent it from surfacing! I must be the one to help it spring forth and smash the concrete around him, and in him. I must be the one to help him dig and search, and dig some more, to find the source. And from that source, life will spring.

Michel Quoist, *With Open Heart*, translated by Colette Copeland, Gill and Macmillan, 1983, page 31

If thou couldst empty all thyself of self,
Like to a shell dishabited,
Then might He find thee on the Ocean shelf,
And say, 'This is not dead,'
And fill thee with Himself instead:
But thou art all replete with very *thou*,
And hast such shrewd activity,
That, when He comes, He says, 'This is enow
Unto itself—Twere better let it be:
It is so small and full, there is no room for Me.'

T.E. Brown, in J.T. Hackett, *My Commonplace Book*, Macmillan and Co., 1923, page 208

There is nothing simpler, safer, more lovely, more fruitful, than this life of the innermost heart. It is not reached by reading and effort of the mind, but by dying to all else but God, and is known and experienced by love only. It is, therefore, rather the work of the Spirit of Christ in us, than our own work. This spirit of love, when we yield ourselves up to Him, pours into us the mind of Jesus Christ, and forms us according to His image, unconsciously to ourselves—leads us ever into a deeper renunciation of all things, and of ourselves, and into an unconditional surrender of ourselves to God.

Gerhard Tersteegen, in Frances Bevan, *Sketches of the Quiet in the Land*, John F. Shaw and Co., 1891, page 390

And many a man carries within him an inheritance of incalculable worth, who is not aware of his immense resources. The richest things are ever hidden from common gaze. The things of God are neither entrusted to the brute, nor to 'the brutish man.' The sensual man can have very little perception of the soul's immortality, for the life to which he has abandoned himself is not immortal. His is the false life, the life that is not lawful *for a man* to live, and there is no eternity which will be any comfort to him. Eternity will most rigorously punish him. But there is no man who reverently, wisely, and perseveringly cultivates his own spiritual life, who is not rewarded far beyond his thoughts.

John Pulsford, Quiet Hours, James Nisbet & Co., 1857, page 216

He insists always that in the last analysis it is Christ in us that saves us, but it was Christ in the flesh, the Christ of Galilee and Golgatha, that revealed to men the way to apprehend the inward and eternal Christ of God. 'The indwelling Christ,' he wrote, 'is all in all. He saves thee. He is thy peace and thy comfort. The outward Christ, the Christ in the flesh, and according to the flesh, cannot save thee in an external way. He must be in thee and thou must abide in Him. Why then did He become man and suffer on the Cross? There are many reasons why, but it was especially that God by the death and suffering of Christ might take the wrath and hostility out of *our* hearts, on account of which we falsely conceive of God as a wrathful enemy to us. He had to deal that way with poor blind men like us and so reconcile us with Himself. There was no need of it on His part. He was always Love and He always loved us, even when we were enemies to Him, but we should never have known it if God had not condescended to show Himself to us in His Son and had not suffered for us.'

Rufus M. Jones, Spiritual Reformers in the 16th and 17th Centuries, Macmillan and Co., 1914, page 141

I think, therefore, that we must go back into ourselves for faith, and away from ourselves into the world for reason. The deeper we go into ourselves the more we throw off forms and find the assurance not only that the great things exist, but that they are the heart of our lives, and, since after all we are of one stock, they must be at the heart of your lives as well as mine. You say there are bad men and wars and cruelties and wrong. I say all these are the collision of undeveloped forms ... Probe inwards, then, and you find the same spring of life everywhere and it is good. Look outwards, and you find, as you yourself admit, the slow movement towards a harmony—which just means that these impulses of primeval energy come, so to say, to understand one another. Every form they take as they grow will provoke conflict, perish, and be cast aside until the whole unites, and there you have the secret of your successive efforts and failures which yet leave something behind them. God is not the creator who made the world in six days, rested on the seventh and saw that it was good. He is growing in the actual evolution of the world.

Professor Hobhouse, 'Questions of War and Peace', in J.T. Hackett, My Commonplace Book, Macmillan and Co.,
1923, page 199

'Live on in me' (John 15:4). It is the Word of God who gives us this command, who expresses this wish. 'Live on in me!' Not just for a few moments, a few passing hours, but *live on*, permanently, habitually. 'Live on in Me,' pray in Me, adore in Me, love in Me, suffer in Me, work, act in Me 'Live on in Me', whoever or whatever comes your way, penetrate ever deeper into the dwelling place which is the true 'wilderness where God speaks to the heart', as the Prophet sang. But to understand this wholly mysterious command, we must not remain, so to speak, on the surface; we must enter ever more deeply into the divine Being, by means of recollection. 'I press on' (Philippians 3:12), cried St Paul, and we too should press on every day down the path into the abyss which is God. Let us slip down this steep incline with a confidence rooted in Love. 'One depth makes answer to another.' (Psalm 42:7). There, in the deepest depths, we shall encounter the divine; there the abyss of our nothingness and misery will find itself face to face with the abyss of the mercy of God and with the immensity of the all of God: there we shall find the strength to die to self and, all selfishness purged away, be transformed by Love. 'Blessed are those who die in the Lord' (Revelation 14:13).

Sister Elizabeth of the Trinity, *Spiritual Writings*, Geoffrey Chapman, 1962, page 141

INTERCESSION

Intercession—interceding, especially by prayer

One afternoon in Bradford, I was doing some random visiting in a block of high-rise flats, near the cathedral. In the course of a busy afternoon, I crossed the threshold of a very difficult situation. An elderly couple lived in the flat I was visiting, and, a few minutes before I knocked on the door, the wife had had a stroke. She was unconscious, and her husband distressed and distraught. The doctor had been summoned, but was yet to arrive. A clergyman at the door was clearly the last person the husband wanted to see, given the circumstances. He coped with me admirably: 'I want you to pray for my wife tonight when you are back at the cathedral, and please come again and visit tomorrow.'

That evening, back at the cathedral, I went to the Chapel of the Holy Spirit, a small chapel specifically set aside for intercessory prayer and healing. There was a table in the chapel on which was placed a cruse of oil, permanently lit. This symbolized the presence of the Holy Spirit, and helped to give the chapel an atmosphere of peace and quiet.

I prayed for the recovery of the wife and for her husband. The next day I called in and was pleasantly surprised to see the wife conscious and sitting in a chair. Her husband was greatly relieved. He told me she had regained consciousness the previous evening. I asked him what time the change had taken place. It transpired she opened her eyes at the very time I was praying for her. This has not been an isolated incident in my ministry. I believe that when intercession takes place 'things happen'.

... he bore the sin of many, and made intercession for the transgressors.
Isaiah 53:12

Be not fainthearted when thou makest thy prayer, and neglect not to give alms.
Ecclesiasticus 7:10 (AV)

Pray at all times in the Spirit, with all prayer and supplication. To that end keep alert with all perseverance, making supplication for all the saints.
Ephesians 6:18

And so, from the day we heard of it, we have not ceased to pray for you, asking that you may be filled with the knowledge of his will in all spiritual wisdom and understanding, to lead a life worthy of the Lord, fully pleasing to him, bearing fruit in every good work and increasing in the knowledge of God.
Colossians 1:9–10

The real meaning of intercession is not telling God in one's words of the needs and sorrows of the world, but through the silent attentive spirit focusing the love of God where the need is greatest.
Anon.

True intercession places another person more firmly in the arms of divine love which will never infringe that person's freedom, but which works through bestowals of awareness and recognition, through evocation and response, through the offer of choice and the glimpse of possibility.

John V. Taylor, *The Go-Between God*, SCM Press, 1973, page 234

To open oneself to another *unconditionally* in love *is* to be with him in the presence of God, and that is the heart of intercession. To pray for another is to expose both oneself and him to the common ground of our being: it is to see one's concern for him in terms of *ultimate* concern, to let *God* into the relationship. Intercession is to *be with* another at that depth, whether in silence or compassion or action.

John Robinson, *Honest to God*, SCM Press, 1963, page 99

While we thus pray and enjoy the presence of God, we remember the world around us with its terrible divisions, sins, sadnesses, needs and frustrations. And we remember our own terrible sins and needs and frustrations because we are part of the miserable world around us. So we intercede; and when we intercede, what do we really do? ... I think this is what we do. We don't start with the world and its needs; we don't start with ourselves and our ideas about the world's needs; we start as far as we can with God, and with God's loving purpose.

The key to intercession is to start by putting ourselves in line with God and his love and his purpose as far as we possibly can. We can think of God's attitude towards the world as one which loves it utterly; is full of goodwill, care, and beneficence; whose love thrusts towards the world like a great stream.

But, because God created the human race in his own image, God in his dealing with the world waits upon the co-operation of human wills in his beneficent purpose towards the world. It is very mysterious, but that is so; it is just a part of the dignity of the human race as free beings in God's own image that it is through them and through their co-operation that God designs his good things for the world.

Michael Ramsey, *Through the Year with Michael Ramsey*, edited by Margaret Duggan, Hodder and Stoughton, 1975, page 41

I said a prayer or two, and then I noticed for the first time a dark outline rising in the centre of the space before the altar. For a moment I was perplexed, and then I saw that it was the nun whose hour it was for intercession ...

First I became aware suddenly that there ran a vital connection from the Tabernacle to the woman ... Something within it beat like a vast Heart and the vibrations of each pulse seemed to quiver through all the ground ... I perceived that this black figure knelt at the centre of reality and force, and with the movements of her will and lips controlled spiritual destinies for eternity. There ran out from this peaceful chapel lines of spiritual power that lost themselves in the distance, bewildering in their profusion and terrible in the intensity of their hidden fire. Souls leaped up and renewed the conflict as this tense will strove for them. Souls even at that moment leaving the body struggled from death into spiritual life, and fell panting and saved at the feet of the Redeemer on the other side of death. Others, acquiescent and swooning in sin, woke and snarled at the merciful stab of this poor nun's prayers ... In my stupid arrogance I had thought that my life was more active in God's world than her's ... It almost seems to me as I look back now as if the air in the chapel were full of a murmurous sound and a luminous mist as the currents of need and grace went to and fro.

Robert Benson, *The Light Invisible*, Isbister & Company, 1903, page 117

When praying for others we allow ourselves to be caught in the current of communication which the Spirit gives between us and another, and most of all between us and God. This is brought home most poignantly in an episode recorded by Archbishop Anthony Bloom from the life of Father Silouan, a Russian artisan who came to Mount Athos to be a monk and was put in charge of one of the workshops where other young peasants from distant villages indented for a year or two to raise a little cash they could get in no other way. For Father Silouan 'management' meant secret prayer for each one: In the beginning I prayed with tears of compassion for Nicholas, for his young wife, for the little child, but as I was praying the sense of the divine presence began to grow on me and at a certain moment it grew so powerful that I lost sight of Nicholas, his wife, his child, his needs, their village, and I could be aware only of God, and I was drawn by the sense of the divine presence deeper and deeper, until of a sudden, at the heart of this presence, I met the divine love holding Nicholas, his wife, and his child, and now it was with the love of God that I began to pray for them again, but again I was drawn into the deep and in the depths of this I again found the divine love.

Such a fading of one's awareness of another human being into one's even more intense awareness of God is the surest safeguard against the wish to use prayer as a means to manipulate other lives by remote control—for their own good, of course—which to some people makes the very idea of intercession distasteful.

John V. Taylor, The Go-Between God, SCM Press, 1973, page 233

Intercession is prayer with, for and on behalf of another person, group of people or even the world, which is undertaken by an individual or group. For true intercession, the intercessor must be in solidarity with God, that is trying to live out faith faithfully. In New Testament terms, the intercessor lives in solidarity with Jesus Christ. 'For there is one God and there is one mediator between God and men, the man Christ Jesus, who gave himself as a ransom for all' (1 Tim. 2:5). Intercession is therefore first an act and way of life in which the intercessor in solidarity with Christ through baptism and a life of faith enters Jesus' life of reconciliation. Jesus' intercession begins with incarnation (John 1:14), immerses him in the world's sin in the Jordan (Matt. 3:13), and brings him through desolation in death (Matt. 27) and resurrection (Mark 16) and intercedes for us (Rom. 8:34).

At another level, intercession is simply seen as praying for someone (sick, in trouble, without faith) or some object (peace in some part of the world, a solution to a dispute, justice in a particular country). Here, modern thought queries what is being attempted. Is it changing God's will, or reminding him of his 'duty'? Normally, the answer is that as Christ enters the world in reconciliation, so the intercessor is part of God's plan, God's economy of salvation. Jesus said: 'Ask and it will be given you' (Matt. 7:7), not explaining how, simply stating the fatherhood of God.

Intercession is work for others. It is an act of faith in God, his caring, his goodness. It is involved in the mystery of God and the freedom of man. We intercede for others because of what we believe about God as loving Father, who works directly, but also through men and women, using their co-operation. Intercession depends on the life of faith, not on words. We intercede with our whole being, opening a door for God, becoming channels, bringing people to God as Aaron did (Ex. 28:29). We can do this by name on a list, on request, because we are aware of need. Results are only sometimes known, and all intercession implies: 'Not my will, but thine, be done' (Lk. 22:42).

Michael Hollings, in Gordon S. Wakefield, editor, A Dictionary of Christian Spirituality, SCM Press, 1986, page 309

JESUS CHRIST

Jesus Christ—the name Jesus refers to the person Jesus of Nazareth
as known from historical research; Christ refers to the 'Messiah', or
'Lord's anointed' of Jewish prophecy, now applied to Jesus as
fulfilling this prophecy; image or picture of Jesus

J.S. Whale in his book *Christian Doctrine* wrote some succinct words about Jesus
Christ. After a long passage listing his human qualities he adds: 'Here in this human life
we meet the living God.'

I have had three experiences of meeting the living God. The first came by way of
Bishop Cuthbert Bardsley. Observing him carefully and listening to him intently I became
convinced he was genuine and living in the Spirit of Jesus Christ. This prompted me to
make a commitment to the living God. The second came through reading the contents of
the four Gospels. These gave me a much clearer image or picture of Jesus, and helped me
on my journey with the living God. The third came six years later. I was looking for a
deeper image or picture of Jesus Christ. A copy of *The Choice is Always Ours* had come
my way. This book enabled me to re-examine the Genesis story of the creation of man. I
noted the divine inbreathing, and man made in the image and likeness of God. I saw
enormous potential in this. I then realized Jesus worked this out in his life, and discovered
the divine in the depths of his being. This divine life, worked out by Christ in all its
fulness, is our spiritual heritage. Baptism, for instance, is about the rebirth of God, Father,
Son and Holy Spirit, in our hearts. Evidence for these insights was forthcoming from the
last 2,000 years of Christian experience. *Visions of Glory* strengthens our meeting with
the living God, focused in Jesus Christ.

'If you had known me, you would have known my Father also; henceforth you know him
and have seen him.'

Philip said to him, 'Lord, show us the Father, and we shall be satisfied.' Jesus said to
him, 'Have I been with you so long, and yet you do not know me, Philip? He who has seen
me has seen the Father; how can you say, "Show us the Father"? Do you not believe that I
am in the Father and the Father in me? The words that I say to you I do not speak on my
own authority; but the Father who dwells in me does his works. Believe me that I am in the
Father and the Father in me; or else believe me for the sake of the works themselves.'

John 14:7–11

... of Christ, in whom are hid all the treasures of wisdom and knowledge.

Colossians 2:2–3

For in him the whole fulness of deity dwells bodily, and you have come to fulness of life in
him.

Colossians 2:9–10

... looking to Jesus the pioneer and perfecter of our faith.

Hebrews 12:2

Jesus is not a figure in a book; He is a living presence.

William Barclay, *The Gospel of Matthew*, The Saint Andrew Press, 1965, volume 1, page 234

Jesus Christ did not come into the world to make life easy; he came to make men great.

Anon.

We need the personal allegiance of love to Christ—such a presentation of Him through the imagination of our minds as will draw forth the soul's enthusiasm and secret life.

Henry Ward Beecher, *Proverbs from Plymouth Pulpit*, Charles Burnet & Co., 1887, page 148

Two thousand years ago, there was One here on this earth who lived the grandest life that ever has been lived yet, a life that every thinking man, with deeper or shallower meaning, has agreed to call Divine.

F.W. Robertson, *Lectures and Addresses*, Smith, Elder & Co., 1858, page 77

But the Wind of heav'n
bloweth where it listeth, and Christ yet walketh the earth,
and talketh still as with those two disciples once
on the road to Emmaus.

Robert Bridges, *The Testament of Beauty*, iv. 1399, Oxford at the Clarendon Press, 1930, page 190

All his loveliness and his glory he keeps for the house of the soul, and there it is that he takes pleasure. Many are the times he comes to the man who lives the inward life, and to him he grants sweet conversation, glad comfort, great peace and amazing friendship.

Thomas à Kempis, *The Imitation of Christ*, translated by Betty I. Knott, William Collins Sons & Co., 1979, page 83

Christ in us and we in Him! Why should the activity of God and the presence of the Son of Man within us not be real and observable? Every day I am thankful to God that I have been allowed to experience the reality of the Divine Image within me.

C.G. Jung, in F.C. Happold, *Religious Faith and Twentieth-Century Man*, Darton, Longman & Todd, 1980, page 71

His is easily the dominant figure in history... A historian without any theological bias whatever should find that he simply cannot portray the progress of humanity honestly without giving a foremost place to a penniless teacher from Nazareth.

H.G. Wells, in William Barclay, *The Gospel of Matthew*, The Saint Andrew Press, 1965, volume 2, page 87

Look on our divinest Symbol: on Jesus of Nazareth, and his Life... and what followed therefrom. Higher has the human Thought not yet reached... a Symbol of quite perennial infinite character; whose significance will ever demand to be anew inquired into, and anew made manifest.

Thomas Carlyle, *Sartor Resartus*, Ward, Lock & Co., page 149

... the Lord suggests that His union with the Father is no more than the perfect form of a relationship open to others and in a certain measure achieved by some; what He has claimed in the phrase censured by the Jews (John 10:32–39) is not necessarily anything unique. It is the perfect Sonship.

William Temple, *Readings in St. John's Gospel*, First and Second Series, Macmillan and Co., 1947, page 173

This Jesus Christ has, somehow, touched, and changed, and set free my soul, my being. He, and only He—His Name, His Person—has had a power over me which is like nothing else. The more I have seen, trusted, loved Him, the more always I have stood clear of sin, of self. I cannot but love Him still.

Handley C.G. Moule, Jesus and the Resurrection, Seeley and Co., 1893, page 8

The immortal Figure of Christ, God's pattern for humanity, stands over against life; and judges it by irradiating it. He sets the standard, shows what man is meant to be, revealing Himself in every demand on our generosity, however homely, and by that demand alone and our response to it separating the real from the unreal, the living from the dead.

Evelyn Underhill, in John Stobbart, editor, The Wisdom of Evelyn Underhill, A.R. Mowbray & Co., 1951, page 10

What was Christ's life? Not one of deep speculations, quiet thoughts, and bright visions, but a life of fighting against evil; earnest, awful prayers and struggles within, continued labour of body and mind without; insult, and danger, and confusion, and violent exertion, and bitter sorrow. This was Christ's life. This was St. Peter's, and St. James's, and St. John's life afterwards.

Charles Kingsley, Daily Thoughts, Macmillan and Co., 1884, page 45

Christ's communion with His Father was the life-centre, the point of contact with Eternity, whence radiated the joy and power of the primitive Christian flock: the classic example of a corporate spiritual life. When the young man with great possessions asked Jesus, 'What shall I do to be saved?' Jesus replied in effect, 'Put aside all lesser interests, strip off unrealities, and come, give yourself the chance of catching the infection of holiness from Me!'

Evelyn Underhill, in John Stobbart, editor, The Wisdom of Evelyn Underhill, A.R. Mowbray & Co., 1951, page 15

It is that experience of unity with God which was constantly both the joy and suffering of Christ: it led Him to be driven by the Spirit into the wilderness because the moment that a man is going to be seriously used by God he will be driven out into the wilderness, he will be driven into the wilderness of the discovering of his real self (i.e. the reality of God in him), tormented by the demon of the false-self which will constantly try to hide the real in the superficial: this tormenting and yet important act of self-discovery can only be done in solitude.

Douglas Rhymes, Prayer in the Secular City, Lutterworth Press, 1967, page 31

It is not Jesus as historically known, but Jesus as spiritually arisen within men, who is significant for our time and can help it. Not the historical Jesus, but the spirit which goes forth from Him and in the spirits of men strives for new influence and rule, is that which overcomes the world...

   The abiding and eternal Jesus is absolutely independent of historical knowledge, and can only be understood by contact with His spirit which is still at work in the world. In proportion as we have the Spirit of Jesus we have the true knowledge of Jesus.

Albert Schweitzer, in George Seaver, Albert Schweitzer: Christian Revolutionary, James Clarke & Co., 1944,
page 104

A Jesus who walked through the world knowing exactly what the morrow would bring, knowing with certainty that three days after his death his Father would raise him up, is a Jesus who can arouse our admiration, but still a Jesus far from us. He is a Jesus far from a mankind that can only hope in the future and believe in God's goodness, far from a mankind that must face the supreme uncertainty of death with faith but without knowledge of what is beyond. On the other hand, a Jesus for whom the future was as much a mystery, a dread, and a hope as it is for us and yet, at the same time, a Jesus who could say, 'Not my will but yours'—this is a Jesus who could effectively teach us how to live, for this is a Jesus who would have gone through life's real trials.

Raymond E. Brown, S.S., *Jesus, God and Man*, Geoffrey Chapman, 1968, page 104

The bottomless and abysmal nature of the human soul comes first into clear revelation in the Person of Christ, who is... truly and essentially both God and Man. In Christ the invisible, eternal, self-existent God has clothed Himself with flesh and become Man, has made Himself visible and vocal to our spiritual eyes and ears, and in Christ God has given us an adequate goal and norm of life, a perfect pattern... to walk by and live by. Here we can see both the character of God and the measure of His expectation for us. But we must not stop with the Christ after the flesh, the Christ without. He first becomes our life and salvation when He is born within us and is revealed in our hearts, and has become the Life of our lives.

Rufus M. Jones, *Spiritual Reformers in the 16th and 17th Centuries*, Macmillan and Co., 1914, page 54

I find it marvellous that Jesus lived for thirty hidden years in Nazareth with his mother and Joseph. No one yet knew he was the Christ, the son of God. He lived family and community life in humility, according to the Beatitudes. He worked with wood and lived the small happenings of a Jewish community in the love of his Father. It was only after he had lived the good news of love that he went out to preach it. The second period of his life was the time of struggle, when he tried to get his message across and used signs to confirm his authority. It seems to me that some Christians are in danger of talking too much about things they do not live: they have their theories on what makes for the 'good life' without knowing whether it is possible, because they haven't lived it. The hidden life of Jesus is the model for all community life.

The third stage of his life was the one when his friends deserted him, and he was persecuted by people outside his community. People who are committed to a community can also go through this third period.

Jean Vanier, *Community and Growth*, Darton, Longman & Todd, 1991, page 302

The poor and the weak have revealed to me the great secret of Jesus. If you wish to follow him you must not try to climb the ladder of success and power, becoming more and more important. Instead, you must walk *down* the ladder, to meet and walk with people who are broken and in pain. The light is there, shining in the darkness, in the darkness of their poverty. The poor with whom you are called to share your life are perhaps the sick and the old; people out of work, young people caught up in the world of drugs, people angry because they were terribly hurt when they were young, people with disabilities or sick with AIDS, or just out of prison; people in slums or ghettos, people in far-off lands where there is much hunger and suffering, people who are oppressed because of the colour of their skin, people who are lonely in overcrowded cities, people in pain.

We are discovering too that the life-giving Jesus is hidden in them. He is truly there. If you become a friend of the poor, you become a friend of Jesus.

If you enter a close relationship with those who are poor, you enter into an intimate relationship with Jesus and you will be led into the heart of the Beatitudes.

Jean Vanier, *The Broken Body*, Darton, Longman & Todd, 1988, page 72

Jesus Christ takes as man a place alike in the realms of ethics and of faith. He gives to us the moral standard of life, the ethical ideal; He discloses the culminating power of the religious consciousness, for He is, in the deep harmony of his relationship with God, the mystic ideal also. While men were labouring to establish relationship with the unseen; while some, failing and despairing, broke into angry revolt against life, and others, deceiving themselves, reached a false repose by shutting out of sight the facts of ugly moral problems; Jesus Christ, keenly alive to evil and warm to defend the weak and the oppressed, keeping the ethical standard high and the ethical perception clear, lived a life of simple and unruffled heart repose. He realizes, and we see that He realizes, the double ideal, the ideal of righteousness and of inward peace. He realizes the perfect harmony, the peace which is no counterfeit; He lives a human life, but we feel that He lives all the time in the serene atmosphere of Heaven. In Him we get a glimpse of what the soul is whose birth and being are from the eternal love. He seems something more than a soul filled with the divine; He seems to be one whose manhood is taken into God, and we no longer wonder that His utterances are sweet and satisfying; we listen to Him, and His teaching comes to us fresh as the breath of the sea and musical as the sound of falling rain.

Bishop Boyd Carpenter, *The Witness to the Influence of Christ*, Archibald Constable & Co., 1905, page 59

JUDGMENT

Judgment—criticism, critical faculty; judgment of mankind by God

There is an old American Indian proverb which goes something like this: 'Don't judge any man until you have walked two moons in his moccassins.' I think this is excellent advice for us to take, especially when tempted to criticize or judge others. Albert Camus states a crucial point on 'Judgment' in his book *The Fall*. 'Don't wait for the Last Judgement,' he writes, 'it takes place every day.' Our tendency is to project judgment into the future—as something which might (or might not) happen at the end of our lives, or at the end of the world. This, we think, helps us. Judgment is kept at a safe distance and made to appear irrelevant in our everyday lives. We then feel free to behave as we like, and if need be, face the consequences later. Here a certain awareness is required. We remember people are not punished *for* their sins but *by* them. I know from my own experience that when I have misbehaved, I have had to face the consequences straight-away. In the parable of the last judgment—about the sheep and the goats—the touchstone question was love. Those who inherited the kingdom were those who responded to the needs of those around them. The acid test was, 'as you did it to the least of these my brethren, you did it to me.'

Hubert van Zeller spells this out perfectly. 'At the judgement I shall be asked if I have loved. If I am not failed on this once and for all, I shall be asked further if I have believed and obeyed, accepted and trusted, prayed and followed as best I could the light that was given me.'

Those who plow iniquity and sow trouble reap the same.

Job 4:8

For God will bring every deed into judgment, with every secret thing, whether good or evil.

Ecclesiastes 12:14

Do not judge by appearances, but judge with right judgment.

John 7:24

God is not mocked, for whatever a man sows, that he will also reap.

Galatians 6:7

Don't wait for the Last Judgment. It takes place every day.

Albert Camus, *The Fall*, translated by Justin O'Brien, Hamish Hamilton, 1957, page 83

... every man must be allowed to judge himself; but he must not be allowed to bury the evidence.

Morris West, *The Salamander*, Heinemann/Octopus, 1977, page 538

Judgement: men of holy hearts and lives best understand holy doctrines and things. Those who have not the *temper* of religion, are not competent judges of the things of religion.

Benjamin Whichcote, *Moral and Religious Aphorims*, iii. 285, Elkin, Mathews & Marrot, 1930

There is to be a day of reckoning. There is a judgment day in the bones, and in the nerves, and in the stomach; in the heart and in the brain.

Henry Ward Beecher, *Proverbs from Plymouth Pulpit*, Charles Burnet & Co., 1887, page 191

In the book of Revelation St John sees in vision the dead standing before God and being judged from books of record. These books are not the book of life, for that is mentioned separately. It has been suggested that they are the books of memory and character.

George Appleton, *Journey for a Soul*, William Collins Sons & Co., 1976, page 228

The world thought that it was judging Christ when Caiaphas rent his clothes, and the people shouted, 'He is worthy of death,' and Pilate gave sentence as they desired. But we know that it was they, and not He, upon whom sentence was then passed.

William Temple, *Readings in St. John's Gospel*, First and Second Series, Macmillan and Co., 1947, page 287

I saw that His love was our judgement; that as the eye must quail before the light of the sun because of the exceeding brightness of that light, so the soul must quail before His love because of the exceeding splendour of that love; and that that love was the greatest of all forces, the perfection of all power.

Father Andrew, S.D.C., *A Gift of Light*, selected and edited by Harry C. Griffith, A.R. Mowbray & Co., 1968, page 20

We can approach God only if we do so with a sense of coming to judgement. If we come having condemned ourselves; if we come because we love him in spite of the fact that we are unfaithful, if we come to him, loving him more than a godless security, then we are open to him and he is open to us, and there is no distance; the Lord comes close to us in an act of compassionate love.

Anthony Bloom, *The Essence of Prayer*, Darton, Longman & Todd, 1989, page 8

What is it like there, in the fields of Hades where the sun does not rise or set, nor seasons alter? Nor do men change; for where change is, life is, and these, who are only shadows of lives past, must keep forever the shape of their earthly selves, whatever they made of them when they walked in daylight. Need the gods judge us further? Surely that is sentence enough, to live with our selves, and to remember.

Mary Renault, *The Bull from the Sea*, Longmans, Green and Co., 1962, page 13

It will not be a case of a puzzled anxious prisoner in the dock waiting in trepidation to hear the verdict of the judge, but one who judges himself. To see burning holiness and then to look at one's own pitiful selfishness and uncleanness, will make one cry out with Isaiah

'Woe is me!' To see perfect love and then to look at one's own mean, miserly soul, will need no verdict and sentence. I shall know: my only hope lies in the fact that judgement has been committed to our Lord, and he is Saviour as well as Lord.

George Appleton, *Journey for a Soul*, William Collins Sons & Co., 1976, page 228

A man in the end will be judged, not by any single act or stage in his life, but by his whole life. Judgment cannot come until the end. A man may make a great mistake, and then redeem himself and, by the grace of God, atone for it by making the rest of life a lovely thing. A man may live an honourable life and then in the end wreck it all by a sudden collapse into sin. No one who only sees the part of a thing can judge the whole thing; and no one who knows only a part of a man's life can judge the whole man.

William Barclay, *The Gospel of Matthew*, The Saint Andrew Press, 1965, volume 2, page 83

No man can justly censure or condemne another, because, indeed no man truly knowes another. This I perceive in my selfe; for I am in the darke to all the world, and my nearest friends behold mee but in a cloud; ... Further, no man can judge another, because no man knowes himselfe; for we censure others but as they disagree from that humour which wee fancy laudable in our selves, and commend others but for that wherein they seeme to quadrate and consent with us. So that in conclusion, all (judgement of others) is but that we all condemne, selfe love.

Sir Thomas Browne, *Religio Medici*, ii. 4, in Geoffrey Keynes, editor, *The Works of Sir Thomas Browne*, Faber and Faber, 1964, volume 1, page 76

He draws us by His love; and men are never so free as when they act from the love in their hearts which love shown to them has called forth. If, then, I come by my own will yet because the Father draws me, so also it is the Father who is taking me away if I depart by my own will. He offers me the love divine; it draws me or repels me, according to the condition of my will. It had repelled Judas ... His going was an act of defiance on his part; it was an act of condemnation and execution on the part of God. This is the thought of judgement everywhere present in this Gospel.

William Temple, *Readings in St. John's Gospel*, First and Second Series, Macmillan and Co., 1947, page 255

... Let us judge ourselves sincerely; let us not vainly content ourselves with the common disorders of our lives, the vanity of our expenses, the folly of our diversions, the pride of our habits, the idleness of our lives, and the wasting of our time, fancying that these are such imperfections as we fall into through the unavoidable weakness and frailty of our natures; but let us be assured, that these disorders of our common life are owing to this, that we have not so much Christianity as to intend to please God in all the actions of our life, as the best and happiest thing in the world.

William Law, *A Serious Call to a Devout and Holy Life*, J.M. Dent & Co., 1898, page 21

In all occasions of challenge and difficulty and suffering the presence of God is both our encouragement and our judge. God's presence is not with us a critical presence, although He cannot be other than a perfect judge. He can only help us perfectly because His judgement is perfect. The only artist who can perfectly help the student is the one whose judgement is absolutely accurate and whose mastery of his art is equally sure. The judgement of God is not the judgement of one who wants to find out where we are wrong in order to condemn us, but the judgement of one who knows we are wrong and wants to help us. So we go on from the common occasions of life to the bigger occasions. When there is something difficult to do, we feel that God is watching us, hoping that we shall play our part, and the thought of His presence will be both a judgement and an encouragement.

It is what *He* thinks that matters, and purity of intention in the big things of life will keep the soul in peace.

Father Andrew, S.D.C., *The Way of Victory*, A.R. Mowbray & Co., 1938, page 28

Remember particularly that you cannot be a judge of anyone. For there can be no judge of a felon on earth, until the judge himself recognizes that he is just such a felon as the man standing before him, and that perhaps he is more than anyone responsible for the crime of the man in the dock. When he has grasped that, he will be able to be a judge. However absurd that may sound, it is true. For if I had been righteous myself, there would, perhaps, have been no criminal standing before me. If you are able to take upon yourself the crime of the man standing before you and whom your heart is judging, then take it upon yourself at once and suffer for him yourself, and let him go without reproach. And even if the law itself makes you his judge, then act in the same spirit as much as you can, for he will go away and condemn himself more bitterly than you have done. If, however, he goes away indifferent to your kisses and laughing at you, do not let that influence you, either; it merely means that his time has not yet come, but it will come in due course; and if it does not come, it makes no difference: if not he, then another in his place will understand and suffer, and will judge and condemn himself, and justice will be done. Believe that, believe it without a doubt, for therein lies all the hope and faith of the saints.

Fyodor Dostoyevsky, *The Brothers Karamazov*, translated by David Magarshack, Penguin Books, 1963, volume 1, page 378

KINGDOM OF GOD

*Kingdom of God—the central theme of the teaching of Jesus,
involving an understanding of his own person and work*

Oscar Wilde provided me with a clue in understanding the kingdom of God. In *De Profundis* he wrote that it is man's soul Christ is always looking for. He calls it 'God's kingdom' and finds it in every one. He compares it to little things, to a tiny seed, to a handful of leaven, to a pearl. That is because one realizes one's soul only by getting rid of all alien passions, all acquired culture, and all external possessions, be they good or evil.

This fits in very closely with the underlying vision in *Visions of Glory*. We recall the 'divine in-breathing' in the Genesis story of the creation of man. This ensured the presence of a tiny seed or spark of divine life in the centre of man's being. We see this coming fully to life in the person of our Lord. As he grew in wisdom and in stature, he found something of the Father in the depths of himself. After his baptism his life was increasingly permeated by the Holy Spirit, indicating a handful of leaven at work. According to St John he was life, light, truth, joy and love. A pearl had been purchased—at a great price—and the kingdom of God was established.

As a consequence of his life we can now find the kingdom of God within ourselves. The cost will be, as we have seen, getting rid of all alien passions, all acquired culture, and all external possessions, whether they are good or evil. We will need to pray, 'Thy Kingdom come; Thy will be done; in earth as it is in heaven.' Reflecting on the material in this section might also be a help.

The kingdom of heaven is like treasure hidden in a field, which a man found and covered up; then in his joy he goes and sells all that he has and buys that field. Again, the kingdom of heaven is like a merchant in search of fine pearls, who, on finding one pearl of great value, went and sold all that he had and bought it.

Matthew 13:44–46

The time is fulfilled, and the kingdom of God is at hand; repent, and believe in the gospel.

Mark 1:15

Neither shall they say, Lo, here! or, lo there! for, behold, the kingdom of God is within you.

Luke 17:21 (AV)

Unless one is born of water and the Spirit, he cannot enter the kingdom of God.

John 3:5

Here are the three pillars upon which the Kingdom of God is raised—faith venturing beyond the unprovable, love forgiving the unpardonable, and hope remaining expectant against all odds.

Colin Morris, *The Hammer of the Lord*, Epworth Press, 1973, page 135

The Kingdom of God is in you and he who searches for it outside himself will never find it, for *apart from God no one can either seek or find God, for he who seeks God, already in truth has Him.*

Rufus M. Jones, *Spiritual Reformers in the 16th and 17th Centuries*, Macmillan and Co., 1914, page 24

'The kingdom of God is within you'—it is written in the very constitution of our being. The laws of the Kingdom are the laws of our being, stamped within our very selves, therefore inescapable. When you revolt against them, you revolt against yourself.

E. Stanley Jones, *Mastery*, Hodder and Stoughton, 1956, page 199

The Kingdom of Heaven is not polite chatter, idle talk, a vague promise, it is an act, it is the encounter between two serious and genuine wills, it is a conversion to light, to love and to life itself, because God is Light, Love, and Life.

Carlo Carretto, *The Desert in the City*, translated by Barbara Wall, William Collins Sons & Co., 1983, page 48

For the orthodox Christian, the coming of the Kingdom is catastrophic and not the peaceful outcome of an ever-widening process of evolution, an intervention of God cutting right *into* history and not springing *from* it. He despairs of earth and lives in apocalyptic hopes of divine intervention.

Sir Sarvepalli Radhakrishnan, *Eastern Religions and Western Thought*, Oxford University Press, 1940, page 74

The kingdom of God is neither prince nor peasant, food nor drink, hat nor coat, here nor there, yesterday nor to-morrow, baptism nor circumcision, nor anything whatever that is external, but peace and joy in the Holy Spirit, unalloyed love out of a pure heart and good conscience, and an unfeigned faith.

Rufus M. Jones, *Spiritual Reformers in the 16th and 17th Centuries*, Macmillan and Co., 1914, page 59

The signs of Christ's kingdom need to be given not only in inner transformations in the soul, but in acts of power in the physical and psychological spheres and, especially, in concrete forms in the life of the local body which he calls to represent him—so that everywhere evidence may be given of the Lord's reign.

Thomas A. Smail, *Reflected Glory*, Hodder and Stoughton, 1975, page 58

...the Church does not, in her full existence ... look forward. She looks centrally, she looks at that which is not to be defined in terms of place and time. It is either the nature of God at which she looks or the nature of things as known in God. It is *now* that the Kingdom of Heaven is fulfilled, generally and individually.

Charles Williams, *The Image of the City*, Oxford University Press, 1958, page 154

The kingdom of which we are speaking is a kingdom of love and it would be superficially, seemingly, so nice to enter it; yet it is not nice, because love has got a tragic side, it means death to each of us, the complete dying out of our selfish, self-centred self, and not dying out as a flower fades away but dying a cruel death, the death of the crucifixion.

Anthony Bloom, *The Essence of Prayer*, Darton, Longman & Todd, 1989, page 38

The kingdom of God, which the Christian wishes to share with others, involves the individual and the community of faith in a process of looking back to the life and ministry of Jesus, in a deep commitment to the present where the kingdom is to be more clearly recognized and established, and in a longing for the future when all the obstacles to the kingdom have been removed and the beauty and perfection of God's love is experienced in all its glory.

Trevor Beeson, *An Eye for an Ear*, SCM Press, 1972, page 28

... the message of God's kingdom is aimed at man in all his dimensions, not only at man's soul but at the *whole* man in his mental and material existence, in his whole concrete, suffering world. And it holds for *all* men; not only the strong, young, healthy, capable, whom the world so likes to exalt, but also the weak, sick, old, incapable, whom the world so likes to forget, to overlook, to neglect. Jesus did not merely talk, but also intervened in the field of sickness and injustice. He has not only the authority to preach, but also the charism of healing. He is not only *preacher* and *adviser.* He is at the same time *healer and helper.*

Hans Küng, *On Being a Christian*, translated by Edward Quinn, William Collins Sons & Co., 1977, page 237

As a matter of fact, that is the one business of man on earth—to co-operate with the divine power. All the activities of life—commercial, industrial, economic, social, political—should be, in their real nature, this co-operation with the divine power for the advancement of humanity. It is not alone when one is ministering to the helpless that he is co-operating with the purposes of God; but also when he is building railroads across the continent, carrying civilisation to new regions, and extending the possibilities of homes and of comfort and happy living; when he is navigating the ocean or the air; when he is inventing new mechanisms to serve the human race; when he is enforcing just and wise laws.

Every avenue through which the forces that make for nobler living may extend themselves is an avenue through which man may co-operate with God. Realising this, how can any hours be poor or desolate?

Lilian Whiting, *Lilies of Eternal Peace*, Gay and Hancock, 1908, page 34

What kind of kingdom will this be?

It will be a kingdom where, in accordance with Jesus' prayer, God's name is truly hallowed, his will is done on earth, men will have everything in abundance, all sin will be forgiven and all evil overcome.

It will be a kingdom where, in accordance with Jesus' promises, the poor, the hungry, those who weep and those who are downtrodden will finally come into their own; where pain, suffering and death will have an end.

It will be a kingdom that cannot be described, but only made known in metaphors: as the new covenant, the seed springing up, the ripe harvest, the great banquet, the royal feast.

It will therefore be a kingdom—wholly as the prophets foretold—of absolute righteousness, of unsurpassable freedom, of dauntless love, of universal reconciliation, of everlasting peace. In this sense therefore it will be the time of salvation, of fulfillment, of consummation, of God's presence: the absolute future.

Hans Küng, *On Being a Christian*, translated by Edward Quinn, William Collins Sons & Co., 1977, page 215

Dominating the whole realm of the moral ideas is the great conception of the Kingdom. It is essentially a *Social Ideal*, a glorious vision of a universe of souls bound together by love. In it, the supreme blessing is a common blessing, a blessing for all and a blessing for each. This Kingdom exists already on earth wherever the principle of love prevails. But its realisation here and now is imperfect. In its perfect form it is the absolute Ideal, the *Summum Bonum*, the great end which all human conduct should strive to realise, for which all should work and pray, and in the realisation of which all its members shall find their eternal realisation. Those who desire to enter this Kingdom must begin as little children. They must recognise their need, their spiritual poverty. They must repent. They must, that is, renounce the evil and worldly life and assume an attitude of spiritual receptivity. Then they will be in a position to acquire the pure heart and sincere mind which are essential to those who would finally arrive at that highest type of character which is modelled upon that of the Great Father Himself. The character of God, marked above all by the supreme attribute of love, is the *Ideal Character*. Thus, both on the side of conduct and on that of character, the moral teaching of our Lord is positive, not negative, as has so often been asserted. On the side of conduct, the rule to 'seek the Kingdom' is essentially an active principle; and on the side of character, the exaltation of the attribute of love throws the emphasis on the positive element in the moral life.

The Kingdom grows, not only in the heart and life of the individual, but also in the life of the human race. To this latter side of moral progress, our Lord devotes a number of striking parables. These teach us that the Kingdom is to be in the world as a great reorganising principle. Like the leaven, it is to spread through the whole till all is leavened. Here our Lord's teaching touches on the political and ecclesiastical organisations of the world, and implies that all will ultimately be made to subserve the coming of the Kingdom. The profound and prophetic character of this part of the teaching, taken together with the history of Christianity, especially in the earlier centuries, shows that our Lord did not omit from the range of His ethical vision all consideration of duty to the State, as superficial critics have frequently asserted.

Lastly, Christ kept steadily before Him the great final realisation of the Ideal. He constantly looked at the present in the light of the future, and He impressed most forcibly on the minds of His hearers the necessity of ever living and working with the great end in view. Thus, He knew, the worker would be lifted above the mere worldly standpoint and would be kept true to the master-rule of all high and holy living. He made His people pray, 'Thy Kingdom come.'

The wonderful presentation of the meaning of human life which we have just outlined would be a mere castle in the air, a thing wholly unpractical, if it were not grounded upon and strengthened by certain great religious ideas. What these ideas are we have already attempted to see. But it would . . . be truer to say that the moral ideas were made effective by a great revelation of God.

Foremost among the principles of this revelation is the Fatherhood of God. The Kingdom is founded in the nature of God. God is love, therefore the Kingdom is. This principle is the bed-rock which underlies every part of the Christian revelation. There is no element in it which does not go deep down below the surface of things to this ultimate truth. The Kingdom, Christ, His Work, His life, His death and resurrection, the functions of the Spirit, all rest upon the Love of the Father. And God is most fully revealed as the Father in the consciousness of Jesus.

There are certain apparently insuperable difficulties in the way of the coming of the Kingdom. There is man's spiritual blindness and the dullness of his heart. There is his selfishness, each one striving for a good which he claims to have and to enjoy without reference to his neighbour. There is sin in all its forms, mighty because of its hold upon man's corrupted nature, and because of its power in the world, that is, its hold upon the social life of man. There is evil as a power in the universe striving against the good.

Our Lord Himself is the means of overcoming these difficulties. He is Himself the revelation of God. He is the glory of God flashing out upon the darkness of this world, so that the dull eyes of sinful men may see it. He is the Love of God so presented that the hard hearts of men may be touched by it. As Incarnate God, He is Himself the bond of union between God and men, and among men of all conditions and races. By His life, death and resurrection He has overcome the evil, redeemed mankind and made pardon and reconciliation possible. By the power of His love He has given to man a moral power never before available. This great revelation of Divine Love and mercy gives to Jesus Christ a supreme claim upon the hearts of men, a claim which He urges with an imperativeness which cannot be mistaken. And why does He so urge His claim? Because faith in Him, the yielding to His claim, is the means by which the Kingdom is to be realised in the hearts and lives of men.

But Jesus Christ has gone from earth, and how can man trust in Him; and how can His army gain victory over evil, when the Lord Himself is not upon the scene of the conflict? But He is here, though unseen, by His great Representative, the Holy Ghost. There is a Divine superintendence of human thoughts and efforts. The Spirit of God is at work in the world, striving with the evil and overcoming it, guiding those who seek for guidance, giving power for moral conquest, overruling the course of this world, bringing in the Kingdom of Eternal Love.

Charles F. D'Arcy, D.D., *Ruling Ideas of Our Lord*, Hodder and Stoughton, 1901, page 135

KNOWLEDGE

Knowledge—the sum of what is known, as every branch of knowledge, personal knowledge, knowledge of God

I have been involved in the pursuit of knowledge as far back as I can remember. My teenage years were taken up in preparation for O and A levels, and these were followed by entrance exams for university. After a respite of two years, doing National Service, I specialized in one particular branch of knowledge and got a law degree.

As Chaplain of University College, Oxford, I am well aware that I belong to an academic institution. We have over forty tutors who are experts in various branches of knowledge, and studying, going to lectures, writing essays, attending tutorials and taking exams form a large part of college and university life. The pursuit of knowledge in the arts and sciences, and training the mind to think, are fundamental tasks of an academic institution.

Harry James Cargas reminds us of a distinction made between two types of knowledge—the knowledge of things created and self-knowledge. He suggests the two should be complementary and held in balance. As a pastoral chaplain most of my work is to do with self-knowledge, which at some point involves a knowledge of God. As William Barclay points out, to *know* God is not merely to have an intellectual knowledge of God. It is to have an intimate relationship with God. He likens this to sexual knowledge: 'Adam knew Eve his wife and she conceived.' Knowing God really means having an inner relationship with God. The material in *Visions of Glory* is designed to foster self-knowledge, leading to a fusion of the whole person.

Talk no more so very proudly, let not arrogance come from your mouth; for the Lord is a God of knowledge.

1 Samuel 2:3

If you cry out for insight and raise your voice for understanding, if you seek it like silver and search for it as for hidden treasures; then you will understand the fear of the Lord and find the knowledge of God. For the Lord gives wisdom; from his mouth come knowledge and understanding.

Proverbs 2:3–6

... to know the love of Christ which surpasses knowledge, that you may be filled with all the fulness of God.

Ephesians 3:19

That their hearts may be encouraged as they are knit together in love, to have all the riches of assured understanding and the knowledge of God's mystery, of Christ, in whom are hid all the treasures of wisdom and knowledge.

Colossians 2:2–3

To know yourself is to realise that you're at once unique and multiple.

Michel Quoist, *With Open Heart*, translated by Colette Copeland, Gill and Macmillan, 1983, page 40

But those who know do not theorize, they merely bear witness to what they have seen and experienced.

Kathleen Raine, *Defending Ancient Springs*, Oxford University Press, 1967, page 118

Ordinary knowledge is awareness of external facts; ordinary belief, conviction on inadequate grounds.

A.R. Orage, *On Love*, The Janus Press, 1957, page 57

I see more and more that the knowledge of one human being, such as love alone can give, and the apprehension of our own private duties and relations, is worth more than all the book learning in the world.

Charles Kingsley, *Daily Thoughts*, Macmillan and Co., 1884, page 151

The highest stage man can reach is to be conscious of his own thoughts and sentiments, to know himself. This affords him the cue for arriving at intricate knowledge even of personalities constituted differently from his own.

Johann Wolfgang von Goethe, *Wisdom and Experience*, selected by Ludwig Curtius, translated and edited by Hermann J. Weigand, Routledge & Kegan Paul, 1949, page 204

Deep subtle wits,
In truth, are master spirits in the world.
The brave man's courage, and the student's lore,
Are but as tools his secret ends to work,
Who hath the skill to use them.

Joanna Baillie, *Basil: A Tragedy*, II. iii, in *A Series of Plays*, Longmans, Hurst, Rees, Orme, and Brown, 1821, volume 1, page 101

The end then of Learning is to repair the ruines of our first Parents by regaining to know God aright, and out of that knowledge to love him, to imitate him, to be like him, as we may the nearest by possessing our souls of true virtue, which being united to the heavenly grace of faith makes up the highest perfection.

John Milton, in *The Works of John Milton*, Columbia University Press, 1931, volume 4, *Of Education*, page 277

What is more wonderful than the delight which the mind feels when it *knows*? This delight is not for anything beyond the knowing, but it is in the act of knowing. It is the satisfaction of a primary instinct. There may be also a divine purpose in this knowing, apart from the gratification of its creature.

Mark Rutherford, *Last Pages From a Journal*, Oxford University Press, 1915, page 282

Knowledge is not something to be packed away in some corner of our brain, but what enters into our being, colours our emotion, haunts our soul, and is as close to us as life itself. It is the over-mastering power which through the intellect moulds the whole personality, trains the emotions and disciplines the will.

Sir Sarvepalli Radhakrishnan, *Indian Philosophy*, George Allen & Unwin, 1923, volume 1, page 431

But though one may be a competent art critic without having ever handled a brush or a chisel, and may legitimately pass judgement upon a book which one could not have written oneself, in the life of the soul there are no such privileges... there is no knowledge at all unless it is also and equally action, and if it is not that, then it is worse than ignorance.

R.H.J. Steuart, S.J., *The Inward Vision*, Longmans, Green and Co., 1929, page 131

That glorious word *know*—it is God's attribute, and includes in itself all others. Love, truth—all are parts of that awful power of *knowing* at a single glance, from and to all eternity, what a thing is in its essence, its properties, and its relations to the whole universe through all Time. I feel awestruck whenever I see that word used rightly, and I never, if I can remember, use it myself of myself.

Charles Kingsley, *Daily Thoughts*, Macmillan and Co., 1884, page 79

He goes so far with his faith in the soul's possibility to return into 'the Original Centre of all Reality' that he declares that a man may sink deep enough into this Original Principle that binds his own soul into union with God so that he can penetrate by an inner Light and experience into the secret qualities and virtues hid in all visible and corporeal things, and may learn to discover the healing and curative powers of metals and plants, and may thus, by inward knowledge, advance all Arts and Sciences.

Rufus M. Jones, *Spiritual Reformers in the 16th and 17th Centuries*, Macmillan and Co., 1914, page 219

We do well to gather in every available fact which biology or anthropology or psychology can give us that throws light on human behaviour, or on primitive cults, or on the richer subjective and social religious functions of full-grown men. But the interior insight got from religion itself, the rich wholeness of religious experience, the discovery within us of an inner nature which defies description and baffles all plumb-lines, and which *can draw out of itself more than it contains*, indicate that we here have dealings with a type of reality which demands for adequate treatment other methods of comprehension than those available to science.

Rufus M. Jones, *Spiritual Reformers in the 16th and 17th Centuries*, Macmillan and Co., 1914, page xviii

What does it mean to know God?
(i) Undoubtedly there is an element of intellectual knowledge here. It means, at least in part, to know what God is like.
To know what God is like does make the most tremendous difference to life... We enter into a new life, we share something of the life of God Himself, when, through the work of Jesus, we discover what God is like. It is eternal life, God's life, to know what God is like.
(ii) But there is something else here. The Old Testament regularly uses the word *know* for sexual knowledge. 'Adam knew Eve his wife, and she conceived, and bare Cain' (Genesis 4:1). Now the knowledge of husband and wife is the most intimate knowledge that there can be. Husband and wife are no longer two; they are one flesh. The sexual act itself is not the important thing; the important thing is the intimacy of heart and mind and soul which ought to precede that act in true love. To *know* God is therefore not merely to have intellectual knowledge of God; it is to have an intimate personal relationship with God, which is like the nearest and dearest and most intimate relationship in life. Knowledge of God is not merely intellectual knowledge of God; it is a personal relationship with God.

William Barclay, *The Gospel of John*, The Saint Andrew Press, 1974, volume 2, page 243

Those for whom religion is real know and accept the reality of mystery. One of the world's great philosophers, Arthur North Whitehead, has said that the measure of a man's intellectual capacity is his sense of mystery, that not ignorance but the ignorance of ignorance is the death of knowledge, and that Mary who pondered in her heart the strange things said about Jesus had the deepest kind of knowledge. We are easily scared; we want to be safe.

Therefore, we do not lift our gaze far enough to see how much we do not and cannot know. The free mind focuses on the depths of mystery on which its clearest seeing must depend.

The thinking mind adjusted to religious distance lives, therefore, by faith. Things nearby he can see and in the light of what he sees he can work. Many things are within his control. He can prepare himself for life and plan to take such thought for living as is possible. The sun by day and the stars by night give light unto his path. But the deep distances and the awful depths he can neither know nor control. Therefore, he accepts mystery as his daily bread and finds in faith his security and his challenge. But although he cannot himself penetrate those distances, he can find One who has come from the region of mystery with the good news that from it he has nothing to fear. He can learn from Him that the God of the illimitable spaces and the deep darknesses is neither a void nor an enemy, but the Great Faithfulness within whom man's little life and knowledge are safely enveloped.

Nels F.S. Ferre, *Making Religion Real*, Harper & Brothers, 1955, page 19

There has long been a distinction made between two types of knowledge. There is the knowledge of things created, and this exerts a proper attraction on most of us. There is, more importantly, self-knowledge which, unfortunately, does not attract us nearly as much. Knowledge of that which is outside ourselves is very important and becomes a problem only when we make that the goal of our journey in life. It complements, in a very important way, self-knowledge but must be held in balance so as not to crowd out our search for the true interior of our beings. For it is deep within ourselves that the meaning of the universe is to be found. Very few persons throughout history seem to have learned the full value of this truth. Socrates is honoured for having taught his pupils to *know thyself*, but he has not been honoured with observance by most of humanity. So much of an emphasis is being placed on community, on social movements, on helping others in a relatively non-ordered way that such activity is used as an excuse to mask a significant observation: that it is too difficult for most of us to attempt to search ourselves for the meaning of the universe. The message the mystics have for us is that while there is indeed a very real world 'out there,' there is a more real world within each of us. What the meaning of this cosmic centre is, each must learn, individually. I am the living text for me and the only text. I cannot learn the lesson from what another has experienced or has written. Some can help me on the periphery, but the heart of the matter is in the heart of my soul. To ignore the *community of individuals* who are the true seekers, who are willing to wrestle and struggle with the difficulties that self-knowledge implies to gain the freedom and light that self-knowledge promises.

Harry James Cargas, *Encountering Myself*, SPCK, 1978, page 120

LIFE

*Life—period from birth to death, birth to the present time, or present
time to death; energy, liveliness, vivacity, animation; vivifying
influence, active part of existence*

'Remember, William, you only get out of life what you are prepared to put into it.' This was the main advice given to me by my parents when I was child. I put this into practice at school, and managed to strike a happy balance between friendships, sporting activities and academic studies. This laid a good foundation for later life. I was able to take National Service in my stride. Six months as a private soldier in the Devon and Dorsets proved to be an invaluable experience. I enjoyed the rigours of the four-month course at Mons Officer Cadet School, and learnt a great deal whilst there. Fourteen months in Singapore with the Gurkhas were one of the happiest periods of my life. I was fascinated by my three years as an undergraduate at Balliol. Perhaps this helps to explain why I have been a college chaplain for twenty-four years.

The quotation I like best in 'Life' is by Alexis Carrel: 'The secret of life is to be found in life itself; in the full organic, intellectual and spiritual activities of the body.' I am a great believer in physical fitness, and in the course of my life have played a great deal of sport. I try to think regularly and the spiritual dimension has become increasingly important to me. I now look to the one of whom it was written, 'In him was life,' and who came that we might 'have life, and have it abundantly'. Ultimately we have a vast resource of life in ourselves, in a unique combination of body, mind and spirit.

As for man, his days are like grass; he flourishes like a flower of the field; for the wind passes over it, and it is gone, and its place knows it no more. But the steadfast love of the Lord is from everlasting to everlasting upon those who fear him, and his righteousness to children's children.

Psalm 103:15–17

Has not the one God made and sustained for us the spirit of life? And what does he desire? Godly offspring. So take heed to yourselves.

Malachi 2:15

If any one thirst, let him come to me and drink. He who believes in me, as the scripture has said, 'Out of his heart shall flow rivers of living water.'

John 7:37–38

I came that they may have life, and have it abundantly.

John 10:10

The secret of life is to be found in life itself; in the full organic, intellectual and spiritual activities of our body.

Alexis Carrel, *Reflections on Life*, translated by Antonia White, Hamish Hamilton, 1952, page 76

Life, as Christianity has always taught, as all clear-eyed observers have known, is a perilous adventure, and a perilous adventure for men and nations it will, I fear and believe, remain.

W. Macneile Dixon, *The Human Situation*, Edward Arnold & Co., 1937, page 50

Life is a unique experience. There is nothing with which to compare it, no measure of its value in terms of some other thing, and money will not purchase it. Yet with this pearl of price we know not what to do.

W. Macneile Dixon, *The Human Situation*, Edward Arnold & Co., 1937, page 85

Life, I repeat, is energy of love
Divine or human; exercised in pain,
In strife, and tribulation; and ordained,
If so approved and sanctified, to pass,
Through shades and silent rest, to endless joy.

William Wordsworth, *The Excursion*, v. 1012, in E. de Selincourt and Helen Darbishire, editors, *The Poetical Works of William Wordsworth*, Oxford at the Clarendon Press, 1959

A woman ... recalls on one occasion when, as a girl, she complained of her hardships, and her mother, who was of pioneer stock, turned on her. 'See here,' said the mother, 'I have given you life; that is about all I will ever be able to give you—life. Now stop complaining and do something with it.'

Harry Emerson Fosdick, *On Being a Real Person*, Harper & Row, 1943, page 77

In what concerns God:
To suffer and offer.
In what concerns others:
To give myself, to pour out myself.
In what concerns me:
To be silent and forget myself.

Elizabeth Leseur, *A Wife's Story—The Journal of Elizabeth Leseur*, Burns & Oates, 1919, page 136

We come fully to life only in meeting one another ... and because we do come fully to life in that meeting we appear to have met not only one another but also God. We appear to have met God in one another, to have addressed God, to have been stirred with a breath of God. Yet that breath is not a breath of immortality but a breath of eternal life.

John S. Dunne, *The Reasons of the Heart*, SCM Press, 1978, page 123

You ask me my theory of life. It is represented in one word, *will*... Life is short, even for those of us who live a long time, and we must live for the few who know and appreciate us, who judge and absolve us, and for whom we have the same affection and indulgence. We ought to hate very rarely, as it is too fatiguing, remain indifferent a great deal, forgive often, and never forget.

Sarah Bernhardt, in Alan Arnold, *Sarah*, Severn House, 1977, page 189

Today, life is a choice of insanities.
Success, failure, love, chastity, debauchery, money or soviets
It is a string of insanities.
All insane.

Why not stay out, and learn to contain oneself?

D.H. Lawrence, 'Today', in Vivian de Sola Pinto and Warren Roberts, *The Complete Poems of D.H. Lawrence*, William Heinemann, 1967, volume 2, page 839

I want to prepare you, to organise you for life, for illness, crisis, and death . . . Live all you can—as complete and full a life as you can find—do as much as you can for others. Read, work, enjoy—love and help as many souls—do all this. Yes—but remember: Be alone, be remote, be away from the world, be desolate. Then you will be near God!

Baron Friedrich von Hügel, *Letters to a Niece*, J.M. Dent & Sons, 1929, page xi

How small a portion of our life it is that we really enjoy! In youth we are looking forward to things that are to come; in old age we are looking backwards to things that are gone past; in manhood, although we appear indeed to be more occupied in things that are present, yet even more that is too often absorbed in vague determination to be vastly happy on some future day, when we have time.

Charles Caleb Colton, *Lacon*, William Tegg, 1866, page 135

Margaret [Schlegel] realized the chaotic nature of our daily life, and its difference from the orderly sequence that has been fabricated by historians. Actual life is full of false clues and signposts that lead nowhere. With infinite effort we nerve ourselves for a crisis that never comes. The most successful career must show a waste of strength that might have removed mountains, and the most unsuccessful is not that of a man who is taken unprepared, but of him who has prepared and is never taken.

E.M. Forster, *Howards End*, Penguin Books, 1981, page 114

. . . Life is the spark which kindles up a soul and opens its capacities to receive the great lessons which it is appointed to learn of the Universe—of Good—of Evil—of accountability—of Eternity, of Beauty, of Happiness. The inestimable moment in which the history of past ages is opened, its own relations to the Universe explained, its dependence and independence shewn; the time to reach itself the affections, and to gratify them, to ally itself in kindly bonds with other beings of like destiny; the time to educate a citizen of unknown spheres; the time to serve the Lord.

Ralph Waldo Emerson, *Journals*, Constable & Co., 1909, volume 1, page 126

One indwelling Life, one animating Soul, lives in and moves through the whole mighty frame of things and expresses its Life through visible things in manifold ways, as the invisible human soul expresses itself through the visible body. Everything is thus, in a fragmentary way, a focus of revelation for the Divine Spirit, whose garment is this vast web of the visible world. But man in a very special way, as a complete microcosm, is a concentrated extract, a comprehensive quintessence of the whole cosmos, visible and invisible—an image of God and a mirror of the Universe.

Rufus M. Jones, *Spiritual Reformers in the 16th and 17th Centuries*, Macmillan and Co., 1914, page 133

If we ask ourselves what *is* life, in its reality, we know that it is not simply existence, that existence which we share with plants and animals. The life of the flower is an expression of vegetable existence, and the life of the animal is the expression of instinctive existence, but when we talk about human life we mean something more than that. It is not something that has its beginning and end in our physical being. Human life is the expression of a spiritual existence, which we know has its glory in spiritual values and in spiritual beauty. 'In the way of righteousness is life,' not in the way of riches or prosperity or health or happiness, but in the way of righteousness which is revealed to be nothing else than the purity of love.

Father Andrew, S.D.C., *The Way of Victory*, A.R. Mowbray & Co., 1938, page 146

Here is a picture-map of the country through which we must expect to travel. First comes the region of beginnings—a wonderful place. It is a green and pleasant land, full of the sights and sounds of spring-time. This is the time of 'conversion' or of a new start. This is followed by a vast expanse of wilderness, with its own lights and shadows, but with much toiling through the shifting sands, or walking along narrow paths through dark and arid gorges—a time of hard going, broken only now and again by an open valley among the mountains, or by an oasis in the sandy desert. This region symbolizes a period in life which is full of difficulty, a time when we are even tempted to give up the journey and settle down at the next stopping-place, or even to lie down and die. This central wilderness is ten times the length of the first region.

Olive Wyon, On the Way, SCM Press, 1958, page 42

Most of the time we tend to think of life as a neutral kind of thing, I suppose. We are born into it one fine day, given life, and in life itself is neither good nor bad except as we make it so by the way that we live it. We may make a full life for ourselves or an empty life, but no matter what we make of it, the common view is that life itself, whatever life is, does not care one way or another any more than the ocean cares whether we swim in it or drown in it. In honesty one has to admit that a great deal of the evidence supports such a view. But rightly or wrongly, the Christian faith flatly contradicts it. To say that God is spirit is to say that life does care, that the life-giving power that life itself comes from is not indifferent as to whether we sink or swim. It wants us to swim. It is to say that whether you call this life-giving power the Spirit of God or Reality or the Life Force or anything else, its most basic characteristic is that it wishes us well and is at work toward that end.

Heaven knows terrible things happen to people in this world. The good die young, and the wicked prosper, and in any one town, anywhere, there is grief enough to freeze the blood. But from deep within whatever the hidden spring is that life wells up from, there wells up into our lives, even at their darkest and maybe especially then, a power to heal, to breathe new life into us. And in this regard, I think, every man is a mystic because every man at one time or another experiences in the thick of his joy or his pain the power out of the depths of his life to bless him. I do not believe that it matters greatly what name you call this power—the Spirit of God is only one of its names—but what I think does matter, vastly, is that we open ourselves to receive it; that we address it and let ourselves be addressed by it; that we move in the direction that it seeks to move us, the direction of fuller communion with itself and with one another. Indeed, I believe that for our sakes this Spirit beneath our spirits will make Christs of us before we are done, or, for our sakes, it will destroy us.

Frederick Buechner, The Magnificent Defeat, Chatto and Windus, 1967, page 114

LIGHT

Light—mental illumination, elucidation, enlightenment, vivacity in a person's face, especially in the eyes, illumination of the soul by divine truth

At Bradford Cathedral we devised a special service for the feast of the Epiphany. The format consisted of lessons, carols and anthems, celebrating the manifestation of Christ (the light of the world) to the Gentiles. Once everyone was in place, lights were switched off and the service started in darkness—symbolic of a world without the light of Christ. Gradually as the service progressed, lights were switched on. By the end of the service the Cathedral was bathed in light. As I recall there was a particular sequence in the readings. The service began with the three wise men, following the star in the East to

Bethlehem, seeking the baby Jesus—a light to lighten the Gentiles. After a suitable item of music we moved to St John's Gospel and to an acknowledgment of light: 'In him was life, and the life was the light of men.' By the middle of the service the spotlight was on the words of Christ: 'I am the light of the world; he who follows me will not walk in darkness, but will have the light of life.' More lights were switched on, with the words: 'Believe in the light, that you may become sons of light,' closely followed by: 'You are the light of the world.' When all the lights had been switched on, we were dismissed with the words: 'Let your light so shine before men, that they may see your good works and glorify your Father who is in heaven.' The sequence of the service mirrored my own journey of faith—of finding light through the person of Jesus Christ.

Yea, thou art my lamp, O Lord, and my God lightens my darkness.

2 Samuel 22:29

The Lord is my light and my salvation; whom shall I fear? The Lord is the stronghold of my life; of whom shall I be afraid?

Psalm 27:1

You are the light of the world.

Matthew 5:14

I am the light of the world; he who follows me will not walk in darkness, but will have the light of life.

John 8:12

Of the great world of light that lies
Behind all human destinies.

Henry Wadsworth Longfellow, 'To a Child', in *The Poetical Works of Longfellow*, Oxford University Press, 1913, page 126

Open your heart to the influence of the light, which, from time to time, breaks in upon you.

Samuel Johnson, *The History of Rasselas*, Oxford University Press, 1971, page 124

A man should learn to detect and watch that gleam of light which flashes across his mind from within, more than the lustre of the firmament of bards and sages.

Ralph Waldo Emerson, 'Self-Reliance', in *The Works of Ralph Waldo Emerson*, George Bell & Sons, 1906, volume 1, *Essays* and *Representative Men*, page 23

Our little systems have their day;
They have their day and cease to be:
They are but broken lights of thee,
And thou, O Lord, art more than they.

Alfred, Lord Tennyson, 'In Memoriam A.H.H.', v, in *The Complete Works of Alfred Lord Tennyson*, Macmillan and Co., 1898, page 247

Before the Sun,
Before the Heavens thou wert, and at the voice
Of God, as with a Mantle didst invest
The rising world of waters dark and deep,
Won from the void and formless infinite.

John Milton, *Paradise Lost*, iii, in H.C. Beeching, editor, *The Poetical Works of John Milton*, Oxford at the Clarendon Press, 1900, page 8

... I thought the Light of Heaven was in this world: I saw it possible, and very probable, that I was infinitely beloved of Almighty God, the delights of Paradise were round about me, Heaven and earth were open to me, all riches were little things; this one pleasure being so great that it exceeded all the joys of Eden.

Thomas Traherne, Centuries, The Faith Press, 1969, page 129

Hail holy light, offspring of Heav'n first-born,
Or of th'Eternal Coeternal beam
May I express thee, unblam'd? since God is light,
And never but in unapproached light
Dwelt from Eternitie, dwelt then in thee,
Bright effluence of bright essence increate.

John Milton, Paradise Lost, iii. 1, in H.C. Beeching, editor, The Poetical Works of John Milton, Oxford at the Clarendon Press, 1900

Let there be Light, said God, and forthwith Light
Ethereal, first of things, quintessence pure
Sprung from the Deep, and from her Native East,
To journie through the airie gloom began,
Sphear'd in a radiant Cloud, for yet the Sun
Was not; she in a cloudie Tabernacle
Sojourn'd the while. God saw the Light was good.

John Milton, Paradise Lost, vii. 244, in H.C. Beeching, editor, The Poetical Works of John Milton, Oxford at the Clarendon Press, 1900

There is a healthy ferment of mind in which one struggles through chaos and darkness, by means of a few clues and threads of light—and—of one great bright pathway, which I find more and more to be *the* only escape from infinite confusion and aberration, *the* only explanation of a thousand human mysteries—I mean the Incarnation of our Lord—the fact that there really is—a God-Man!

Charles Kingsley, Daily Thoughts, Macmillan and Co., 1884, page 291

The doctrine of Christ in every man, as the indwelling Word of God, the Light who lights every one who comes into the world, is no peculiar tenet of the Quakers, but one which runs through the whole of the Old and New Testaments, and without which they would both be unintelligible, just as the same doctrine runs through the whole history of the Early Church for the first two centuries, and is the only explanation of them.

Charles Kingsley, Daily Thoughts, Macmillan and Co., 1884, page 259

The supreme experience of his life—and one of the most remarkable instances of 'illumination' in the large literature of mystical experiences—occurred when Boehme was twenty-five years of age, some time in the year 1600. His eye fell by chance upon the surface of a polished pewter dish which reflected the bright sunlight, when suddenly he felt himself environed and penetrated by the Light of God, and admitted into the innermost ground and centre of the universe. His experience, instead of waning as he came back to normal consciousness, on the contrary deepened.

Rufus M. Jones, Spiritual Reformers in the 16th and 17th Centuries, Macmillan and Co., 1914, page 159

Jesus said: 'He who follows me will not walk in darkness, but he will have the light of life.' The phrase *the light of life* means two things. In the Greek it can mean, either, the light which issues from the source of life, or, the light which gives life to men. In this passage it means both things. Jesus is the very light of God come among men; and Jesus is the light which gives men life. Just as the flower can never blossom when it never sees the sunlight, so our lives can never flower with the grace and beauty they ought to have until they are irradiated with the light of the presence of Jesus Christ.

William Barclay, *The Gospel of John*, The Saint Andrew Press, 1965, volume 2, page 13

It is wonderful to observe how plants will appear simply in answer to the presence of light, be it but a lamp. Go into a cave. Venture right into the underground world opened up by the spelaeologists. This is the realm of darkness. Here little grows. Yet if the spelaeologists have fixed lanterns here and there upon the walls of the tunnels, and have kept them continuously shining, green plants will grow around them. You can see them in Wookey Hole in Somerset; wherever there is a lamp, then growing in the crevices of the damp rock, we see a cluster of green vegetation. How did they get there? It is hard to say. Light had called them, and they came.

John Stewart Collis, *The Vision of Glory*, Charles Knight & Co., 1972, page 20

How shall I get true knowledge? Knowledge which will be really useful, really worth knowing. Knowledge which I shall know accurately and practically too, so that I can use it in daily life, for myself and others? Knowledge, too, which shall be clear knowledge, not warped or coloured by my own fancies, passions, prejudices, but pure and calm and sound; *Siccum Lumen*, 'Day Light,' as the greatest of philosophers called it of old.

To all such who long for light, that by the light they may live, God answers through His only begotten Son: 'Ask and ye shall receive, seek and ye shall find.'

Charles Kingsley, *Daily Thoughts*, Macmillan and Co., 1884, page 177

'The Light is the first Principle of Religion; for, seeing there can be no true Religion without the knowledge of God, and no knowledge of God without this Light, Religion must necessarily have this Light for its first Principle.' 'Without thyself, O Man,' he concludes, 'thou hast no means to look for, by which thou mayest know God. Thou must abide within thyself; to the Light that is in thee thou must turn thee; there thou wilt find it and nowhere else. God is nearest unto thee and to every man. He that goes forth of himself to any creature, thereby to know God, departs from God. God is nearer unto every man than himself, because He penetrates the most inward and intimate parts of man and is the Light of the inmost spirit. Mind, therefore, the Light that is in thee.'

Rufus M. Jones, *Spiritual Reformers in the 16th and 17th Centuries*, Macmillan and Co., 1914, page 130

There are times when we sense the light within us, urging us forth to delight in truth, the truth in our own being, the truth of the word of God, of reality, of people. The light urges us to separate ourselves from anything which is not true, from all that is darkness, lies of illusion, for we sense that it is the truth which will set us free.

We begin to love the universe, this extraordinary universe with the stars and the moon and the sun, the winds, the seasons, the lands, the animals and the people.

We begin to look at the music and the suffering of the world. We begin to discover the beauty of the word of God and we love it. And thus gradually lose our heaviness and we begin to grow in hope. The wings of our being come forth. We begin to urge and to yearn. We are reborn in hope.

This is the light which grows in us, which urges us on to greater understanding of the beauties of people and of the universe and gradually calls us forth to wonderment and contemplation. We begin to look at this universe and at Jesus with the eyes of a child, with the peace, the excitement, the adoration of a child. This is the light as it grows in us: to love reality.

Jean Vanier, *Be Not Afraid*, Griffin House, 1975, page 120

Beholding His Glory is only half our job. In our souls too the mysteries must be brought forth; we are not really Christians till that has been done. 'The Eternal Birth,' says Eckhart, 'must take place in *you*.' And another mystic says human nature is like a stable inhabited by the ox of passion and the ass of prejudice; animals which take up a lot of room and which I suppose most of us are feeding on the quiet. And it is there between them, pushing them out, that Christ must be born and in their very manger He must be laid—and they will be the first to fall on their knees before Him. Sometimes Christians seem far nearer to those animals than to Christ in His simple poverty, self-abandoned to God.

The birth of Christ in our souls is for a purpose beyond ourselves: it is because His manifestation in the world must be through us. Every Christian is, as it were, part of the dust-laden air which shall radiate the glowing Epiphany of God, catch and reflect His golden Light. *Ye are the light of the world*—but only because you are enkindled, made radiant by the One Light of the World. And being kindled, we have got to get on with it, be useful. As Christ said in one of His ironical flashes, 'Do not light a candle in order to stick it under the bed!' Some people make a virtue of religious skulking.

Evelyn Underhill, Light of Christ, Longmans, Green and Co., 1944, page 41

The sun is the source of material light, and all light comes from it. In the same way all spiritual light, the light of beauty of thought, of purity of love, of goodness in people everywhere, has come from the one source of light, which is God. We have the power of assimilating light, but we cannot of ourselves create light. If our eyes are normal, we can use the light though we cannot ourselves provide it. So we have spiritual eyes to see what is beautiful and fair, but we have not in ourselves the power of creating light.

Jesus is the Light of the World. He has taken a human nature and in that human nature He has set the light of the Divine Nature, so revealing what human nature was meant for. It was meant for this great end, that in it should shine the Divine Light. When we look at our Lord, we see a humanity which is utterly lovely and perfectly pure, and yet so completely human that to Him went those two types who more than any other cry out for what is human, the sinner and the child.

If people have bad eyes, they cannot stand the light. It is not the fault of the light, it is the fault of their eyes. If people do not love Jesus, it is always because they have had some wrong impression of Him, or because in some way their organs of spiritual vision have become diseased. God has given the light of the sun to bless our eyes, and the light of His dear Son to bless our souls, the true Light which shines upon every man.

Father Andrew, S.D.C., Meditations For Every Day, A.R. Mowbray & Co., 1941, page 122

MAN

*Man—a human being—male or female, the human race, inner,
outer, the spiritual, material parts of man*

During the Nigerian Civil War in 1968 I teamed up with an American, and we took in some relief supplies to Enugu. This garden city of the Eastern State had just been captured by the Federal forces, and there was a great need for food and medical supplies. The route took us through an area where a battle had recently been fought. We paused to look at a wrecked armoured-car, and were shocked to see the remains of a dead soldier in the driving seat. I was suddenly filled with a horror of war and angry at the destructive nature of man. Henry Ward Beecher, in this section, sums up accurately this aspect of human nature: 'There is the same fierce, destructive nature in man that there is in the lion and tiger; the same combative nature that there is in the wolf; the same cunning, artful nature that there is in the fox. We have not descended from animals, we are with them yet.' Happily this is only one aspect of human nature. Nikos Karantzakis restores the balance in his *Report to Greco*. He writes, 'Every man is half God, half man; he is both spirit and flesh.' As we have seen, man is made in the image and likeness of God, with a vast spiritual potential in the depths of his being. The lives of the saints furnish us with many examples of those who have made this a living reality. A change has taken place and basic human nature transformed into something wholesome and sublime. The saints would attribute this not to their own efforts but to the grace of God at work in their lives. They continue to be an inspiration to the human race.

God said, 'Let us make man in our image, after our likeness; and let them have dominion over the fish of the sea, and over the birds of the air, and over the cattle, and over all the earth, and over every creeping thing that creeps upon the earth.'

Genesis 1:26

Yet thou hast made him little less than God, and dost crown him with glory and honour. Thou hast given him dominion over the works of thy hands; thou hast put all things under his feet.

Psalm 8:5–6

Thus it is written, 'The first man Adam became a living being'; the last Adam became a life-giving spirit.

1 Corinthians 15:45

What is man that thou art mindful of him, or the son of man, that thou carest for him? Thou didst make him for a little while lower than the angels, thou hast crowned him with glory and honour, putting everything in subjection under his feet.

Hebrews 2:6–8

Christ is the one great typical man; and all high manhood necessarily conforms to Christ.

Henry Ward Beecher, Proverbs from Plymouth Pulpit, Charles Burnet & Co., 1887, page 148

A man passes for that he is worth. What he is engraves itself on his face, on his form, on his fortunes, in letters of light.

Ralph Waldo Emerson, 'Spiritual Laws', in *The Works of Ralph Waldo Emerson*, George Bell & Sons, 1906, volume 1, *Essays* and *Representative Men*, page 86

But man, cut off from his supra-human environment, may be dwarfed to an infra-human stature and become the slave of impersonal determinisms—as our civilization is now finding out.

F.R. Barry, *Secular and Supernatural*, SCM Press, 1969, page 57

For there's not a man
That lives who hath not known his god-like hours,
And feels not what an empire we inherit
As natural beings in the strength of Nature.

William Wordsworth, *The Prelude*, iii. 193, in E. de Selincourt and Helen Darbishire, editors, *The Poetical Works of William Wordsworth*, Oxford at the Clarendon Press, 1959, page 81

So long as a man is capable of self-renewal he is a living being ... The soul must be for ever recreating itself, trying all its various modes, vibrating in all its fibres, raising up new interests for itself.

Henri Frédéric Amiel, *Amiel's Journal*, translated by Mrs Humphry Ward, Macmillan and Co., 1918, page 186

The essence of man lies in this, in his marvellous faculty for seeking truth, seeing it, loving it, and sacrificing himself to it.—Truth, that over all who possess it spends the magic breath of its puissant health!

Romain Rolland, *John Christopher IV, The Journey's End*, translated by Gilbert Cannan, William Heinemann, 1913, page 395

There is the same fierce, destructive nature in man that there is in the lion and the tiger; the same combative nature that there is in the wolf; the same cunning, artful nature that there is in the fox. We have not descended from animals, we are with them yet.

Henry Ward Beecher, *Proverbs from Plymouth Pulpit*, Charles Burnet & Co., 1887, page 17

Man who man would be,
Must rule the empire of himself; in it
Must be supreme, establishing his throne
On vanquished will, quelling the anarchy
Of hopes and fears, being himself alone.

Percy Bysshe Shelley, 'Sonnet: Political Greatness', line 10, in Thomas Hutchinson, editor, *The Complete Poetical Works of Percy Bysshe Shelley*, Oxford University Press, 1935, page 636

What is an intelligent man? A man who enters with ease and completeness into the spirit of things and the intention of persons, and who arrives at an end by the shortest route. Lucidity and suppleness of thought, critical delicacy and inventive resource, these are his attributes.

Henri Frédéric Amiel, *Amiel's Journal*, translated by Mrs Humphry Ward, Macmillan and Co., 1918, page 254

Man has set up camp in a tiny little corner of himself. From time to time, he ventures out of his tent to fetch some water from a stream close by. But he never goes beyond the boundaries of his camp territory.

Man is undiscovered territory.

Michel Quoist, *With Open Heart*, translated by Colette Copeland, Gill and Macmillan, 1983, page 179

In every man there is a tension; every man is a walking civil war; there is a constant battle between the higher and the lower side of man; man is always torn between the desire for good and the desire for evil; he hates his sins and loves his sins at one and the same time.

William Barclay, *The Letters to the Galatians and Ephesians*, The Saint Andrew Press, 1958, page 77

In truth 'spiritual animal' wer a term for man
nearer than 'rational' to define the genus;
Faith being the humanizer of his brutal passions,
the clarifer of folly and medicine of care,
the clue to reality, and the driving motiv
of thatt self-knowledge which teacheth the ethick of life.

Robert Bridges, *The Testament of Beauty*, iv. 1132, Oxford at the Clarendon Press, 1930, page 179

If in the man Christ Jesus we have a man in perfect response to the acts of God through which we are related to him, then in the same Christ we have in actual and perfect expression the human pole of the relation between God and man, as redemption restores it under the conditions of our present life; and to know this would be to know the Christian doctrine of man in the only way possible to us here.

Austin Farrer, *Interpretation and Belief*, SPCK, 1976, page 76

Man? I am a man, thou art a woman—not by reason of bones and muscles, nerves and brain, which I have in common with apes, and dogs, and horses—I am a man, thou art a man or woman, not because we have a flesh, God forbid! but because there is a spirit in us, a divine spark and ray which nature did not give, and which nature cannot take away. And therefore, while I live on earth, I will live to the spirit, not to the flesh, that I may be indeed a man.

Charles Kingsley, *Daily Thoughts*, Macmillan and Co., 1884, page 89

... Man—as individual and as society—remains incapable of mastering his world, because he tries to cope with everything except himself. As he seems to be gaining the whole world, he is threatened with the loss of his own soul: in routine, bustling activity, endless talk, in disorientation and futility. This has little to do with the wickedness of man or of particular individuals. It is the legal constraints of the technocratic society itself, as we have seen, which threaten to crush man's personal dignity, freedom and responsibility.

Hans Küng, *On Being a Christian*, translated by Edward Quinn, William Collins Sons & Co., 1977, page 58

The fundamental fact of man's nature ... is personal *freedom*. Starting with no theological presuppositions he is under no obligation to make the primary assumption common to all Augustinian systems that man is devoid of any native capacities which have to do with spiritual salvation. He begins instead with man as he knows him—a sadly marred and hampered being, but still possessed of a potentially Divine nature, and capable of co-operating, by inward choices and decisions, with the ceaseless effort of God to win him completely to Himself.

Rufus M. Jones, *Spiritual Reformers in the 16th and 17th Centuries*, Macmillan and Co., 1914, page 22

The men we see in each other do not give us the image and likeness of God. The men we see are whipped through the world; they are harried, wrinkled, anxious; they all seem hacks of some invisible riders. How seldom we behold tranquillity! We have never seen a man. We do not know the majestic manners that belong to him, which appease and exalt the beholder. There are no divine persons with us, and the multitude do not hasten to be divine. And yet we hold fast, all our lives long, a faith in a better life, in better men, in clean and noble relations, notwithstanding our total inexperience of a true society.

Ralph Waldo Emerson, *Society and Solitude, Domestic Life*, J.M. Dent & Sons, 1912, page 58

... there is something in the 'very make of man' which links the human spirit to the Divine Spirit and which thus makes it as natural for man to be religious as it is for him to seek food for his body. There is a 'seminal principle,' 'a seed of God,' 'something that comes immediately from God,' in the very structure of man's inner nature, and this structural possession makes it as natural and proper for man's mind to tend toward God, 'the centre of immortal souls,' as it is for heavy things to tend toward their centre. 'God,' he elsewhere says, 'is more inward to us than our own souls,' and we are more closely 'related to God than to anything in the world.'

Rufus M. Jones, *Spiritual Reformers in the 16th and 17th Centuries*, Macmillan and Co., 1914, page 296

The Incarnation is the act of God. He was made man and dwelt among us, and in His manhood He was absolutely loyal to human nature and all its limitations. Our Lord had two great loyalties. One was His complete loyalty to His human nature. He met man's temptations with man's weapons and no others. He shared the limitations and conditions and the knowledge of the times in which He lived. He knew the aches and pains of man, the tiredness of man, the temptations of man, the agony of man, the death of man. He asked to be exempt from no handicap that human nature knows as human nature. That is one perfect loyalty which we see in Christ. The second is His perfect loyalty to divine ideals. In the spiritual sphere He was as loyal to the divine ideals as in the human sphere He was loyal to human limitations. As God in man's nature He interpreted God to man as perfectly as He, as man represented man to God.

Father Andrew, S.D.C., *Meditations for Every Day*, A.R. Mowbray & Co., 1941, page 22

... they took Adam as a type of the unspoiled man, and they saw writ large in him the possibilities and potentialities of man. What had been originally possible in Adam became, according to their thought, actual realization in Jesus Christ—the form and type of man, the true Head of the race—and in spite of the havoc and spoiling, which sin had wrought, that original possibility, that divine potentiality, still reappears in every child, who comes now, as Adam did, made in the image of God, with the breath of God in him, and with creative freedom of will to settle his own destiny. Some of the Reformers whom I am studying centre this image of God, this immense divine potentiality, in the ideal man, in man as God conceives him in his perfect state, or as God by His Grace intends him to be, and they do not go the whole bold way of asserting that this man we know, this man who lives in time and space, who loves and sins and suffers, has and always has, in the very structure of his inmost moral and rational being, a divine, unlost, inalienable, soul-centre which is unsundered from God, and bears eternal witness to our origin from Him, our potential likeness to Him, and our capacity to receive illumination from Him. But this latter bolder view of the inherent greatness of man's essential nature is the prevailing tendency of these men.

Rufus M. Jones, *Spiritual Reformers in the 16th and 17th Centuries*, Macmillan and Co., 1914, page xxxi

Every man is half God, half man; he is both spirit and flesh.

That is why the mystery of Christ is not simply a mystery for a particular creed; it is universal. The struggle between God and man breaks out in everyone, together with the longing for reconciliation. Most often this struggle is unconscious and short-lived. A weak soul does not often have the endurance to resist the flesh for very long. It grows heavy, becomes flesh itself, and the contest ends. But among responsible men, men who keep their eyes rivetted day and night upon the Supreme Duty, the conflict between flesh and spirit breaks out mercilessly and may last until death.

The stronger the soul and the flesh, the more fruitful the struggle and the richer the final harmony. God does not love weak souls and flabby flesh. The spirit desires to wrestle with flesh which is strong and full of resistance. It is a carnivorous bird which is incessantly hungry; it eats flesh and, by assimilating it, makes it disappear.

Struggle between flesh and the spirit, rebellion and resistance, reconciliation and submission, and finally—the supreme purpose of the struggle—union with God: this was the ascent taken by Christ, the ascent which He invites us to take as well, following in His bloody tracks.

Nikos Kazantzakis, *Report to Greco*, translated by Carmino J. deCatanzaro, Faber and Faber, 1973, page 290

MEDITATION

*Meditation—the verb means to plan mentally, design; exercise the
mind in contemplation on (upon) a subject, thinking about or
reflecting on something spiritual or religious*

I began meditation at theological college. We had an official quiet time each day, before breakfast, lasting for half an hour. When the weather was fine I used to go to the nearby University Parks and walk down to the river. I started with a sentence from the Psalms—'Be still and know that I am God'—and used to repeat this phrase quietly to myself as I strolled around the Parks. The beauty of nature added another dimension to the meditation. When the weather was bad I stayed in my room, and carried out the same exercise, sitting in a comfortable chair.

My practice of meditation slowly developed. I carefully searched the Scriptures and noted suitable phrases for meditation. Later I made a collection of short phrases and sentences from novels and spiritual classics. I then began to keep a spiritual diary or journal. With the aid of a pen and clipboard I would write out thoughts and feelings that came to the surface in meditation. A further stage was reached on discovering an anthology by Victor Gollancz—*A Year of Grace*. I decided to work through the contents systematically. It took six months to complete. Eventually I decided to compile my own anthology with material collected over the years. The result has been four compilations, *Visions of Faith, Hope, Love* and *Glory*. My hope is others might benefit from this valuable practice of meditation.

Blessed is the man who walks not in the counsel of the wicked, nor stands in the way of sinners, nor sits in the seat of scoffers; but his delight is in the law of the Lord, and on his law he meditates day and night. He is like a tree planted by streams of water, that yields its fruit in its season, and its leaf does not wither. In all that he does, he prospers.

Psalm 1:1–3

I will meditate on all thy work, and muse on thy mighty deeds. Thy way, O God, is holy.

Psalm 77:12–13

The good man out of the good treasure of his heart produces good... for out of the abundance of the heart his mouth speaks.

Luke 6:45

Whatever is true, whatever is honourable, whatever is just, whatever is pure, whatever is lovely, whatever is gracious, if there is any excellence, if there is anything worthy of praise, think about these things.

Philippians 4:8

He plainly began, while still very young, to revolt from the orthodox theology of his time, and his years of reading and of silent meditation and reflection were the actual preparation for what seemed finally to come to him like a sudden revelation, or, to use his own common figure, as 'a flash'.

Rufus M. Jones, *Spiritual Reformers in the 16th and 17th Centuries*, Macmillan and Co., 1914, page 155

A man will be effective to the degree that he is able to concentrate! Concentration is not basically a mode of *doing* but above all a mode of being.

We meditate to find, to recover, to come back to something of ourselves we once dimly and unknowingly had and have lost without knowing what it was or where or when we lost it.

Lawrence LeShan, *How to Meditate*, Turnstone Press, 1983, page 9

Mental prayer, by way of meditation, is very easy, even to the meanest capacities; it requires nothing but a good will, a sincere desire of conversing with God, by thinking of him, and loving him. In effect, the great business of mental prayer is *thinking* and *loving*; and who is there that can even live without *thinking* and *loving*?

Richard Challoner, in Gordon S. Wakefield, editor, *A Dictionary of Christian Spirituality*, SCM Press, 1986, page 85

After the act of the imagination there follows the act of the understanding, which we call meditation. This is nothing other than one or more considerations made in order to raise up our affections to God and heavenly things. Hence, meditation is different from study and other thoughts and reflections which do not have the love of God or our spiritual welfare for their object.

St Francis de Sales, *Introduction to the Devout Life*, translated and edited by John K. Ryan, Longmans, Green and Co., 1962, page 63

Within a cavern of man's trackless spirit
Is throned an Image, so intensely fair
That the adventurous thoughts that wander near it
Worship, and as they kneel, tremble and wear
The splendour of its presence, and the light
Penetrates their dreamlike frame
Till they become charged with the strength of flame.

Percy Bysshe Shelley, 'Cancelled passage of the Ode To Liberty', in Thomas Hutchinson, editor, *The Complete Poetical Works of Percy Bysshe Shelley*, Oxford University Press, 1935, page 604

After having placed yourself in the presence of God, by an act of loving faith, you must read something that is substantial, and stop gently upon it; not that you may reason, but only to fix your mind, remembering that the principal exercise ought to be the (practice of the presence) of God, and that the subject should serve more to stay your mind than to employ your reason.

Madame Guyon, *A Method of Prayer*, James Clarke & Co., 1902, page 9

Unless one takes the time to turn inward and be silent, meditation and the spiritual quest will not get very far. We seldom find God in a hurry, or in bits and pieces of reflection on a day of busy activity. I am told that Dr. Jung once remarked, 'Hurry is not *of* the Devil, it *is* the Devil.' There is simply no better way to keep ourselves out of relationship with God than by simply having no time for Him, having no time to look within in meditation.

Morton T. Kelsey, *The Other Side of Silence*, SPCK, 1977, page 83

Living things need an appropriate climate in order to grow and bear fruit. If they are to develop to completion, they require an environment that allows their potential to be realized. The seed will not grow unless there is soil that can feed it, light to draw it from, warmth to nurture and moisture that unlocks its vitality. Time is also required for its growth to unfold...

Meditation is the attempt to provide the soul with a proper environment in which to grow and to become.

Morton T. Kelsey, *The Other Side of Silence*, SPCK, 1977, page 31

Meditation is a way of liberation from all fear. Fear is the greatest impediment to fullness of life. The wonder of the vision proclaimed by Jesus is that the great power of love which dispels fear is the power that we make contact with in the depths of our own being. The power of love is the energy that sweeps all before it. What we need to understand and what we need to proclaim if we are going to proclaim the Christian message to the world is that in prayer we begin to live fully from the life force that is set free in our inmost being and that life force is love because it is God.

John Main, O.S.B., *Moment of Christ*, Darton, Longman & Todd, 1984, page 31

One of the main purposes of meditation is to expose us to the reality of the Father in such a way that we can become the kind of people who are able to love. His life radiating through us cleanses, heals and transforms us. Then we can truly love in the way that Jesus asked of us. He did not tell us that we are His followers when we are great at meditating and religious activities, but only when we love one another as He loved us. This is the ultimate criterion of our lives, which can be fully realized only as we turn inward and open ourselves to God.

Morton T. Kelsey, *The Other Side of Silence*, SPCK, 1977, page 65

The end of meditation is to love God better. That is a very simple thing to say. In earthly friendships two friends do not analyse one another's characters; they just love one another. The best meditation is that which is most fruitful in love. We should love God with simplicity, not seek to know how much we love Him. Our gaze at God has to be a gaze into a darkness, for it is the finite creature gazing at the infinite Creator, but that darkness becomes more precious than any earthly light, and faith finds sufficient light, as Browning says in *The Ring and the Book*, 'for us in the dark to rise by.' But if we seek to measure our love for God, or to gauge it by our feelings and emotions, we immediately harm our power of loving God. The measure of our love to Him, says St. Bernard, is that we love Him without measure.

Father Andrew, S.D.C., *In the Silence*, A.R. Mowbray & Co., 1947, page 57

Meditation is one of the ways in which the spiritual man keeps himself awake. It is not really a paradox that it is precisely in meditation that most aspirants for religious perfection grow dull and fall asleep.

Meditative prayer is a stern discipline, and one which cannot be learned by violence. It requires unending courage and perseverance, and those who are not willing to work at it patiently will finally end in compromise. Here, as elsewhere, compromise is only another name for failure.

To meditate is to think. And yet successful meditation is much more than 'affections,' much more than a series of prepared 'acts' which one goes through.

In meditative prayer, one thinks and speaks not only with the mind and lips, but in a certain sense with one's *whole being*. Prayer is not then just a formula of words or a series of desires springing up in the heart—it is the orientation of our whole body, mind and spirit to God in silence, attention, and adoration. All good meditative prayer is a *conversion of our entire self to God*.

Thomas Merton, *Thoughts in Solitude*, Burns & Oates, 1958, page 41

... the subject of Christian meditation is God. Its aim is to help us to turn away from ourselves, *our* needs, *our* thoughts and plans, and to turn towards God, in His Glory and Love and Power. A good motto for meditation would be: 'Think glorious thoughts of God, and serve Him with a quiet mind.' For the purpose of meditation is to lead us to know, love and serve God. All that God wants from us is this humble readiness to love and serve, not fine thoughts and heightened emotion. Meditation may sometimes give us delight, and God may often give us these gleams of joy, but in this exercise, as in every other part of our life, we need to learn more and more only to want to *give*. Sometimes people say: But what is the use of meditation? Why should we do it? First of all, it is necessary in order that we may assimilate what we already know *about* God, till it becomes part of us. We need to 'feed' upon the Word of God if we are to become convinced Christians, with the love of God in our very bones. Then, too, meditation teaches us to see our own position more plainly: we begin to see how sinful and helpless we are, and how we need to depend upon God for everything. Meditation is not an end in itself; it is a means to an end: in it we listen to God that we may hear, and obey Him.

There are many methods of meditation; most of us can find our own way, and choose the one which makes it easiest for us to pray. The simplest is that which most of us do without calling it 'meditation': to read a passage in the Bible, think about it for a few moments, and then pray. This is a good way of using the Bible in connexion with prayer, but it can be carried further with advantage. For instance we can take an incident from the Gospel story. We pray for the guidance of the Holy Spirit. Then we try to picture the scene very vividly. We look at Jesus; we listen to what He says; we see what He does; we notice the way He treats the people in the story. And if we throw ourselves into the story with sufficient knowledge and imagination we may feel we have been 'there'. Then we keep quiet and wait, and very gradually some thought will come... and we know that God has spoken to us—even to us—through His Word... Finally, in order that this thought and prayer may lead to action, we make a very simple definite resolution: something we can do that day, almost at once, however small it may seem as a response to something great and wonderful. Many people find it a help to choose some word from the passage, and especially some word from the teaching of Jesus, to treasure in their minds and repeat in their hearts throughout the day. We can, of course, use any part of the Bible for such Meditations on an incident or narrative, but for most of us the Four Gospels will give us all we need for many years. For the Gospels are windows into the heart of God.

Olive Wyon, *On the Way*, SCM Press, 1958, page 118

MIRACLES

Miracles—marvellous events due to some supernatural agency; remarkable occurrence; remarkable specimen (of ingenuity, impudence, etc.)

In *Visions of Hope*, in the introductory paragraphs of 'Healing' and 'Petition', I wrote accounts of what I took to be two experiences of the miraculous. In both instances there was a laying on of hands with prayer, and something occurred which resulted in healing. In *Visions of Glory* I have recorded two further instances, in my introductions to 'Grace' and 'Intercession', when some form of miraculous healing took place.

I sometimes feel we need to look more closely at what is going on all around us, to see the miraculous. A friend of mine, a scientist, was filled with feelings of awe and wonder when he witnessed the birth of his daughter. Excitedly he came to see me shortly afterwards and talked of this everyday occurrence in terms of the miraculous.

Of all the contributions in this section on 'Miracles' the one I like best is by W. Macneile Dixon from his book *The Human Situation*. He mentions the starry worlds in time and space, the pageant of life, the process of growth and reproduction, the instincts of animals, the inventiveness of nature, the rising and setting sun, and a whole host of other phenomena. Through reading this passage, I have had my eyes opened and now find I am surrounded by the miracles of nature. In the arts and sciences we are further confronted with the miraculous. Miracles? I see evidence of miracles everywhere, in the Gospels and in everyday life.

They forgot what he had done, and the miracles that he had shown them. In the sight of their fathers he wrought marvels.

Psalm 78:11

Remember the wonderful works that he has done, his miracles, and the judgments he uttered.

Psalm 105:5

But if I do them, even though you do not believe me, believe the works, that you may know and understand that the Father is in me and I am in the Father.

John 10:38

To one is given through the Spirit the utterance of wisdom, and to another the utterance of knowledge according to the same Spirit, to another faith by the same Spirit, to another gifts of healing by the one Spirit, to another the working of miracles...

1 Corinthians 12:8–10

Seeing, hearing, feeling, are miracles, and each part and tag of me is a miracle.

Walt Whitman, 'Song of Myself', in *The Complete Poems*, edited by Francis Murphy, Penguin Books, 1982, page 87

A miracle, remember, is not a breach of natural law, but a revelation of spiritual law.

Hugh Redwood, *Residue of Days*, Hodder and Stoughton, 1958, page 35

A miracle is not a condition of faith; faith is the condition of experiencing a miracle.

Peter de Rosa, *Jesus who became Christ*, William Collins Sons & Co., 1975, page 151

A miracle is not the breaking of the laws of the fallen world, it is the re-establishment of the laws of the kingdom of God.

Anthony Bloom, *The Essence of Prayer*, Darton, Longman & Todd, 1989, page 69

A miracle is a law-abiding event by which God accomplishes His redemptive purposes through the release of energies which belong to a plane of being higher than any with which we are normally familiar.

Leslie Weatherhead, *Psychology, Religion and Healing*, Hodder and Stoughton, 1952, page 45

God does not shake miracles into Nature at random as if from a pepper-caster. They come on great occasions: they are found at the great ganglions of history—not of political or social history, but of that spiritual history which cannot be fully known by men.

C.S. Lewis, *Miracles*, William Collins Sons & Co., 1960, page 171

There comes a moment when people who have been dabbling in religion ('Man's search for God'!) suddenly draw back.

Supposing we really found Him? We never meant it to come to *that*! Worse still, supposing He had found us!

So it is a sort of Rubicon. One goes across; or not. But if one does, there is no manner of security against miracles. One may be in for *anything*.

C.S. Lewis, Miracles, William Collins Sons & Co., 1960, page 98

What is a miracle?

A miracle, my friend, is an event which creates faith. That is the purpose and nature of miracles. They may seem very wonderful to the people who witness them, and very simple to those who perform them. That does not matter: if they confirm or create faith they are true miracles... Frauds deceive. An event which creates faith does not deceive: therefore it is not a fraud, but a miracle.

George Bernard Shaw, St. Joan, ii, The Bodley Head, 1973, page 105

... the people who witness such an event do not feel themselves religiously elevated and inwardly edified... Instead they are shocked and frightened, so that they ask in complete bewilderment, 'How can he do these things?' They can even suppose that Jesus is in league with the dark powers of magic. Thus it is not edification but shock that results from a miracle; not insight into higher worlds but a claim of God that pins one down and forces a decision. *That* is the effect of a miracle, and we can observe it time after time.

Helmut Thielicke, I Believe: The Christian's Creed, translated by John W. Doberstein and H. George Anderson,
William Collins Sons & Co., 1969, page 47

The spirit and meaning of Christ are present and perceptible to us even without the aid of miracles. Miracles appeal only to the understanding of those who cannot perceive the meaning. They are mere substitutes for the not understood reality of the spirit. This is not to deny that the living presence of the spirit is not occasionally accompanied by marvellous physical happenings; I only wish to emphasize that these happenings can neither replace nor bring about knowledge of the spirit, which is the essential thing.

C.G. Jung, Answer to Job, translated by R.F.C. Hull, Routledge & Kegan Paul, 1954, page xii

But the real miracle is in fact more astounding than the healing of the sick, the raising of the dead, or the moving of mountains: for the birth of a universal personality is the equivalent, if not more than the equivalent, of the sudden appearance of a new species in nature. Through the creation and incarnation of a universal persona, or mask, a whole civilization may not merely alter its composite face but deeply change many other dynamic constituents of its character. By strenuous discipline and devout imitation, each follower of the new prophet assumes the mask for himself, and in time his own very bones and flesh begin, as it were, to fill in these ideal outlines: by a second birth he achieves a nature no less distinctive than that given by his first birth.

Lewis Mumford, The Conduct of Life, Secker & Warburg, 1952, page 98

It is in connection both with the teaching and the example of Jesus that the miracles may be with most advantage considered. They must not be regarded as external credentials of supernatural power to enforce the authority of Jesus as teacher. That teaching appeals to reason, conscience, affection, and aspiration, and needs no such enforcement. The miracles are necessary constituents of His message and mission of grace, in which He revealed the love of the Father to men, and showed the characteristics of His own religious experience, moral character, and mediatorial function. We shall not accordingly give the miracles their due place in this work if we lay stress on the supernatural power which may have been displayed and not on their witness to His confidence in God and compassion for man.

Alfred E. Garvie, *The Christian Doctrine of the Godhead*, Hodder and Stoughton, 1925, page 69

According to the Christian case, the miracles of Christ belong to the life and work of One who has changed, and changed immeasurably for the better, the moral and religious condition of great nations, and whose power after the lapse of eighteen centuries is still unspent. In the narratives which record the miracles of Christ the miracles are not the most wonderful elements: His teaching, His unique Personality, the Divine perfection revealed under human conditions in His character and history, are more wonderful still. Finally, His appearance has proved to be the transcendent fulfilment of a great hope which, for many centuries, had been the stay, the strength, and the consolation of the race from which He sprang, a race to which had come an exceptional knowledge of God. That Christ should have worked miracles does not surprise me. It would have surprised me if He had not.

R.W. Dale, *The Living Christ and the Four Gospels*, Hodder and Stoughton, 1890, page 101

A philosopher friend of mine could never, he told me, bring himself to believe in his own existence. A future life would be a miracle, and you find it difficult to believe in miracles? I, on the contrary, find it easy. They are to be expected. The starry worlds in time and space, the pageant of life, the processes of growth and reproduction, the instincts of animals, the inventiveness of nature, the rising and the setting sun, the affections and passions, the character of thought, of will, intuition, consciousness, these singly and together plunge the human mind into profound amazement to be in their midst. They are all utterly unbelievable, miracles piled upon miracles.

If there be a sceptical star I was born under it, yet I have lived all my days in complete astonishment. What does this fine reason of ours tell me to believe or disbelieve? When you come to me with your explanations of all the world contains I am profoundly interested. Not, indeed, in your explanations, which are, of course, like all others, supremely ridiculous, but in the bright-eyed simplicity of the human mind, and its explanatory prattle. Explain to me, for I am all attention, some of the everyday familiar things; how, for example, a stimulus to a nerve produces a sensation, by what process we recall a name or a fact, 'how a peacock's tail builds up a series of perfect eyes out of hundreds of separate feathers, each with its thousands of separate branches'.

Miracles? For my part I see miracles everywhere. I see nothing but works of magic. Miracles are not rare birds. They fly in flocks, they darken the air in their multitudes. So much for miracles. Nature is not natural, but supernatural, delighting in marvels, in confounding us with the astounding and impossible.

W. Macneile Dixon, *The Human Situation*, Edward Arnold & Co., 1937, page 430

MYSTICS AND MYSTICISM

Mystics, mysticism—a type of religion which puts the emphasis on immediate awareness of relation with God, on direct and immediate consciousness of the divine presence; religion in its most acute, intense and living stage

I like this definition of mystics and mysticism. The words have given me an insight into the character and personality of Jesus Christ. I now feel to be in a much better position to understand his life and work. The same applies to St Paul. I often wondered what lay behind his power and genius. Now I think I know. Many saints down the ages have spoken of an immediate awareness of relation with God. In prayer and contemplation they found rich resources of divine life welling up in themselves, and were not disappointed. The great mystical poets George Herbert and John Donne found their inspiration in a direct and immediate consciousness of the divine presence. The contents of their poems continue to delight the ear today. A modern composer, Ralph Vaughan Williams, discovered the source of his genius in mysticism. His music still enchants those of us who listen to his works. The artist Fra Angelico used to meditate before painting, and attributed his genius to a divine source. Perhaps this helps to explain why there is something special in his art. According to our definition, mysticism is religion in its most acute, intense and living stage. Long ago, Henri Frédéric Amiel claimed we had lost the mystical sense. Perhaps this helps us to understand why the Church is in the doldrums. A rediscovery of mysticism might well bring about a much-needed regeneration.

The secret things belong to the Lord our God; but the things that are revealed belong to us and to our children for ever, that we may do all the words of this law.
Deuteronomy 29:29

And behold, the Lord passed by, and a great and strong wind rent the mountains, and broke in pieces the rocks before the Lord, but the Lord was not in the wind; and after the wind an earthquake, but the Lord was not in the earthquake; and after the earthquake a fire, but the Lord was not in the fire; and after the fire a still small voice.
1 Kings 19:11–12

The Spirit searches everything, even the depths of God.
1 Corinthians 2:10

The mystery was made known to me by revelation . . . the mystery of Christ . . . was not made known to the sons of men in other generations as it has now been revealed to his holy apostles and prophets by the Spirit . . . I was made a minister . . . to preach to the Gentiles the unsearchable riches of Christ, and to make all men see what is the plan of the mystery hidden for ages in God who created all things; that through the church the manifold wisdom of God might now be made known to the principalities and powers.
Ephesians 3:3–5, 7–10

We have lost the mystical sense; and what is religion without mysticism?
Henri Frédéric Amiel, *Amiel's Journal*, translated by Mrs Humphry Ward, Macmillan and Co., 1918, page 80

The ultimate gift of conscious life is a sense of the mystery that encompasses it.
Lewis Mumford, *The Conduct of Life*, Secker & Warburg, 1952, page 57

. . . mysticism is wisdom or knowledge that is found through love; it is loving knowledge.
William Johnston, *The Inner Eye of Love*, William Collins Sons & Co., 1978, page 20

Without mysticism nothing great, nothing fine can be accomplished in this world.
André Gide, *The Counterfeiters*, Alfred A. Knopf, 1928, page 179

God is an Unutterable sigh in the Human Heart, said the German mystic. And thereby said the last word.
Havelock Ellis, *Impressions and Comments*, Constable & Co., 1914, page 190

For the mystics, the great aim of all religious experience is the vision of God and union with him.
William Barclay, *The Letters to the Corinthians*, The Saint Andrew Press, 1988, page 256

'Mysticism'... the simple childlike intercourse of the believing soul with God, by no effort of the mind, but by the working of the Holy Spirit.

Gerhard Tersteegen, in Frances Bevan, *Sketches of the Quiet in the Land*, John F. Shaw and Co., 1891, page 396

Other faiths have their mystics but only in Jesus, I believe, can we find such spontaneous and personal communion with God combined with such a passionate ethical concern for humanity. Both awareness of God and awareness of the world attain their zenith in him.

John V. Taylor, *The Go-Between God*, SCM Press, 1973, page 225

The typical mystic is the person who has a certain first-hand experience and knowledge of God through Love; and the literature of mysticism tells us, or tries to tell us, what the finite human spirit has come to know through love of the relation between the little half-made spirit of man and the Infinite Spirit of God.

Evelyn Underhill, in John Stobbart, editor, *The Wisdom of Evelyn Underhill*, A.R. Mowbray & Co., 1951, page 22

The problem of mysticism is to endow the mind and will of man with a supernatural experience of God as He is in Himself and, ultimately, to transform a human soul into God by a union of love. This is something that no human agency can perform or merit or even conceive by itself. This work can be done only by the direct intervention of God.

Thomas Merton, *The Waters of Silence*, Hollis and Carter, 1950, page 20

That which makes Christian mysticism so rich, deep, life-giving, and beautiful is the Christian doctrine of the nature and action of God. It is different because it is based upon the Incarnation, the redemptive self-giving of the Eternal Charity. The Christian mystic tries to continue in his own life Christ's balanced life of ceaseless communion with the Father and lonely service to the crowd.

Evelyn Underhill, in John Stobbart, editor, *The Wisdom of Evelyn Underhill*, A.R. Mowbray & Co., 1951, page 23

Mysticism for the mystic himself is characterized by a personal experience through which the ordinary limitations of life and the passionate pursuits of the soul are transcended, and a self-evident conviction is attained that he is in communion, or even in union, with some self-transcending Reality that absolutely satisfies and is what he has always sought. 'This is He, this is He,' the mystic exclaims: 'There is no other: This is He whom I have waited for and sought after from my childhood!'

Rufus M. Jones, *Spiritual Reformers in the 16th and 17th Centuries*, Macmillan and Co., 1914, page xix

In her autobiography St Theresa compares these degrees of mystical prayer with four ways of watering a garden. At first the water has to be drawn up by hand as from a deep well; a great deal of human effort is called for. Then things become easier. The senses have been stilled and it is as if the well had been fitted with a windlass; more water can be got by less effort. Later still, when all voluntary activities of the mind have ceased, it is as if a little river ran through the garden. In the last and highest degree it is as if God Himself watered the garden with His rain.

F.C. Happold, *Mysticism*, Penguin Books, 1981, page 74

Mysticism keeps men sane. As long as you have mystery you have health; when you destroy mystery you create morbidity. The ordinary man has always been sane because the ordinary man has always been a mystic. He has permitted the twilight. He has always had one foot in earth and the other in fairyland. He has always left himself free to doubt his gods; but (unlike the agnostic of to-day) free also to believe in them. He has always cared more for truth than for consistency. If he saw two truths that seemed to contradict each other, he would take the two truths and the contradiction along with them.

G.K. Chesterton, Orthodoxy, The Bodley Head, 1935, page 46

But intuition, though it includes the testimony of will and feeling, is never fully attained without strenuous intellectual effort. It cannot dispense with the discipline of reason and the technique of proof. Religion itself may take three forms, primitive or sensuous, reflective, and mystical.

Religion in the mystic sense is not a mere speculation of reason or a feeling of dependence or a mode of behaviour. It is something which our entire self is, feels, and does; it is the concurrent activity of thought, feeling, and will. It satisfies the logical demand for abiding certainty, the aesthetic longing for repose, and the ethical desire for perfection. In the great mystics... holiness and learning, purity of soul, and penetration of understanding are fused in an harmonious whole.

Sir Sarvepalli Radhakrishnan, Eastern Religions and Western Thought, Oxford University Press, 1940, page 63

Mysticism in the proper sense is an intense realisation of God within the self, and the self embraced within God in vivid nearness.

It is a phenomenon known in a number of religions, and in those religions very similar language is used in describing the experience. There is deep darkness, the darkness of not knowing, and there is light, with flashes in which the self knows the unknowable to be terribly near, and knows itself as never before.

Now, through the centuries Christian teaching has emphasised that the significant thing is not just the mystic experience in itself, but its place and context within the whole life of a Christian. The experience is given by God sometimes to one who seeks God in a life of humility and charity, turned towards righteousness as well as the beauty of God. And the effect of the experience of mystic union, sometimes described as 'passive contemplation', is not to cause the person to long to have the experience again, but to long to serve God, and to do his will.

Those who have had the mystic experience will not want to tell everyone about it: they will have a longing to serve God in daily life, for in his *will* is our peace.

Michael Ramsey, Through the Year with Michael Ramsey, edited by Margaret Duggan, Hodder and Stoughton, 1975, page 164

There is another limitation which must always attach to religion of the purely mystical type. In so far as it is an *experience* of the inward type, it is indescribable and incommunicable. That does not mean or imply any lessened value in the experience itself, it only means that it is very difficult to mint it into the universal coinage of the world. The recovery of faith, after some catastrophic bankruptcy of spiritual values, as with Job or Dante or Faust, cannot be described in analytic steps. The loss of faith in the rationality of the universe, the collapse of the 'beautiful world' within, can be told step by step; the process of integration and reconstruction, on the other hand, always remains somewhat of a mystery, though it is plain enough that a new and richer inner world has been found. So, too, with Mysticism. The experience itself may, and often does, bring to the recipient an indubitable certainty of spiritual realities, revealing themselves within his own spirit, and, furthermore, it is often productive of permanent life-results, such as augmented conviction, heightened tone of joy, increased unification of personality, intense moral passion and larger conquering power, but he, nevertheless, finds it a baffling matter to draw from his mystical experience concrete information about the nature and character of God, or to supply, from the experience alone, definite contributions that can become part of the common spiritual inheritance of the race.

Rufus M. Jones, Spiritual Reformers in the 16th and 17th Centuries, Macmillan and Co., 1914, page xxiii

If the consecrated religions are doomed to pass away, and dogma and liturgy to become matters of learning or of poetry, there will still be mystics and mysticism: already, indeed, we see that the crumbling of the old faiths has enriched the soil for many strange forms of lawless, emotional religion. Men will believe something about the nature of the Cause and about the high meaning of man. But apart from this, which is perhaps vanity and hubris, there is another reason why Mysticism will always be in the world, and will grow as the sacred, the communal faiths wane. Through religions and through literature and the arts and through the ceaseless widening of the common knowledge of human life, there has sprung in man a greater pity, the beginning of a deeper love; and once the religions with their neat promises of future redressing have ceased to set consciences too easily at rest, there must come a new brooding over the meaning of the world, a new searching after all justice and beauty and perfection.

Henceforth men must always find in themselves a gnawing greed for a good that the world does not give; if they cease to pray to God, they will all the more, and all the more imploringly, consult their own Highest, which is but God more nearly seen; all the old words of the mystics they will re-read in their own, the new sense, and they will find new words of their own for the new revelations of life's meanings and duties.

Stephen MacKenna, *Journal and Letters*, Constable & Co., 1936, page 119

The mystic only gradually becomes aware of the faculty he has been given of perceiving the indefinite fringe of reality surrounding the totality of all created things, with more intensity than the precise, individual core of their being.

For a long time, thinking he is the same as other men, he will try to see as they do, to speak their language, to find contentment in the joys with which they are satisfied.

For a long time, seeking to appease his mysterious but obsessive need for plenitude of being, he will try to divert it on to some particularly stable or precious object to which, among all the accessory pleasures of life, he will look for the substance and overflowing richness of his joy.

For a long time he will look to the marvels of art to provide him with that exaltation which will give him access to the sphere—his own sphere—of the extrapersonal and the suprasensible; and in the unknown of nature he will strive to hear the heartbeats of that higher reality which calls him by name.

Happy the man who fails to stifle his vision.

Happy the man who will not shrink from a passionate questioning of the Muses and of Cybele concerning his God.

But happy above all he who, rising beyond aesthetic dilettantism and the materialism of the lower layers of life, is given to hear the reply of all beings, singly and all together: 'What you saw gliding past, like a world, behind the song and behind the colour and behind the eyes' glance does not exist just here or there but is a Presence existing equally everywhere: a presence which, though it now seems vague to your feeble sight, will grow in clarity and depth. In this presence all diversities and all impurities yearn to be melted away.'

Pierre Teilhard de Chardin, *Hymn of the Universe*, William Collins Sons & Co., 1981, page 78

OBEDIENCE

Obedience—obeying the will of God; doing God's will rather than one's own

The crunch came in my early twenties. I took a step of faith and made a commitment to God, as revealed in Jesus Christ. What followed was an attempt to obey the will of God. The outcome was an inner civil war in which I was pulled in two different directions. One part of me wanted to observe the plea of the Psalmist: 'Teach me thy way, O Lord.' Another part was fully alive and kicking. I was bent on following the dictates of my own will.

Two years later, a major step was taken in obedience to the will of God, and I set out on the path to ordination. The inner battle intensified. In those next few years I learnt something of the truth of John J. Vincent's words in this section: The 'obedience' of Jesus is not simply submission, but real striving, cooperation, and activity.' The outcome, after theological college, was four busy years on the staff of Bradford Cathedral. In my role as a part-time hospital chaplain, I visited some 14,000 patients in the Bradford Royal Infirmary in that period—and this was only one facet of my work as Chaplain of the Cathedral.

A change of job led to a change in my practice of obedience. I was appointed Chaplain to University College, London. Here I learned to 'listen' to the will of God, through times of reflection and the keeping of a journal. This form of self-discipline gave me a clearer idea of what was required and a stronger will to do what was bidden. The civil war continues at University College, Oxford, but the inner battles are more gentle—and the outcome more productive and creative.

Teach me thy way, O Lord.
Psalm 27:11

If you are willing and obedient, you shall eat the good of the land.
Isaiah 1:19

Every one then who hears these words of mine and does them will be like a wise man who built his house upon the rock; and the rain fell, and the floods came, and the winds blew and beat upon that house, but it did not fall, because it had been founded on the rock.
Matthew 7:24–25

What you have learned and received and heard and seen in me, do.
Philippians 4:9

Lord, make my heart like yours.
Brother Lawrence, *The Practice of the Presence of God*, introduction by Dorothy Day, Burns & Oates, 1977, page 123

Obedience is much more seen in little things, than in great.
Thomas Fuller, *Gnomologia*, Stearne Books, 1733, page 157

If within us we find nothing over us we succumb to what is around us.

P.T. Forsyth, *Positive Preaching and the Modern Mind*, Independent Press, 1949, page 32

The 'obedience' of Jesus is not simply submission, but real striving, cooperation, activity.

John J. Vincent, *Secular Christ*, Lutterworth Press, 1968, page 199

We can only have power if we are obedient. If we are disobedient, all power falls from us, because we are living in our own strength, in our own way.

Father Andrew, S.D.C., *A Gift of Light*, selected and edited by Harry C. Griffith, A.R. Mowbray & Co., 1968, page 89

... there are various paths to Christian obedience. The essential point, however, is that this obedience can only be measured by its commitment to the world.

Paul Oestreicher, in Hans Jürgen Schultz, *Conversion to the World*, SCM Press, 1967, page 12

Men should find their hearts with a sense of fidelity, of generosity, and of obedience to God, and then let God take care of the result.

Henry Ward Beecher, *Proverbs from Plymouth Pulpit*, Charles Burnet & Co., 1887, page 179

There is but one single faculty in the whole roll of the soul's faculties to which every one in the nature of man consents to be obedient. This is the faculty of LOVE.

Henry Ward Beecher, *Proverbs from Plymouth Pulpit*, Charles Burnet & Co., 1887, page 206

Son of heav'n and earth,
Attend: that thou art happy, owe to God;
That thou continuest such, owe to thy self,
That is, to thy obedience; therein stand.

John Milton, *Paradise Lost*, v. 520, in H.C. Beeching, editor, *The Poetical Works of John Milton*, Oxford at the Clarendon Press, 1900, page 285

In practical terms obedience is in line with the very root of the word which suggests 'listening to'—listening to the will of God by listening *to* each other and listening *with* each other to its varied manifestations.

Sister Madeleine, OSA, *Solitary Refinement*, SCM Press, 1972, page 49

... such delight hath God in Men
Obedient to his will, that he vouchsafes
Among them to set up his Tabernacle,
The holy One with mortal Men to dwell.

John Milton, *Paradise Lost*, xii. 246, in *The Works of John Milton*, Columbia University Press, 1931, volume 2, part 2, page 387

'If,' said a Celtic saint of the ninth century, 'If a man does his own will he walks with a shadow on the heart, but if with Christ's power in thee, thou doest God's will, thou shalt walk in a circle of light.'

Alistair MacLean, *The Quiet Heart*, Allenson & Co., 1940, page 186

O let thy sacred will
All thy delight in me fulfill!
Let me not think an action mine own way,
But as thy love shall sway,
Refining up the rudder to thy skill.

George Herbert, *The Church, Obedience*, in *The Poems of George Herbert*, Oxford University Press, 1979, page 95

To take the vow of obedience is primarily to consecrate one's freedom to God. It is to recognise the pre-existing fact that in human life freedom is limited by the demands made upon us by God: he is the author of our freedom, the object of this freedom, the master of this freedom.

Basil Hume, O.S.B., *Searching for God*, Hodder and Stoughton, 1979, page 55

Therefore doth Heaven divide
The state of man in divers functions,
Setting endeavour in continual motion;
To which is fixed, as an aim or butt,
Obedience: for so work the honey-bees.

William Shakespeare, *Henry V*, I. ii. 183

O my God, since Thou art with me, and I must now, in obedience to Thy commands, apply my mind to these things, I beseech Thee to grant me the grace to continue in Thy presence; and to this end do Thou prosper me with Thy assistance, receive all my works, and possess all my affections.

Brother Lawrence, *The Practice of the Presence of God*, A.R. Mowbray & Co., 1977, page 21

Jesus lays hold on the individual and summons him to *obedience to God*, who is to embrace his whole life. These are simple, transparent, liberating appeals, dispensing with arguments from authority or tradition, but providing examples, signs, tokens, for transforming one's life.

Hans Küng, *On Being a Christian*, translated by Edward Quinn, William Collins Sons & Co., 1977, page 244

God... lays claim not to half the will, but the whole. He demands not only external acts which can be observed and controlled, but also internal responses which cannot be controlled or checked. He demands man's heart. He wants not only good fruits, but the good tree: not only action but being; not something, but myself—and myself wholly and entirely.

Hans Küng, *On Being a Christian*, translated by Edward Quinn, William Collins Sons & Co., 1977, page 246

The time of suffering is not a time for speech upon the ultimate problems of the universe. It is a time for the upward look and trustful silence. Some people are so strong in faith, and so sure of God, that they can praise Him in pain, and pass through the valley of the shadow with songs on their lips. But they are rare souls. For most people it is a time for mute obedience.

W.E. Sangster, *He is Able*, Hodder and Stoughton, 1936, page 24

Let us not meddle with the future, and matters which are too high for us, but refrain our souls, and keep them low like little children, content with the day's food, and the day's schooling, and the day's play-hours, sure that the Divine Master knows that all is right, and how to train us, and whither to lead us; though we know not and need not know, save this, that the path by which He is leading each of us, if we will but obey and follow step by step, leads up to everlasting life.

Charles Kingsley, *Daily Thoughts*, Macmillan and Co., 1884, page 129

It was the obedience of Jesus which brought glory to God. There is only one way in which anyone can show that he loves and admires and trusts a leader and that is by obeying that leader, if need be to the bitter end. The only way in which an army can really honour a leader, is by unquestioningly following his leadership. The only way in which a child can honour a parent is by obeying that parent. Jesus gave the supreme honour and the supreme glory to God, because He gave to God the supreme obedience, the obedience which obeyed even unto a Cross.

William Barclay, *The Gospel of John*, The Saint Andrew Press, 1965, volume 2, page 172

In the religious life all obedience is to God the Holy Ghost, Who calls the soul to follow Christ. All right and legitimate rule is of God. Any other obedience would be calamitous. The Holy Ghost calls, and the soul that has a vocation knows that it must obey. True obedience will be the outcome of a childlike spirit, and is the heart self-surrender of trustful love. It is an act of union with the will of God, taught by the Holy Spirit.

If God calls a soul into the wilderness He does not leave it, but abides with it to infuse it with that grace which is to lead it on. There are still many cords to be broken before the will is really surrendered. Our obedience should be prompt, no less in calls onward than in the first call to leave the world. If we are not prompt in following, we lose our capacity for following. Father Benson says: 'Our Lord moves on. If we do not follow, His voice gets fainter, and His form begins to disappear.' Delay may spoil an act of obedience. Promptness is a great secret of growth in grace, and a real and practical way of self-surrender. We learn to obey by obeying. A simple heart to love and serve God is the fruit of the counsel of obedience lovingly persevered in.

The lowliest detail of obedience provides a means of union with our Lord. He is our example, and He never did one single thing just because He liked it. The end of His obedience seemed so disappointing, and yet that disappointment was its consummation. Our obedience must go on, even when it seems to no purpose, even to Calvary. Our failure may be our greatest offering to His glory.

Father Andrew, S.D.C., *Meditations for Every Day*, A.R. Mowbray & Co., 1941, page 309

OTHER FAITHS

Other faiths—the relationship of Christianity to Judaism, Islam, Buddhism, Hinduism, etc.

Three things have altered the way I look at people of other faiths. The first is the Genesis story of the creation of man. In this story God is depicted as fashioning and shaping man in his own image and likeness, and the last thing he does is breathe into man, and man becomes a living being. This means all men and women, irrespective of race, creed, caste and colour, have something of the divine latent in them.

The second is a passage in this section by William Barclay. He wrote: 'There are many ways to God. God has His own secret stairway into every heart. God fulfils Himself in many ways; and no man, and no Church, has a monopoly of the truth of God.'

The third is a passage, not in this book, by Mahatma Gandhi, in which he states his attitude to other faiths. 'After long study and experience I have come to these conclusions that: 1) all religions are true; 2) all religions have some error in them; 3) all religions are almost as dear to me as my own Hinduism. My veneration for other faiths is the same as for my own faith. Consequently, the thought of conversion is impossible... Our prayer for others ought never to be: "God! give them the light thou has given to me!" But: "Give them all the light and truth they need for their highest development."'

My attitude is to be loyal to the truths of Christ, and open to truths of God to be found in people of other faiths, and from different backgrounds.

I was sent only to the lost sheep of the house of Israel.

Matthew 15:24

... a woman, whose little daughter was possessed by an unclean spirit, heard of him, and came and fell down at his feet. Now the woman was a Greek, a Syrophoenician by birth.

Mark 7:25–26

And I have other sheep, that are not of this fold.

John 10:16

Now among those who went up to worship at the feast were some Greeks. So these came to Philip, who was from Bethsaida in Galilee, and said to him, 'Sir, we wish to see Jesus.'

John 12:20–21

As all men are alike (tho' infinitely various), So all Religions &, as all similars, have one source.
    The true Man is the source, he being the Poetic Genius.

William Blake, *Complete Writings*, edited by Geoffrey Keynes, Oxford University Press, 1974, page 98

There are many ways to God. God has His own secret stairway into every heart. God fulfils Himself in many ways; and no man, and no Church, has a monopoly of the truth of God.

William Barclay, *The Gospel of Luke*, The Saint Andrew Press, 1965, page 132

... we believe we may speak not only of the unknown God of the Greeks but also of the *hidden Christ of Hinduism*—hidden and unknown and yet present and at work because he is not far from any one of us.

Raimundo Panikkar, *The Unknown Christ of Hinduism*, Darton, Longman & Todd, 1981, page 168

The humble, meek, merciful, just, pious, and devout souls, are everywhere of one religion; and when death has taken off the mask, they will know one another, though the diverse liveries they wear have made them strangers.

William Penn, *Fruits of Solitude*, A.W. Bennett, 1863, page 63

The Church has never declared that the Judeo-Christian tradition was alone in possessing revealed Scriptures, sacraments, and supernatural knowledge about God. It has never declared that there was no affinity at all between Christianity and the mystical traditions of countries other than Israel.

Simone Weil, *Gateway to God*, William Collins Sons & Co., 1974, page 147

The Christian doctrine is a doctrine not of Immortality but of Resurrection. The difference is profound. The method of all non-Christian systems is to seek an escape from the evils and misery of life. Christianity seeks no escape, but accepts these at their worst, and makes them the material of its triumphant joy. That is the special significance in this connection of the Cross and Resurrection of Jesus Christ.

William Temple, *Nature, Man and God*, Macmillan and Co., 1934, page 461

'But the Jews, the Mohammedans, the Confucians, the Buddhists—what of them?' he put to himself the dilemma that had threatened him before. 'Can those hundreds of millions of human beings be deprived of that greatest of blessings without which life has no meaning?' he pondered, but immediately pulled himself up. 'But what is it that I want to know?' he said to himself. 'I am asking about the relation to the Deity of all the different religions of mankind.'

Leo Tolstoy, *Anna Karenin*, translated by Rosemary Edmonds, Penguin Books, 1983, page 851

I say quite plainly, as a student of comparative religion for many years, that the best this world has ever learned about religion centres in Jesus Christ. I pay my willing tribute to whatever learning has come to our poor race by the illumination of great and good men everywhere. I speak with reverence of the holy books of other faiths: the Talmud, the Koran, the Analects, and all the rest of them, but God, who 'at sundry times and in divers manners' has spoken in time past by the sages of many religions, spoke at the last unto us by His Son, and that revelation supersedes all others.

W.E. Sangster, *Westminster Sermons*, Epworth Press, 1961, volume 2, *At Fast and Festival*, page 127

The Catholic Church rejects nothing of what is true and holy in these religions... In Hinduism, men explore the divine mysteries and express it both in the limitless riches of myth and the accurately defined insights of philosophy... Buddhism in its various forms testifies to the essential inadequacy of this changing world. It proposes a way of life by which men can, with confidence and trust, attain a state of perfect liberation... The Church has also a high regard for the Muslims. They worship God, who is one, living and subsistent, merciful and almighty... they venerate Jesus as a prophet... Since Christians and Jews have such a common spiritual heritage, this sacred Council wishes to encourage and further mutual understanding and appreciation.

Vatican Council II, in Austin Flannery, O.P., General Editor, *The Conciliar and Post-conciliar Documents*, Fowler Wright Books, 1981, page 739

What we must strive for is an independent, unselfish Christian ministry to human beings in the religions. We must do this in a spirit of open-mindedness which is more than patronizing accommodation; which does not lead us to deny our own faith, but also does not impose any particular response; which turns criticism from outside into self-criticism and at the same time accepts everything positive; which destroys nothing of value in the religions, but also does not incorporate uncritically anything worthless. Christianity therefore should perform its service among the world religions in a dialectical unity of recognition and rejection, as critical catalyst and crystallization point of their religious, moral, meditative, ascetic, aesthetic values.

Hans Küng, *On Being a Christian*, translated by Edward Quinn, William Collins Sons & Co., 1977, page 112

C.F. Andrews, one of the most influential missionaries who ever went to India, said of his approach to Hindus, Buddhists, Muslims, there, 'I always assume that they are Christian; and, after I have talked with them awhile, I sometimes see the light of Christ in their eyes.' What did Andrews mean by assuming that they were Christian? Clearly, he meant that if Christian faith and experience are true—as he believed them to be—they cannot be merely local, isolated, shut in by boundaries of race or special formulations of religion. They must have universal ingredients which men everywhere, in one degree or another, seek after and sometimes find. As another Christian missionary put it, 'How is it possible to hold a firm, deep vibrant Christian faith, wholehearted and committed, without knowing that God meets other men in other ways?'

Harry Emerson Fosdick, *Dear Mr Brown*, William Collins Sons & Co., 1962, page 110

... when the deepest foundations of all the religions of the world have been laid free and restored, who knows but that those very foundations may serve once more, like the catacombs, or like the crypts beneath our old cathedrals, as a place of refuge for those who, to whatever creed they may belong, long for something better, purer, older and truer... Though leaving much behind of what is worshipped or preached in Hindu temples, in Buddhist viharas, in Mohammedan mosques, in Jewish synagogues, and Christian churches, each believer may bring down with him into that quiet crypt what he values most—his own pearl of great price... That crypt, though as yet but small and dark, is visited even now by those few who shun the noise of many voices, the glare of many lights, the conflict of many opinions. Who knows but that in time it will grow wider and brighter, and that the Crypt of the Past may become the Church of the Future.

F. Max Muller, *Lectures on the Origin and Growth of Religion*, Longmans, Green and Co., 1891, page 385

Islam is the most transcendent of all the higher religions; in no other is the complete 'otherness' of God so strongly emphasized. Yet out of it came one of the most beautiful and profound upsurges of mystical insight in the whole history of mysticism. In Sufism, as this manifestation is called, one finds a most subtle blending of the experience of God as the Divine Lover and of utter self-loss in Him. While the Hindu deity is an abstract deity, in Sufism He is the Beloved. The Beloved is, however, also the 'Truth', and the 'Truth' admits of no duality either in fact or idea; the union must be complete, the self must die absolutely.

There is a story which expresses this idea very vividly. The lover knocks at the door of the Beloved. 'Who is there?' asks the Beloved. 'It is I,' replies the lover. 'This house will not hold Me and thee,' comes the reply. The lover goes away and weeps and prays in solitude. After a long time he returns and knocks again. The Voice asks, 'Who is there?' 'It is Thou.' Immediately the door opens; lover and Beloved are face to face at last.

F.C. Happold, *Mysticism*, Penguin Books, 1981, page 96

There have been times when the Christian Church has rightly claimed to have an exclusive role. This was particularly so in its beginnings. If Christianity had not claimed to be the final and only true revelation in its own Mediterranean world and refused to become merely one of the many religions of that world, it could never have become the inspiration of European civilisation. Those days are now past. The Spirit of God is moving in the world, leading men into a wider vision, which does not destroy but fulfils and is in part contained within all the earlier partial visions. Christianity, and this is true of all higher religions, is now called upon, within the divine economy, to become universal, not by each religion ceasing to be itself, or watering down its own particular revelation, not by an attempt to iron out differences at the intellectual level, so that all may be lost in some nebulous World Faith, but by each seeing itself within the other, by each becoming incarnate within the other. This intersection of faiths in charity and spiritual understanding cannot but seem to each to be a sacrifice; for it involves the abandonment of every shred of exclusiveness.

For Christians, conditioned by the centuries-old conviction of being a 'chosen people', the favoured guardians of the one true and complete revelation, it will be more difficult than for, for instance, Hindus, whose religion has never had the same exclusiveness. But in this sacrifice of love no religion is called upon to sacrifice its own particular insights. It is a sacrifice by each religion of its self that in losing itself it may find it again. It is a dying in order to rise again in a yet more glorious body.

There is no need to seek for a World Religion. It is here already in that ultimate mystical experience, known to the contemplative saints of every religious faith. For the Christian it is here already, if he can only see it, in the actual and potential universality of his own revelation.

F.C. Happold, *The Journey Inwards*, Darton, Longman & Todd, 1974, page 128

Our purpose is to take God and his love to the poorest of the poor, irrespective of their ethical origin or the faith that they profess. Our discernment of all is not the belief but the necessity. We never try to convert those who receive to Christianity but in our work we bear witness to the love of God's presence and if Catholics, Protestants, Buddhists or agnostics become for this better men—simply better—we will be satisfied. Growing up in love they will be nearer to God and will find him in his goodness.

Every human being comes from the hand of God and we all know what is the love of God for us. My religion is everything to me but for every individual, according to the grace God has given that soul, God has his own ways and means to work in the hearts of men and we do not know how close they are to him but by their actions we will always know whether they are at his disposal or not. Whether you are a Hindu, a Moslem or a Christian, how you live your life is the proof that you are fully his or not. We must not condemn or judge or pass words that will hurt people. Maybe a person has never heard of Christianity. We do not know what way God is appearing to that soul and what way God is drawing that soul, and therefore who are we to condemn anybody?

It matters to the individual what Church he belongs to. If that individual thinks and believes that this is the only way to God for him or her, this is the way God comes into their life—his life. If he does not know any other way and if he has no doubt so that he does not need to search then this is his way to salvation. This is the way God comes into his life. But the moment a soul has the grace to know and to want to know more about God, more about faith, more about religion, then he has to search and if he does not search then he goes astray. God gives to every soul that he has created a chance to come face to face with him, to accept him or reject him.

People throughout the world may look different, or have a different religion, education or position, but they are all the same. They are all people to be loved. They are all hungry for love. The people you see in the streets of India or Hong Kong are hungry in body, but the people in London or New York have also a hunger which must be satisfied. Every person needs to be loved.

Some call him Ishwar, some call him Allah, some simply God, but we all have to acknowledge that it is he who made us for greater things: to love and to be loved. What matters is that we love. We cannot love without prayer and so whatever religion we are we must pray together.

Mother Teresa of Calcutta, *In the Silence of the Heart*, compiled by Kathryn Spink, SPCK, 1983, page 81

PARADISE

*Paradise—place of exceptional happiness and delight; often used as
a synonym for heaven and for the Garden of Eden before the
expulsion of Adam and Eve*

The word is probably of Persian origin, denoting an enclosed park or pleasure-ground in which the king frequented. Hence to be in paradise meant to be in the presence of God.

I have experienced exceptional happiness and delight in places of nature, at the seaside, in the mountains and by streams and rivers. Occasionally I have felt 'a presence that disturbs me with the joy of elevated thoughts', and find I can relate to these words of William Wordsworth.

Thomas Merton suggests we forget our vain cares and enter into our own hearts, which God has made to be his paradise and our own. 'If we have God dwelling within us, making our souls His paradise, then the world around us can also become for us what it was meant to be for Adam—his paradise.'

Reflection is a simple method for making this possible. We set aside our vain cares, choose a topic, and ponder over the contents in silence. Before long something stirs in the depths of our being and new life comes to the surface. Our thoughts, feelings and intuitions act as channels of grace, giving us a feel of paradise. It is not unknown for people to see the world differently after a period of reflection. For George Fox, all things were new, and all creation gave another smell than before, beyond what words can utter. If we experience paradise now, we shall not worry too much about our last migration into paradise, for we shall know a good deal about it already.

And he said, 'Jesus, remember me when you come into your kingdom.' And he said to him, 'Truly, I say to you, today you will be with me in Paradise.'

Luke 23:42–43

I know a man in Christ who fourteen years ago was caught up to the third heaven—whether in the body or out of the body I do not know, God knows. And I know that this man was caught up into Paradise—whether in the body or out of the body I do not know, God knows—and he heard things that cannot be told, which man may not utter.

2 Corinthians 12:2–4

He who has an ear, let him hear what the Spirit says to the churches. To him who conquers I will grant to eat of the tree of life, which is in the paradise of God.

Revelation 2:7

And I heard a voice from heaven saying, 'Write this: Blessed are the dead who die in the Lord henceforth.' 'Blessed indeed,' says the Spirit, 'that they may rest from their labours, for their deeds follow them!'

Revelation 14:13

He that will enter into Paradise, must have a good key.

George Herbert, *Outlandish Proverbs*, number 895, in F.E. Hutchinson, editor, *The Works of George Herbert*, Oxford at the Clarendon Press, 1945, page 350

'Paradise,' he said, 'is hidden in every one of us. It is hidden in me, too, now, and I have only to wish and it will come to me in very truth and will remain with me for the rest of my life.'

Fyodor Dostoyevsky, *The Brothers Karamazov*, translated by David Magarshack, Penguin Books, 1963, volume 1, page 356

The word *Paradise* comes from a Persian word which means *a walled-garden*. When a Persian king wished to confer a very special honour on someone specially dear to him, he made him *a companion of the garden* and gave him the right to walk in the royal gardens with him in intimate companionship.

William Barclay, *The Letters to the Corinthians*, The Saint Andrew Press, 1988, page 257

I have been a foolish, greedy and ignorant man;
Yet I have had my time beneath the sun and stars;
I have known the returning strength and sweetness of the seasons,
Blossom on the branch and the ripening of fruit,
The deep rest of the grass, the salt of the sea,
The frozen ecstasy of mountains.
The earth is nobler than the world we have built upon it;
The earth is long-suffering, solid, fruitful;
The world is still shifting, dark, half-evil.
But what have I done that I should have a better world,
Even though there is in me something that will not rest
Until it sees Paradise...?

J.B. Priestley, *Johnson over Jordan*, act III, William Heinemann, 1939, page 115

All nature is meant to make us think of paradise. Woods, fields, valleys, hills, the rivers and the sea, the clouds travelling across the sky, light and darkness, sun and stars, remind us that the world was first created as a paradise for the first Adam, and that in spite of his sin and ours, it will once again become a paradise when we are all risen from death in the second Adam. Heaven is even now mirrored in created things. All God's creatures invite us to forget our vain cares and enter into our own hearts, which God Himself has made to be His paradise and our own. If we have God dwelling within us, making our souls His paradise, then the world around us can also become for us what it was meant to be for Adam—his paradise. But if we seek paradise outside ourselves, we have no peace with what is all around us. Only the man who is free from attachment finds that creatures have become his friends. As long as he is attached to them, they speak to him only of his own desires. Or they remind him of his sins. When he is selfish, they serve his selfishness. When he is pure, they speak to him of God.

Thomas Merton, *No Man is an Island*, Burns & Oates, 1974, page 101

What is the destiny of a Christian?

Christ and the apostles give us some clear intimations in their teaching. Christ said to the thief who was dying, crucified near to him in his own last dying hours, 'Today, you shall be with me in paradise'.

Paradise did not mean a place of final perfection. Literally meaning a park, it was a word used comprehensively of the place of all departed spirits who are not lost. 'With me': the thief who died was to be with Jesus, and plainly this means a conscious existence with human fellowship and fellowship with God.

But it is not revealed to us that after death perfection is immediately attained. The fact of God's holiness, and the need for us to become holy like him, precludes the idea that the mere event of death enables a sort of moral jump from our present imperfection to a final perfection. Hence, we believe in growth, a purgation, a movement onwards, a being made perfect, after death. And if in this there is the pain of purgation, there is (can we doubt?) the joy of the growing fellowship with Christ.

Michael Ramsey, *Through the Year with Michael Ramsey*, edited by Margaret Duggan, Hodder and Stoughton, 1975, page 250

Shall we know one another in paradise?

If, as we have endeavoured to show, we shall be, in the Intermediate-World, the same living, thinking and speaking beings as on earth, what will constitute an important factor in the continuity of our life in that sphere?

The re-establishment of intercourse between ourselves and those with whom we have before been in contact.

We may, perhaps, never have reflected that *how* we think and feel; *how* we regard things; and *how* the tone and complexion has been imparted to our character, is very greatly due to our intercourse with others. In the moral universe, as in the physical world, an independent existence is impossible.

For example. You have a certain attribute, or quality, called love; it may be for wife, parent, child or friend. It is part of your consciousness, and consequently, part of your Self. Take it away, and you will have got rid of part of that Self.

Without it, you will be less a consciousness than you would be with it, in the same way as a body wanting a limb will be less a body than another in which the defect does not exist.

Arthur Chambers, *Our Life after Death*, Charles Taylor, 1894, page 72

What is the basis for the Christian belief in a life beyond death? Is it, as some of our Easter hymns and sermons affirm, the resurrection of Jesus? In fact both Jesus and his disciples, as Jews who were in this respect of the Pharisaic tradition, already believed in the resurrection of the dead. Today we believe as Christians in 'the life everlasting' for two basic intertwined reasons. One is that Jesus believed this. Several of his parables depict our present phase of existence as leading to another phase and urge us to take account now of this larger context. The other reason centres upon the Christian understanding of God as our loving heavenly Parent. If God loves each one of us and is seeking to draw us into a perfect relationship both with one another and with the divine Thou, does it not follow that God will hold us in being beyond the end of this short earthly life? Could it be an expression of infinite love to create us with immense spiritual potentialities but with so short a career, and often in such inauspicious circumstances, that those potentialities are normally destined never to be fulfilled? It has been claimed by some that in addition to these religious considerations there is evidence for a life after death in the findings of parapsychology or psychical research. This evidence consists both in mental interactions between the living, labelled 'telepathy', which do not seem to be physically mediated and which thus suggest that the mind is capable of functioning other than through the physical nervous system; and also in supposed communications, through trance mediums, automatic writing, visions, etc., from people who have died. Christian opinion remains strongly divided concerning the value of this evidence, but the obligation to take it seriously becomes increasingly evident.

John Hick, in Alan Richardson and John Bowden, editors, *A New Dictionary of Christian Theology*, SCM Press, 1985, page 331

POWER

Power—ability to do or act; particular faculty of body or mind,
vigour, energy; influential person, body or thing

In the Wisdom of Solomon we find a summarized version of the Genesis story of the creation of man. The writer wrote of 'the One who shaped him, who breathed an active soul into him, and inspired a living spirit'. Mystics, such as Meister Eckhart, believe we are born with a seed or spark of divine power in the depths of ourselves. An awareness of this power was experienced by the prophets. Micah, for instance, acknowledged he was 'filled with power, with the Spirit of the Lord, and with justice and might'. In the Gospels, we find the consequences of the divine inbreathing fully worked out in the life of Christ. We note the power of his preaching, teaching and healing. We remember his claim at the end of his ministry: 'All power is given unto me in heaven and earth.' Paul reminds us the gift of power is part of our spiritual heritage and a direct consequence of Christ's life, death and resurrection. He prays for the members of the early Church: 'May you be strengthened with all power, according to his glorious might, for all endurance and patience with joy, giving thanks to the Father, who has qualified us to share in the inheritance of the saints in light.'

Today we have lost sight of the divine power to be found in ourselves. We need to return to that source. A few years ago one of our reflection groups contained some very able sportsmen. They met on a regular basis for what they called 'their hour of power'. I am looking forward to the outcome. We might well have had a future Prime Minister in that group.

With God are wisdom and might; he has counsel and understanding.

Job 12:13

But as for me, I am filled with power, with the Spirit of the Lord, and with justice and might.

Micah 3:8

All power is given unto me in heaven and in earth.

Matthew 28:18 (AV)

That the God of our Lord Jesus Christ, the Father of glory, may give you a spirit of wisdom and of revelation in the knowledge of him, having the eyes of your hearts enlightened, that you may know what is the hope to which he has called you, what are the riches of his glorious inheritance in the saints, and what is the immeasurable greatness of his power in us who believe, according to the working of his great might.

Ephesians 1:17–19

The power of God is the worship He inspires.

Alfred North Whitehead, *Science and the Modern World*, The New American Library, 1964, page 172

Man is a born child, his power is the power of growth.

Rabindranath Tagore, 'Stray Birds', xxv, in *Collected Poems and Plays of Rabindranath Tagore*, Macmillan and Co., 1936, page 290

God's great power is in the gentle breeze, not in the storm.

Rabindranath Tagore, 'Stray Birds', cli, in *Collected Poems and Plays of Rabindranath Tagore*, Macmillan and Co., 1936, page 306

His power [that of Kahlil Gibran] came from some great reservoir of spiritual life else it could not have been so universal and so potent, but the majesty and beauty of the language with which he clothed it were all his own.

Claude Bragdon, in the Introduction of Kahlil Gibran, *The Prophet*, William Heinemann, 1923

There is a power which lapses into the human soul, and by that divine power all the faculties of a man become competent to do or to be what they cannot do or be when they are left to the laws of society or to the laws of nature.

Henry Ward Beecher, *Proverbs from Plymouth Pulpit*, Charles Burnet & Co., 1887, page 155

For man, discovering that knowledge is power, uses that power to dominate. The power within him is not the power of a great personality, the power which is sure and strong and is therefore able to be gentle and tolerant. This is the true power of God, the power of an infinite understanding, and it can only exist in a context of eternity.

Stuart B. Jackman, *The Numbered Days*, SCM Press, 1954, page 31

Christianity is not, as it is sometimes presented and sometimes practised, an additional burden of observances and obligations to weigh down and increase the already heavy load, or to multiply the already paralysing ties of our life in society. It is, in fact, a soul of immense power which bestows significance, beauty and a new lightness on what we are already doing.

Pierre Teilhard de Chardin, *Le Milieu Divin*, William Collins Sons & Co., 1960, page 43

The astronomical world is *not* all there is. We are in touch with other dimensions, other levels of life. And from among the powers that spring from these *other levels* there rises up one Power, all the more terrible because it refuses to practise cruelty, a Power that is neither Capitalist, nor Communist, or Fascist, nor Democratic, nor Nazi, a Power *not of this world at all*, but capable of inspiring the individual soul with the wisdom of the serpent and the harmlessness of the dove.

John Cowper Powys, *Autobiography*, Macdonald & Co., 1967, page 652

It was at the baptism that the Spirit came upon Jesus with power... The Jewish word for Spirit is *ruach*, which is the word which means *wind*. To the Jew there was always three basic ideas of Spirit. The Spirit was *power*, power like a mighty rushing wind; the Spirit was *life*, the very centre and soul and essence of life, the very dynamic of the existence of man; the Spirit was *God*; the power and the life of the Spirit were beyond mere human achievement and attainment. The coming of the Spirit into a man's life was the coming of God.

William Barclay, *The Gospel of John*, The Saint Andrew Press, 1965, volume 1, page 66

Working in a garden, in contact with the earth and the elements of Nature, gives me a deeper consciousness of the power which governs and is the source of all life. It makes me realize my dependence upon that power, and at the same time gives me the feeling of working together with God. It is the divine spark in the soul of man which unites him with the divine power and calls upon him to do his share in the partnership—to understand and minister to the needs of divine creation in whatever form it is manifested: plant, animal and, above all, human.

Pauline Rose, *Window on Mount Zion*, W.H. Allen, 1973, page 49

To become a Christian... is to pass over one of the most decisive watersheds in the universe, to go from one kingdom to another kingdom of a higher rank. The *process*—for it is a vital process—is from beginning to end in the realm of experience. By the exercise of faith in the crucified, risen and glorified God-Man, as the life-giving Spirit, real power from a higher world streams into the soul. Something 'pneumatic,' something which belongs ontologically to a higher spiritual world-order, comes into the person as a divinely bestowed germ-plasm, with living, renewing, organizing power.

Rufus M. Jones, *Spiritual Reformers in the 16th and 17th Centuries*, Macmillan and Co., 1914, page 71

The omnipotence of God is indemonstrable by any logic, because the power of love can only be truly apprehended from within, or rather by those in whom it already dwells. Selfish people can never understand it; and most of us have to learn with difficulty to recognize a new sort of power, before we can judge of the truth of God's almightiness as Christian saints have believed it. It is to those who believe, says St Paul, that the Cross is the power of God. It can be no matter of surprise to a Christian that many even intelligent people should reckon him either a fool or a hypocrite when he says that he believes in God the Father Almighty.

Oliver Quick, *Doctrines of the Creed*, James Nisbet & Co., 1938, page 66

All outward power that we exercise in the things about us is but as a shadow in comparison of that inward power that resides in our will, imagination, and desires; these communicate with eternity and kindle a life which always reaches either Heaven or hell... here lies the ground of the great efficacy of prayer, which when it is the prayer of the heart, the prayer of faith, has a kindling and creating power, and forms and transforms the soul into everything that its desires reach after: it has the key to the Kingdom of Heaven and unlocks all its treasures, it opens, extends and moves that in us which has its being and motion in and with the divine nature, and so brings us into real union and communion with God.

William Law, in Stephen Hobhouse, editor, *Selected Mystical Writings of William Law*, Rockliff, 1948, page 53

The cultivation of this quality [energy] is of the greatest importance; resolute determination in the pursuit of worthy objects being the foundation of all true greatness of character. Energy enables a man to force his way through irksome drudgery and dry details, and carries him onward and upward in every station of life. It accomplishes more than genius, with not one-half the disappointment and peril. It is not eminent talent that is required to ensure success in any pursuit, so much as purpose—not merely the power to achieve, but the will to labour energetically and perseveringly. Hence energy of will may be defined to be the very central power of character in a man—in a word, it is the Man himself. It gives impulse to his every action, and soul of every effort. True hope is based on it, and it is hope that gives the real perfume of life.

Samuel Smiles, *Self-Help*, S.W. Partridge & Co., 1912, page 147

The effects of such a [mystical] experience are (1) the birth of an inner conviction of God's immediate and environing Presence amounting to axiomatic certainty—faith through experience has become 'the substance,' and 'is now one spirit with God'; (2) The radiation of the whole being with 'a joy like that which parents have at the birth of their first-born child'—the joy now of the soul crying, 'Abba'; (3) A vastly heightened perception of what is involved in the eternal nature of the religious life and in the spiritual relation between the soul and God, *i.e.* increased ability to see what promotes and furthers the soul's health and development; (4) A unification, co-ordination, and centralizing of the inner faculties, so that there is an increment of power revealed in the entire personality; and (5) An increase of clarity and a sharpening of focus in the perception of moral distinctions with a distinctly heightened moral and social passion.

Rufus M. Jones, *Spiritual Reformers in the 16th and 17th Centuries*, Macmillan and Co., 1914, page 205

We live in a world where there are terrible abuses of power. In some countries there is torture, brainwashing, religious and political persecution, deliberate distortion of truth.

Man's ingenuity has produced terrible armaments, and there is the ever-present threat of nuclear war. These abuses of power are the result of men's choice of evil rather than good. They can only be remedied by a responsible use of power. Jesus contrasted the despotic use of power with that of his own life-style (Mark 10:41–5). 'And when the ten heard it, they began to be indignant at James and John. And Jesus called them to him and said to them, "You know that those who are supposed to rule over the Gentiles lord it over them, and their great men exercise authority over them. But it shall not be so among you; but whoever would be great among you must be your servant, and whoever would be first among you must be slave of all. For the Son of man also came not to be served but to serve, and to give his life as a ransom for many." '

Christians are not called to turn their back on power but to use it responsibly.

Hugh Montefiore, *Confirmation Notebook*, Fifth Edition, SPCK, 1985, page 7

One fine summer night in June 1933 I was sitting on a lawn after dinner with three colleagues, two women and one man. We liked each other well enough but we were certainly not intimate friends, nor had any one of us a sexual interest in another. Incidentally, we had not drunk any alcohol. We were talking casually about everyday matters when, quite suddenly and unexpectedly, something happened. I felt myself invaded by a power, which, though I consented to it, was irresistible and certainly not mine. For the first time in my life I knew exactly—because, thanks to the power, I was doing it—what it means to love one's neighbour as oneself. I was also certain, though the conversation continued to be perfectly ordinary, that my three colleagues were having the same experience. (In the case of one of them, I was able to confirm this.) My personal feelings towards them were unchanged—they were still colleagues, not intimate friends—but I felt their existence as themselves to be of infinite value and rejoiced in it.

I recalled with shame the many occasions on which I had been spiteful, snobbish, selfish, but the immediate joy was greater than the shame, for I knew that, so long as I was possessed by this spirit, it would be literally impossible for me deliberately to injure another human being. I also knew that the power would, of course, be withdrawn sooner or later and that, when it did, my greeds and self-regard would return. The experience lasted at its full intensity for about two hours when we said good-night to each other and went to bed. When I awoke next morning, it was still present, though weaker, and it did not vanish completely for two days or so. The memory of that experience has not prevented me from making use of others, grossly and often, but it has made it much more difficult for me to deceive myself about what I am up to when I do. And among the various factors which several years later brought me back to the Christian faith in which I had been brought up, the memory of this experience and asking myself what it could mean was one of the most crucial, though, at the time it occurred, I thought I had done with Christianity for good.

W.H. Auden, in Anne Fremantle, editor, *The Protestant Mystics*, The New English Library, 1955, page 30

PRAYER

Prayer—solemn request to God or object of worship; formula used in praying, practice of praying; entreaty to a person; thing prayed for

I was taught to say my prayers by our school chaplain. He gave us a simple technique in preparing us for Confirmation. We were to say our prayers at night, just before going to bed. First we were to start with thanksgiving, giving thanks for the many blessings we enjoyed. Secondly we were to move on to confession, owning up to all that had gone wrong in our lives—in thought, word, deed and omission—ending with an acceptance of God's forgiveness. Thirdly we were to say the Lord's Prayer. Fourthly we were to pray for other people, especially those who were in any kind of need. Finally we were to pray for ourselves and our own particular needs.

I used this technique for several years, and then gradually stopped saying my prayers. I was looking for a change. I came across *The Choice is Always Ours*. The emphasis of this book is on God's presence in the depths of ourselves. Tennyson's words struck a chord: 'Closer is He than breathing, and nearer than hands and feet.' Most of my prayer life so far had concentrated on talking to God. The time had come for a humbler approach on my part. Instead of doing all the talking I had to learn to keep quiet and listen. I found this difficult at first. Keeping a journal was a help. Gradually I learnt to reflect, meditate and contemplate. The material in *Visions of Faith, Hope, Love* and *Glory* is an aid, supporting this reflective way of prayer.

Now my eyes will be open and my ears attentive to the prayer that is made in this place. For now I have chosen and consecrated this house that my name may be there for ever; my eyes and my heart will be there for all time.

2 Chronicles 7:15–16

Then you will delight yourself in the Almighty, and lift up your face to God. You will make your prayer to him, and he will hear you.

Job 22:26–27

When you pray, go into your room and shut the door and pray to your Father who is in secret.

Matthew 6:6

And in the morning, a great while before day, he rose and went out to a lonely place, and there he prayed.

Mark 1:35

Prayer takes place in the heart, not in the head.

Carlo Carretto, *The Desert in the City*, translated by Barbara Wall, William Collins Sons & Co., 1983, page 23

Prayer is the Divine in us appealing to the Divine above us.

C.H. Dodd, in William Barclay, *The Letter to the Romans*, The Saint Andrew Press, 1969, page 116

My words fly up, my thoughts remain below:
Words without thoughts never to heaven go.

William Shakespeare, *Hamlet*, III. iii. 97

Let never day nor night unhallow'd pass,
But still remember what the Lord hath done.

William Shakespeare, *II King Henry VI*, II. i. 85

The exercise of prayer, in those who habitually exert it, must be regarded by us doctors as the most adequate and normal of all the pacifiers of the mind and calmers of the nerves.

William James, *Essays on Faith and Morals*, Longmans, Green and Co., 1943, page 235

You pray best when the mirror of your soul is empty of every image except the image of the invisible Father. This image is the Wisdom of the Father, the Word of the Father ... the glory of the Father.

Thomas Merton, *Thoughts in Solitude*, Burns & Oates, 1958, page 91

Prayer places our understanding in the divine brightness and light and exposes our will to the warmth of heavenly love. There is nothing that so effectually purges our understanding of its ignorance and our will of its depraved affections.

St Francis de Sales, *Introduction to the Devout Life*, Longmans, Green and Co., 1962, page 54

Prayer is the responsibility to meet others with *all* that I have, to be ready to encounter the unconditional in the conditional, to expect to meet God in the way, not to turn aside from the way.

John Robinson, *Honest to God*, SCM Press, 1963, page 100

Prayer should never be regarded as a science or reduced to a system—that ruins it, because it is essentially a living and personal relationship, which tends to become more personal and also more simple, as one goes on.

Evelyn Underhill, in Charles Williams, editor, *The Letters of Evelyn Underhill*, Longmans, Green and Co., 1947, page 271

So true prayer demands that we be more passive than active; it requires more silence than words, more adoration than study, more concentration than rushing about, more faith than reason.

Carlo Carretto, *Letters from the Desert*, translated by Rose Mary Hancock, Darton, Longman & Todd, 1972, page 55

Do not forget to say your prayers. If your prayer is sincere, there will be every time you pray a new feeling containing an idea in it, an idea you did not know before, which will give you fresh courage; you will then understand that prayer is education.

Fyodor Dostoyevsky, *The Brothers Karamazov*, translated by David Magarshack, Penguin Books, 1963, volume 1, page 375

Prayer is the sum of our relationship with God.
We are what we pray.
The degree of our faith is the degree of our prayer.
The strength of our hope is the strength of our prayer.
The warmth of our charity is the warmth of our prayer.

Carlo Carretto, *Letters from the Desert*, translated by Rose Mary Hancock, Darton, Longman & Todd, 1972, page 35

Prayer ardent opens heaven, lets down a stream
Of glory on the consecrated hour
Of man, in audience with the Deity.
Who worships the great God, that instant joins
The first in heaven, and sets his foot on hell.

Edward Young, *Night Thoughts*, viii. 721, in *The Complete Works of Edward Young*, William Tegg and Co., 1854, volume 1, page 168

Love to pray—feel the need to pray often during the day and take the trouble to pray. If you want to pray better, you must pray more. Prayer enlarges the heart until it is capable of containing God's gift of himself. Ask and seek and your heart will grow big enough to receive him and keep him as your own.

Mother Teresa of Calcutta, *In the Silence of the Heart*, compiled by Kathryn Spink, SPCK, 1983, page 17

Summe up at night, what thou hast done by day;
And in the morning, what thou hast to do.
Dresse and undresse thy soul: mark the decay
And the growth of it: if with thy watch, that too

Be down, then winde up both; since we shall be
Most surely judg'd, make thy accounts agree.

George Herbert, 'The Church Porch', in *The Poems of George Herbert*, Oxford University Press, 1961, page 20

God will always answer our prayers; *but He will answer them in His way*, and His way will be the way of perfect wisdom and of perfect love. Often if He answered our prayers as we at the moment desire, it would be the worst thing possible for us, for in our ignorance we often ask for gifts which would be our ruin.

William Barclay, *The Gospel of Matthew*, The Saint Andrew Press, 1965, volume 1, page 275

Prayer means turning to Reality, taking our part, however humble, tentative and half-understood, in the continual conversation, the communion, of our spirits with the Eternal Spirit; the acknowledgement of our entire dependence, which is yet the partly free dependence of the child. For prayer is really our whole life toward God: our longing for Him, our 'incurable God-sickness,' as Barth calls it, our whole drive toward Him. It is the humble correspondence of the human spirit with the Sum of all Perfection, the Fountain of Life. No narrower definition than this is truly satisfactory, or covers all the ground.

Evelyn Underhill, *The Spiritual Life*, Harper & Row, 1936, page 61

Prayer is speaking to God; so the first necessity is that you should be directing your mind towards God. That is the best part and the most important part of prayer anyhow, and without it all the rest is useless... Our Lord says that when you come into the presence of God you should forget all about yourself and your needs, even your sins; you should be so filled with the thought of God that what you want above all things is that God's Name may be hallowed—reverenced—throughout the world. You are to ask for that first, because you ought to want it most. And next, that He may be effectively King of the world He has made, so that all men obey His law; and then, that His whole purpose of love shall be carried out unspoiled by the selfishness of men.

William Temple, *Christian Faith and Life*, SCM Press, 1963, page 113

The effect of prayer is union with God, and, if someone is with God, he is separated from the enemy. Through prayer we guard our chastity, control our temper and rid ourselves of vanity. It makes us forget injuries, overcomes envy, defeats injustice and makes amends for sin. Through prayer we obtain physical well-being, a happy home, and a strong, well-ordered society... Prayer is the seal of virginity and a pledge of faithfulness in marriage. It shields the wayfarer, protects the sleeper, and gives courage to those who keep vigil... It will refresh you when you are weary and comfort you when you are sorrowful. Prayer is the delight of the joyful as well as the solace of the afflicted... Prayer is intimacy with God and contemplation of the invisible... Prayer is the enjoyment of things present and the substance of things to come.

Gregory of Nyssa, in William Barclay, *The Letter to the Romans*, The Saint Andrew Press, 1969, page 7

To pray is essentially:
to come to Jesus and to drink,
to come to him as to a friend,
to be in communion with him,
to remain in his love,
to trust him,
and to follow him;
it is to rest in him.

To pray is to cry out to Jesus and to the Paraclete, the One who answers the cry, when we cannot go on or when we fall and touch our pain and brokenness. It is to offer all this pain and the pain of the world, with him and in him to the Father. It is to let the Holy Spirit penetrate into our brokenness and to lead us to wholeness and teach us how to love as he loves.

Prayer is to be in contact with our own centre; it is to be close to our own source; it is to let Jesus make his home in us and to make our home in him. It is to be guided by Jesus, our good shepherd.

Jean Vanier, *The Broken Body*, Darton, Longman & Todd, 1988, page 115

First of all, it is very important to remember that prayer is an encounter and a relationship, a relationship which is deep, and this relationship cannot be forced either on us or on God. The fact that God can make Himself present or can leave us with the sense of His absence is part of this live and real relationship. If we could mechanically draw Him into an encounter, force Him to meet us, simply because we have chosen this moment to meet Him, there would be no relationship and no encounter. We can do that with an image, with the imagination, or with the various idols we can put in front of us instead of God; we can do nothing of the sort with the living God, any more than we can do it with a living person. A relationship must begin and develop in mutual freedom. If you look at the relationship in terms of *mutual* relationship, you will see that God could complain about us a great deal more than we about Him. We complain that He does not make Himself present to us for the few minutes we reserve for Him, but what about the twenty-three and a half hours during which God may be knocking at our door and we answer 'I am busy, I am sorry' or when we do not answer at all because we do not even hear the knock at the door of our heart, of our minds, of our conscience, of our life. So there is a situation in which we have no right to complain of the absence of God, because we are a great deal more absent than He ever is.

Anthony Bloom, *School for Prayer*, Darton, Longman & Todd, 1970, page 2

PRESENCE

Presence—being present; real presence, place where person is

There was a time when I tended to think of God miles above the sky and therefore absent from everyday living. Christ was seen primarily as someone who lived nearly 2,000 years ago and distanced from us by time. My eyes were opened to the presence of God by an experience recorded by Joseph Estlin Carpenter. One afternoon he went for a walk in the country. He had not gone far before he became conscious of the presence of someone else. He was unable to describe it. He felt he had as direct a perception of the being of God all about him, as if he were with a friend. For him, it was an act of spiritual apprehension. This experience never happened to him again but the effects never left him. The sense of a direct relation to God then generated in his soul became a part of his habitual thought and feeling.

William James recorded someone else who had a similar experience, which I have included in this section. The original comes from his book *The Varieties of Religious Experience.* I am also indebted to Brother Lawrence, a Carmelite lay brother of the seventeenth century. He developed a form of prayer called *The Practice of the Presence of God.* In this simple mode of prayer use is made of the imagination and intellect. For years he ran the monastery kitchen. Amid the noise and clatter of his kitchen he was able to possess God in as great a tranquillity as if he was upon his knees at the Blessed Sacrament. Perhaps we should take a leaf out of his book and practice the presence of God.

> My presence will go with you, and I will give you rest.
> Exodus 33:14

Fear not, for I am with you, be not dismayed, for I am your God; I will strengthen you, I will help you, I will uphold you with my victorious right hand.
> Isaiah 41:10

> I am with you always, to the close of the age.
> Matthew 28:20

All who keep his commandments abide in him, and he in them. And by this we know that he abides in us, by the Spirit which he has given us.
> 1 John 3:24

> Faith is the realisation of an invisible presence of truth.
> Henry Ward Beecher, *Proverbs from Plymouth Pulpit*, Charles Burnet & Co., 1887, page 183

Drench your spirit in the palpitating consciousness of the Presence! Then let an astonished world behold the resultant change!
> F.W. Boreham, *A Late Lark Singing*, Epworth Press, 1945, page 160

People are hungry for the word of God that will give peace, that will give unity, that will give joy. But you cannot give what you don't have. That's why it is necessary to deepen your life of prayer. Allow Jesus to take you, pray with you and through you, and then you will be a real, true contemplative in the heart of the world.
> Mother Teresa, *Jesus, the Word to be Spoken*, compiled by Brother Angelo Devananda, William Collins Sons & Co., 1990, page 74

The presence of God which sanctifies our souls is the indwelling of the Blessed Trinity, who take up their abode in the depths of our hearts when we submit to the divine will; for the presence of God that results from contemplation effects this intimate union in us only in the same way as other things which are part of God's design.
> Jean-Pierre de Caussade, S.J., *Self-Abandonment to Divine Providence*, William Collins Sons & Co., 1972, page 42

Practice ... the presence of God ... Let us thus think often that our only business in this life is to please God, that perhaps all besides is but folly and vanity ... Let us think of Him perpetually. Let us put all our trust in Him ... We cannot have too much in so good and faithful a Friend, Who will never fail us in this world or in the next.
> Brother Lawrence, *The Practice of the Presence of God*, A.R. Mowbray & Co., 1977, page 50

What Christians claim in 'Christian experience' is not to pick up a body of wrought-out knowledge on the cheap, and to have a pat reply to all the mysteries of the universe, but to be aware of a Presence ...

As the Christian responds to the Presence and ventures forward, he becomes acquainted with a Person—holy, loving and merciful, and One who proves His personal care over all who turn to Him in trust.
> W.E. Sangster, *Give God a Chance*, Epworth Press, 1968, page 104

At the same time they became conscious by degrees of an usual yearning of the soul for stillness and solitude, and for a rest and quietness in which all the natural powers are hushed and silent. And their hearts seem to them to be drawn away into a region where all external things become distasteful, and pass into forgetfulness. And they are drawn sweetly and gently in the hidden power of love, to God Himself, and *awaken to a sense of His presence.*

Gerhard Tersteegen, in Frances Bevan, Sketches of the Quiet of the Land, John F. Shaw and Co., 1891, page 384

It is the presence of God which makes anywhere heaven or hell or what we call purgatory. The presence of God is the heaven of those who love His presence; the presence of God is the hell of those who do not love His presence; and the presence of God is the sweet purification of the penitent who longs to be worthy of His presence. The presence of God is everywhere, and it is our reaction to it which makes us either good or peaceful people, or rebellious, defiant people, or penitent, learning people.

Father Andrew, S.D.C., The Symbolism of the Sanctuary, A.R. Mowbray & Co., 1927, page 18

'Walk before Me, and be thou perfect.' (Gen. 17:1).

They are the words of God to Abraham, instructing us, that to live in the Presence of God is the way to perfection. We never depart from that way, but by losing sight of God, and forgetting our dependence upon Him. God is the Light by which we see, and the end at which we should aim. In all the business and events of life we should consider only the order of His Providence, and we shall maintain a sense of His Presence in the midst of our business, as long as we have no other intention in performing it, but purely that of obeying Him.

François de la M. Fénelon, Spiritual Thoughts for Busy People, SPCK, 1894, page 85

Lord, what a change within us one short hour
Spent in thy presence will prevail to make,
What heavy burdens from our bosoms take,
What parched grounds refresh, as with a shower.
We kneel, and all around us seems to lower;
We rise, and all, the distant and the near,
Stands forth in sunny outline, brave and clear;
We kneel how weak, we rise how full of power.
Why therefore should we do ourselves this wrong,
Or others—that we are not always strong,
That we are ever overborne with care,
That we should ever weak or heartless be,
Anxious or troubled, when with us is prayer,
And joy and strength and courage are with Thee?

Richard Chenevix Trench, 'Sonnet', in Poems, Macmillan and Co., 1885, volume 1, page 196

God is more real to me than any thought or thing or person. I feel his presence positively, and the more as I live in closer harmony with his laws written in my body and mind. I feel him in the sunshine or rain; and awe mingled with a delicious restfulness most nearly describes my feelings. I talk to him as to a companion in prayer and praise, and our communion is delightful. He answers me again and again, often in words so clearly spoken that it seems my outer ear must have carried the tone, but generally in strong mental impressions. Usually a text of Scripture, unfolding some new view of him and his love for me, and care for my safety. I could give hundreds of instances, in school matters, social problems, financial difficulties, etc. That he is mine and I am his never leaves me, it is an abiding joy. Without it life would be a blank, a desert, a shoreless, trackless waste.

Quoted by William James, in The Varieties of Religious Experience, William Collins Sons & Co., 1974, page 85

Men of acknowledged and pre-eminent saintliness agree very closely in what they tell us about God. They tell us that they have arrived gradually at an unshakeable conviction, not based on inference but on immediate experience, that God is a Spirit with whom the human spirit can hold intercourse; that in Him meet all that they can imagine of goodness, truth, and beauty; that they can see His footprints everywhere in nature, and feel His presence within them as the very life of their life, so that in proportion as they come to themselves they come to Him. They tell us that what separates us from Him and from happiness is, first, self-seeking in all its forms; and, secondly, sensuality in all its forms; that these are the ways of darkness and death, which hide from us the face of God; while the path of the just is like a shining light, which shineth more and more unto the perfect day. As they have toiled up the narrow way, the Spirit has spoken to them of Christ and has enlightened the eyes of their understandings, till they have at least *begun* to know the love of Christ which passeth knowledge, and to be filled with all the fulness of God.

W.R. Inge, *Christian Mysticism*, Methuen & Co., 1912, page 325

Having found different ways of attaining to God and different practices of the spiritual life in many different books, I came to the conclusion that they would serve to hinder rather than to help me in my quest, which was for nothing else but a way of becoming wholly God's. So I made up my mind to give all to gain all, and, after giving myself up entirely to God... I renounced everything in the world that came between Him and me... I looked on Him as my Father and my God, worshipping Him as often as I was able, and recollecting myself whenever my mind was distracted from His holy presence. I found no little difficulty in this exercise, but I persevered in spite of my failures not worrying or blaming myself when my distractions were involuntary. I did this not only at my set times of prayer, but at all times driving away from my mind everything that could displace the thought of God, every hour, every minute, even at my busiest moments.

Such... has been my practice ever since I entered religion, and, though I have grievously given way to slackness and weakness, I have received very great benefits thereby. That I owe to the mercy and goodness of God I know well enough; for we can do nothing without Him... But by keeping ourselves faithfully in His presence and setting Him always before our eyes, not only do we hinder ourselves from displeasing Him, at any rate wilfully, but we also gain a holy liberty to ask for those graces of which we stand in need. In fact, by so often repeating these acts they become habitual, and the presence of God becomes, as it were, natural.

Brother Lawrence, *The Practice of the Presence of God*, introduction by Dorothy Day, Burns & Oates, 1977, page 96

Many of us would say that God knows all and sees all. Yet few of us act consistently with this *apparent* belief. If we did, how could we act in the manner we do, how can we contrive to dwell on the thoughts that we do? The holy men and women urge us to strive to live in the presence of God, to be conscious of God being fully with us every moment. Brother Lawrence, a seventeenth-century advocate of such practice and a simple, unsophisticated person as the world judges, lived his life in the presence of God for half a century. This humble man has said that it is not difficult to acquire the habit, that it does not take particularly long. The initial effort requires a great spiritual struggle—hard work that is—but soon the habit of mind can be cultivated, developed. Then God takes over. It is as if God has seen that we are sincere in our efforts to live continually in the divine presence, and so when we have the human tendency to lapse, God assists us. But God does not initiate the attitude in us. We are allowed our freedom here, as in all other things. But when we choose the spiritual path of trying to experience God's divine presence in us at all times, ceaselessly, then we will receive the assistance that we need. We can imagine the tremendous, the significant effect such an ongoing experience will have on our lives. If I am a political figure, all my votes and decisions would be based on moral considerations. As a teacher, my work for the students would be my work for God—no more skimping on class preparations or short-tempered responses to those who don't catch on as quickly as I would wish. Again, our imagination can help us to project the effect living in the divine presence might have on us as spouses, drivers, neighbours, members of a racial or economic group, citizens—the list is as long as each of us wishes to make it. Asking God's help to be with God and working toward this end can lead to 'ordinary' life lived on a heroic level.

Harry James Cargas, *Encountering Myself*, SPCK, 1978, page 64

PRIDE

Pride—overweening opinion of one's own qualities, merits, etc;
arrogant bearing or conduct; exalted position, consciousness of this,
arrogance; also proper pride—a sense of what befits one's position,
preventing one from doing an unworthy thing

The Gurkhas are a good illustration of a proper sense of pride. They have an honourable outlook on life and an infectious enthusiasm for their work. They are the smartest soldiers in the world, both on and off parade. They have a well-deserved reputation for loyalty, cheerfulness and bravery. I remember an occasion when a rifleman was picked up for a fault in his arms drill. Late that evening he was hard at work, ironing out the fault. He, like the others, had a proper sense of pride which insisted on doing a good job and producing top quality work. I was very privileged to serve with them.

We all know of instances of the other kind of pride. For the writer of Ecclesiasticus, the beginning of human pride is to desert the Lord, and to turn one's heart away from one's maker. Linking this up with the Genesis story of the creation of man, we are left with two choices, either to centre ourselves on 'the God within' or on ourselves. Most of us choose the latter and end up in pride. Seen from this perspective, we can understand why pride is designated the first of the seven deadly sins. Not only are we caught up in an inordinate self-love, but at one and the same time we shut ourselves off from 'the God within' and a vast resource of 'life' in the depths of our being.

The Lord tears down the house of the proud.

Proverbs 15:25

The beginning of human pride is to desert the Lord, and to turn one's heart away from one's maker.

Ecclesiasticus 10:12 (JB)

He has scattered the proud in the imagination of their hearts, he has put down the mighty from their thrones.

Luke 1:51–52

None of you may be puffed up in favour of one against another. For who sees anything different in you? What have you that you did not receive? If then you received it, why do you boast as if it were not a gift?

1 Corinthians 4:6–7

His own opinion was his law.

William Shakespeare, *Henry VIII*, IV. ii. 37

Self-blinded are you by your pride.

Alfred, Lord Tennyson, 'The Two Voices', line 23, in *The Works of Alfred Lord Tennyson*, Macmillan and Co., 1898, page 31

A *Proud* man hath no *God*: for he hath put God down, and set Himself up.

Benjamin Whichcote, *Morals and Religious Aphorisms*, ix. 801, Elkin, Mathews & Marrot, 1930, page 90

Pride: ignorant presumption that the qualities and status of the organism are due to merit.

A.R. Orage, *On Love*, The Janus Press, 1957, page 60

Intellectual pride inflicts itself upon everybody. Where it dwells there can be no other opinion in the house.

Cardinal Manning, *Pastime Papers*, Burns & Oates, 1892, page 27

Pride, like the magnet, constantly points to one object, self; but, unlike the magnet, it has no attractive pole, but at all points repels.

Charles Caleb Colton, *Lacon*, William Tegg, 1866, page 248

Perverted pride is a great misfortune in men; but pride in its original function, for which God created it, is indispensable to a proper manhood.

Henry Ward Beecher, *Proverbs from Plymouth Pulpit*, Charles Burnet & Co., 1887, page 26

Now, if this thought that you deliberately conjure up, or harbour, and dwell lovingly upon, is natural worth or knowledge, charm or station, favour or beauty—then it is *Pride*.

The Cloud of Unknowing, translated by Clifton Wolters, Penguin Books, 1971, page 68

We need to avoid pride. Pride destroys everything. That's why Jesus told his disciples to be meek and humble. He didn't say contemplation is a big thing—but being meek and humble with one another. If you understand that, you understand your vocation. To live his way is the key to being meek and humble.

Mother Teresa, *Jesus, the Word to be Spoken*, compiled by Brother Angelo Devananda, William Collins Sons & Co., 1990, page 20

As all things are God's, so all things are to be used and regarded as the things of God. For men to abuse things on earth, and live to themselves, is the same rebellion against God, as for angels to abuse things in Heaven; because God is just the same Lord of all on earth, as He is the Lord of all in Heaven.

William Law, *A Serious Call to a Devout and Holy Life*, J.M. Dent & Co., 1898, page 39

The self-centred or self-concerned soul, making itself the object of its contemplation, and seeing all else as related to itself, is trying to feed upon itself. The food may be congenial, but the process is inevitably one of wastage. Such a soul must shrink and shrivel, suffering at last both the pain of unsatisfied hunger and the pain of contraction.

William Temple, *Nature, Man and God*, Macmillan and Co., 1934, page 421

In the last resort there are only two pivots about which human life can revolve, and we are always organising society and ourselves about one or other of them. They are self and God. In the great book with which the Bible closes, these two principles are set before us under the symbolical figures of the 'Lamb standing, as it had been slain'—the symbol of love that uses sacrifice as its instrument—and the great wild beast, the symbol of self-will or pride, whose instrument is force.

William Temple, *Christian Faith and Life*, SCM Press, 1963, page 132

... the one kind of pride which is wholly damnable is the pride of the man who has something to be proud of. The pride which, proportionally speaking, does not hurt the character, is the pride in things which reflect no credit on the person at all. Thus it does a man no harm to be proud of his country, and comparatively little harm to be proud of his remote ancestors. It does him more harm to be proud of having made money, because in that he has a little more reason for pride. It does him more harm still to be proud of what is nobler than money—intellect. And it does him most harm of all to value himself for the most valuable thing on earth—goodness.

G.K. Chesterton, *Heretics*, The Bodley Head, 1938, page 167

Pride which for good reason is reckoned to be the principal sin, has been defined in a number of ways, as an exaggerated self-love, as an excessive concern for one's dignity, as a refusal to acknowledge dependence...

Vanity is a form of pride which relies on the approbation of others to maintain a superior self-image. The admiration of others helps to keep at bay my feelings of worthlessness. Pride can be seen as a kind of idolatry, the worship of a self-image and the overvaluation of objects, persons, causes, institutions, which are relied upon to make the self-image seem secure. Pride leads a person to seek security for himself apart from God. The proud person may not be an atheist intellectually but his attitude implies atheism.

Christopher Bryant, S.S.J.E., *The Heart in Pilgrimage*, Darton, Longman & Todd, 1980, page 37

Simple people, between whom and God there is no barrier of pride, whose minds are not clouded or confused by the innumerable theories and hypotheses of experimental science, who, moreover, are not the possessors of great material wealth or highly organized by subdivision of labour for the production of wealth for others, such people, such souls are readily attuned to divine wind. For them it seems most natural and most reasonable that all the things of earth should be analogues of the divine reality, echoes of the divine voice, material counterparts of the divine ideas. And if the trees and rocks, the thunder and the sea, the frightful avidity of animal life and the loveliness of flowers are so many hints of God who made them, how much more obviously are the things of humanity analogues of the things of God.

Eric Gill, *Art Nonsense and Other Essays*, Cassell and Co., 1929, page 199

Pride is the root sin. Here Self takes the place of God; hence it is both rebellion and idolatry. It takes many forms, all closely interrelated; they can be summed up under three heads: pride of power, pride of knowledge, and pride of virtue. Yet most of us are so deeply infected with pride that we fail to recognize it in ourselves though we are quick to detect it in others. Sometimes it comes out in a sneer of contempt for 'Poor So-and-so'; it is very evident in excessive self-regard: if our instinctive question is always: 'What will suit *me*?' if we are always trying to be in the centre of the picture, this is an evidence of pride. Boasting, even of an inverted refined kind, is another symptom; and so of course is every brand of conceit and vanity, the desire of praise, intolerance and opinionatedness, presumption and exaggerated love of independence, and unwillingness to receive from others. Personal ambition and the desire to dominate are obvious signs of this sin.

Olive Wyon, *On the Way*, SCM Press, 1958, page 50

Man's arrogance never ceases to amaze me. He has become so high and powerful, so much in control of so much of the universe... yet he doesn't see that there are still things he hasn't yet discovered and that his science is only in its infancy.

He has penetrated the subconscious enough to gain great knowledge and discover the source of man.

He is very advanced in his study of man in society and within its economic and political structures and knows what he should know: he can analyse all society and all structures and measure their value and influence. Finally when those who study the universe, man and society have studied and understood everything, they will still be faced with the unknown, the incomprehensible—the monumental mystery of the 'senses' which, for all their science and knowledge, they will never fathom.

Yes, I'm amazed that man should still be so arrogant because it seems to me that the more knowledge and power he acquires, the more he should be aware of his own ignorance and weakness.

Michel Quoist, *With Open Heart*, translated by Colette Copeland, Gill and Macmillan, 1983, page 92

But a vain man is a nauseous creature: he is so full of himself, that he has no room for anything else, be it ever so good or deserving. It is I, at every turn, that does this, or can do that. And as he abounds in his comparisons, so he is sure to give himself the better of everybody else; according to the proverb, 'All his geese are swans.' They are certainly to be pitied that can be so much mistaken at home. And yet I have sometimes thought, that such people are, in a sort, happy, that nothing can put out of countenance with themselves, though they neither have, nor merit, other people's. But at the same time, one would wonder they should not feel the blows they give themselves, or get from others, from this intolerable and ridiculous temper; nor shew any concern at that, which makes others blush for, as well as at them, viz. their unreasonable assurance. To be a man's own fool is bad enough; but the vain man is everybody's. This silly disposition comes of a mixture of ignorance, confidence, and pride: and as there is more or less of the last, so it is more or less offensive, or entertaining. And yet, perhaps, the worst part of this vanity is its unteachableness. Tell it anything, and it has known it long ago; and out-runs information and instruction, or else proudly puffs at it. Whereas the greatest understandings doubt most, are readiest to learn, and least pleased with themselves; this, with nobody else. For though they stand on higher ground, and so see further than their neighbours, they are yet humbled by their prospect, since it shows them something so much higher above their reach.

And truly then it is that sense shines with the greatest beauty when it is fed in humility.

William Penn, *Fruits of Solitude*, A.W. Bennett, 1863, page 91

RECONCILIATION

Reconciliation—a healing, a restoration of relationships,
a re-establishment of friendship

A short time ago, I was taking part in a reflection group. The topic selected by members of the group was 'guilt'. We spent the first half-hour in silence, each of us reflecting on some twenty quotations about guilt. The second half-hour was spent in discussion. I triggered this off by asking if anyone in particular had chosen 'guilt'? One of the group said he was the one who made a bid for 'guilt'. I asked him if there was any reason for his choice of topic. 'Yes,' he said, 'several years ago I was very positive about life. I was keen on my studies and worked hard. Physically I was extremely fit and eager to excel in sport. I was also interested in meeting people and wanted to be socially successful. Now, it has all gone. I have been caught up in several forms of self-indulgence and lost my zest for life. I really want to get back to where I was.' I asked him if he had found anything helpful. Yes, there were a number of points he wanted to follow up and explore.

In the discussion which followed I was reminded of the parable of the prodigal son; how he left home to do his own thing. He eventually 'came to himself' and returned home. He was welcomed back by his father, forgiven, restored, and a loving reconciliation took place. I wonder if the secret of reconciliation lies in a 'coming to ourselves' and discovering 'a loving Father' in the depths of our being. Seen this way we can be welcomed back by God, forgiven, restored, reconciled, and made ready for a new start in life.

Agree with God, and be at peace; thereby good will come to you.
Job 22:21

A fool is too arrogant to make amends; upright men know what reconciliation means.
Proverbs 14:9 (NEB)

If you are offering your gift at the altar, and there remember that your brother has something against you, leave your gift there before the altar and go; first be reconciled to your brother, and then come and offer your gift.
Matthew 5:23–24

For he is our peace, who has made us both one, and has broken down the dividing wall of hostility, by abolishing in his flesh the law of commandments and ordinances, that he might create in himself one new man in place of the two, so making peace, and might reconcile us both to God in one body through the cross, thereby bringing the hostility to an end.
Ephesians 2:14–16

When powers and institutions are reconciled to God, they become more modest, and take on their proper place in His purposes.
David Sheppard, *Bias to the Poor*, Hodder and Stoughton, 1983, page 173

... refers to a change of attitude from hostility to amity, of God toward humanity, of humanity toward God, and of individuals toward each other.

Oliver O'Donovan, in James F. Childress and John Macquarrie, editors, *A New Dictionary of Christian Ethics*, SCM Press, 1986, page 528

There is a dark
Invisible workmanship that reconciles
Discordant elements, makes them move
In one society.

William Wordsworth, *The Prelude*, i. 341, in E. de Selincourt and Helen Darbishire, editors, *The Poetical Works of William Wordsworth*, Oxford at the Clarendon Press, 1959, page 22

This very beautiful word is one of the key words of the New Testament. There has been a very wrong thought that an angry God demanded to be propitiated by the sacrifice of an innocent victim, that He has been reconciled to us by the innocent suffering of His dear Son. The New Testament story is not the tale of a God Who had to be got to forgive men by the pleading of the Saviour, but of how God Himself went out as a Good Shepherd to find the wanderer, how God took the initiative and set against man's sin His own perfect love. It is not that God has to be reconciled to us, but it is that by God's love we can be reconciled to Him. We can be brought back to the peace of a happy relationship with our God.

Father Andrew, S.D.C., *Christ the Companion*, A.R. Mowbray & Co., 1945, page 111

Looking back on my own experiences they all converge towards a kind of insight to which I cannot help ascribing some metaphysical significance. The keynote of it is invariably a reconciliation. It is as if the opposites of the world, whose contradictoriness and conflict make all our difficulties and troubles, were melted into unity. Not only do they, as contrasted species, belong to one and the same genus, but *one of the species*, the nobler and better one, *is itself the genus, and so soaks up and absorbs its opposite into itself.*

This is a dark saying, I know, when thus expressed in terms of common logic, but I cannot wholly escape from its authority.

William James, *The Varieties of Religious Experience*, William Collins Sons & Co., 1974, page 374

The priest is still the *minister of reconciliation*; and by this office he links the common life of the Church to the gospel of divine forgiveness upon which its common life depends.

Now the priest today is only one among many skills and agencies designed to help people in their troubles. The psychiatrist, the doctor, the welfare officer, the marriage guidance counsellor, and many kinds of social worker bring relief to the problems with which people get entangled. The parson's monopoly has long ceased, and the confessional no longer stands pre-eminent as the seat of counsel and direction. Yet amidst all the various activities for the putting right of human ills there is so often a whole dimension missing, the dimension of sin and forgiveness. It not seldom happens that psychiatry, instead of liberating the patient into the realm of moral responsibility and the issues of conscious sin and forgiveness, can substitute medicine for moral responsibility. It is this dimension of sin and forgiveness which the priest keeps alive by an office which represents the forgiving Church and the forgiving Lord Jesus. He will do this by his ministry in Confession and Absolution and by his preaching of the gospel of God's reconciliation. He will bear witness to the cost of forgiveness to the divine holiness, and he will remember that the familiar phrase in 2 Corinthians 5:20 which we translate 'the ministry of reconciliation' means 'the ministry of *the reconciliation*', the reconciliation once for all wrought on the hill of Calvary and subsequently to be applied through the centuries to every penitent heart. 'Whose sin thou dost forgive they are forgiven.'

Michael Ramsey, *The Christian Priest Today*, SPCK, 1983, page 8

The whole Gospel of S. Luke is full of the spirit of reconciliation, the reconciliation of man with God, of person with person. The spirit of reconciliation is necessary in all ages. We may have perfect organization and perfect machinery, but, unless we have a right spirit behind them, they will not effect much. The forces of coercion on one side and revenge on the other will never do any good. Christ's religion reveals His spirit, and it is a reconciling spirit. Some people, wherever they go, bring trouble, and others bring blessing and healing, as did this great tender doctor, who was with S. Paul to the end, and must have had so sweet a character.

It is of the first importance that the world should be educated, and rightly educated. If a boy is taught to write beautifully, without a true teaching of morality, he may become a clever forger. If a man is taught the science of medicine without religious faith, he may become an inventor of poisonous drugs. One need not be afraid of education, but only of a bad education; nor need we be afraid of the truth, but only of a half-truth. Our religion teaches us that the whole of life is one thing. The interest of India is the interest of England; the interest of Germany is the interest of France; the interest of men is the interest of women. We are one great family, and, as we are created in the image of our Father, it must be our joy, as it is our duty, to produce the perfect life of the true children of God, the life of men and women who can look into each other's eyes with courageous love, because they have the faith that can face any future without fear.

Father Andrew, S.D.C., *Meditations for Every Day*, A.R. Mowbray & Co., 1941, page 320

The sacrament of reconciliation is part of our Lord's warming love expressed through the ministry of healing. Neither of the older terms, confession and penance, conveys a purpose beyond the mechanics of sincere regret and contrition. To confess and yet remain captive to feelings of guilt is to miss the reality of the Church's commission and Christ's command.

Pardon comes through sincere repentance and our deep desire to put matters right before God and those whom we have wronged. The free-flowing power of God's love will only become a reality for us when individually and willingly we confess our sins.

To know how to do this, without wasting emotional energy in self-delusion and being irrelevant, we need the guidance of a spiritual director who will help us to build our lives on three great guidelines: a rule of life suited to our needs, on-going spiritual direction, and regularity in the sacrament of reconciliation. Faithfully followed these will ensure peace of mind and purpose in life, literally becoming saving grace during times of need or stress.

The sacrament of reconciliation has always been public and/or private. In the Anglican Church the guideline has always been, *all may, none must, some should—and many ought*. This is totally confidential and the priest who hears a confession is under a sacred oath never to reveal the contents under any circumstances. Through the proper guidance of a priest the sacrament of reconciliation can be an enormously cleansing experience. Spiritual direction will enable you to discover a deepened awareness about daily living.

Reconciliation commits us to
asking God for discernment to see our sins
being truly sorry
confessing our sins and determining to do better
giving thanks for such cleansing,
and fresh opportunities to do better.

Giles Harcourt, *Dawn through our Darkness*, William Collins Sons & Co., 1985, page 231

REDEMPTION

Redemption—redeeming or being redeemed; thing that redeems,
purchase the freedom of another, oneself

In 1960 I went up to Balliol to read for a law degree. In our First Public Examinations (Law Mods) we had to take a paper in Roman law. I remember there was a certain procedure for the freeing of slaves, called manumission. The outcome was as follows. A wealthy man went to the slave market. He bought a slave and assumed property rights over him. He then renounced his rights in manumission and set the slave free. By this he broke the fetters of slavery and *redeemed* the slave.

Christ's crucifixion was viewed from this legal background. His death on the cross was interpreted as the cost of our redemption. The fetters of sin were broken and we were set free from slavery. The process of *redemption* was complete.

I prefer to look at redemption from a different perspective. The starting point is the now familiar Genesis story of the creation of man. God fashions and shapes man in his own image and likeness and breathes something of his nature into man. Man becomes a living being. That which is fashioned and shaped in the image and likeness of God is taken from the dust of the earth. Man, as well as having a divine potential, is at one and the same time earthy and creaturely. Sadly, the earthy and creaturely predominated.

In his life, Christ *redeemed* fallen human nature. The divine in him accepted and integrated the earthy and creaturely, and thereby transformed human nature. The outcome was a whole full-blooded human being, very God and very man. This process of redemption, at one level complete, needs to be repeated in our lives.

I will redeem you with an outstretched arm and with great acts of judgment, and I will take you for my people, and I will be your God; and you shall know that I am the Lord your God.
Exodus 6:6–7

For with the Lord there is steadfast love, and with him is plenteous redemption.
Psalm 130:7

Blessed be the Lord God of Israel, for he has visited and redeemed his people.
Luke 1:68

But when the time had fully come, God sent forth his Son, born of woman, born under the law, to redeem those who were under the law, so that we might receive adoption as sons.
Galatians 4:4–5

Redemption is the ultimate actualization of potentialities—to 'be what we must be'.
A.R. Orage, *On Love*, The Janus Press, 1957, page 60

If you are cut down in a movement that is designed to save the soul of a nation, then no other death could be more redemptive.
Martin Luther King, *The Words of Martin Luther King*, selected by Coretta Scott King, William Collins Sons & Co., 1986, page 67

Sin is always loving badly, or not loving at all.
Redemption is Jesus Christ restoring to the world the full weight of love, of which man robbed it through his sin.
Michel Quoist, *With Open Heart*, translated by Colette Copeland, Gill and Macmillan, 1983, page 223

There is nothing in this world or the next, absolutely nothing, which cannot, and will not, be turned into the valid currency we need to buy the one pearl of great price. That is what is meant when we say that we are redeemed.

H.A. Williams, C.R., *True Wilderness*, William Collins Sons & Co., 1983, page 53

After the forgiveness of sin must come the cure of sin. And that cure, like most cures, is a long and a painful process.

But there is our comfort, there is our hope—Christ the great Healer, the great Physician, can deliver us, and will deliver us, from the remains of our old sins, the consequences of our own follies. Not, indeed, at once, or by miracle, but by slow education in the new and nobler motives, in purer and more unselfish habits.

Charles Kingsley, *Daily Thoughts*, Macmillan and Co., 1884, page 169

To the eye of Faith the common life of humanity, not any abnormal or unusual experience, is material of God's redeemimg action. As ordinary food and water are the stuff of the Christian sacraments, so it is the ordinary pain and joy, tension and self-oblivion, sin and heroism of normal experience that His moulding and transfiguring work is known. The Palestinian glow which irradiates the lovely mysteries of the Gospel, and gives to them the quality of eternal life, lights up for Faith the slums and suburbs, the bustle, games and industries of the modern world.

Evelyn Underhill, in John Stobbart, editor, *The Wisdom of Evelyn Underhill*, A.R. Mowbray & Co., 1951, page 18

All things are blessed now, but sin; for all things, excepting sin, are redeemed by the life and death of the Son of God. Blessed are wisdom and courage, joy and health and beauty, love and marriage, childhood and manhood, corn and wine, fruit and flowers, for Christ redeemed them by His life ...

Blessed is death, and blessed the unknown realms where souls await the Resurrection Day, for Christ redeemed them by His death. Blessed are all days, dark as well as bright, for all are His, and He is ours; and all are ours, and we are His for ever.

Charles Kingsley, *Daily Thoughts*, Macmillan and Co., 1884, page 289

Now here is opened to us the true reason of the whole process of our Saviour's incarnation, passion, death, resurrection and ascension into Heaven. It was because fallen man was to go through all these stages as necessary parts of his return to God; and therefore, if man was to go out of his fallen state there must be a son of this fallen man, who, as a head and fountain of the whole race, could do all this, could go back through all these gates and so make it possible for all the individuals of human nature, as being born of Him, to inherit His conquering nature and follow Him through all these passages to eternal life. And thus we see, in the strongest and clearest light, both why and how the holy Jesus is become our great Redeemer.

William Law, in Stephen Hobhouse, editor, *Selected Mystical Writings of William Law*, Rockliff, 1948, page 59

The great weakness of all doctrines of redemption since the Primitive Christian is that they represent a man as wholly concerned with his own individual redemption, and not equally with the coming of the Kingdom of God. The one thing needful is that we should work for the establishment of a Christianity, which does not permit those who allow their lives to be determined by Christ to be 'of little faith' in regard to the future of the world. However much circumstances may suggest to them this want of faith, Christianity must compel them to realise that to be a Christian means to be possessed and dominated by a hope of the Kingdom of God, and a will to work for it, which bids defiance to external reality. Until this comes about Christianity will stand before the world like a wood in the barrenness of winter.

Albert Schweitzer, *The Mysticism of Paul the Apostle*, A. & C. Black, 1931, page 384

By the fall of our first father we have lost our first glorious bodies, that eternal, celestial flesh and blood which had as truly the nature of paradise and Heaven in it as our present bodies have the nature, mortality and corruption of this world in them: if, therefore, we are to be redeemed there is an absolute necessity that our souls be clothed again with this first paradisaical body or heavenly flesh and blood, or we can never enter into the Kingdom of God. Now this is the reason why the Scriptures speak so particularly, so frequently, and so emphatically of the powerful blood of Christ, of the great benefit it is to us, of its redeeming, quickening, life-giving virtue; it is because our first life or heavenly flesh and blood is born again in us, or derived again into us from this blood of Christ.

William Law, in Stephen Hobhouse, editor, *Selected Mystical Writings of William Law*, Rockliff, 1948, page 63

Accustom thyself to the Holy Service of this inward Temple. In the midst of it is the Fountain of Living Water, of which thou mayest drink, and live for ever. There the Mysteries of thy Redemption are celebrated, or rather opened in Life and Power. There the Supper of the Lamb is kept; the *Bread that came down from Heaven, that giveth Life to the World*, is thy true Nourishment: all is done, and known in real Experience, in a living Sensibility of the Work of God on the Soul. There the Birth, the Life, the Sufferings, the Death, the Resurrection and Ascension of Christ, are not merely remembered, but inwardly found, and enjoyed as the real States of thy Soul, which has followed Christ in the Regeneration. When once thou art well grounded in this *inward Worship*, thou wilt have learnt to live unto God *above Time*, and *Place*. For every Day will be *Sunday* to thee, and wherever thou goest, thou wilt have a *Priest*, a *Church*, and an *Altar* along with Thee.

William Law, in Sidney Spencer, editor, *The Spirit of Prayer*, James Clarke & Co., 1969, page 51

As faith in Christ is something wholly different from the belief that Matthew, Mark, Luke, and John wrote the four narratives of our Lord's earthly life contained in the New Testament, so it is wholly different from a belief in the authenticity of these narratives. If, when my heart is dark with the sense of guilt, and all my strength is broken through despair of the Divine mercy, I trust in Christ for forgiveness, and the awful weight which crushed me is removed, and the light breaks, and I am conscious that in the mystery of my personal relations to the Eternal a great change has come, and that God has absolved me; if, having known in past days the blessedness of living in the presence of God, I am lonely and desolate because no sign or intimation of the presence of God is given me, and I trust in Christ to restore me to God, and the vision and the power and the glory return; if when the springs of life seem to have dried up, and there is apathetic indifference to all those invisible and eternal things which once filled me with awe, kindled fire of love for God and for man, created an exulting hope, transfigured the world, exalted the ideal of conduct, and inspired strength and resolution to attempt to achieve it—if then I trust in Christ to have pity on me, and the 'river of water of life clear as crystal, proceeding out of the throne of God,' returns to its deserted channels, and rises and overflows its banks; if, I say, Christ in answer to my faith does the great things for me, what more direct, appropriate, decisive evidence can I have that He is the Redeemer and Lord of men? It is the precise kind of evidence that I need to authenticate and confirm my faith in Him.

R.W. Dale, *The Living Christ and the Four Gospels*, Hodder and Stoughton, 1890, page 36

The concept is derived from one of the most basic features of human life in society: the urge to exchange something in one's own possession for something possessed by another. All kinds of objects have been exchanged, normally with the conviction that what was received was equal to or even more valuable than what was given.

Redemption, meaning *buying back*, implies that a situation has existed in which an individual or a society has been brought into some kind of bondage. This may have been of an earthly kind, e.g. an individual may have become a slave, or a tribe may have been subjugated by a stronger nation. Alternatively the bondage may have been of a superhuman kind, e.g. an individual may believe himself to have been paralysed by a spell or a taboo or by some demonic agent; a society may be deemed to lie under a ban or a sentence of condemnation. It is because of the manifold ways in which humans have felt themselves to be confined, oppressed, threatened, doomed that the prospect of *redemption* has captured the human imagination...

The central theme represented by such words as redemption, deliverance, liberation is that of divine compassion leading to active succour on behalf of those oppressed and unable to help themselves. The danger of redemption theology has been a tendency to compare the divine action with that of victorious warriors or of champions using physical force. The writers of the New Testament insist that the divine redemption involved identification with the human lot, refusal to use physical instruments of compulsion, submission to man's last enemy, death. By identifying himself with humans in their temptations, trials, hopelessness, suffering and death he paid an immeasurably costly price and brought into being a new humanity, bearing his own image and committed to following his example.

The most eloquent celebration of Christian redemption is found in the Epistle to the Ephesians (1:7, 14; 4:30). Here the cost, the immediate effects and the final goal of redemption are vividly portrayed. All earthly deliverances are but types and models of the *eternal redemption* (Heb. 9:14) which Christ has obtained for us.

F.W. Dillistone, in Alan Richardson and John Bowden, editors, *A New Dictionary of Christian Theology*, SCM Press, 1985, page 487

RELIGION

Religion—monastic condition; practice of sacred rites; one of the prevalent systems of faith and worship; human recognition of superhuman controlling power and especially of a personal God entitled to obedience, effect of such recognition on conduct and mental attitude

Of all the quotations in this section the one I like best is by Henry Ward Beecher— 'Religion is a state of the soul. The kingdom of God within us.' In my opinion the author of this proverb gets right to the heart of the matter. The soul is the meeting-place of God in man. Here, we can find something of the presence of the Father, the Son and the Holy Spirit. This includes the gifts of the Holy Spirit—wisdom, knowledge, counsel, understanding, might (power), fear (feelings of awe and reverence) and the Spirit of the Lord. If we accept these gifts and live by them we can also experience the fruits of the Spirit—love, joy, peace, patience, kindness, goodness, faithfulness, gentleness and self-control. The sum total of all this is the kingdom of God within us. This is, however, only half the story. An experience of the kingdom of God within us opens our eyes to discover the kingdom of God outside us—in nature, in other people, in art, in music, in poetry, in literature, in science, etc.—in the whole living process.

The central message of Jesus is this kingdom of God. His life was an inauguration of the kingdom, and he promised a similar experience to those who were prepared to follow him. This is the essence of what we mean by religion in *Visions of Glory*.

I perceive that in every way you are very religious.

Acts 17:22

Great indeed, we confess, is the mystery of our religion: He was manifested in the flesh, vindicated in the Spirit, seen by angels, preached among the nations, believed on in the world, taken up in glory.

1 Timothy 3:16

For men will be lovers of self, lovers of money, proud, arrogant, abusive, disobedient to their parents, ungrateful, unholy, inhuman, implacable, slanderers, profligates, fierce, haters of good, treacherous, reckless, swollen with conceit, lovers of pleasure rather than lovers of God, holding the form of religion but denying the power of it.

2 Timothy 3:2–5

If any one thinks he is religious, and does not bridle his tongue but deceives his heart, this man's religion is vain. Religion that is pure and undefiled before God and the Father is this: to visit orphans and widows in their affliction, and to keep oneself unstained from the world.

James 1:26–27

Religion is a state of the soul. The kingdom of God within us.

Henry Ward Beecher, Proverbs from Plymouth Pulpit, Charles Burnet & Co., 1887, page 123

The gauge of religion is the intensity and the productiveness of the love-principle.

Henry Ward Beecher, Proverbs from Plymouth Pulpit, Charles Burnet & Co., 1887, page 116

All religion is of the Life, and the Life of Religion is the doing of good.

Emanuel Swedenborg, Doctrine of Life for the New Jerusalem, The Swedenborg Society, 1897, page 1

Religion hath its *inwards*, as well as its *outwards*; which hold proportion to *spirit* and *flesh*.

Benjamin Whichcote, Moral and Religious Aphorisms, iv. 363, Elkin, Mathews & Marrot, 1930

Institutional religion will always exasperate us because it is carried on in the words and deeds of inadequate and sinful human beings.

J. Neville Ward, Five for Sorrow, Ten for Joy, Epworth Press, 1971, page 31

The object of religion is not to make dreaming speculators, but real, earnest, vigorous men. It is not to remove the burden from our path, but to enable us to bear it.

Henry Ward Beecher, Proverbs from Plymouth Pulpit, Charles Burnet & Co., 1887, page 119

Religion is intended to fit a man for life—to teach him how to carry himself in his business, his pleasures, and his pains, as much as to aid him when he dies.

Henry Ward Beecher, Proverbs from Plymouth Pulpit, Charles Burnet & Co., 1887, page 121

Religion is a thing not alien to us. It has to be evolved out of us. It is always within us: with some, consciously so; with others, quite unconsciously. But it is always there.

Mohandas K. Gandhi, in C.F. Andrews, Mahatma Gandhi's Ideas, George Allen & Unwin, 1929, page 66

Religion will not regain its old power until it can face change in the same spirit as does science. Its principles may be eternal, but the expression of those principles requires continual development.

Alfred North Whitehead, Science and the Modern World, The New American Library, 1964, page 168

To him [Mahatma Gandhi] Religion is an intensely practical thing. It underlies all action. Politics, morals, commerce—all that has to do with conscience must be Religion. He can only think in this way.

C.F. Andrews, *Mahatma Gandhi's Ideas*, George Allen & Unwin, 1929, page 66

... a religion of universal validity, brought to birth by the discovery of God in Christ as revealed in the Gospel, and made continuously effective anew by personal experience of the same Christ as Divine Revealer in the lives of men.

Rufus M. Jones, *Spiritual Reformers in the 16th and 17th Centuries*, Macmillan and Co., 1914, page 238

Religious sentimentality instead of the numinosum of divine experience: this is the well-known characteristic of a religion that has lost the living mystery. It is easily understandable that such a religion is incapable of giving help or of having any other moral effect.

C.G. Jung, *Psychological Reflections*, selected and edited by Jolande Jacobi, Routledge & Kegan Paul, 1953, page 313

Religion... is shown not in some intellectual or verbal formulations but in one's total orientation to life. Religion is whatever the individual takes to be his ultimate concern. One's religious attitude is to be found at that point where he has a conviction that there are values in human existence worth living and dying for.

Rollo May, *Man's Search for Himself*, Souvenir Press, 1975, page 210

Religion is... thought of as the normal way of life, as the true fulfilment of human nature and as complete inward health. 'Holiness,' he says, 'is our right constitution and temper, our inward health and strength.' Sin and selfishness carry a man below the noble Creation which God made in him, and Religion is the return to the true nature and capacity of God's Creation in man.

Rufus M. Jones, *Spiritual Reformers in the 16th and 17th Centuries*, Macmillan and Co., 1914, page 298

His religion is not of the theoretical kind, but it is a constant, earnest, sincere practice. It is neither demonstrative nor loud, but manifests itself in a quiet practical way, and is always at work. It is not aggressive, which sometimes is troublesome, if not impertinent. In him, religion exhibits its loveliest features; it governs his conduct...

H.M. Stanley, *How I Found Livingstone*, Sampson, Low, Marston, Low, and Searle, 1872, page 434

... the reality of religion is so completely bound up with the whole personal life of man and with his conjunct life in the social group and in the world of nature; it is, in short, so much an affair of man's whole of experience, of his spirit in its undivided and synthetic aspects, that it can never be adequately dealt with by the analytic and descriptive method of this wonderful new god of science, however big with results that method may be.

Rufus M. Jones, *Spiritual Reformers in the 16th and 17th Centuries*, Macmillan and Co., 1914, page xviii

One suspects... that religion has a long while yet to run before its work is over. For in its innermost and intensest meaning religion has concerned itself with the release, emancipation, salvation, growth of the soul. Behind its disguises of theory and ritual, all great religion has one common centre: it sees human life as the adventure of the soul. Its insistent question is: 'For what shall it profit a man, if he shall gain the whole world, and lose his own soul?' To religious insight the most important truth about man is that he has been entrusted with himself, capable on the one hand of dismal failure, or on the other of high adventure into the life that is life indeed.

Harry Emerson Fosdick, *Twelve Tests of Character*, Hodder and Stoughton, 1923, page 105

The early stage of religion is characterized by externals, and only after long processes of tutorship and discipline does the soul learn how to live by the Seed of life and Light of truth within. The early stage is legalistic, during which the person is 'hedged about' with promises and threats, 'walled in' with laws and ordinances, 'living in a perpetual alarm of fears,' 'shut up to rules, retirements and forms'—but it is far better to serve God from fear and by outward rules than not to serve Him at all. The true way of progress is to move up from fear and law to love and freedom, and from outward rules to the discovery of a central Light of God, a Heavenly Image, in the depths of one's own spirit.

Rufus M. Jones, *Spiritual Reformers in the 16th and 17th Centuries*, Macmillan and Co., 1914, page 285

A man who is religious, is religious morning, noon, and night; his religion is a certain character, a mould in which his thought, words, and actions are cast, all forming parts of one and the same whole. He sees God in all things; every course of action he directs towards those spiritual objects which God has revealed to him; every occurrence of the day, every event, every person met with, all news which he hears, he measures by the standard of God's will. And a person who does this may be said almost literally to pray without ceasing; for, knowing himself to be in God's presence, he is continually led to address Him reverently, whom he sets always before him, in the inward language of prayer and praise, of humble confession and joyful trust.

John Henry Newman, in Erich Przymara, S.J., editor, *The Heart of Newman*, Burns & Oates, 1963, page 174

A religion true to its nature must also be concerned about man's social conditions. Religion deals with both earth and heaven, both time and eternity. Religion operates not only on the vertical plane but also on the horizontal. It seeks not only to integrate men with God but to integrate men with men and each man with himself. This means, at bottom, that the Christian gospel is a two-way road. On the one hand, it seeks to change the souls of men and thereby unite them with God; on the other hand, it seeks to change the environmental conditions of men so that the soul will have a chance after it is changed. Any religion that professes to be concerned with the souls of men and is not concerned with the slums that damn them, the economic conditions that strangle them, and the social conditions that cripple them is a dry-as-dust religion. Such a religion is the kind the Marxists like to see—an opiate of the people.

Martin Luther King, *The Words of Martin Luther King*, selected by Coretta Scott King, William Collins Sons & Co., 1986, page 66

Religion begins for us with an awareness that our life is not of ourselves alone. There is another, greater life, enfolding and sustaining us. Religion as man's search for this greater self will not accept any creeds as final or any laws as perfect. It will be evolutionary, moving ever onward. The witness to this spiritual view is borne, not only by the great religious teachers and leaders of mankind, but by the ordinary man in the street, in whose inmost being the well of the spirit is set deep. In our normal experience events happen which imply the existence of a spiritual world. The fact of prayer or meditation, the impulse to seek and appeal to a power beyond our normal self, the moving sense of a revelation which the sudden impact of beauty brings, the way in which decisive contacts with certain individuals bring meaning and coherence into our scattered lives, suggest that we are essentially spiritual. To know oneself is to know all we can know and all we need to know. A spiritual as distinct from a dogmatic view of life remains unaffected by the advance of science and criticism of history. Religion generally refers to something maternal, a system of sanctions and consolations, while spirituality points to the need for knowing and living in the highest self and raising life in all its parts. Spirituality is the core of religion and its inward essence, and mysticism emphasises this side of religion.

Sir Sarvepalli Radhakrishnan, *Eastern Religions and Western Thought*, Oxford University Press, 1940, page 61

And an old priest said, Speak to us of Religion.
And he said:
Have I spoken this day of aught else?
Is not religion all deeds and all reflection,
And that which is neither deed or reflection, but a wonder and a surprise ever springing in the soul, even while the hands hew the stone or tend the loom?
Who can separate his faith from his actions, or his belief from his occupations?
Who can spread his hours before him, saying, 'This for God and this for myself; This for my soul and this other for my body'? ...
Your daily life is your temple and your religion.
Whenever you enter into it take with you your all.
Take the plough and the forge and the mallet and the lute,
The things you have fashioned in necessity or for delight ...
And take with you all men:
For in adoration you cannot fly higher than their hopes nor humble yourself lower than their despair.
And if you would know God, be not therefore a solver of riddles.
Rather look about you and you shall see Him playing with your children. And look into space; you will see Him walking in the cloud, outstretching His arms in the lightning and descending in rain.
You shall see Him smiling in flowers, then rising and waving His hands in trees.

Kahlil Gibran, The Prophet, William Heinemann, 1970, page 90

RENUNCIATION

Renunciation—renouncing, self-denial, giving up of things

At University College, London, I used to organize a speaker meeting called *Forum*. One of our guest speakers was a doctor, who combined conventional medicine with spiritual healing. He was scheduled to speak in Lent. He warned us beforehand he would be fasting— on a diet of bread and water only—for forty days. I expected to see a thin, emaciated man but he turned out to be a picture of health, with bright shining eyes, like those of an eagle. Fasting, he claimed, made him lucid, and vastly improved his powers of concentration and discernment.

Since his talk, I have come to look at *renunciation* in a much more positive way. We give up something to make way for something better or greater. A writer, H.H. Leavitt, states this combination perfectly. 'Fasting,' he wrote, 'is the attitude of, "Lord, empty me of self." Prayer is the insistent cry of one's soul, "Lord, fill me with thyself." '

I try to put into practice these words on a daily basis. Fasting in the sense of 'Lord, empty me of self' means a death to the dominance of the ego, to the prior place sometimes occupied by the earthy and creaturely. Prayer in the sense of 'Lord, fill me with thyself' means spending time in reflection, being open to receive something of the divine. This form of self-discipline can be seen in the Gospels, in the life of Christ, and in the lives of the saints down the ages. The experts of spirituality see *renunciation* as a healthy exercise, leading to fulness of life. *Visions of Glory* can be used to foster this practice.

For the wicked boasts of the desires of his heart, and the man greedy for gain curses and renounces the Lord. In the pride of his countenance the wicked does not seek him; all his thoughts are, 'There is no God.'

Psalm 10:3–4

218

Thou hast renounced the covenant with thy servant; thou hast defiled his crown in the dust.

Psalm 89:39

We have renounced disgraceful, underhanded ways; we refuse to practice cunning or to tamper with God's word, but by the open statement of the truth we would commend ourselves to every man's conscience in the sight of God.

2 Corinthians 4:2

I count everything as loss because of the surpassing worth of knowing Christ Jesus my Lord. For his sake I have suffered the loss of all things, and count them as refuse, in order that I may gain Christ.

Philippians 3:8

For in what measure we put off the creature, in the same measure are we able to put on the Creator; neither more nor less.

Theologia Germanica, translated by Susanna Winkworth, Stuart & Watkins, 1966, page 36

Denying the world does not mean that we do not possess it in courageous use of all its possibilities, but only that we do not allow it to possess us.

John Oman, *Natural and Supernatural*, Cambridge at the University Press, 1931, page 471

Deliverance is not for me in renunciation. I feel the embrace of freedom in a thousand bonds of delight. Thou ever pourest for me the fresh draught of thy wine of various colours and fragrance, filling this earthen vessel to the brim.

My world will light its hundred different lamps with thy flame and place them before the altar of thy temple.

No, I will never shut the doors of my senses. The delights of sight and hearing and touch will bear thy delight.

Yes, all my illusions will burn into illumination of joy, and all my desires ripen into fruits of love.

Rabindranath Tagore, *Gitanjali*, Macmillan and Co., 1971, page 68

... if we desire to have our souls moulded to this holy frame, to become partakers of the divine nature, and have Christ formed in our hearts, we must seriously resolve and carefully endeavour to avoid and abandon all vicious and sinful practices. There can be no treaty of peace, till once we lay down those weapons of rebellion, wherewith we fight against heaven: nor can we expect to have our distempers cured, if we be daily feeding on poison. Every wilful sin gives a mortal wound to the soul, and puts it at a greater distance from God and goodness; and we can never hope to have our hearts purified from corrupt affections, unless we cleanse our hands from vicious actions. Now in this case we cannot excuse ourselves by the pretence of impossibility, for sure our outward man is some way in our power, we have some command of our feet, and hands, and tongue, nay, and of thoughts and fancies too, at least so far as to divert them from impure and sinful objects, and to turn our mind another way; and we should find this power and authority much strengthened and advanced, if we were careful to manage it and exercise it. In the mean while, acknowledge our corruptions are so strong, and our temptations so many, that it will require a great deal of steadfastness and resolution, of watchfulness and care, to preserve ourselves even in this degree of innocence and purity.

Henry Scougal, *The Life of God in the Soul of Man*, C.J.G. & F. Rivington, 1829, page 45

Our next essay must be to wean our affections from created things, and all the delights and entertainments of the lower life, which sink and depress the souls of men, and retard their motions towards God and heaven; and this we must do by possessing our minds with a due persuasion of the vanity and emptiness of worldly enjoyments. This is an ordinary theme, and every body can make declamations upon it: but alas! how few understand and believe what they say! These notions float in our brains, and come sliding off our tongues, but we have no deep impression of them in our spirits, we feel not the truth which we pretend to believe. We can tell that all the glory of splendour, all the pleasures and enjoyments of the world, are vanity and nothing; and yet these nothings take up all our thoughts, and engross all our affections; they stifle the better inclinations of the soul, and inveigle us into many a sin. It may be in a sober mood, we give them the slight, and resolve no longer to be deluded with them; but these thoughts seldom outlive the next temptations; the vanities which we have shut out at the door get in at the postern; there are still some pretentions, some hopes that flatter us; and after we have been frustrated a thousand times, we must be continually repeating the experiment; the least difference of circumstances is enough to delude us, and make us expect that satisfaction in one thing, which we have missed in another: but could we once get clearly off, and come to a real and serious contempt of worldly things, this were a very considerable advancement in our way. The soul of man is of a vigorous and active nature, and hath in it a raging and inextinguishable thirst, and immaterial kind of fire, always catching at some object or other, in conjunction wherewith it thinks to be happy; and were it once rent from the world, and all bewitching enjoyments under the sun it would quickly search after some higher and more excellent object, to satisfy its ardent and importunate cravings, and being no longer dazzled with glittering vanities, would fix on that supreme and all-sufficient Good, where it would discover such beauty and sweetness, as would charm and overpower all its affections.

Henry Scougal, *The Life of God in the Soul of Man*, C.J.G. & F. Rivington, 1829, page 53

Our blessed Saviour and His Apostles are wholly taken up in doctrines that relate to common life. They call us to renounce the world, and differ in every temper and way of life, from the spirit and the way of the world: to renounce all its goods, to fear none of its evils, to reject its joys, and have no value for its happiness: to be as new-born babes that are born into a new state of things: to live as pilgrims in spiritual watching, in holy fear, and heavenly aspiring after another life: to take up our daily cross, to deny ourselves, to profess the blessedness of mourning, to seek the blessedness of poverty of spirit: to forsake the pride and vanity of riches, to take no thought for the morrow, to live in the profoundest state of humility, to rejoice in worldly sufferings: to reject the lust of the flesh, the lust of the eyes, and the pride of life: to bear injuries, to forgive and bless our enemies, and to love mankind as God loveth them: to give up our whole hearts and affections to God, and strive to enter through the strait gate into a life of eternal glory.

This is the common devotion which our blessed Saviour taught, in order to make it the common life of all Christians. Is it not therefore exceeding strange that people should place so much piety in the attendance upon public worship, concerning which there is not one precept of our Lord's to be found, and yet neglect these common duties of our ordinary life, which are commanded in every page of the Gospel? I call these duties the devotion of our common life, because if they are to be practised, they must be made parts of our common life; they can have no place anywhere else.

If contempt of the world and heavenly affection is a necessary temper of Christians, it is necessary that this temper appear in the whole course of their lives, in their manner of using the world, because it can have no place anywhere else. If self-denial be a condition of salvation, all that would be saved must make it a part of their ordinary life. If humility be a Christian duty, then the common life of a Christian is to be a constant course of humility in all its kinds. If poverty of spirit be necessary, it must be the spirit and temper of every day of our lives. If we are to relieve the naked, the sick, and the prisoner, it must be the common charity of our lives, as far as we can render ourselves able to perform it. If we are to love our enemies, we must make our common life a visible exercise and demonstration of that love. If content and thankfulness, if the patient bearing of evil be duties to God, they are the duties of every day, and in every circumstance of our life. If we are to be wise and holy as the new-born sons of God, we can no otherwise be so, but by renouncing every thing that is foolish and vain in every part of our common life.

William Law, A Serious Call to a Devout and Holy Life, J.M. Dent & Co., 1898, page 7

REPENTANCE

Repentance—a change of heart and mind, sometimes brought about
by regret, remorse, sorrow and contrition; a turning round
involving a change of priorities

Jesus called people to 'repent, for the kingdom of heaven is at hand'. A good example of repentance is Saul on the road to Damascus. He was on his way to track down disciples of the Lord and bring them bound to Jerusalem for the high priest. Suddenly a light from heaven flashed about him and he fell to the ground. He heard a voice, saying, 'Saul, Saul, why do you persecute me?' And he said, 'Who are you, Lord?' And the voice said, 'I am Jesus, whom you are persecuting; but rise and enter the city, and you will be told what you are to do.' In the space of a few days, Saul experienced a major change of heart and mind—a *repentance*—and spent the rest of his days an apostle.

The Greek word for repentance (*metanoia*) means more than a change of heart and mind but 'involves turning to God and changing one's ways'. Think of this in the context of the Genesis story of the creation of man. On the one hand there is the divine inbreathing and a source of divine life in the heart of man. On the other hand there is the presence of the earthy and creaturely. Most of us are well aware this side of human nature has dominated our lives down the ages. Imagine now a repentance involving a complete turn-around, in which we centre ourselves on God and relegate the earthy and creaturely. This *repentance* would certainly lead to a change of heart and mind, and lead to an upheaval in our way of life. Centring ourselves on God, we would experience the kingdom of heaven—close at hand.

Wash yourselves; make yourselves clean; remove the evil of your doings from before my eyes; cease to do evil, learn to do good; seek justice, correct oppression; defend the fatherless, plead for the widow.

Isaiah 1:16–17

Repent and turn from all your transgressions, lest iniquity be your ruin. Cast away from you all the transgressions which you have committed against me, and get yourselves a new heart and a new spirit!

Ezekiel 18:30–31

Repent, for the kingdom of heaven is at hand.

Matthew 3:2

Repent therefore, and turn again, that your sins may be blotted out, that times of refreshing may come from the presence of the Lord.

Acts 3:19

The seeds of repentance are sown in youth by Pleasure, but the harvest is reaped in age by Pain.

Charles Caleb Colton, *Lacon*, William Tegg, 1866, page 262

Confess yourself to heaven;
Repent what's past; avoid what is to come.

William Shakespeare, *Hamlet*, III. iv. 150

If a man turns to Christ, nothing in him is to be left behind. Every passion must be brought to Him to be transformed by Him. Otherwise the man does not come, but only a part of him.

Said by a friend to Mark Rutherford, in Mark Rutherford, *More Pages From a Journal*, Oxford University Press, 1910, page 245

Whatever, therefore, is foolish, ridiculous, vain, or earthly, or sensual, in the life of a Christian, is something that ought not to be there; it is a spot and a defilement that must be washed away with tears of repentance.

William Law, *A Serious Call to a Devout and Holy Life*, J.M. Dent & Co., 1898, page 132

Turning and becoming a child must... mean at least jettisoning this need for position, for 'standing', and so being willing to be knocked down. It means being exposed and vulnerable.

J. Neville Ward, *Five for Sorrow, Ten for Joy*, Epworth Press, 1971, page 23

Christ calls us to repentance, not so that we shall remain at this introspective stage, but so that, forgiven and set free, we can throw ourselves into action, and bring forth fruit, as he himself insists.

Paul Tournier, *The Person Reborn*, SCM Press and William Heinemann, 1967, page 209

He said: 'I don't know how to repent.' That was true: he had lost the faculty. He couldn't say to himself that he wished his sin had never existed, because the sin seemed to him now so unimportant—and he loved the fruit of it.

Graham Greene, *The Power and the Glory*, William Heinemann, 1940, page 159

Presume not that I am the thing I was;
For God doth know, so shall the world perceive,
That I have turn'd away my former self;
So will I those that kept me company.

William Shakespeare, *II Henry IV*, V. iv. 56

Jesus called the people to 'repent, for the kingdom of heaven is at hand' (Matt. 4:17). Repentance (*metanoia*, a change of mind) presupposes regret, remorse, sorrow and contrition for one's unrighteousness, and it involves turning to God and changing one's ways.

James F. Childress, in James F. Childress and John Macquarrie, editors, *A New Dictionary of Christian Ethics*, SCM Press, 1986, page 534

This, then, is the philosophy of fasting. It expresses repentance, and it uncovers the life of God. 'Come down, my pride; stand back my passions; for I am wicked, and I wait for God to bless me.' You see what I mean by fasting. It is the voluntary disuse of anything innocent in itself, with a view to spiritual culture. It does not apply to food alone. It applies to everything which a man may desire.

Phillips Brooks, *The Candle of the Lord and other Sermons*, Macmillan and Co., 1881, page 206

In ordinary use, the word refers to a person's regret of a past action or thought deemed unacceptable. In scripture, however, repentance (*metanoia*) implies acceptance of the challenge to human beings to respond to God's call in Jesus Christ that they 'repent, for the kingdom of God is at hand'. This response consists of a turning away from a life of rebellion, inertia or perversity, and a turning to God in Christ in faith. In this context, repentance is not a single act, but an ongoing responsiveness to the will of God, a continuous experience made possible through the gift of grace. The gospel enables the person to be gracious when confronted with the reality of his or her failures and with the magnitude of the gulf between the individual and the perfect will of God. But concrete steps are necessary for the renewal of life in Jesus Christ to occur. The genuineness of one's repentance is demonstrated by actual changes in actions, thoughts and feelings: through one's evaluation of their life in the light of scripture, through honesty in confession, and through receptivity to forgiveness. Thus does repentance enable a person to grow ever closer to God in Christ.

Lewis R. Rambo, in Alan Richardson and John Bowden, editors, *A New Dictionary of Christian Theology*, SCM Press, 1985, page 499

When Jesus urged men to repent, he was urging them to become as little children. He wasn't asking them to eat the dust. He was confronting them with the necessity of a radical change of outlook, a fundamental reorientation of their lives, so that they would no longer trust for security in the persona they had built up—the drama of being me which I continuously stage for my own benefit—so that they would no longer trust that, but have the courage to become as receptive as little children, with all the openness to life, the taking down of the shutters and the throwing away of the armour which that entails...

That is what repentance means: discovering that you have more to you than you dreamt or knew, becoming bored with being only a quarter of what you are and therefore taking the risk of surrendering to the whole, and thus finding more abundant life...

It is obvious how important repentance is for the Christian. It was part of the basic message of Jesus. He began his ministry by telling men to repent and believe in the gospel.

Unless, therefore, we are willing to repent, we cannot be his disciples.

H.A. Williams, C.R., *True Wilderness*, William Collins Sons & Co., 1983, pages 72, 76 and 78

What does repentance mean? The word originally meant an *afterthought*. Often a second thought shows that the first thought was wrong; and so the word came to mean *a change of mind*. But, if a man is honest, a change of mind demands *a change of action*. Repentance must involve both change of mind and change of action. A man may change his mind and come to see that his actions were wrong but be so much in love with his old ways that he will not change them. A man may change his ways but his mind remains the same, changing only because of fear or prudence. True repentance involves a change of mind *and* a change of action.

When repentance comes something happens *to the past*. There is God's forgiveness for what lies behind. Let us be quite clear that the *consequences* of sins are not wiped out. Not even God can do that. When we sin we may well do something to ourselves and to others which cannot be undone. Let us look at it this way. When we were young and had done something bad there was an invisible barrier between us and our mother. But when we went and said we were sorry, the old relationship was restored and we were right with her again. Forgiveness does not abolish the consequences of what we have done but it puts us right with God.

When repentance comes something happens *for the future*. We receive *the gift of the Holy Spirit* and in that power we can win battles we never thought to win and resist things which by ourselves we would have been powerless to resist.

William Barclay, *The Acts of the Apostles*, The Saint Andrew Press, 1979, page 28

When we take sin seriously, it is obvious that we 'must do something about it'. If we have even a glimmering of an idea of what the love of God means, and of all that He suffers to bring us back to Himself, we feel the very least we can do is to say with all our hearts: 'I will arise and go to my Father, and will say unto Him, 'I have sinned...' When we realize too that our sin affects others, known and unknown, we long to break the chains which bind us to ourselves, and give ourselves up to God and His service. A very saintly man once said: 'My own return to God is the greatest good I could do to anyone else.' One of the greatest sins of religious people is the refusal to believe certain sins are forgiven.

Repentance involves penitence and confession of sin. The first step in confession is to be honest with ourselves, to admit that in a particular instance we have *sinned*. Then we turn to God, asking Him to forgive us, and set us free. For some people, this secret and private confession to God is all they require. Their repentance is thorough and deep. To others the practice of confession is essential. It is a very ancient practice, of immense value. Whether we confess to a priest, and receive absolution through the Church, or informally to a trusted Christian friend, the practice of confession, wisely used, is a great safeguard against some of the dangers to the spiritual life, and indeed to life as a whole.

Definite repentance, leading to confession of sin, followed by reparation or restitution where this is possible, liberates the whole personality, and sets it free for God's service.

This freedom springs from the grateful acceptance of the free forgiveness of God in Christ. Bunyan's matchless words express this best:

'Up this way therefore did burdened Christian run, but not without great difficulty, because of the load on his back. He ran thus till he came to a place somehow ascending: and upon that place stood a Cross, and a little below, in the bottom, a sepulchre. So I saw in my dream, that, just as Christian came up with the Cross, his burden loosed from off his shoulders, and fell from off his back, and began to tumble... till it came to the mouth of the sepulchre, where it fell in, and I saw it no more. Then was Christian glad and lightsome, and said with a merry heart, "He hath given me rest by His sorrow, and life by His death".'

Olive Wyon, *On the Way*, SCM Press, 1958, page 54

RESURRECTION

Resurrection—rising from the dead, especially the Resurrection of Christ; rising again of men at the last day; revival from disuse or inactivity

Three observations have helped me to believe in the resurrection of Christ. The first comes from some words of Martin Luther, writing about nature: 'Our Lord has written the promise of the Resurrection, not in books alone, but in every leaf in springtime.' The wistaria outside my rooms in the Radcliffe Quad look to be dead in winter, and yet each springtime there is a 'resurrection'—leaves re-appear, followed by those familiar pale purple flowers.

The second observation comes from some words of Emil Brunner, the Swiss theologian: 'You believe in the Resurrection, not because it is reported by the Apostles but because the Resurrected One Himself encounters you in a living way.' I would like to link this statement with the experience of Archbishop Anthony Bloom, recorded in the last quotation of this section. At a time of his life when he was an atheist the resurrected one encountered him in a living way, and proved to be the decisive factor in his journey of faith.

The third observation follows on from the Genesis story of the creation of man, and the life of Christ. In the practice of reflection, it is possible to experience a 'resurrection', a *re-surrection*—a rising of the divine from the depths of ourselves where we have 'entombed' him. This, too, can be decisive on our journey of faith.

These observations have helped me to believe in the reality of the historic resurrection, and to a life of faith, hope, love and glory.

For I know that my Redeemer lives,
and at last he will stand upon the earth;
and after my skin has been thus destroyed,
then from my flesh I shall see God.

Job 19:25–26

Jesus said to her, 'I am the resurrection and the life; he who believes in me, though he die, yet shall he live, and whoever lives and believes in me shall never die.'

John 11:25–26

Yet a little while, and the world will see me no more, but you will see me; because I live, you will live also.

John 14:19

Blessed be the God and Father of our Lord Jesus Christ! By his great mercy we have been born anew to a living hope through the resurrection of Jesus Christ from the dead, and to an inheritance which is imperishable, undefiled, and unfading, kept in heaven for you.

1 Peter 1:3–4

Jesus's resurrection makes it impossible for man's story to end in chaos—it has to move inexorably towards light, towards life, towards love.

Carlo Carretto, *The Desert in the City*, translated by Barbara Wall, William Collins Sons & Co., 1983, page 103

The Resurrection is not a miracle like any other. It is a unique manifestation within this world of the transition God makes for us out of this way of being into another.

Austin Farrer, *Saving Belief*, Hodder and Stoughton, 1964, page 83

What is more difficult, to be born or to rise again; that what has never been should be, or that what has been should be again? Is it more difficult to come into existence than to return to it?

Blaise Pascal, *Pensées*, translated by W.F. Trotter, Random House, 1941, page 77

The friends of Jesus saw him and heard him only a few times after that Easter morning, but their lives were completely changed. What seemed to be the end proved to be the beginning; what seemed to be a cause for fear proved to be a cause for courage; what seemed to be defeat proved to be victory; and what seemed to be the basis for despair proved to be the basis for hope. Suddenly a wall becomes a gate, and although we are not able to say with much clarity or precision what lies beyond that gate, the tone of all that we do and say on our way to the gate changes drastically.

Henri J.M. Nouwen, *Seeds of Hope*, edited by Robert Durback, Darton, Longman & Todd, 1989, page 137

Resurrection is a mighty act of God. Remember that in the New Testament the language used is not of Jesus rising, but of Jesus being raised by God. Jesus did not 'achieve' resurrection: rather did he make himself naught, and when all was dark, when human possibilities were exhausted, God raised him by a mighty act of his power.

This truth about resurrection colours the whole process of man's movements towards his goal, whether in this world or the next. It is not that man, even under God's grace, gets gradually better and better, and so attains to saintliness here, and to heaven hereafter. Rather does the grace of God work surprises, turning defeats into deliverances, 'calling things that are naught as though they are', and acting beyond any laws of progress or expectation.

Michael Ramsey, *Through the Year with Michael Ramsey*, edited by Margaret Duggan, Hodder and Stoughton, 1975, page 178

Christ is the first-born of this new creation. He is the first 'new Adam,' who by His triumphant life and victorious resurrection has become for ever 'a life-giving Spirit,' the creative Principle of a new humanity. In Christ the Word of God, the actual Divine Seed of God, became flesh, entered into our human nature and penetrated it with Spirit and with Life, conquered its stubborn bent toward sin, and transfigured and transformed this human flesh into a divine and heavenly substance. By obedience to the complete will of God, even to the extreme depths of suffering, sacrifice, and death on the Cross for the love of men, Christ glorified human flesh, exalted it from flesh to spirit, and in His resurrected heavenly life He is able to unite Himself inwardly with the souls of believers, so that His spiritual resurrected flesh and blood can be their food and drink, and He can become the life-giving source of a new order of humanity, the spiritual Head of a new race.

Rufus M. Jones, *Spiritual Reformers in the 16th and 17th Centuries*, Macmillan and Co., 1914, page 70

All the New Testament proclamations about the person of Jesus and all the narratives relating his history are set against the horizon of Easter. The appearances of the crucified Jesus in the splendour of divine glory call into being the confession of faith in 'Christ the Lord'. Christian faith is the acknowledgement of the lordship of Christ through public testimony, through new fellowship and through lived life. Christian existence is new life in Christ's sphere of influence. Confession and life in the lordship of Christ are founded on faith in his resurrection from the death through God the Father. Conversely, this faith in the resurrection is only alive in acknowledgement of the present lordship of Christ (Romans 10:9f.). Without new life, without the ability to love and the courage of hope in the lordship of Christ, faith in the resurrection would decay into belief in particular facts, without any consequences. Without faith in the resurrection new life in the lordship of Christ would cease to be a radical alternative to human forms of sovereignty and—adapting itself religiously, morally or politically—would lose its power to overcome the world. Where there is certainty that death has lost its power there is an alternative to those power structures that are built up on the threat of death. The removal of death's power brings to light a life which overcomes the systems of domination and oppression and demonstrates freedom in fellowship. Faith in the resurrection and a life of liberty in the lordship of Christ therefore belong indissolubly together and mutually interpret one another.

Jürgen Moltmann, *The Church in the Power of the Spirit: A Contribution to Messianic Eschatology*, translated by M. Kohl, SCM Press, 1977, page 98

Without the Resurrection the Christian movement would have petered out in ignomiy, and there would have been no Christianity. It is not too much to say that without the Resurrection the phenomenon of Christianity in the apostolic age and since is scientifically unaccountable. It is also true to say that without the Resurrection Christianity would not be itself, as the distinctiveness of Christianity is not its adherence to a teacher who lived long ago but its belief that 'Jesus is Lord' for every generation through the centuries.

The Resurrection is something that 'happened' a few days after the death of Jesus. The apostles became convinced that Jesus was alive, and that God had raised him to life. It is not historically scientific to say only that the apostles came to realise the divine meaning of the Crucifixion for them, or that the person of Jesus now became contagious to them. Something *happened* so as to vindicate for them the meaning of the Cross, and to make the person of Jesus contagious to them. The evidence for a stupendous happening, which the New Testament writers mention, was the survival of the Church, the appearance of Jesus in a visible and audible impact on the apostles, and the discovery that the tomb was empty.

The several elements in this threefold evidence no doubt had different degrees of evidential weight for different people, and they have had such varying degrees ever since. As to significance: if it were the existential encounter of Jesus which alone mattered, then the empty tomb would have little or no significance. If, however, Jesus has a *cosmic* meaning with cosmic effects, then the empty tomb has great significance, akin to the significance of the Incarnation itself.

Michael Ramsey, *Through the Year with Michael Ramsey*, edited by Margaret Duggan, Hodder and Stoughton, 1975, page 71

The Christian belief is that after death individuality will survive, that you will still be you and I will still be I. Beside that we have to set another immense fact. To the Greek the body could not be consecrated. It was matter, the source of all evil, the prison-house of the soul. But to the Christian the body is not evil. Jesus, the Son of God, has taken this human body upon him and therefore it is not contemptible because it has been inhabited by God. To the Christian, therefore, the life to come involves the total man, body and soul.

Now it is easy to misinterpret and to caricature the doctrine of the resurrection of the body. Celsus, who lived about A.D. 200, a bitter opponent of Christianity, did this very thing long ago. How can those who have died rise with their identical bodies? he demands. 'Really it is the hope of worms! For what soul of a man would any longer wish for a body that had rotted?' It is easy to cite the case of a person smashed up in an accident or dying of cancer.

But Paul never said that we would rise with the body with which we died. He insisted that we would have a spiritual body. What he really meant was that a man's *personality* would survive. It is almost impossible to conceive of personality without a body, because it is through the body that the personality expresses itself. What Paul is contending for is that after death the individual remains. He did not inherit the Greek contempt of the body but believed in the resurrection of the whole man. He will still be himself; he will survive as a person. That is what Paul means by the resurrection of the body. Everything of the body and of the soul that is necessary to make a man a person will survive, but, at the same time, all things will be new, and body and spirit will alike be very different from earthly things, for they will alike be divine.

William Barclay, *The Letter to the Corinthians*, The Saint Andrew Press, 1988, page 141

I began to look for a meaning in life other than what I could find through purposefulness. Studying and making oneself useful for life didn't convince me at all. All my life up to now had been concentrated on immediate goals, and suddenly these became empty. I felt something immensely dramatic inside myself, and everything around me seemed small and meaningless.

Months passed and no meaning appeared on the horizon. One day—it was during Lent, and I was then a member of one of the Russian youth organisations in Paris—one of the leaders came up to me and said, 'We have invited a priest to talk to you, come.' I answered with violent indignation that I would not. I had no use for the Church. I did not believe in God. I did not want to waste any of my time. The leader was subtle—he explained that everyone who belonged to my group had reacted in exactly the same way, and if no one came we would all be put to shame because the priest had come and we would be disgraced if no one attended his talk. 'Don't listen,' the leader said, 'I don't care, but just sit and be a physical presence.' That much loyalty I was prepared to give to my youth organisation, so I sat through the lecture. I didn't intend to listen. But my ears pricked up. I became more and more indignant. I saw a vision of Christ and Christianity that was profoundly repulsive to me. When the lecture was over I hurried home in order to check the truth of what he had been saying. I asked my mother whether she had a book of the Gospel, because I wanted to know whether the Gospel would support the monstrous impression I had derived from his talk. I expected nothing good from my reading, so I counted the chapters of the four Gospels to be sure I read the shortest, not to waste time unnecessarily. I started to read St. Mark's Gospel.

While I was reading the beginning of St. Mark's Gospel, before I reached the third chapter, I suddenly became aware that on the other side of my desk there was a presence. And the certainty was so strong that it was Christ standing there that it has never left me. This was the real turning-point. Because Christ was alive and I had been in his presence I could say with certainty that what the Gospel said about the crucifixion of the prophet of Galilee was true, and the centurion was right when he said 'Truly he is the Son of God'. It was in the light of the Resurrection that I could read with certainty the story of the Gospel, knowing that everything was true in it because the impossible event of the Resurrection was to me more certain than any event of history. History I had to believe, the Resurrection I knew for a fact. I did not discover, as you see, the Gospel beginning with its first message of the Annunciation, and it did not unfold for me as a story which one can believe or disbelieve. It began as an event that left all problems of disbelief behind because it was a direct and personal experience.

… I became absolutely certain within myself that Christ is alive and that certain things existed. I didn't have all the answers, but having touched that experience, I was certain that ahead of me there were answers, visions, possibilities. This is what I mean by faith—not doubting in the sense of being in confusion and perplexity, but doubting in order to discover the reality of the life, the kind of doubt that makes you want to question and discover more, that makes you want to explore.

Anthony Bloom, *School for Prayer*, Darton, Longman & Todd, 1970, page xi

REVELATION

Revelation—disclosing of knowledge, to man by divine or supernatural agency; knowledge so disclosed

In the opening verses of the Bible we read of God creating 'the heavens and the earth … and the Spirit of God was moving over the face of the waters'. As a result of these words I expect to see some evidence of the Creator in the creation. Consequently nature has always been an important source of revelation for me.

The opening words of St John's Gospel point us to a revelation not only in the words of Scripture, but specifically in the person of Jesus Christ: 'In the beginning was the Word, and the Word was with God, and the Word was God … And the Word became flesh and dwelt among us, full of grace and truth; we have beheld his glory, glory as of the only Son from the Father.' Consequently the Gospels have always been for me an important media for the revelation of God as seen in the person of Jesus Christ.

I have also found the saints an important source of revelation of God as experienced in their lives. Two biographies have been particularly helpful, both by George Seaver: *Edward Wilson of the Antarctic* and *Albert Schweitzer: The Man and his Mind*. I have singled these out in particular; others, no doubt, will have their favourites. Close allies are other people, and their experience in art, music, poetry, literature, drama, philosophy, science, etc. All these are potential sources of revelation. Mention must also be made of worship, the sacraments, and prayer—the passive forms of reflection, meditation and contemplation.

In the beginning God created the heavens and the earth. The earth was without form and void, and darkness was upon the face of the deep; and the Spirit of God was moving over the face of the waters.

Genesis 1:1–2

Surely the Lord God does nothing, without revealing his secret to his servants the prophets.

Amos 3:7

He who has my commandments and keeps them, he it is who loves me; and he who loves me will be loved by my Father, and I will love him and manifest myself to him.

John 14:21

Now to him who is able to strengthen you according to my gospel and the preaching of Jesus Christ, according to the revelation of the mystery which was kept secret for long ages but is now disclosed and through the prophetic writings is made known to all nations, according to the command of the eternal God, to bring about the obedience of faith—to the only wise God be glory for evermore through Jesus Christ!

Romans 16:25–27

The world is charged with the grandeur of God.

Gerard Manley Hopkins, 'God's Grandeur', in The Poems of Gerard Manley Hopkins, Oxford University Press, 1967, page 66

Man is the revelation of the Infinite, and it does not become finite in him. It remains the Infinite.

Mark Rutherford, More Pages From a Journal, Oxford University Press, 1910, page 251

We affirm, then, that unless all existence is a medium of Revelation, no particular Revelation is possible.

William Temple, Nature, Man and God, Macmillan and Co., 1934, page 306

The purpose of revelation is restoration, the renewal in us of that likeness to God which man lost by sin.

Stephen Neil, Christian Holiness, Lutterworth Press, 1960, page 96

For it was in the act of God's recovering man that man saw how low he had fallen. The revelation of a depth implies the revelation of a height, and both were revealed by the act which lifted man from the one to the other.

Austin Farrer, Interpretation and Belief, SPCK, 1976, page 74

The revelation which has won our acceptance has not been concerned with mere disclosure of things invisible or systems of supersensible being, but always with what has happened, is happening, or will happen; events in which the prophet claims to trace the hand and purpose of God.

J. Neville Ward, Five for Sorrow, Ten for Joy, Epworth Press, 1971, page 106

We know that he will appear unexpectedly and with great joy to all who love him. He works in secret, yet he wills to be seen. His appearing will be delightful and unexpected. His will is that we trust him, him who is utterly kind and unassuming. Blessings on him!

Julian of Norwich, *Revelations of Divine Love*, translated by Clifton Wolters, Penguin Books, 1976, page 79

We are at last beginning to know and understand the value of the myth, as it has been elaborated in 'primitive' and archaic societies—that is, among those groups of mankind where the myth happens to be the very foundation of social life and culture... in such societies the myth is thought to express the *absolute truth*, because it narrates a *sacred history*; that is, a transhuman revelation which took place... in the holy time of the beginnings.

Mircea Eliade, *Myths, Dreams and Mysteries*, Harvill Press, 1976, page 23

God, Who hideth Himself from the great and from the wise, revealeth and communicateth Himself to babes and to the simple-minded. The transformed soul is the spiritual man, of whom S. Paul speaketh, that is to say, the man who is moved and led by grace in the way of pure faith. Oftentimes, by grace and by experience, such a soul hath, for its conduct in the exercises and trials of pure love, a light which the learned lack, who have more of pure human knowledge and wisdom than of spiritual experience and divine grace.

François de la M. Fénelon, in B.W. Randolph, *Maxims of the Mystics*, translated by W.W. Williams, A.R. Mowbray & Co., 1909, page 103

The ordinary work of my morning had come to its close, and before going to take my bath I stood for a moment at my window overlooking a market-place on the bank of a dry river bed, welcoming the first flood of rain along its channel. Suddenly I became conscious of a stirring of soul within me. My world of experience in a moment seemed to become lighted, and facts that were detached and dim found a great unity of meaning. The feeling which I had was like that which a man, groping through a fog without knowing his destination, might feel when he suddenly discovers that he stands before his own house.

Rabindranath Tagore, *The Religion of Man*, George Allen & Unwin, 1931, page 94

It is true that all creation manifests the Creator. 'The heavens declare the glory of God and the firmament sheweth his handiwork' (Psalm 19:1). But we see all this awry until we have first learnt to see God in Jesus Christ. We cannot ascertain the character of God by induction from what He has done and is doing in history. But when we have found it in Jesus Christ we can begin to trace it there also. As we look back we can see that the special revelation in Christ is the crown of the general revelation in nature and history; but if we start with this and look forward, we cannot even adumbrate that only true revelation.

William Temple, *Readings in St. John's Gospel*, First and Second Series, Macmillan and Co., 1947, page 155

Now and again they have a vague longing for something which the saint seems to possess. There are many people who would like to have the vision of God, but they will not pay anything for it. Sometimes in the hour of terrible stress they cry out for light and strength. Then when nothing much seems to happen, they conclude that all this religious talk is just dreaming. It never seems to enter their minds that God's entrance into the human heart must always wait for an open door. They seem to be unaware that a revelation is dependent not only upon the giver, but also upon the receiver. But some things are not available to anything except moral and spiritual purity.

Gerald Kennedy, in *The Interpreter's Bible*, Abingdon Press, 1956, volume 6, page 375

God reveals Himself also in art of all kinds—written, visual, audible. For art, when true to itself, attempts to bring into the sharpest possible focus some aspect or other of reality, how it threatens and ennobles, destroys and creates, its tragedies and triumphs, thus waking us up from our comforting dreams and consoling illusions—or maybe from our nightmares.

... There is the story of Charles Gore, encountered one evening 'in the corridor of the Queen's Hall after the orchestra had played a Brandenburg concerto. His almost unconscious comment on the music showed where it had led his thoughts: 'If *that* is true, everything must be all right.'

Wherever reality of any kind is revealed, there God must be.

For it is only in His light that we can see light, which means also that it is only in His light that we can perceive darkness.

H.A. Williams, C.R., The Joy of God, Mitchell Beazley, 1980, page 65

But it is clear that a purely intellectual appeal would make religion the monopoly of the learned. That is God's problem, to make Himself known in such a way that He can give a message to every one of His children. 'How am I to touch the child, the philosopher, the ignorant person, the very learned person? Where am I to find a common thing which all these people have?' The divine answer is in the Incarnation. As soon as ever a baby can begin to take notice, he can be shown another Baby in a little nest of straw, a Baby like himself, and be taught that that is his God, the God Who loved him and became a Baby for him. The philosopher, whose whole life is thought, can be shown the philosopher brooding in the wilderness and saying, 'I came to bring them life that they might have it more abundantly.' The ordinary, unlearned person, who loathes books, can be shown the human Christ at the wedding-feast. Conversion is just falling in love with God as revealed to us by Christ.

Father Andrew, S.D.C., The Romance of Redemption, A.R. Mowbray & Co., 1954, page 33

The revelations which the guidance of the Divine Spirit breathes forth within our souls are always truths of universal significance, truths that are already implicitly revealed in the Bible, truths that carry their own self-evidence to any rational mind. But these revelations, these discoveries of what God means and what life may become, are possible only to those who prepare themselves for inward converse and who centre down to the deeper Roots of their being: 'Unless a man takes himself sometimes out of the world, by retirement and self-reflection, he will be in danger of losing *himself* in the world.' Where God is not discovered, something is always at fault with man. 'As soon as he is abstracted from the noise of the world, withdrawn from the call of the Body, having the doors of the senses shut, the Divine Life readily enters and reveals Itself to the inward Eye that is prepared for it.'

Rufus M. Jones, Spiritual Reformers in the 16th and 17th Centuries, Macmillan and Co., 1914, page 299

The Christian revelation gives precision and purpose and assurance to the inchoate striving of all men for a life that is fully human. On the other hand a rigid interpretation of the great metaphors and symbols that have been used from the beginning to embody and express that revelation has succeeded in making the whole Christian idea seem to the majority of educated people (and through them to millions of less educated ones) at best a comforting illusion to be outgrown and at worst a formidable obstacle to the honest and unselfish thinking that leads to real human progress. And in many cases it is those who reject the Christian idea as they know it who can actually do most to make clear the real human meaning of the faith that Christians profess.

To become holy is to become human. A fully matured and perfected humanity is capable of the vision of God in the life of the resurrection.

Rosemary Haughton, On Trying To Be Human, Geoffrey Chapman, 1966, page 33

One of the mistakes which men sometimes make is to identify God's revelation *solely* with the Bible. That would be to say that since about A.D. 120, when the latest book in the New Testament was written, God has ceased to speak, that since then there has been no more revelation from God. God's Spirit is *always* revealing Himself. It is true that God's supreme and unsurpassable revelation came in Jesus Christ; but Jesus is not a figure in a book. He is a living person, and in Him God's revelation goes on. God is still leading us into a greater and greater realization of what Jesus means ... It is quite wrong to think of God's revelation as being confined to what we might call theological truth. The theologians and the preachers are not the only persons who are inspired. When a great poet delivers to men a great message in words which defy time, he is inspired ... A great musician is inspired ... When a scientist discovers something which will help the world's toil and make life better for men, when a surgeon discovers a new technique which will save men's lives and ease their pain, when someone discovers a new treatment, a new drug, which will bring life and hope to suffering humanity, that is a revelation from God. It actually happens in a way that we can see.

William Barclay, *The Gospel of John*, The Saint Andrew Press, 1974, volume 2, page 227

There is, however, through the ages a steady ripening of the Divine Harvest, a gradual and progressive onward movement of the spiritual process, ever within the lives of men: 'Time brings roses. He who thinks that he has all the fruit when strawberries are ripe forgets that grapes are still to come. We should always be eagerly looking for something better.' There are, he says, three well-marked stages of revelation: (1) The stage of the law, when God, the Father, was making Himself known through His external creation and by outward forms of training and discipline; (2) the stage of self-revelation through the Son, that men might see in Him and in His personal activity the actual character and heart of God; and (3) the stage of the Holy Spirit which fills all deeps and heights, flows into all lives, and is the One God revealed in His essential nature of active Goodness—Goodness at work in the world. Externals of every type—law, ceremonies, rewards and punishments, historical happenings, written Scriptures, even the historical doings and sufferings of Christ—are only pointers and suggestion-material to bring the soul to the living Word within, 'to the Lord Himself who is never absent,' and who will be spiritually born within man. 'God,' he says, 'has once become flesh in Christ and has revealed thus the hidden God and, as happened in a fleshly way in Mary, even so Christ must be spiritually born in us.' So, too, everything which Christ experienced and endured in His earthly mission must be re-lived and reproduced in the life of His true disciples. There is no salvation possible without the new birth of Christ in us, without self-surrender and the losing of oneself, without being buried with Christ in a death to self-will and without rising with Him in joy and peace and victory.

Rufus M. Jones, *Spiritual Reformers in the 16th and 17th Centuries*, Macmillan and Co., 1914, page 41

SALVATION

Salvation—saving of the soul; deliverance from sin and its consequences and admission to heaven brought about by Christ; acquisition of wholeness

William Law gave me a valuable insight into the meaning of salvation: 'There is but one salvation for all mankind,' he wrote, 'and that is the life of God in the soul.' He added that God's intent is to 'introduce or generate His own life, light, and Spirit in them, that all may be as so many images, temples and habitations of the Holy Trinity'.

Baptism is about the birth of the life of God in the soul. In this sacrament we are baptized in the name of (nature of) the Father, the Son, and the Holy Spirit. The seed or spark of God already in us is triggered off and catalysed. The gifts of the Holy Spirit, latent within us, are brought to life and activated. From that moment onwards we can expect to grow in wisdom, understanding, counsel, knowledge, fear, might and the Spirit of the Lord. As we grow and develop we experience the presence of the fruits of the Spirit in our lives—love, joy, peace, patience, kindness, goodness, faithfulness, gentleness and self-control. Through prayer, reflection, meditation and contemplation our bodies become temples and habitations of the Holy Trinity.

I have previously mentioned the presence of the earthy and creaturely in our lives. In the process of salvation, the life of God thus generated in the soul accepts the earthy and creaturely and brings about an integration. A valuable part of our nature, thought to be fallen, is transformed and becomes a vital source of energy. The result is salvation, the acquisition of wholeness.

The Lord is my strength and my song, and he has become my salvation.
Exodus 15:2

Surely his salvation is at hand for those who fear him, that glory may dwell in our land.
Psalm 85:9

For the gate is narrow and the way is hard, that leads to life, and those who find it are few.
Matthew 7:14

Work out your own salvation with fear and trembling; for God is at work in you, both to will and to work for his good pleasure.
Philippians 2:12–13

Our salvation, thank God! depends much more on His love of us than of our love of Him.
Father Andrew, S.D.C., *Meditations for Every Day*, A.R. Mowbray & Co., 1941, page 164

... the man who is saved, made whole, is the man who responds to a vision of God's life in Christ.
Frank Wright, *The Pastoral Nature of the Ministry*, SCM Press, 1980, page 16

God both represents to us what we are to become and shows us both the way to become it. Union with God is the goal and the love of God is the way.

Don Cupitt, *Taking Leave of God*, SCM Press, 1980, page 9

Man needs, above all else, salvation. He needs to turn round and see that God is standing there with a rope ready to throw to him if only he will catch it and attach it to himself. Then life can start all over again for him.

Norman Goodacre, *Laymen's Lent*, A.R. Mowbray & Co., 1969, page 31

Salvation does not come from not going along, or from running away. Nor does it come from letting oneself be carried along without willing. Salvation comes from complete self-surrender, and one's gaze must be directed upon a centre.

C.G. Jung, *The Integration of the Personality*, Kegan Paul, Trench, Trubner & Co., 1941, page 158

The believer is one who places a particular kind of interpretation on his past—he sees it as salvation. And he does this, not by selecting from it what suits him; not by ignoring the less pleasant bits. He ignores nothing. He accepts it *all* as the way God brought him; learns from it all, but is bowed down by none of it. His past becomes not the history of failure, but the history of what God has done to him, and for him, and with him.

Henry McKeating, *God and the Future*, SCM Press, 1974, page 8

It was something in which they were *being saved*. It is interesting to note that in the Greek this is a present tense, and not past. It would be strictly correct to translate it not, 'in which you have been saved,' but 'in which you are being saved'. Salvation goes from glory to glory. It is not something which is ever completed in this world. There are many things in this life which we can exhaust, but the meaning of salvation is something which a man can never exhaust.

William Barclay, *The Letters to the Corinthians*, The Saint Andrew Press, 1988, page 143

Those who are in the Universities and Churches of men have Christ in their mouths, and they have a measuring-reed by their side—the inhabitants of God's Church on the other hand have the Life of Christ and the testing-standing within themselves. Those who are 'nominal professors' hang salvation on a literal knowledge of the merit secured by Christ's death; the true believer knows that salvation is never a purchase, is never outwardly effected, but is a new self, a new spirit, a new relation to God: 'Man must cease to be what he is before he can come to be another kind of person.'

Rufus M. Jones, *Spiritual Reformers in the 16th and 17th Centuries*, Macmillan and Co., 1914, page 147

Salvation… is wholly an inward process, initiated from above through the Divine Word, the Christ, whom we know outwardly as the historical Person of the Gospel, and whom we know inwardly as the Revealer of Light and Love, the Witness in us against sin, the Voice of the Father to our hearts, calling us home, the Goal of our spiritual quest, the Alpha and the Omega of all religious truth and all spiritual experience. The Way to God… is Christ inwardly and spiritually known. But however audible the Word may be; however vivid the illumination; however drawing the Love, there is never compulsion. The soul itself must hear and see and feel; must say *yes* to the appeal of Love, and must co-operate by a continuous adjustment of the personal will to the Will of God and 'learn to behave as a child of God.'

Rufus M. Jones, *Spiritual Reformers in the 16th and 17th Centuries*, Macmillan and Co., 1914, page 27

We must desire passionately, wholly, only, to find the way out. We must understand what Christ meant in saying that the Kingdom is a pearl of great price, to purchase which every other asset and security is liquidated. We must attend to what Buddha meant when he vowed that he would die in his tracks unless he could find the path of Deliverance, the way of Life. We must recall the story sometimes told of him that when he had found the way and thousands were flocking to him, one man coming into his presence was told to follow him—for it was bathing time—to the river. Thinking this meant a ritual purification, the seeker gladly followed. As soon, however, as they were at some depth in the stream, he found himself pushed under and held, until at his last gasp, with a desperate wrench, he forced his head above water. To the quiet question, 'When you thought you were going to be drowned, what did you desire most?' he gasped with some exasperation, 'Air!'—'When you want salvation as much as you wanted air,' came the reply, 'then you will get it.'

Gerald Heard, *The Code of Christ*, Cassell and Company, 1944, page 74

God always saves the many by the few, and both the many and the few are saved by One, our Lord Jesus Christ himself. It is out of the nucleus of praying, suffering, witnessing Christians in their dedicated groups, groups which know the power of Christ's resurrection even while they are conformed to Christ's death, that the new things will come, for the Church and for the world through the Church. The world's resurrection is indeed bound up with the Church's resurrection.

And we want a resurrection for ourselves—not apart from the Church but within it, not apart from the world but within it. 'Of those who have companied with us all the time that the Lord Jesus went in and went out among us, beginning from the baptism of John, unto the day that he was received up from us, must one become a witness with us of his resurrection.' This is the qualification for apostleship—'a witness with us of the resurrection'. '*With us.*' A corporate, yet an intensely individual-within-that corporate, resurrection. There are many forms of resurrection, all pointing to a final resurrection—recovery from illness, recovery from fear, recovery from anxiety, recovery from sin, recovery from guilt; and it is through prayer and faith and repentance, through forgiveness and absolution, through being 'accepted in the Beloved', through being justified, for 'while we were yet sinners, Christ died for the ungodly'.

We do not make our salvation, nor our absolution, nor our resurrection. God does that. He prepares our salvation, absolution, resurrection before we even think of repenting. But we can dispose ourselves towards receiving that salvation, absolution and resurrection.

Eric Symes Abbott, *The Compassion of God and the Passion of Christ*, Geoffrey Bles, 1963, page 41

What every man looks for in life is his own salvation and the salvation of the men he lives with. By salvation I mean first of all the full discovery of who he himself really is. Then I mean something of the fulfilment of his own God-given powers, in the love of others and of God. I mean also the discovery that he cannot find himself in himself alone, but that he must find himself in and through others. Ultimately, these propositions are summed up in two lines of the Gospel: 'If any man would save his life, he must lose it,' and, 'Love one another as I have loved you.' It is also contained in another saying from St. Paul: 'We are members one of another.'

The salvation I speak of is not merely a subjective, psychological thing—a self-realization in the order of nature. It is an objective and mystical reality—the finding of ourselves in Christ, in the Spirit, or, if you prefer, in the supernatural order. This includes and sublimates and perfects the natural self-realization which it to some extent presupposes, and usually effects, and always transcends. Therefore this discovery of ourselves is always a losing of ourselves—a death and a resurrection. 'Your life is hidden with Christ in God.' The discovery of ourselves in God, and of God in ourselves, by a charity that also finds all other men in God with ourselves is, therefore, not the discovery of ourselves but of Christ. First of all, it is the realization that 'I live, now not I, but Christ liveth in me,' and secondly it is the penetration of that tremendous mystery which St Paul sketched out boldly—and darkly—in his great Epistles: the mystery of the recapitulation, the summing up of all in Christ. It is to see the world in Christ, its beginning and its end. To see all things coming forth from God in the *Logos* who becomes incarnate and descends into the lowest depths of His own creation and gathers all to Himself in order to restore it finally to the Father at the end of time. To find 'ourselves,' then, is to find not only our poor, limited, perplexed souls, but to find the power of God that raised Christ from the dead and 'built us together in Him unto a habitation of God in the Spirit' (Ephesians 2:22).

Thomas Merton, No Man is an Island, Burns & Oates, 1974, page xiv

There is but one salvation for all mankind, and that is the life of God in the soul. God has but one design or intent towards all mankind and that is to introduce or generate His own life, light, and Spirit in them, that all may be as so many images, temples and habitations of the Holy Trinity. This is God's will to all Christians, Jews, and heathens. They are all equally the desire of His heart; His light continually waits for an entrance into all of them; His wisdom crieth, she putteth forth her voice, not here or there, but everywhere, in all the streets of all the parts of the world.

Now there is but one possible way for man to attain this salvation or life of God in the soul. There is not one for the Jew, another for a Christian, and a third for the heathen. No; God is one, human nature is one, salvation is one, and the way to it is one; and that is, the desire of the soul turned to God. When this desire is alive and breaks forth in any creature under Heaven, then the lost sheep is found and the shepherd has it upon his shoulders. Through this desire the poor Prodigal Son leaves his husks and swine and hastes to his father: it is because of this desire that the Father sees the son while yet afar off, that he runs out to meet him, falleth on his neck and kisses him. See here how plainly we are taught that no sooner is desire arisen and in motion towards God, but the operation of God's Spirit answers to it, cherishes and welcomes its first beginnings—signified by the father's seeing and having compassion on his son whilst yet afar off, that is, in the first beginnings of his desire. Thus does this desire do all, it brings the soul to God and God into the soul, it unites with God, it co-operates with God, and is one life with God. Suppose this desire not to be alive, not in motion, either in a Jew or a Christian, and then all the sacrifices, the service, the worship, either of the Law or the Gospel are but dead works that bring no life into the soul nor beget any union between God and it. Suppose this desire to be awakened and fixed upon God, though in souls that never heard either of the Law or Gospel, and then the divine life or operation of God enters into them, and the new birth in Christ is formed in those who never heard of His name. And these are they 'that shall come from the East, and from the West, and sit down with Abraham and Isaac in the Kingdom of God.'

O my God, just and good, how great is thy love and mercy to mankind, that Heaven is thus everywhere open, and Christ thus the common Saviour to all that turn the desire of their hearts to thee! O sweet power of the Bruiser of the Serpent, born in every son of man, that stirs and works in every man and gives every man a power and desire to find his happiness in God! O holy Jesus, heavenly light that lightest every man that cometh into the world, that redeemest every soul that follows thy light, which is always within him! O Holy Trinity, immense ocean of divine love in which all mankind live and move and have their being! None are separated from thee, none live out of thy love, but all are embraced in the arms of thy mercy, all are partakers of thy divine life, the operation of thy Holy Spirit, as soon as their heart is turned to thee! O plain and easy and simple way of salvation, wanting no subtleties of art or science, no borrowed learning, no refinements of reason, but all done by the simple natural motion of every heart that truly longs after God. For no sooner is the finite desire of the creature in motion towards God but the infinite desire of God is united with it, co-operates with it. And in this united desire of God and the creature is the salvation and life of the soul brought forth. For the soul is shut out of God and imprisoned in its own dark workings of flesh and blood, merely and solely because it desires to live to the vanity of this world. This desire is its darkness, its death, its imprisonment and separation from God.

When, therefore, the first spark of a desire after God arises in thy soul, cherish it with all thy care, give all thy heart into it, it is nothing less than a touch of the divine loadstone that is to draw thee out of the vanity of time into the riches of eternity. Get up, therefore, and follow it as gladly as the Wise Men of the East followed the star from Heaven that appeared to them. It will do for thee as the star did for them: it will lead thee to the birth of Jesus, not in a stable in Bethlehem in Judea, but to the birth of Jesus in the dark centre of thy own fallen soul.

William Law, in Stephen Hobhouse, editor, *Selected Mystical Writings of William Law*, Rockliff, 1948, page 102

SERVICE

Service—doing of work, or work done, for another or for a community, etc.; assistance or benefit given to someone, readiness to perform this

One of my duties in Nigeria was to teach in a local school—The Good Samaritan School for Handicapped Children. This unique school had been founded, a few years previously, by an elderly missionary couple, Mr and Mrs Patey. The pupils were small in number, but because of their physical and mental disabilities required a great deal of attention. I used to go to the school on a Friday morning to teach for two hours. I was impressed by Mr and Mrs Patey. They accommodated the children in their own home, looked after them, fed them, taught them and nursed them, twenty-four hours a day. Somehow, in spite of all the demands on their time and energy, they remained cheerful and produced a happy atmosphere. A warm friendly spirit pervaded the school—a consequence of costly service.

In the end the cost proved to be too great. I went in one Friday morning and found them both delirious, suffering from malaria. They were admitted to hospital and eventually were invalided back to England. It transpired they had not gone on holiday for twelve years, and this largely contributed to the breakdown of their health.

Jesus realized the importance of service. He said of himself: 'I am among you as one who serves.' He was also aware of the demands of service and warned his disciples to count the cost beforehand. Even the Good Samaritan needed to share the burden of service with the innkeeper.

Know the God of your father, and serve him with a whole heart and with a willing mind.

1 Chronicles 28:9

Behold my servant, whom I uphold, my chosen, in whom my soul delights; I have put my Spirit upon him.

Isaiah 42:1

When you have done all that is commanded you, say, 'We are unworthy servants; we have only done what was our duty.'

Luke 17:10

I am among you as one who serves.

Luke 22:27

Life is given to us, we earn it by giving it.

Rabindranath Tagore, 'Stray Birds', lvi, in *Collected Poems and Plays of Rabindranath Tagore*,
Macmillan and Co., 1936, page 294

Great works do not always lie in our way, but every moment we may do little ones excellently, that is, with great love.

St Francis de Sales, *On the Love of God*, Methuen & Co., 1902, page 94

Service of man... does not replace service of God. But the service of God never excuses from service of man: it is in service to man that service to God is proved.

Hans Küng, *On Being a Christian*, translated by Edward Quinn, William Collins Sons & Co., 1977, page 253

The service of the fruit is precious, the service of the flower is sweet, but let my service be the service of the leaves in its shade of humble devotion.

Rabindranath Tagore, 'Stray Birds', ccxvii, in *Collected Poems and Plays of Rabindranath Tagore*,
Macmillan and Co., 1936, page 315

Abide in me and I in you... All truth and depth of devotion, all effectiveness in service springs from this. It is not a theme for words, but for the deeper apprehensions of silence.

William Temple, *Readings in St. John's Gospel*, First and Second Series, Macmillan and Co., 1947, page 258

Who love their fellows even to the death;
Who feel the giant agony of the world;
And more, like slaves to poor humanity,
Labour for mortal good?

John Keats, 'The Fall of Hyperion', line 156, in Miriam Allott, editor, *The Poems of John Keats*, Longman, 1986, page 668

The lives of the saints have always been for Christians the reminder that in this life men and women of all kinds, temperaments and cultures have touched the heights of Christian experience and have committed themselves utterly to the service of their fellows.

E.G. Rupp, in Alan Richardson and John Bowden, editors, *A New Dictionary of Christian Theology*, SCM Press, 1985,
page 441

What an unspeakable privilege to be allowed to do anything for God at all! Fancy being accepted into His service and 'put upon the strength'; actually allowed—with the unaffected brightness of a Christian—to wear His livery and call oneself by His Name.

W.E. Sangster, *Westminster Sermons*, Epworth Press, 1960, volume 1, *At Morning Worship*, page 24

The way to call anyone into fellowship with us is, not to offer them service, which is liable to arouse the resistance of their pride, but to ask service from them. Of course the request must be prompted by a real need... So the Almighty God seeks to win us to fellowship with Himself by putting some part of His purpose into our hands.

William Temple, *Readings in St. John's Gospel*, First and Second Series, Macmillan and Co., 1947, page 66

Service is sometimes *costly*, very costly. It takes toll of us in various ways. It takes its toll when we hear ourselves unjustly charged with ulterior motives: when those we have helped with pure intent discuss what we were 'getting out of it' ourselves, and fling our kindness in our face. In such an hour it is hard to be poised and to go on serving.

W.E. Sangster, *He is Able*, Hodder and Stoughton, 1936, page 115

The ideal of philanthropy commends a love of humankind that issues in concrete deeds of service to others. These gifts of service can take the form of goods, time, or money. They help either to meet the basic needs of others (food, shelter, and medical care) or to foster their excellence (support for art, culture, research, parks, museums, public buildings, and education).

William F. May, in James F. Childress and John Macquarrie, editors, *A Dictionary of Christian Ethics*, SCM Press, 1986, page 474

'We can become like God—only in proportion as we are of use,' said —. 'I did not see this at once. I tried to be good, not knowing what good meant. I tried to be good, because I thought it would pay me in the world to come. But at last I saw that all life, all devotion, all piety, were only worth anything, only Divine, and God-like and God-beloved, as they were means to that one end—to be of use.

Charles Kingsley, *Daily Thoughts*, Macmillan and Co., 1884, page 225

Ah yes, men must learn to serve
not for money, but for life.
Ah yes, men must learn to obey
not a boss, but the gleam of life on the face of a man
who has looked into the eyes of the gods.
Man is only perfectly human
when he looks beyond humanity.

D.H. Lawrence, 'Service', in Vivian de Sola Pinto and Warren Roberts, editors, *The Complete Poems of D.H. Lawrence*, William Heinemann, 1967, volume 2, page 650

Everybody can be great. Because anybody can serve. You don't have to have a college degree to serve. You don't have to make your subject and your verb agree to serve. You don't have to know about Plato and Aristotle to serve. You don't have to know Einstein's theory of relativity to serve. You don't have to know the second theory of thermo-dynamics in physics to serve. You only need a heart full of grace. A soul generated by love.

Martin Luther King, *The Words of Martin Luther King*, selected by Coretta Scott King, William Collins Sons & Co., 1986, page 17

Only the pure in heart can love God and love man. Suffering love is the miracle of the spirit by which, though the wrongs of others are borne on our shoulders, we feel a sense of comfort deeper and more real than any given by purely selfish pleasures. At such moments we understand that nothing in the world is sweeter than the knowledge that we have been able to give a moment's happiness to another, nothing more precious than the sense that we have shared another's sorrow. Perfect compassion untouched by condescension, washed clean of pride, even of the pride of doing good, is the highest religious quality.

Sir Sarvepalli Radhakrishnan, *Mahatma Gandhi*, George Allen & Unwin, 1949, page 18

I'm not saying 'God exists, I've met him,' but 'God exists, he has embraced me.' I'm still sustained by those few deeply moving encounters with God in which he touched me, and marked me incurably. Anyone who hasn't been gripped by such an encounter and held his breath in the embrace of God, can't live his life for God and in the service of his brothers.

I will never regret the seminary which, despite the stupidity of certain rules and regulations, offered me a long sojourn in the desert—where silence and simplicity encourage encounters with God.

Is it an illusion? Over-reaction? No, not if the encounter results in a lifetime commitment.

What proves the authenticity of such encounters? The strength they give one to live in the service of others, demanding nothing in return.

Michel Quoist, *With Open Heart*, translated by Colette Copeland, Gill and Macmillan, 1983, page 85

Availability for service is one of the most marvellous gifts that we can find in community. People who have this gift trust those in authority and the community itself, and take on whatever is proposed to them. And if they do not know how to cope, they ask help of the Holy Spirit and of their brothers and sisters.

There is a tendency nowadays to decry obedience, perhaps because authority has been abused in the past. This means that people are more ready to take on positions than to grow spiritually and personally. And it has to be admitted, too, that obedience can be servile and morose.

But it is marvellous for a community to have among its members people with this child-like spirit, who are ready to assume whatever is asked of them. They have confidence that it would not be asked if they were not capable of doing it, by the grace of the spirit and the trust of their brothers and sisters.

Jean Vanier, *Community and Growth*, Darton, Longman & Todd, 1991, page 261

God has created me to do Him some definite service; He has committed some work to me which He has not committed to another. I have my mission—I may never know it in this life, but I shall be told it in the next. Somehow I am necessary for His purposes, as necessary in my place as an Archangel in his—if, indeed, I fail, He can raise another, as He could make the stones children of Abraham. Yet I have a part in this great work; I am a link in a chain, a bond of connexion between persons. He has not created me for naught. I shall do good, I shall do His work; I shall be an angel of peace, a preacher of truth in my own place, while not intending it, if I do but keep His commandments and serve Him in my calling.

Therefore I will trust Him. Whatever, wherever I am, I can never be thrown away. If I am in sickness, my sickness may serve Him; in perplexity, my perplexity may serve Him; if I am in sorrow, my sorrow may serve Him. My sickness, or perplexity, or sorrow may be necessary causes of some great end, which is quite beyond us. He does nothing in vain; He may prolong my life, He may shorten it; He knows what He is about. He may take away my friends, He may throw me among strangers, He may make me feel desolate, make my spirits sink, hide the future from me—still He knows what He is about.

John Henry Newman, *Meditations and Devotions*, Longmans, Green, and Co., 1893, page 400

Crossing a range of mountains in a heavy snowstorm he was joined by a Tibetan who was afraid of going alone. The cold was so intense that they had already begun to despair of reaching their destination alive, when they saw a man who had slipped down a slope of snow some thirty feet below the path, lying unconscious. The Sadhu asked his companion to help him carry the man to the village. The Tibetan, telling him that he was a fool to try to help another man when he could barely save himself, left him and hurried on ahead. The Sadhu went down the slope and just managed to get back on to the road again with the man on his shoulders and struggled slowly along. Some distance farther on he perceived his former companion sitting by the wayside. He called, but there was no answer—he was frozen dead. The Sadhu himself meanwhile had become thoroughly warmed by his exertions and, as a result of this warmth and of the friction between their bodies, the man he carried also gradually became warmer and came to; and both reached the village alive and full of thankfulness.

Sadhu Sundar Singh, in B.H. Streeter and A.J. Appasamy, *The Sadhu*, Macmillan and Co., 1921, page 87

SIN

Sin—transgression, a transgression against the divine law or principles of morality

Father Andrew writes in this section: 'Sin is that condition in which a man makes himself the centre of his own life, and either ignores God or pushes Him on to the circumference. Fallen human nature is self-centred human nature.'

Seen in the context of the Genesis story of the creation of man, man chooses to centre himself on the earthy and creaturely, and ignores the fact he is made in the image and likeness of God. The divine life, latent in the depths of his being, is ignored altogether or pushed out on to the circumference of life. The outcome is a serious condition called sin. This leads to the commission of sins, and to a deadening of life.

Father Andrew goes on to point out: 'The human nature Christ brought to earth is God-centred.' Looking at the life of Christ as revealed in the Gospels we notice he centred his life on God, and brought about an integration of the earthy and creaturely. The outcome was wholeness or salvation. Today we need to centre our lives on God in like manner, integrating the earthy and creaturely.

George Macleod gives us a timely reminder of the word Jesus used for sin—*hamartia*—a word taken from the arena and archery practice. In the thought of Jesus, to miss the target is to be off-centre and the result is *hamartia*, sin. We thereby miss the very essence of life, and seek compensation elsewhere. To be on target is to be centred on God, and find there something of that more abundant life.

Be sure your sin will find you out.

Numbers 32:23

The way of the faithless is their ruin.

Proverbs 13:15

For from within, out of the heart of man, come evil thoughts, fornication, theft, murder, adultery, coveting, wickedness, deceit, licentiousness, envy, slander, pride, foolishness. All these evil things come from within, and they defile a man.

Mark 7:21–23

The next day he saw Jesus coming towards him, and said, 'Behold, the Lamb of God, who takes away the sin of the world!'

John 1:29

The root of sin of indolence of heart.

Alan Ecclestone, *The Night Sky of the Lord*, Darton, Longman & Todd, 1980, page 142

Know this, O man, the sole root of sin in thee
Is not to know thine own divinity!

James Rhoades, in Ralph Waldo Trine, *My Philosophy and my Religion*, George Bell and Sons, 1926, page 27

... The principle of sin which is man's self-centred desire to secure his independence against God.

G.W.H. Lampe, in A.R. Vidler, editor, *Soundings*, Cambridge at the University Press, 1962, page 186

All sins tend to be addictive, and the terminal point of addiction is what is called damnation.

W.H. Auden, *A Certain World*, Faber and Faber, 1982, page 181

Sin burdens the hearts of men; spoils the modesty of intellectual nature; and disposes men for evil.

Benjamin Whichcote, *Moral and Religious Aphorisms*, vi. 571, Elkin, Mathews & Marrot, 1930

It is only when we have lost all love of ourselves for our own sakes that our past sins cease to give us the anguish of shame.

Thomas Merton, *Elected Silence*, Hollis and Carter, 1949, page 247

The appalling thing about sin is that man does not appear to be able to create in that realm, it is always the same old thing man has been doing all along.

J. Neville Ward, *The Use of Praying*, Epworth Press, 1967, page 45

Original sin? It is probably the malice that is ever flickering within us. Seen thus, it is a grievous error for those who manage human affairs not to take original sin into account.

Eric Hoffer, *The Passionate State of Mind*, Secker & Warburg, 1956, page 70

... means the determined or lackadaisical refusal to live up to one's essential humanity. It is the torpid unwillingness to revel in the delights or to share in the responsibilities of being fully human.

Harvey Cox, *God's Revolution and Man's Responsibility*, SCM Press, 1969, page 40

Sin has always been an ugly word, but it has been made so in a new sense over the last half-century. It has been made not only ugly, but passé. People are no longer sinful, they are only immature or underprivileged or frightened or, more particularly, sick.

Phyllis McGinley, *The Province of the Heart*, The World's Work (1913), 1962, page 35

Sin is that condition in which a man makes himself the centre of his own life, and either ignores God or pushes Him on to the circumference. Fallen human nature is self-centred human nature. The human nature Christ brought to earth is God-centred. God cannot condone sin and remain holy: He cannot be vindictive to the sinner and remain Love: so He Himself as Man accepts all the consequences of sin, and on the Cross reveals in one perfect classic occasion His own condemnation of sin and His own love of sinners. Nobody can look at the Crucifix and think God condones sin. There is the punishment of human nature. Nobody can look at it and say God does not love sinners.

Father Andrew, S.D.C., *The Good Shepherd*, A.R. Mowbray & Co., 1949, page 12

Sin grows out of our fear and resentment against the limitations of our life, and our proud illusion that we can defy the conditions that bind us to earth and death. From the root spring our anxieties about ourselves; our fear and weakness in facing crises; our coveting of the things others have; our craving for reputation, publicity, excitement, and luxury, for love that is really pampering of our self-regard, and for success that consists in the inflation of our egos. All these are troubling enough for any one of us to manage in his own private life. But they become disastrous when they intrude into our common life with others. And when a whole world becomes inhabited with individuals driven, by fear of death, to act as though they were gods, then we have such a tragic, imperilled and despairing world as the one in which our generation is living.

John L. Casteel, *Rediscovering Prayer*, Hodder and Stoughton, 1955, page 56

Sin means . . . the *free choice* of something for one's private and particular self in place of life-aims that fulfil the good of the whole and realize the universal Will of God. To live for the flesh instead of for the spirit, to pursue the aims of a narrow private self where they conflict with the spirit of universal love, to turn from the Word of God in the soul to follow the idle voices of the moment—that is the very essence of sin. It is not inherited, it is self-chosen, and yet there is something in our disposition which sets itself in array against the divine revelation within us. The Adam-story is a genuine life-picture. It is a chapter out of the book of the ages, the life of humanity. We do not sin and fall because he did; we sin and fall because we are human and finite, as he was, and choose the darkness instead of the Light, prefer Satan to God, pursue the way of death instead of the way of Life, as he did.

Rufus M. Jones, *Spiritual Reformers in the 16th and 17th Centuries*, Macmillan and Co., 1914, page 62

Where we need more precision and definition is in our interpretation of Sin as opposed to sins. Our sins are local manifestations, the out-croppings, of our attitude to life; Sin is that attitude, when it is wrong-headed, immature, rebellious or evasive. But to say that all Sin is selfishness, or an offence against God, or a flouting of the Law, is not, in my view, adequate; it is too moralistic, too legalistic. I prefer William Blake's assessment of sin as the refusal to be creative. 'The man who is not an artist is not a Christian.' Sin is being mechanical where one should be vital, being imitative where one should be original, being submissive to an external authority where one should be responsive to the ever-renewed, ever-changing, voice of the living God. My own private definition of sin, whereby I measure my own actions and those of others, may not sound very theological but I think it has the root of the matter in it. 'Sin is any and every action that I perform without the full consent of my whole personality.'

W.B.J. Martin, *Five Minutes to Twelve*, William Collins Sons & Co., 1957, page 139

We can reach the point where it becomes possible for us to recognise and understand Original Sin, that dark counter-centre of evil in our nature—that is to say, though it *is* not our nature, it is *of* it—that something within us which rejoices when disaster befalls the very cause we are trying to serve, or misfortune overtakes even those we love.

Life in God is not an escape from this, but a way to gain full insight concerning it: it is not our depravity which forces a fictitious religious explanation upon us, but the experience of religious reality which forces the 'Night Side' out into the light.

It is when we stand in the righteous all-seeing light of love that we can dare to look at, admit, and *consciously* suffer under this something in us which wills disaster, misfortune, defeat to everything outside the sphere of our narrowest self-interest. So a living relation to God is the necessary precondition for the self-knowledge which enables us to follow a straight path, and so be victorious over ourselves, forgiven by ourselves.

Dag Hammarskjöld, *Markings*, translated by Leif Sjorberg and W.H. Auden, with a foreword by W.H. Auden, Faber and Faber, 1964, page 128

I am often struck by the word Jesus used for sin. It comes from archery practice; to sin (in the thought of Jesus) means to miss the mark: miss the target. To miss the target at least implies that you are aiming at something. However wide of the mark the shots are going, a sinner is aiming at something. Take the lecherous man, the sex addict. What's he aiming at? A real experience of love surely—mad though his efforts be ever so to find it. Take the gambler: what is he aiming at? Surely making a big thing out of life: taking real risks to get it; real risks and terrifying. Isn't he playing (however upside down) with that precious gift called Faith? He risks all on an Act. And our drunkards . . . what are they aiming at? Most solemnly I say it, they want to be filled: filled with life, filled with spirit. They want to recover hope. Faith, hope and love—that's their real target, all of them—Life! They want to be filled with it: they take appalling risks for it: they are determined to live; determined to love. I am not condoning it. Poor souls, they don't condone it themselves. They are missing the mark; and they don't know it. But at least they go on demanding Life. Dare we say this is why Jesus loved them? I am sure the sinners crowded round Him (in the market-place and pub) because they knew He understood. He didn't just love sinners; He liked them. He saw their possibility. He loved sinners—not as the Pharisees did, because it was their duty to save; He loved them for wanting something badly: for wanting Life at all costs.

G.F. Macleod, in Christopher Woodard, *Healing Words,* Max Parish and Co., 1958, page 138

We cannot understand ourselves aright, nor can we understand what sin is, save in the light of the Christian revelation. In that light we see two things; first, that man has been made in the image of God; that is why we have these longings for God and for goodness; that is why even a person who has repeatedly fallen away from God, or who has fallen into gross sin, is perpetually haunted by the sense of being 'recalled' to a better life. We are homesick for God, from whom we come, and for whom we have been made. 'Thou hast made us for Thyself, and our hearts are restless until they rest in Thee.' At the same time we see that a dark streak runs right across our human nature, our true nature out of shape. This 'dark streak', which disfigures human nature, is 'sin'.

As Christians we all have some knowledge of this fact of sin, not only as we see it in the world around us, but in our own lives and hearts. We become aware that we are 'sinners' by the fact that we commit obvious 'sins', in thought, word, and act. Gradually we realize that we sin quite as much by what we do not do, as by what we do; our hearts condemn us in the sight of God. Slowly we begin to realize our sinfulness: we see that we are infected with a poison which affects everything; that we have a downward tendency, which is constantly trying to drag us away from God and goodness. We have begun to feel the 'sinfulness of sin'.

What then, is sin? this sin which seems to spring from something deeper still which we call 'sinfulness'? something which is 'there' before it is expressed in word or act?

Briefly, there are four things to say about sin:

(a) From the religious point of view, *sin is rebellion,* rebellion against God; it is the attempt to take the place that belongs to God. This is a profound truth, often carelessly expressed in a phrase such as: 'He wants to set himself up as a little tin god.' Behind man's presumptuous effort to raise himself to the throne of the universe (or of that part over which he wants to rule) is his fundamental sense of insecurity, against which he rebels; sin is defiance of God.

(b) *Sin is apostasy:* it is a personal act. In this sense sin is the desire and effort to get rid of God, the desire to be wholly independent; it denies God to His face. It is a total act; the whole personality is involved, not merely some part of it...

(c) From the moral and social point of view, *sin is injustice.* The man who sets himself upon a pedestal, and regards himself as the centre of existence, naturally wants to dominate other people, and then, of course, he treats them unjustly. When a group, or a party, or a nation, is filled with this spirit, we get a Colour Problem, or a Class Problem, or a Race Problem, or a Political Problem, with all the misery, hatred and injustice that lies behind these phrases.

(d) *Sin is universal:* we see this most clearly in the light of the Cross. Here we all come under the same condemnation; good, bad, and indifferent—we are all in the same boat— we are all sinners, all guilty, all responsible.

Olive Wyon, *On the Way,* SCM Press, 1958, page 48

SONS OF GOD

Sons of God—a consequence of the Genesis story of the creation of man, fully worked out in the life of our Lord, activated by baptism and nurtured by prayer, grace and sacramental worship

We have already noted the divine inbreathing of the Genesis story of the creation of man. The writer of Deuteronomy was conscious of this truth and wrote: 'You are the sons of the Lord your God.' The Psalmist in turn backed this up and recorded: 'You are gods, sons of the Most High.' Our Lord worked out in his life and person what was meant by the phrase 'Son of God'. He was the pioneer and prototype of a new way of life, opened up to all who were prepared to receive him. We read of this in St John's Gospel: 'But to all who received him, who believed in his name, he gave power to become children of God; who were born, not of blood nor of the will of the flesh nor of the will of man, but of God.' St Paul discovered that what Christ had experienced in his life we can all experience in some measure. Hence his words to the church in Rome: 'But you have received the spirit of sonship. When we cry, "Abba! Father!" it is the Spirit himself bearing witness with our spirit that we are children of God, and if children, then heirs, heirs of God and fellow heirs with Christ.'

We receive the Spirit of sonship in baptism, a sacrament concerned with spiritual rebirth. Grace becomes operative in our lives and we realize our spiritual heritage in prayer and worship. The outcome is summarized by Martin Luther King: 'Every man is somebody because he is a child of God.'

You are the sons of the Lord your God . . . a people holy to the Lord your God, and the Lord has chosen you to be a people for his own possession.

Deuteronomy 14:1–2

You are gods, sons of the Most High.

Psalm 82:6

But to all who received him, who believed in his name, he gave power to become children of God; who were born, not of blood nor of the will of the flesh nor of the will of man, but of God.

John 1:12–13

For all who are led by the Spirit of God are sons of God. For you did not receive the spirit of slavery to fall back into fear, but you have received the spirit of sonship. When we cry, 'Abba! Father!' it is the Spirit himself bearing witness with our spirit that we are children of God, and if children, then heirs, heirs of God and fellow heirs with Christ, provided we suffer with him in order that we may also be glorified with him.

Romans 8:14–17

Sons of God: they who understand and consciously co-operate.

A.R. Orage, *On Love*, The Janus Press, 1957, page 47

A man, Jesus says, is God's child. When a man realizes that he has a Father, a pedigree, a family, traditions, he has a peace within him that no one can take away. That is a very simple foundation of religious belief.

Father Andrew, S.D.C., *The Romance of Redemption*, A.R. Mowbray & Co., 1954, page 70

Now let me say that the next thing we must be concerned about if we are to have peace on earth and good will toward men is the non-violent affirmation of the sacredness of all human life. Every man is somebody because he is a child of God.

Martin Luther King, *The Words of Martin Luther King,* selected by Coretta Scott King, William Collins Sons & Co., 1986, page 83

In hours of doubt it seems labour thrown away to undertake to change the great human race. It is only when looking into the eyes of Jesus which carry light everywhere that we can have hope that every man can be changed into a son of God.

Henry Ward Beecher, *Proverbs from Plymouth Pulpit,* Charles Burnet & Co., 1887, page 20

When one finds himself in a disposition that comes oftener and oftener, that is sponta-neous, and that rises through an atmosphere of sympathising love toward God, that atmospheric condition of the soul is witness of God that he is His son.

Henry Ward Beecher, *Proverbs from Plymouth Pulpit,* Charles Burnet & Co., 1887, page 187

All men are the sons of God in the sense that all men owe to God the creation and the preservation of their lives; but only some men *become* the sons of God in the real depth and intimacy of the true father and son relationship.

William Barclay, *The Gospel of John,* The Saint Andrew Press, 1965, volume 1, page 42

... he succeeded in presenting the principle of the Inward Word as the basis of religion without giving any encouragement to libertinism or moral laxity, for he found the way of freedom to be a life of growing likeness to Christ, he held the fulfilling of the law to be possible only for those who accept the burdens and sacrifices of love, and he insisted that the privileges of blessedness belong only to those who *behave like sons.*

Rufus M. Jones, *Spiritual Reformers in the 16th and 17th Centuries,* Macmillan and Co., 1914, page 30

The acts of God, instead of being events beyond human control such as floods and storms and earthquakes, are the communication of love to those who are languishing, of life to those who are dead, of light to those who are in darkness. And the children of God, instead of being those who are afflicted and who are outside the human circle, are those who pass from languishing to love, from death to life, from darkness into light.

John S. Dunne, *The Reasons of the Heart,* SCM Press, 1978, page 15

If we are to have the nature of Christ regenerated in us, as the life of Adam is born in us; if we are to be like Him in nature as we are like to Adam in nature; if we are to be the heavenly sons of the one as we are the earthly sons of the other, then there is an absolute necessity that that which was done and born in the Virgin Mary be also by the same power of the Holy Ghost done and born in us, by a seed of life derived into us from Christ our regenerator... Jesus Christ therefore stands as our regenerator, to help us by a second birth from Him to such a holy, pure, and undefiled nature, as He Himself received in the Blessed Virgin and which we should have received in paradise from our first father...

William Law, in Stephen Hobhouse, editor, *Selected Mystical Writings of William Law,* Rockliff, 1948, page 28

The life of Adam, that is to say, the 'breath' which was to give actuality and existence and movement to the whole person of man, had mysteriously proceeded from the intimate depths of God's own life. Adam was created not merely as a living and moving animal who obeyed the command and will of God. He was created as a 'son' of God because his life shared something of the reality of God's own breath or Spirit. For 'breath' is the same as 'spirit'...

If the expression may be permitted, Adam's very existence was to be a kind of 'inspiration.' God intended not only to conserve and maintain Adam's bodily life. He would also foster and increase, even more directly and intimately, the spiritual life and activity which were the main reason for Adam's existence. Adam, then, was meant from the very first to live and breathe in unison with God, for just as the soul was the life of Adam's body, so the Spirit of God, dwelling in Adam, was to be the life of the soul. For him, then, to live would mean to 'be inspired'—to see things as God saw them, to love them as he loved them, to be moved in all things ecstatically by the Spirit of God.

Thomas Merton, The New Man, Burns & Oates, 1962, page 36

The doctrine of Jesus consisted in the elevation of the Son of man, that is, in the recognition on the part of men, that he, man, was the son of God. In his own individuality Jesus personified the man who has recognized the filial relation with God. He asked his disciples whom men said that he was—the Son of man? His disciples replied that some took him for John the Baptist and some for Elijah. Then came the question. '*But whom say ye that I am?*' And Peter answered, '*Thou art the Messiah, the Son of the living God.*' Jesus responded, '*Flesh and blood hath not revealed it unto thee, but My Father which is in heaven*'; meaning that Peter understood, not through faith in human explanations, but because, feeling himself to be the son of God, he understood that Jesus was also the Son of God. And after having explained to Peter that the true faith is founded upon the perception of the filial relation to God, Jesus charged his other disciples that they should tell no man that he was the Messiah. After this, Jesus told them that although he might suffer many things and be put to death, he, that is his doctrine, would be triumphantly re-established.

Leo Tolstoy, What I Believe ('My Religion'), C.W. Daniel, 1922, page 145

This Jesus lived with men: with the consciousness of unutterable majesty, he joined a lowliness, gentleness, humanity, and sympathy which have no example in human history. I ask you to contemplate this wonderful union. In proportion to the superiority of Jesus to all around him, was the intimacy, the brotherly love, with which he bound himself to them. I maintain that this is *a character wholly remote from human conception*. To imagine it to be the production of imposture or enthusiasm, shows a strange unsoundness of mind. I contemplate it with a veneration second only to the profound awe with which I look up to God. It bears no mark of human invention. It was real. It belonged to, and it manifested, the beloved Son of God . . .

Here I pause; and indeed I know not what can be added to heighten the wonder, reverence, and love which are due to Jesus. When I consider him, not only as possessed with the consciousness of an unexampled and unbounded majesty, but as recognizing a kindred nature in human beings, and living and dying to raise them to a participation of his divine glories; and when I see him, under these views, allying himself to men by the tenderest ties, embracing them with a spirit of humanity, which no insult, injury, or pain could for a moment repel or overpower—I am filled with wonder as well as reverence and love. I feel that this character is not of human invention; that it was not assumed through fraud, or struck out by enthusiasm; for it is infinitely above their reach. When I add this character of Jesus to the other evidence of his religion, it gives, to what before seemed so strong, a new and a vast accession of strength: I feel as if I could not be deceived. *The Gospels must be true: they were drawn from a living original; they were founded on reality.* The character of Jesus is not a fiction: *he was what he claimed to be, and what his followers attested.* Nor is this all. Jesus not only *was, he is still, the Son of God, the Saviour of the world.* He exists now: he has entered that heaven to which he always looked forward on earth. There he lives and reigns. With a clear, calm faith, I see him in that state of glory; and I confidently expect, at no distant period, to see him face to face. We have, indeed, no absent friend whom we shall so surely meet. Let us, then, my hearers, by imitation of his virtues and obedience to his word, prepare ourselves to join him in those pure mansions, where he is surrounding himself with the good and pure of our race, and will communicate to them for ever his own spirit, power, and joy.

William Ellery Channing, *The Complete Works of William Ellery Channing*, Routledge & Sons, 1848, page 242

SOUL

Soul—the spiritual or immaterial part of man, often regarded as immortal; the moral or emotional or intellectual nature of a person; the meeting-place of God in man

The Authorized Version of the Bible uses a different terminology in the Genesis story of the creation of man from the one we have been using. Genesis 2:7 reads: 'And the Lord God formed man of the dust of the ground, and breathed into his nostrils the breath of life; and man became a living soul.' This was the beginning of the meeting-place of God in man.

To summarize, we have seen this fully worked out in the life and person of Jesus Christ. In his life he found the presence of the Father in his soul, as well as the Holy Spirit and divine attributes such as life, light, joy, truth and love. By his life, death and resurrection, he opened up our spiritual heritage, activated by baptism and nurtured by prayer and worship. The lives of the saints, prophets and martyrs testify to the reality of the soul, and are examples of this way of life.

Non-biblical language may help us to understand more about the nature of the soul. Richard Jefferies in *The Story of My Heart*, wrote of a desire for 'a greatness of soul, an irradiance of mind, a deeper insight, a broader hope... By the word soul, or psyche, I mean an inner consciousness which aspires.' For Henry Ward Beecher, 'The human soul is God's treasury, out of which He coins unspeakable riches.' This insight points to the role of the priest and the 'cure of souls'—enabling people to come to wholeness by releasing the divine in them. We have now largely abandoned this role through unbelief.

My soul yearns for thee in the night, my spirit within me earnestly seeks thee.
Isaiah 26:9

... the One who shaped him, who breathed an active soul into him, and inspired a living spirit.
Wisdom of Solomon 15:11 (JB)

My soul magnifies the Lord.
Luke 1:46

Beloved, I pray that all may go well with you and that you may be in health; I know that it is well with your soul. For I greatly rejoiced when some of the brethren arrived and testified to the truth of your life, as indeed you do follow the truth. No greater joy can I have than this, to hear that my children follow the truth.
3 John 2–4

What is a soul? The thing that keeps the body alive.
James A. Froude, *Thomas Carlyle*, Longmans, Green, and Co., 1884, volume 2, page 35

The raging, unquiet soul which craves to tear itself to pieces and cure itself of being human.

Ugo Betti, *Crime on Goat Island*, act I, translated by Henry Reed, Samuel French, 1960, page 18

And it is with the soul that we grasp the essence of another human being, not with the mind, not even with the heart.

Henry Miller, *The Books in My Life*, Village Press, 1974, page 212

There is a direct in-shining, a direct in-breathing, a direct in-reaching of the Divine Soul upon the human soul.

Henry Ward Beecher, *Proverbs from Plymouth Pulpit*, Charles Burnet & Co., 1887, page 153

We shall know some day that death can never rob us of that which our soul has gained, for her gains are one with herself.

Rabindranath Tagore, 'Stray Birds', cccxii, in *Collected Poems and Plays of Rabindranath Tagore*, Macmillan and Co., 1936, page 327

Love unites the soul with God, and, the more degrees of love the soul has, the more profoundly does it enter into God and the more is it centred in Him.

St John of the Cross, *Living Flame of Love*, translated by E. Allison Peers, Image Books, 1962, page 40

When he is in possession of his soul, then will man be fully alive, caring nothing for immortality and knowing nothing of death.

Henry Miller, *The Books in My Life*, Village Press, 1974, page 193

The sphere that is deepest, most unexplored, and most unfathomable, the wonder and glory of God's thought and head, is our own soul!

Henry Ward Beecher, *Proverbs from Plymouth Pulpit*, Charles Burnet & Co., 1887, page 27

I desire a greatness of soul, an irradiance of mind, a deeper insight, a broader hope. Give me power of soul, so that I may actually effect by its will that which I strive for.

Richard Jefferies, *The Story of My Heart*, Macmillan and Co., 1968, page 8

The human soul is God's treasury, out of which He coins unspeakable riches. Thoughts and feelings, desires and yearnings, faith and hope—these are the most precious things which God finds in us.

Henry Ward Beecher, *Proverbs from Plymouth Pulpit*, Charles Burnet & Co., 1887, page 31

The soul is a temple; and God is silently building it, by night and by day. Precious thoughts are building it; disinterested love is building it; all-penetrating faith is building it.

Henry Ward Beecher, *Proverbs from Plymouth Pulpit*, Charles Burnet & Co., 1887, page 31

But with Western man the value of the self sinks to zero. Hence the universal depreciation of the soul in the West. Whoever speaks of the reality of the soul or psyche is accused of 'psychologism.'

C.G. Jung, *The Collected Works of C.G. Jung*, translated by R.F.C. Hull, Routledge & Kegan Paul, 1953, volume 12, page 8

By nature the core of the soul is sensitive to nothing but the divine Being, unmediated. Here God enters the soul with all he has and not in part. He enters the soul through the core and nothing may touch that core except God himself.

Meister Eckhart, *Meister Eckhart*, translated by Raymond B. Blakney, Harper & Row, 1941, page 97

There is, they say, (and I believe there is)
A spark within us of th'immortal fire,
That animates and moulds the grosser frame;
And when the body sinks escapes to heaven,
Its native seat, and mixes with the Gods.

John Armstrong, *The Art of Preserving Health*, iv. 11, printed for T. Cadell, Jun. and W. Davies, 1795, page 124

It is man's soul that Christ is always looking for. He calls it 'God's Kingdom,' and finds it in every one. He compares it to little things, to a tiny seed, to a handful of leaven, to a pearl. That is because one realises one's soul only by getting rid of all alien passions, all acquired culture, and all external possessions, be they good or evil.

Oscar Wilde, *De Profundis*, in *The Works of Oscar Wilde*, William Collins Sons & Co., 1948, page 870

If we wish to respect men we must forget what they are, and think of the ideal which they carry hidden within them, of the just man and the noble, the man of intelligence and goodness, inspiration and creative force, who is loyal and true, faithful and trustworthy, of the higher man, in short, and that divine thing we call a soul. The only men who deserve the name are the heroes, the geniuses, the saints, the harmonious, puissant, and perfect samples of the race.

Henri Frédéric Amiel, *Amiel's Journal*, translated by Mrs Humphry Ward, Macmillan and Co., 1918, page 247

But whither went his Soul, let such relate
Who search the Secrets of the future State:
Divines can say but what themselves believe;
Strong Proofs they have, but not demonstrative:
For, were all plain, then all Sides must agree,
And Faith it self be lost in Certainty.
To live uprightly then is sure the best,
To save our selves, and not to damn the rest.

John Dryden, 'Palamon and Arcite', iii. 844, in James Kinsley, editor, *The Poems of John Dryden*, Oxford at the Clarendon Press, 1958, volume 4, page 1521

... the Garden-of-Eden story is a mighty parable of the human soul. All that is told in the Genesis account is told of what goes on in the mysterious realm within us. It is told as though it were an external happening, it is in reality an internal affair. The Paradise and the Fall, the Voice of God and the tempting voice of the serpent, the Tree of Life and the Tree of the knowledge of Good and Evil, are all in our own hearts as they were in the heart of Adam. Heaven and Hell are there. The one stands fully revealed in the triumphant Adam, who is Christ; the other is exhibited in its awfulness in the disobedient Adam of the Fall.

Rufus M. Jones, *Spiritual Reformers in the 16th and 17th Centuries*, Macmillan and Co., 1914, page 57

This true and inner life is no questionable or new thing. It is the old primeval service of the heart to God; it is Christian life in its beauty, and its own peculiar form.

These souls, alive with the inner life, form no special sect. If each one were simply to follow the teaching, and live the life of Christ, the world would be full of such mystics; that is to say, people who had not only an outward show of Christianity, but also the hidden man of the heart, the ornament of a meek and quiet spirit, so precious in the sight of God.

Gerhard Tersteegen, in Frances Bevan, *Sketches of the Quiet in the Land*, John F. Shaw and Co., 1891, page 391

With all the energy the sunbeams had powered unwearied on the earth since Sesostris was conscious of them on ancient sands; with all the life that had been lived by vigorous men and beauteous women since first in dearest Greece the dream of the gods was woven; with all the soul-life that had flowed a long stream down to me, I prayed that I might have a soul more than equal to, far beyond my conception of, these things of the past, the present, and the fulness of all life. Not only equal to these, but beyond, higher, and more powerful than I could imagine. That I might take from all their energy, grandeur, and beauty, and gather it into me. That my soul might be more than the cosmos of life.

Richard Jefferies, The Story of My Heart, Macmillan and Co., 1968, page 10

There is something in us that seems deeper and truer than the mind, and we call it the soul: I sometimes find myself thinking that the soul is nearer to the body than the mind is: perhaps it is the eternity of the body: for, like the body, it is self-centred, dark, little changing, little answering: it too goes its own way, muttering to itself, and the mind playing by its skirts can guess only dimly at its thoughts. The mind seems little more than a flickering, bubbling stream that may sometimes catch and throw up for a moment the Image of an Image: the body, I have thought, may be God or, as the Hebrews seem to have deeply conceived, the Image of God; sometimes the body seems beautiful enough to be mysteriously That; always it is strange enough to be That, or the fallen image of That, for it is shapely and stately and most wonderfully coloured and it has too its strange share of ugliness, of evil: beauty and ugliness. The Good and The Evil, is there not in that strange blend something akin to the God? but the body dies? And if it does? is it not good Pauline lore that it shall rise again, even as the God that died rose again?

Stephen MacKenna, Journal and Letters, Constable & Co., 1936, page 126

Meanwhile within man is the soul of the whole; the wise silence; the universal beauty, to which every part and particle is equally related; the eternal ONE.

From within or from behind, a light shines through us upon things, and makes us aware that we are nothing, but the light is all. A man is the facade of a temple wherein all wisdom and all good abide. What we commonly call man, 'the eating, drinking, planting, counting man,' does not, as we know him, represent himself, but misrepresents himself. Him we do not respect, but the soul, whose organ he is, would he let it appear through his action, would make our knees bend. When it breathes through his intellect, it is genius; when it breathes through his will, it is virtue; when it flows through his affection, it is love. And the blindness of the intellect begins, when it would be something of itself. The weakness of the will begins, when the individual would be something of himself. All reform aims, in some one particular, to let the soul have its way through us; in other words to engage us to obey.

Of this pure nature every man is at some time sensible.

Language cannot paint it with his colours. It is too subtle. It is undefinable, unmeasurable, but we know that it pervades and contains us. We know that all spiritual being is in man. A wise old proverb says, 'God comes to see us without bell;' that is, as there is no screen or ceiling between our heads and the infinite heavens, so is there no bar or wall in the soul where man, the effect, ceases, and God, the cause, begins. The walls are taken away. We lie open on one side to the deeps of spiritual nature, to the attributes of God. Justice we see and know, Love, Freedom, Power. These natures no man ever got above, but they tower over us, and most in the moment when our interests tempt us to wound them.

Ralph Waldo Emerson, 'Essay on the Over-Soul', in The Works of Ralph Waldo Emerson, George Bell & Sons, 1906, volume 1, Essays and Representative Man, page 144

SUFFERING

Suffering—undergoing pain, loss, grief, defeat, disablement, change, punishment, wrong, etc.

The Director of the Health Centre in University College, London, asked me if I could befriend a post-graduate student from Nepal. A few weeks previously he had been diagnosed as having T.B. and was admitted to hospital. He was treated with a drug, one of the known side-effects being that it could damage one's eyesight. Sadly our man from Kathmandu had not been warned. He was cured of his T.B. at the cost of his eyesight. He had recently been discharged from hospital and was now almost completely blind. The Director knew I had spent some time in Nepal, and asked if I could possibly befriend him.

I found him very depressed. Gradually we became friends. One of the first things we did was go to the Royal Society for the Blind and fix him up with a white stick and various aids. Befriending him took us into a High Court action for medical negligence. Liability was admitted and he was awarded damages of £90,000. Four years went by and he was still depressed. He kept on asking why this had happened to him and not to someone else. He refused to come to terms with what had happened and ended up deeply embittered.

Suffering poses many questions and provides few answers. Perhaps asking why this has happened is the wrong question. A better approach is to accept suffering, and concentrate on working out what our response is going to be. This is a positive response to suffering. Sometimes with the passage of time we find our own answers and come to value this period of suffering.

When the righteous cry for help, the Lord hears, and delivers them out of all their troubles. The Lord is near to the broken-hearted, and saves the crushed in spirit.

Psalm 34:17–18

When you pass through the waters I will be with you; and through the rivers, they shall not overwhelm you; when you walk through fire you shall not be burned, and the flame shall not consume you.

Isaiah 43:2

Although he was a Son, he learned obedience through what he suffered; and being made perfect he became the source of eternal salvation to all who obey him.

Hebrews 5:8–9

And after you have suffered a little while, the God of all grace, who has called you to his eternal glory in Christ, will himself restore, establish, and strengthen you.

1 Peter 5:10

We must somehow believe that unearned suffering is redemptive.

Martin Luther King, *The Words of Martin Luther King*, selected by Coretta Scott King, William Collins Sons & Co., 1986, page 67

Deep, unspeakable suffering may well be called a baptism, a regeneration, the initiation into a new state.

George Eliot, *Adam Bede*, J.M. Dent & Sons, 1960, page 409

God is weak and powerless in the world, and that is exactly the way, the only way, in which he can be with us and help us... Only a suffering God can help.

Dietrich Bonhoeffer, *Letters and Papers from Prison*, William Collins Sons & Co., 1963, page 122

There are powerful kinds of good that can come into life only where something has gone terribly wrong. That does not justify even the smallest area of life going wrong; it just happens to be one aspect of the composition of things.

J. Neville Ward, Friday Afternoon, Epworth Press, 1982, page 97

... the bad things that happen to us in our lives do not have a meaning when they happen. But we can redeem these tragedies from senselessness by imposing meaning on them. In the final analysis, the question is not why bad things happen to good people, but how we respond when such things happen.

Rabbi H. Kushner, When Bad Things Happen to Good People, Pan Books, 1982, page 142

Only by saying 'Amen' ('So be it') explicitly or implicitly—despite everything—can suffering be endured if not explained. Saying 'Amen' is the translation of the Old Testament noun 'belief' (*heemen*). The world with its enigma, its evil and suffering, can be affirmed because of God. Not otherwise. The mystery of the Incomprehensible in his goodness embraces also the misery of our suffering.

Hans Küng, On Being a Christian, translated by Edward Quinn, William Collins Sons & Co., 1977, page 299

Job never found an answer to the problem of unmerited suffering. The problem remained insoluble, but in it he met God. That is where man always meets God. That is where man most frequently meets his fellows. For he is so constituted that he needs problems more than solutions. His soul thrives on questions but grows sickly on answers—especially answers served up by others and, most of all, answers laid down by authority.

John V. Taylor, The Go-Between God, SCM Press, 1973, page 146

My faith in God is most acutely tested by the existence of suffering which seems to have no special wrongdoing at base. Indeed, belief that God is almighty and all-loving is strained for the sensitive Christian until he goes on to see the divine way of dealing with suffering in the Cross of Christ. There the answer comes.

But it is an answer which is not speculative, but practical, for it is an answer that is valid only when something like the spirit of Christ has been translated into human lives— lives which show what can be made of human suffering in terms of heroic saintliness. Such lives are faith's most powerful witnesses, for just when the problem of evil oppresses us they assault us with the problem of good. Faith is a costly thing, valid only in terms of the challenge to a costly way of life. Those who possess it have found it to be not an escape from life's conflicts, but a way of meeting those conflicts with the certainty that the power of God and of goodness will prevail.

Michael Ramsey, Through the Year with Michael Ramsey, edited by Margaret Duggan, Hodder and Stoughton, 1975, page 39

In order to give glory to God and overcome suffering with the charity of Christ:

Suffer without reflection, without hate, suffer with no hope of revenge or compensation, suffer without being impatient for the end of suffering.

Neither the beginning of suffering is important nor its ending. Neither the source of suffering is important nor its explanation, provided it be God's will. But we know that He does not will useless, that is to say sinful, suffering.

Therefore in order to give Him glory we must be quiet and humble and poor in all that we suffer, so as not to add to our sufferings the burden of a useless and exaggerated sensibility.

In order to suffer without dwelling on our own affliction, we must think about a greater affliction, and turn to Christ on the Cross. In order to suffer without hate we must drive out bitterness from our heart by loving Jesus. In order to suffer without hope of compensation, we should find all our peace in the conviction of our union with Jesus. These things are not a matter of ascetic technique but of simple faith: they mean nothing without prayer, without desire, without the acceptance of God's will.

In the end, we must seek more than a passive acceptance of whatever comes to us from Him, we must desire and seek in all things the positive fulfilment of His will. We must suffer with gratitude, glad of a chance to do His will. And we must find, in this fulfilment, a communion with Jesus, who said: 'With desire have I desired to eat this Pasch with you before I suffer' (Luke 22:15).

Thomas Merton, *No Man is an Island*, Burns & Oates, 1974, page 82

It would be surprising to find, in a bouquet, flowers which were ill-formed or sickly, since these flowers are picked one by one and artificially grouped together in a bunch. But on a tree which has had to struggle against the inner accidents of its own development and external accidents of climate, the broken branches, the torn leaves, and the dried or sickly or wilted blossoms have their place: they reveal to us the greater or lesser difficulties encountered by the tree itself in its growth.

Similarly in a universe where each creature formed a little enclosed unit, designed simply for its own sake and theoretically transposable at will, we should find some difficulty in justifying in our own minds the presence of individuals whose potentialities and upward-soaring drives had been painfully impeded. Why this gratuitous inequality, these gratuitous frustrations?

If on the other hand the world is in truth a battlefield whereon victory is in the making—and if we are in truth thrown at birth into the thick of the battle—then we can at least vaguely see how, for the success of this universal struggle in which we are both fighters and the issue at stake, there must inevitably be suffering. Seen from the viewpoint of our human experience and drawn to our human scale, the world appears as an immense groping in the dark, an immense searching, an immense onslaught, wherein there can be no advance save at the cost of many setbacks and many wounded. Those who suffer, whatever form their suffering may take, are a living statement of this austere but noble condition: they are simply paying for the advance and the victory of all. They are the men who have fallen on the battlefield.

Pierre Teilhard de Chardin, *Hymn of the Universe*, William Collins Sons & Co., 1981, page 104

There is a dark side to this universe which, at least at first sight, seems utterly inconsistent with faith in a good God. Consider what we have recently read in newspapers. A volcano erupts, killing people, burning villages, ruining farmlands. An earthquake, followed by a tidal wave, strikes North America, destroying a whole city and slaying thousands.

Lightning blasts an airplane, which falls a blazing mass upon a home and kills all the family, as well as all the passengers. Rivers overflow their banks in disastrous floods, demolishing churches, homes, schools, exhibiting a ruthless indifference to everything that Christian faith holds sacred...

Why the ruthless evolutionary process—parasites, insects, beasts with claws and beaks, preying on one another? Why cancer cells and polio? Why little children born blind, deformed... And when one turns from nature's pitiless acts to man's the suffering is so dreadful that one wonders how any God there may be can stand it...

Moreover, this question is nowhere presented in so acutely difficult a form as in the Christian faith. For there God's goodness is pictured in such terms of mercy and compassion that one sometimes despairs of reconciling such grace with the world's hideous evils and mankind's frightful sufferings. 'God is love', 'God so loved the world that he gave his only begotten Son'—against that background you are right in feeling the problem of evil reaches its most difficult form...

Let us start, then, with the proposition that God is, and try to see what light we can shed on the mystery of evil. We may help ourselves by imagining ourselves in the place of God, facing the responsibility of creating and managing the universe. Just what would we do about the major causes of human suffering?

First, there is the law-abiding nature of the universe. A little child falls out of a tenth-story window, and the law of gravitation is merciless. Cause and consequence, bound together in unbreakable succession—how much of the world's agony springs from that! But if omnipotence were put into our hands, would we abolish nature's law-abiding order, and let creation become chaotic, haphazard, fortuitous, undependable? . . . despite all the agony that nature's law-abiding forces inflict on mankind we would not dare substitute a lawless for a law-abiding world.

Second, obviously our world is not finished yet. It is in the making—a creative process is afoot here, with a long evolutionary story behind us and unforeseeable possibilities ahead. Call that exciting if you will, but think of the suffering that has been and still is involved in being born into a world racked by growing pains. Conceivably, God might have made a finished universe, perfect, static, all-complete, with nothing more to be done in it. Let your imagination dwell on that possibility! Do you like it? Can you conceive anything more intolerably boring? Could creative minds or courageous characters ever develop in such a finished paradise? No! Despite the agony involved in an evolutionary universe, we would not dare to substitute a static world with no progress in it, no future of open doors before it, nothing to work and fight for, nothing to surpass and improve.

Third, we have the power of choice. If I should tell you that Gene Neely made the all-American team in football, played a crack centrefield in baseball, that he would handle a golf course in the eighties, and was a master at tennis, you would say, would you not, that he must have had a magnificent physique. On the contrary he had only one arm. He lost the other as the result of a gunshot wound. But, you see, he was not a mere thing, a robot helplessly pushed about by circumstance; he was a person with the power of decision, who could choose his own kind of response to any situation, and stand up to life, saying, Come on now, I'll show you! Just because we are human beings we are not automatons; we do make choices and decisions, we do exercise this power of personal initiative. But think of the evil that mankind suffers from the misuse of this marvellous power! Most of what Gibbon calls 'the crimes, follies, and misfortunes of mankind' come from the ignorant or wicked abuse of our free will. All the way from intimate personal hurts and tragedies to the vast catastrophe of war, how much of human agony springs from the personal choice of evil instead of good! . . .

Nevertheless, if you were in charge of the universe, would you dare to take from man his freedom of choice and make him a mere puppet, a marionette mechanically pulled by the strings of circumstance, with no liberty to shape his own conduct, no power to make decisions? Well, when I think of Gene Neely and millions like him, I am sure that I would take the calculated risk which the Creator took when he gave man power to choose between good and evil.

Fourth, another source of human suffering is the fact that we are not merely separate individuals, but woven together, by loyalty, love, mutual need and interdependence, into homes, friendships, communities. This fact of inescapable fellowship is alike the source of our deepest joys and our most heartbreaking tragedies. 'Where I love, I live' is at once a beautiful and a dreadful fact. A catastrophe befalling my children or grand-children would be to me a far more tragic hurt than anything that could happen to me as an individual.

Let your imagination play upon this universal source of heartbreak, until you feel how much of mankind's agony is due to the very relationships which make life most worth living, but in which the ills that happen to one thereby happen to all who most dearly love him. Then picture yourself as the Creator managing this universe, and tell me whether you would have made men and women isolated individuals, incapable of affection or loyalty, with no families, no friendships, no capacity for fellowship or fraternity. What an utterly useless, meaninglessness world that would be!

You see what I am driving at. These four factors—the law abiding order of the world, the progressive, evolutionary nature of the world, the human power to choose and to decide, and the human loves and loyalties that create homes and friendships—account for all the tragedy and suffering on earth. And yet, were we possessed of the power to eradicate a single one of the four, we would not dare to do so. Do not misunderstand me! I do not think that this answers all our questions. Countless protests and queries still confront our minds. Why cancer?—to that kind of question I can find no adequate reply. Why did the evolutionary process have to involve such beastly cruelty. Why the kind and degree of deprivation and suffering which, far from building character, almost inevitably cause madness and depravity? Nevertheless, from the facing of the fourfold source of human suffering, I do come to a reassuring conclusion: on the basis of no-God I can see no possible explanation of the problem of good, but on the basis of faith in God I can see the wide-open possibility of Mind and Purpose here and of an ultimate outcome which will vindicate the Creator.

Harry Emerson Fosdick, *Dear Mr Brown*, William Collins Sons & Co., 1962, page 63

TEMPTATION

*Temptation—tempting or being tempted, incitement especially to
wrongdoing; attractive thing or course of action; archaic putting to the test*

In this section I like the verse from 'A Prayer, in the Prospect of Death', written by Robert Burns. These words are very expressive and seem to get to the heart of temptation.

*Thou know'st that Thou hast formed me,
With Passions wild and strong;
And list'ning to their witching voice
Has often led me wrong.*

The first couplet reminds me of the Genesis story of the creation of man, particularly that we are formed from the dust of the earth. Not only are we born earthy and creaturely, but we have within us the primitive instincts and passions of the animals, stimulated by mind and imagination. I am glad we are born with these 'Passions wild and strong'. They contain within them valuable sources of power and energy, and properly channelled, lead to dynamism and many forms of creativity.

The second couplet reminds me of Christ's temptations in the wilderness. Was he listening to 'their witching voice' when tempted to turn stones into bread, throw himself from a pinnacle of the temple, and opt for the glory of worldly power? Led by the Spirit into the wilderness he resisted the pull of the passions and showed us how to deal with temptation. Overall these words of Robert Burns ring true to my own experience, and form a graphic introduction to this section on temptation.

My son, if sinners entice you, do not consent.
Proverbs 1:10

My son, if you aspire to serve the Lord, prepare yourself for an ordeal. Be sincere of heart, be steadfast, and do not be alarmed when disaster comes. Cling to him and do not leave him, so that you may be honoured at the end of your days. Whatever happens to you, accept it, and in the uncertainties of your humble state, be patient, since gold is tested in the fire, and chosen men in the furnace of humiliation. Trust him and he will uphold you, follow a straight path and hope in him.
Ecclesiasticus 2:1–6 (JB)

Watch and pray that you may not enter into temptation; the spirit indeed is willing, but the flesh is weak.
Matthew 26:41

No temptation has overtaken you that is not common to man. God is faithful, and he will not let you be tempted beyond your strength, but with the temptation will also provide the way of escape, that you may be able to endure it.
1 Corinthians 10:13

All temptations are founded either in hope or fear.

Thomas Fuller, *Gnomologia*, Stearne Brock, 1733, page 21

He did not say, 'You will never have a rough passage, you will never be over-strained, you will never feel uncomfortable,' but he *did* say 'You will never be overcome.'

Julian of Norwich, *Revelations of Divine Love*, translated by Clifton Wolters, Penguin Books, 1976, page 185

Yet temptations often bring great benefits, even if they are disagreeable and a great burden; for in temptation a man is humbled, purified and disciplined.

Thomas à Kempis, *The Imitation of Christ*, translated by Betty I. Knott, William Collins Sons & Co., 1979, page 53

Thou know'st that Thou hast formed me,
With Passions wild and strong;
And list'ning to their witching voice
Has often led me wrong.

Robert Burns, 'A Prayer, in the Prospect of Death', in James Kinsley, editor, *The Poems and Songs of Robert Burns*, Oxford at the Clarendon Press, 1968, volume 1, page 20

Pray! Have I prayed! When I'm worn with all my praying!
When I've bored the blessed angels with my battery of prayer!
It's a proper thing to say—but it's only saying, saying,
And I cannot get to Jesus for the glory of her hair.

G.A. Studdert Kennedy, *The Unutterable Beauty*, Hodder and Stoughton, 1964, page 24

Temptation in the New Testament means any testing situation. It includes far more than the mere seduction to sin; it covers every situation which is a challenge to and a test of a person's manhood and integrity and fidelity. We cannot escape it, but we can meet it with God.

William Barclay, *The Gospel of Luke*, The Saint Andrew Press, 1965, page 146

Man is not entirely safe from temptation as long as he is alive, because the source of temptation lies within us—we are born in concupiscence. When one trial or temptation leaves us, another takes its place, and we will always have something to endure, because we have lost the blessing of human happiness.

Thomas à Kempis, *The Imitation of Christ*, translated by Betty I. Knott, William Collins Sons & Co., 1979, page 53

The drunken Rip Van Winkle in Jefferson's play excuses himself for every fresh dereliction by saying, 'I won't count this time!' Well, he may not count it, and a kind Heaven may not count it, but it is being counted none the less. Down among his nerve-cells and fibres the molecules are counting it, registering and storing it up to be used against him when the next temptation comes.

William James, *The Principles of Psychology*, Macmillan and Co., 1890, volume 1, page 127

But temptations have their right uses, if they are met in a right way. Temptation tries us, and one of the Psalmist's prayers was, 'Try me, O God, search the ground of my heart, and see if there be any weakness within me.' Temptations do prove our genuineness. That English word 'try' means 'test.' If we want to know if a rope will bear a weight, we put a strain upon the rope to see if it will bear it. In the same kind of way, temptations put a strain on our character. They prove whether we can bear pain with courage, whether we can bear ill-treatment with love, whether we can bear being humbled without resentment. Those things temptation does for us. It is not a small thing to be made into a saint.

Father Andrew, S.D.C., *In the Silence*, A.R. Mowbray & Co., 1947, page 17

I was still under great temptations sometimes, and my inward sufferings were heavy; but I could find none to open my condition to but the Lord alone, unto whom I cried night and day. I went back into Nottinghamshire, and there the Lord shewed me that the natures of those things which were hurtful without, were within, in the hearts and minds of wicked men. I cried to the Lord, saying, 'Why should I be thus, seeing I was never addicted to commit those evils?' and the Lord answered that it was needful I should have a sense of all conditions, how else should I speak to all conditions, and in this I saw the infinite love of God. I saw also that there was an ocean of darkness and death, but an infinite ocean of light and love which flowed over the ocean of darkness. In that also I saw the infinite love of God; and I had great openings.

George Fox, *The Journal of George Fox*, J.M. Dent & Sons, 1924, page 11

The Temptation was real, not a mere semblance. Our Lord, under stress of genuine temptation, had to win the victory, in man and for man, by evincing self-denial, self-control, disregard for selfish advantage; absolute renunciation of power, honour, and self-gratification; and complete self-surrender to His Heavenly Father's will. If the struggle had not been an actual struggle, there would have been no significance in the victory. The Gospels represent Jesus as subject to temptations from without, not only at this crisis, but during all His life. He said to Peter, 'Get thee behind Me, Satan: thou art a *stumbling-block* unto Me'; and He said to His Apostles, 'Ye are they which have continued with Me in My temptations.' The only difference between the temptations of Christ and our own is that His came from without, but ours come also from within. In Him 'the tempting opportunity' could not appeal to 'the susceptible disposition.' With us sin acquires its deadliest force, because we have yielded to it. We can only conquer it when, by the triumph of God's grace within us, we are able to say with the dying hero of Azincour, 'Get thee hence, Satan; thou hast no part in me; my part is in the Lord Jesus Christ.'

Dean F.W. Farrar, *The Life of Lives*, Cassell and Company, 1900, page 251

Some of the most difficult and perplexing experiences in life come to us in temptation. We have given ourselves to God; we have begun to pray in earnest; we are trying to order our lives—so far as we can—in accordance with the will of God. And then, when we think that we have made a good start... we are suddenly over-whelmed by a storm of temptations. Sins that we thought we had overcome renew their attacks, and a host of new and bewildering temptations come upon us. This is both painful and bewildering...

The first thing to remember is this: *temptation is not sin.* This is a most elementary truth, but it is often ignored. Jesus himself was tempted, over and over again, but 'without sin'. We only commit sin when we give way to temptation. Everything turns on our consent. To *feel* cross with everyone all day long is not sin unless we give way to it, and vent our feelings on others in angry, impatient words and actions. To *feel* tempted to tell *lies*, to *feel* tempted to steal something, to *feel* tempted to cheat, to *feel* tempted to give way to thoughts which we know are bad for us, does not mean that we have sinned. If we resist the temptation, if we turn away from evil thoughts we have not consented; we have not fallen into sin...

Why are we allowed to fall into temptation? Briefly: for several reasons. God has His own reasons, which we do not know or understand; we have to take this on trust. But experience shows us that temptation, trying as it is, has many good effects: it wakes us up; it makes us realize the power of sin, and our own weakness; it teaches us humility; it purifies our desires and our hearts; it makes us depend upon God for everything.

But not all temptations are as obvious and as easy to detect with a vigorous 'no'... Very often the temptation is so subtle that we do not perceive it for some time; it finds an entrance into our hearts in disguise. It creeps in as a half-truth, or as evil disguised as good. In such a case temptation is not so much an attraction to sin... it is rather an illusion:

seeming 'good' is shown to us, and we do not see that it is a sham ... Such an experience is painful and searching, but if it drives us to a very earnest prayer for light, and a more complete obedience to God, the experience will have taught us a great deal, and we shall know that we have been delivered from temptations ...

One of the disquieting features of the spiritual life is the recurrence of temptations which we thought we had left behind many years ago. Whatever form this temptation may take, at bottom it is the same one: it is the fundamental temptation against faith. When we are faced with this kind of experience one of two things may happen: either we shall give way to discouragement and depression; or we shall become defiant; we feel disgusted with ourselves and this brings on an overpowering desire to 'do what we like for once', and to throw off the shackles of a steady, disciplined life of prayer, for 'after all, perhaps it is all illusion!' This temptation, strange to say, may occur after many years of devoted Christian life; our desire to 'throw it all up' is a simple fit of rebellion. Why? Why, after years of faithful life and service, do we feel like this? The reason seems to be that, although with our *will* we have been serving God faithfully all these years, we may have forgotten that our human nature is still 'there'; that we are not by any means all 'spiritual', but that we have bodies and natural instincts and self-willed desires which are not yet brought fully under obedience to God. The 'dark streak' in our nature is still inclined to rebellion—the fundamental sin against God. So when we are thrown into a furnace of temptation we should not be too greatly surprised. Casting ourselves upon God for deliverance we shall be able to endure, and, though we do not know what is happening, we shall come out of this experience humbled and purified, and stronger, because we know ourselves and our weakness better than ever before.

Olive Wyon, *On the Way*, SCM Press, 1958, page 55

THANKSGIVING

Thanksgiving—expression of gratitude, especially to God

I shall always remember a sermon preached on the phrase—'Learn to count your blessings, name them one by one.' I have tried to put this into practice on a daily basis ever since. The first few weeks of being a part-time hospital chaplain at the Bradford Royal Infirmary were particularly difficult and demanding. At the beginning of each week I would visit a hundred sick people and spend about five minutes with each patient. At the end of each session I was physically and mentally exhausted. On my way back to the clergy house I would 'count my blessings'. I would go over the session in the wards. I had met a man about to have his leg amputated. How thankful I was having both legs functioning properly, and able to walk and run. I had spent a few minutes with a woman who had a constriction in her throat. She had been fed solely on liquids for the last two months. How thankful I was, able to eat solid foods. I had come across a blind person, and someone else who was deaf. How thankful I was, able to see and hear without difficulty. By the time I had reached the clergy house I was well on the road to recovery and ready for the evening meal—and more work.

My life has had its ups and downs, but thanksgiving, practised on a daily basis, has brought me through setbacks and disappointments, and enabled me to extract value from them. William Law has some good advice: 'If anyone would tell you the shortest, surest way to all happiness, and all perfection, he must tell you to make a rule to yourself, to thank and praise God for everything that happens to you.'

O give thanks to the Lord, for he is good; for his steadfast love endures for ever!

1 Chronicles 16:34

O give thanks to the Lord, call on his name, make known his deeds among the peoples!

Psalm 105:1

Continue steadfastly in prayer, being watchful in it with thanksgiving.

Colossians 4:2

Rejoice always, pray constantly, give thanks in all circumstances; for this is the will of God in Christ Jesus for you. Do not quench the Spirit.

1 Thessalonians 5:16–19

... the chief idea of my life ... the doctrine I should always have liked to teach. That is the idea of taking things with gratitude, and not taking things for granted.

G.K. Chesterton, *Autobiography*, Hutchinson & Co., 1969, page 330

Thank God, carefully and wonderingly, for your continuing privileges, and for every experience of his goodness. Thankfulness is a soil in which pride does not easily grow.

Michael Ramsey, *Through the Year with Michael Ramsey*, edited by Margaret Duggan, Hodder and Stoughton, 1975, page 82

Gratitude was surely implanted in our hearts by our great Creator, and to fail in its observance, is acting against the dictates of conscience and humanity.

Elizabeth Helme, *St. Margaret's Cove; or, The Nun's Story*, printed for Earle and Hemet, 1801, volume 2, page 141

Thank God that those times which strain faith so hard come only occasionally in life. For the most part we travel a sunlit road, and when we are unaware of the love of God it is often because we have not looked for it. To see the evidence of God's mercies you have only to look.

W.E. Sangster, *Westminster Sermons*, Epworth Press, 1961, volume 2, *At Fast and Festival*, page 140

Thou that hast giv'n so much to me,
Give one thing more, a gratefull heart ...
Not thankfull, when it pleaseth me;
As if thy blessings had spare dayes:
But such a heart, whose pulse may be
Thy Praise.

George Herbert, 'Gratefulnesse', in *The Poems of George Herbert*, Oxford University Press, 1961, page 114

Certainly a marked feature of Christ's character was his perennial gratefulness of spirit. Run through His prayers and you will be surprised how large a place thanksgiving holds in them, how often He gave eager praise for what would have soured you and me, and made us feel quite certain that God had forgotten to be gracious. Did He not take the cup, that awful symbol of things so near and so fearsome, and even then give thanks?

A.J. Gossip, *From the Edge of the Crowd*, T. & T. Clark, 1925, page 37

We cannot of course always live thankfully, though this is the Christian ideal. We need help with the dark side of life which always provokes resentment. Most people cannot understand how one could possibly be thankful for what one dislikes in life, how resentment could possibly become thankfulness. Part of the meaning of the Eucharist is that this extraordinary transfiguration of life is possible, but only when life is interpreted in terms of the whole event of Christ as the Church understands Christ. When life is so interpreted it becomes all thankfulness.

J. Neville Ward, *The Use of Praying*, Epworth Press, 1967, page 29

Would you know who is the greatest saint in the world? It is not he who prays most or fasts most; it is not he who gives most alms, or is most eminent for temperance, chastity or justice; but it is he who is always thankful to God who wills everything that God willeth, who receives everything as an instance of God's goodness, and has a heart always ready to praise God for it . . .

If anyone would tell you the shortest, surest way to all happiness, and all perfection, he must tell you to make a rule to yourself, to thank and praise God for everything that happens to you. For it is certain that whatever seeming calamity happens to you, if you thank and praise God for it, you turn it into a blessing. Could you therefore work miracles, you could not do more for yourself than by this thankful spirit; for it heals with a word speaking and turns all that it touches into happiness.

William Law, *A Serious Call to a Devout and Holy Life*, J.M. Dent & Co., 1898, page 231

Thanksgiving is the expression of both faith and gratitude. Its effect in proportion to its genuineness is to strengthen the sense of dependence on God and trust in him. Thanksgiving for all that is enjoyable in life strengthens the sense of creaturely dependence on the author of all that is good. But even in the midst of acute tribulation a person can give thanks for the love which is at work bringing good out of evil. The focus of thanksgiving for the Christian is Jesus Christ, crucified and risen. The figure of Christ in the believer's imagination releases a rush of gratitude and the energy to live for God and the kingdom. Thanksgiving for redemption, expressed corporately and sacramentally in the eucharist, colours all fully Christian prayer and gives it its characteristic note of joy.

Christopher Bryant, S.S.J.E., in Gordon S. Wakefield, editor, *The Dictionary of Christian Spirituality*, SCM Press, 1986, page 318

Gratitude . . . is more than a mental exercise, more than a formula of words. We cannot be satisfied to make a mental note of things which God has done for us and then perfunctorily thank him for favours received.

To be grateful is to recognize the Love of God in everything he has given us—and he has given us everything. Every breath we draw is a gift of his love, every moment of existence is a grace, for it brings with it immense graces from him. Gratitude therefore takes nothing for granted, is never unresponsive, is constantly awakening to new wonder and to praise of the goodness of God. For the grateful man knows that God is good, not by hearsay but by experience. And that is what makes all the difference.

Thomas Merton, *Thoughts in Solitude*, Burns & Oates, 1958, page 37

I will thank Him for the pleasures given me through my senses, for the glory of the thunder, for the mystery of music, the singing of birds and the laughter of children. I will thank Him for the pleasures of seeing, for the delights through colour, for the awe of the sunset, the beauty of flowers, the smile of friendship and the look of love; for the changing beauty of the clouds, for the wild roses in the hedges, for the form and beauty of birds, for the leaves on the trees in spring and autumn, for the witness of the leafless trees through the winter, teaching us that death is sleep and not destruction, for the sweetness of flowers and the scent of hay. Truly, O Lord, the earth is full of thy riches! And yet, how much more I will thank and praise God for the strength of my body enabling me to work, for the refreshment of sleep, for my daily bread, for the days of painless health, for the gift of my mind and the gift of my conscience, for His loving guidance of my mind ever since it first began to think, and of my heart ever since it first began to love.

Edward King, *Sermons and Addresses*, Longmans, Green and Co., 1911, page 37

Thanksgiving . . . is an integral part of the practice of prayer. It includes both the fervent and spontaneous praise for whatever moves us to thank God from the bottom of our hearts, and the obligation to reflect upon the signs of God's goodness in our own lives, and in the world around us, and in the riches of the Christian revelation, and to give thanks for them all. 'In everything, give thanks,' says St Paul, and we recall how he and Silas in the darkness of the night, in the painful discomfort of the prison of Philippi, sang the praises of God so fervently that the whole prison sang with them. Sooner or later, Evelyn Underhill used to say, 'we all have to go on the night-shift', and the more steadily we have made our thanksgivings on principle the better shall we be able to sing God's praises in the night...

The range of our thanksgiving should be both wide and deep. A study of St Paul's great prayers in the Epistles to the Philippians and the Colossians shows us thanksgiving to God. So we give thanks for all things, small and great: for food and Sacrament, for work and health, for suffering and joy, for disappointment and for success, for the love of God and the laughter of children, for humour and for truth, and indeed for all the experiences of life.

Most people find it easier to practise thanksgiving if we ascend up a ladder which is firmly planted on the earth; that is, we begin with what is nearest and most obvious—though too often neglected because we take the good things of every day for granted, without a thought. From that we rise to the next step by reflection, and note God's goodness to us in certain incidents or events which we might otherwise take for granted, again without thought. Then for all the delights of human life, for games and dancing up to the joys of art and literature and every worth-while activity, including hard work. Thomas Traherne, for instance, overflows with thanksgiving for the beauty of the world which 'discovers the being of God unto you, opens His nature, and shews you His wisdom, goodness and power... it entertains you with many perpetual praises and thanksgivings, it enflames you with the love of God, and is the link of your union and communion with Him.' Then come the deeper experiences of human life, the pleasant and the less pleasant, which make up the warp and woof of life, and so on, up to joy in God Himself. So we rise gradually from the ground into the upper air where we are able to give thanks to God 'for His great glory'.

Olive Wyon, *On the Way*, SCM Press, 1958, page 99

THEOLOGY

Theology—science of (especially Christian) religion; natural theology (dealing with the knowledge of God as gained from his works by light of nature and reason); positive, revealed theology (based on revelation); dogmatic theology (dealing with authoritative teaching of the Scriptures and the Church); speculative theology (giving scope to human speculation, not confined to revelation); systematic theology (methodical arrangement of the truths of religion in their natural connexion)

According to this definition there are five categories of theology. *Visions of Glory* uses all five, which together make up another category which I call 'living theology'. This consists of the truths by which we live our everyday lives. The starting point was natural theology, closely followed by positive, revealed theology, focusing on the person of Jesus Christ. I moved on through dogmatic and systematic theology, ending up with speculative theology. At this point my faith came to a grinding halt.

I was helped forward by *A Year of Grace* and *From Darkness to Light*, both by Victor Gollancz. These two books helped me to make a start on 'living theology'. A big step forward was taken with the discovery of *The Choice is Always Ours*, edited by Dorothy Berkley Phillips. Twenty years have gone by since that book first came into my hands. For the development of 'living theology' I have branched out into poetry, literature, drama, art, music, history, philosophy, science, psychology, and included insights from a wide variety of sources. *Visions of Faith, Hope, Love* and *Glory* are the outcome, along with the practice of reflection.

Talk no more so very proudly, let not arrogance come from your mouth; for the Lord is a God of knowledge.

1 Samuel 2:3

Teach me good judgment and knowledge, for I believe in thy commandments.

Psalm 119:66

'How is it that this man has learning, when he has never studied?' So Jesus answered them, 'My teaching is not mine, but his who sent me.'

John 7:15–16

I myself am satisfied about you, my brethren, that you yourselves are full of goodness, filled with all knowledge, and able to instruct one another.

Romans 15:14

Theology is nothing but mental philosophy applied to the divine mind and the divine government.

Henry Ward Beecher, *Proverbs from Plymouth Pulpit*, Charles Burnet & Co., 1887, page 25

F.D. Maurice knew better than many of his contemporaries that Christian truth is about every man and woman and child.

Theology is about them, or it is not about God at all.

Michael Ramsey, *Through the Year with Michael Ramsey*, edited by Margaret Duggan, Hodder and Stoughton, 1975, page 31

Theological truth is the truth of God's relationship with man and it is the fruit not of learning but of experience. In this sense all theology, properly so called, is written in blood.

H.A. Williams, C.R., foreword in W.H. Vanstone, *Love's Endeavour, Love's Expense*, Darton, Longman and Todd, 1978, page xi

The study of theology, or at least of Christian theology, cannot survive in a healthy state apart from the life of prayer and the search for holiness. The theologian is essentially a man of prayer.

Kenneth Leech, *Soul Friend*, Sheldon Press, 1977, page 35

... mysticism is the very centre of religion and theology. I discovered that mysticism is the exquisitely beautiful queen before whom the other branches of theology bow down with awe and reverence like lowly handmaids.

William Johnston, *The Inner Eye of Love*, William Collins Sons & Co., 1978, page 10

The more ... the theologian knows of this world, through the natural sciences, psychology, sociology, philosophy, and—today less than ever to be forgotten—history, but most of all through his own experience, so much the better will he be able to fulfill his theological task.

Hans Küng, *On Being a Christian*, translated by Edward Quinn, William Collins Sons & Co., 1977, page 87

A theological system is supposed to satisfy two basic needs: the statement of the Christian message and the interpretation of this truth for every new generation. Theology moves back and forth between two poles, the eternal truth of its foundation and the temporal situation in which the eternal truth must be received.

Paul Tillich, *Systematic Theology*, James Nisbet & Co., 1964, volume 1, page 3

There can be no theological statement that remains unaffected by changing cultural conditions, no timeless expression of faith that speaks equally to every generation; on the other hand, a theology that is 'with it' in a cultural sense but has no roots in the tradition is not a Christian theology at all.

John Macquarrie, *The Faith of the People of God*, SCM Press, 1972, page 4

Theology is an encounter with the living God, not an uncommitted academic exercise. This encounter cannot survive if its only *locus* is the lecture theatre or the library. It needs the nourishment of sacramental worship, of solitude, of pastoral care and the cure of souls. Theology must arise out of and be constantly related to a living situation.

Kenneth Leech, *Soul Friend*, Sheldon Press, 1977, page 36

Theology has always made a distinction between *natural* theology and *revealed* theology. Revealed theology deals with the truths that came to us directly from God in the words of the prophets, the pages of His Book, and supremely in Jesus Christ. Natural theology deals with the truths that man could discover by the exercise of his own mind and intellect on the world in which he lives.

William Barclay, *The Gospel of John*, The Saint Andrew Press, 1965, volume 1, page 36

The Christian is not seeking a solitary walk with God, a private mystical trip, a flight of the alone to the Alone. He is involved in a corporate search for humanity, renewal, the Kingdom of God, the transfigured cosmos, the Body of Christ. It is within the context of the flock or the Body that mystical theology is practised, and there are very serious hazards and dangers when the spiritual quest occurs outside that framework.

Kenneth Leech, *Soul Friend*, Sheldon Press, 1977, page 37

There is, therefore, no Christian mysticism without theology; but, above all, there is no theology without mysticism... It is an existential attitude which involves the whole man: there is no theology apart from experience; it is necessary to change, to become a new man. To know God one must draw near to Him. No one who does not follow the path of union with God can be a theologian. The way of the knowledge of God is necessarily the way of deification.

Vladimir Lossky, *The Mystical Theology of the Eastern Church*, James Clarke & Co., 1957, page 9

We need theologians to help us reflect on our experiences of trying to create a just and caring society, for which the Church is there to offer its life. What we do *not* need is white, male, middle-class theologians writing books to each other in universities, in jargon which hardly anyone except themselves can understand. It's time they stopped writing books and started to work for the Church. They are the people who should provide the critical, prophetic part of the Church's ministry.

Donald Reeves, in Gerald Priestland, *Priestland's Progress*, BBC Publications, 1982, page 22

Ascetical theology is the practical doctrine of prayer, its techniques, methods and the disciplines which help to support and nurture it. Spiritual direction is its application, by one skilled in this doctrine, to the personal needs of individual people. It all adds up to a science of co-operation with grace, of using the grace which God gives us, not only in the fight against temptation and sin, but in the positive development of those spiritual gifts and human graces which God bestows far more generously than we sometimes suppose.

Martin Thornton, *The Purple Headed Mountain*, The Faith Press, 1962, page 14

There is one thing I would like to tell the theologians: something which they know and others should know. They hold the sole truth which goes deeper than the truth of science, on which the atomic age rests. They hold a knowledge of the nature of man that is more deeply rooted than the rationality of modern times. The moment always comes inevitably when our planning breaks down and we ask and will ask about this truth. The present bourgeois status of the Church is no proof that men are really asking about Christian truth. This truth will be convincing when it is lived.

Carl Friedrich von Weizsacker, in Hans Küng, *On Being a Christian*, translated by Edward Quinn, William Collins Sons & Co., 1977, page 83

The priest is the teacher and preacher, and as such he is the *man of theology*. He is pledged to be a dedicated student of theology; and his study need not be vast in extent but it will be deep in its integrity, not in order that he may be erudite but in order that he may be simple. It is those whose studies are shallow who are confused and confusing. The Church's hold upon the faith requires those who in theology are 'learned', concentrated, dedicated, and deep; and by his service of the laity in this role, the priest will be helping them to be better witnesses. But this work will be a partnership; and the contrast between *discens* and *docens* melts away as the priest learns from the laity much about the contemporary world and about the meaning of divine truth in its human context. Together they, from their several kinds of knowledge, will work out the meaning of the Word of God as it bears upon life's problems and upon the various spheres of the Church's witness. It can be a wonderful partnership, and within it ordained priesthood finds its role. Thus in new guises the old 'didactic' and 'kerygmatic' roles of the priests are carried on. The 'kerygmatic' role still stands, for it is the presence of the divine Word and its proclamation to, and with, and by, the Church that the Church is still *ecclesia Dei*.

Michael Ramsey, *The Christian Priest Today*, SPCK, 1983, page 7

Theologians have long been an important group of the members of the Christian community. However, there may be some misunderstanding regarding who they are. This is particularly true in our era when people can get university degrees in theology and are thus generally looked on as theologians. But a true theologian is not to be judged by the amount of subject matter mastered. Rather, a theologian in the fullest sense is a man or woman in whom God is prayerfully present. Scholarship is not absent from this person's experience; it is, however, embraced in a contemplative tradition—part of the Christian meditative historical process that gives theological knowledge its special illumination. The holy woman or man, ignorant of theological schools and trends, is far more worthy to be considered a theologian than is a person with various college degrees, who 'knows' the field but leads a life which is not virtuous. Just as a politician may not necessarily be the best 'American' nor a wealthy man a good man, nor a beautiful woman a kind one, nor a well-read person a good teacher, nor a strong man a courageous one, neither is every one who is called a theologian actually a true one. Perhaps we might consider that each of us is called, in a certain way, to be more a theologian than we had at first suspected. Knowledge of theological matters is a good something for which we may profitably strive as Christians. But this knowledge must be planted in the soil of the contemplative awareness of Christ in our lives if it is to be rooted so that it might develop within us. The combination, then, of the awareness of the mystery of God in us and the wisdom stemming from the union of this experience with what has been called the science of God, is a combination that could lead us to the fuller life for which we search. We need not feel that true theologians are those other people. Each of us is able to be a theologian by virtue of a mature love of God in union with the intellectual search.

Harry James Cargas, *Encountering Myself*, SPCK, 1978, page 126

Everybody who can do so ought to acquire something of a theologian's accuracy and sharpness in appreciating the true sense of dogma. Every Christian ought to have as deep a comprehension of his belief as his state will allow him. And this means that every one ought to breathe the clean atmosphere of orthodox tradition and be able to explain his belief in correct terminology—and terminology with a content of genuine ideas.

Yet true contemplation is not arrived at by an effort of the mind. On the contrary, a man could easily lose his way in the forest of technical details which concern a professional theologian. But God gives true theologians a hunger born of humility, which cannot be satisfied with formulas and arguments, and which looks for something closer to God than analogy can bring you.

This serene hunger of the spirit penetrates the surface of words and goes beyond the human formulations or mysteries and seeks, in the humiliation of silence, intellectual solitude and interior poverty, the gift of a supernatural apprehension which words cannot truly signify.

Beyond the labour of argument it finds rest in faith and beneath the noise of discourse it apprehends the Truth, not in distinct and clear-cut definitions but in the limpid obscurity of a single intuition that unites all dogmas in one simple Light, shining into the soul directly from God's eternity, without the medium of created concept, without the intervention of symbols or of language or the likeness of material things.

Here the Truth is One whom we not only know and possess but by whom we are known and possessed. Here theology ceases to be a body of abstractions and becomes a Living Reality who is God Himself. And He reveals Himself to us in our total gift of our lives to Him. Here the light of truth is not something that exists for our intellect but One in whom and for whom all minds and spirits exist, and theology does not truly begin to be theology until we have transcended the language and separate concepts of theologians.

Thomas Merton, *New Seeds of Contemplation*, Burns & Oates, 1962, page 115

TRINITY

*Trinity—union of three persons (Father, Son, Holy Spirit) in one
Godhead, the doctrine of the Trinity*

I remember going on a university chaplains' conference in Durham some years ago. A small group of chaplains, influenced by the charismatic movement, made a bid to take over the conference. The gifts of healing, speaking in tongues and baptism of the Spirit were all highlighted in an attempt to win us over to their position. Most of the chaplains dug in their heels and resisted these overtures. By the time we had started the plenary session the atmosphere was tense and somewhat hostile. One of the members of the organizing committee suddenly spotted Archbishop Michael Ramsey sitting quietly amongst us. 'What do you think about this, Archbishop?' he asked. There was a pregnant pause, and the hall became strangely silent. The white bushy eyebrows went into overdrive. The Archbishop quietly replied, 'We all know, don't we, that when one member of the Trinity is over-emphasized at the expense of the other two, there is always trouble, always trouble.' A huge sigh of relief went round the hall. In one brief sentence the Archbishop had resolved the issue once and for all and restored an equilibrium.

I think this is one reason why we believe in the Trinity—for a balanced faith, with some breadth and depth. I find it helpful to think of our bodies as temples of the Trinity. After our baptism we should expect to find something of the Father, Son and Holy Spirit in the depths of our being. This fits in well with the Genesis story of the creation of man and gives us a practical working model of the Trinity.

Go therefore and make disciples of all nations, baptizing them in the name of the Father and of the Son and of the Holy Spirit.

Matthew 28:19

The grace of the Lord Jesus Christ and the love of God and the fellowship of the Holy Spirit be with you all.

2 Corinthians 13:14

The Trinity... is seen by the heart; the doctrine of the Trinity arises out of a vision of the heart.

John S. Dunne, *The Reasons of the Heart*, SCM Press, 1978, page 51

The union of the Christian with Christ in 'one spirit' is the means whereby the whole *koinonia* of the Blessed Trinity becomes present in the generate life of man.

L.S. Thornton, *The Common Life in the Body of Christ*, A. & C. Black, 1950, page 442

Some things I see clearly and hold with desperate clutch. A Father in heaven for all, a Son of God incarnate for all, and a Spirit of the Father *and* the Son—who works to will and to do of His own good pleasure in every human being in whom there is one spark of active good, the least desire to do right or to be of use—the Fountain of all good on earth.

Charles Kingsley, *Daily Thoughts*, Macmillan and Co., 1884, page 146

What we have in the experience of being known and understood is not the doctrine of the Trinity but, perhaps we could say, the roots of that doctrine. It is the human experience of intimacy with God, of being accessible to God in the loneliest depths of one's being and of having access thereby to God. It points to the intimacy that is seen within God in that doctrine.

John S. Dunne, *The Reasons of the Heart*, SCM Press, 1978, page 47

The doctrine of the Holy Trinity is wholly practical; it is revealed to us, to discover our high original and the greatness of our fall, to show us the deep and profound operation of the triune God in the recovery of the divine life in our souls; that by the means of this mystery thus discovered, our piety may be rightly directed, our faith and prayer have their proper objects, that the workings and aspiring of our own hearts may co-operate and correspond with that triune life in the Deity, which is always desiring to manifest itself in us.

William Law, in Stephen Hobhouse, editor, *Selected Mystical Writings of William Law*, Rockcliff, 1948, page 41

To discover the Trinity is to discover a deeper solitude. The love of the Three Divine Persons holds your heart in its strength and builds about you a wall of quiet that the noise of exterior things can only penetrate with difficulty. You no longer have to strive to resist the world or escape it: material things affect you little. And thus you use and possess them as you should, for you dominate them, in making them serve the ends of prayer and charity, instead of letting them dominate you with the tyranny of your own selfishness and cupidity.

Thomas Merton, *The Sign of Jonas*, Sheldon Press, 1976, page 74

It is this eternal, unbeginning Trinity in unity of fire, light, and spirit, that constitutes eternal nature, the Kingdom of Heaven, the heavenly Jerusalem, the divine life, beatific visibility, the majestic glory and presence of God. Through this Kingdom of Heaven, or eternal nature, is the invisible God, the incomprehensible Trinity eternally breaking forth, and manifesting itself in a boundless height and depth to blissful wonders, opening and displaying itself to all its creatures as in an infinite variation and endless multiplicity of its powers, beauties, joys and glories.

William Law, in Stephen Hobhouse, editor, *Selected Mystical Writings of William Law*, Rockcliff, 1948, page 46

Yes, the mystery of God is the mystery of the Person and, in last analysis, we who are created 'in His own image' (Gen 1:27) follow in His traces.

God is immanent in the Cosmos and at the same time He is transcendent to it.

The mystery of the Trinity is the mystery of the Transcendence of God that can never be conditioned by the unicity of His Nature. What liberates from conditioning is Love.

Life, which is from the Father, says to Light which is the Son: 'I love you'.

From this statement and from the rejoiner, 'I love you too', proceeds Love which is the Holy Spirit.

And communication is made.

Carlo Carretto, *The Desert in the City*, translated by Barbara Wall, William Collins Sons & Co., 1983, page 31

The Old Testament proclaimed the Father openly, and the Son more obscurely. The New manifested the Son, and suggested the Deity of the Spirit. Now the Spirit Himself dwells among us, and supplies us with a clearer demonstration of Himself. For it was not safe, when the Godhead of the Father was not yet acknowledged, plainly to proclaim the Son; nor when that of the Son was not yet received to burden us further (if I may use so bold an expression) with the Holy Ghost... but that by gradual additions... and advances progress from glory to glory, the Light of the Trinity might shine upon the more illuminated... You see lights breaking upon us gradually; and the order of Theology, which it is better for us to keep, neither proclaiming things too suddenly, nor yet keeping them hidden to the end.

St Gregory of Nazianzus, in *A Select Library of Nicene and Post-Nicene Fathers of the Christian Church*, James Parker and Company, 1894, volume 7, page 326

I wonder if an analogy will help. There are three ways in which a man might know Beethoven. One man might know Beethoven the composer and be an expert student of his works. Another man might know Beethoven the performer, hearing him play and rejoicing in his skill. Another man might know Beethoven as an intimate friend, living in his home as a comrade and companion. Beethoven has three 'personae,' he reveals himself in three characters—composer, performer, friend. But what if a man could know Beethoven all three ways at once! Then he would indeed know him, and the crown and consummation of that whole experience would be that Beethoven the composer and performer had become his friend.

Harry Emerson Fosdick, *Dear Mr Brown*, William Collins Sons & Co., 1962, page 120

The doctrine of the Trinity may seem to some at a first superficial glance difficult to accept, and the creed that is called the Creed of S. Athanasius a tangle of phrases, but doctrine and creed stand for the one satisfying faith, that in the Divine Life there is a perfection of relationships, the holiness of a full life and not just a divine loneliness. It would be difficult to find joy in the worship of a God who had in Himself no joy, or to believe that there could be joy in a Life which had within itself no relationships, a God who had to wait for an object of His own creation to give Him a purpose for living and a reason for loving. Could God be an adorable Being if He had no relationships within Himself? Could there be a Love that had nothing to love? Is not the formula of the Holy Trinity, which sets our Lord Jesus Christ in the heart of the Godhead, the only satisfactory expression of what we feel in our inmost being ought to be true about the being of God—that in Him are relationships, a Lover, a Love, and a Beloved?

Father Andrew, S.D.C., *The Adventure of Faith*, A.R. Mowbray & Co., 1933, page 55

One of the comparisons or likenesses I am speaking of is taken from the most glorious object which our eyes see, the sun. That ball of light and heat, which we call most properly the Sun, may be compared to the Father, from whom both the Word and the Spirit come.

From this sun the light issues, and is as it were a part of it, and yet comes down to our earth and gives light to us. This we may compare to the Word, who came forth from the Father, and came down to earth, and was made man, and who, as St. John tells us, is 'the true light, which lighteth every man that cometh into the world.' But beside this there is the heat, which is a different thing from the light: for we all know, there may be heat without light: and so may there be light—moonlight for example, and starlight—without any perceivable heat. Yet the two are blended and united in the sun; so that the same rays, which bring us light to enlighten us, bring us heat also to warm us, and to ripen the fruits and herbs of all kinds which the earth bears. This heat of the sun may not unfitly be compared to the Holy Spirit, the Lord and Giver of life, as the Creed calls him, for heat is the great fosterer of life: as we see for example in an egg. As that is hatched by the warmth of the parent bird, sitting on it lovingly, and brooding over it, until it is quickened into life; just so does the Holy Spirit of God brood with more than dove-like patience over the heart of the believer, giving it life and warmth; and though he be driven away again and again by our backslidings, he still hovers round our hearts, desiring to return to them, and to dwell in them, and cherish them for ever. Moreover, if any seed of the Word has begun to spring up in any heart, the Spirit descends like a sunbeam upon it, and ripens the ear, and brings the fruit to perfection. Thus have we first the sun in the sky, secondly, the light, which issues from the sun, and thirdly, the heat, which accompanies the light—three separate and distinguishable things; yet distinct as they are, what can be more united than the sun and its rays, or than the light and heat which those rays shed abroad?

Augustus William Hare, 'Holy Branches: or why was the Trinity revealed?' in R. Nye, editor, *The English Sermon*, Carcanet Press, 1976, volume 3, page 119

TRUST

Trust—firm belief in the honesty, veracity, justice, strength, etc., of a person or thing—as our trust is in God

In my early twenties I came to trust in God, and took a simple step of faith. I accepted as true the contents of the Gospels, and the person they revealed—Jesus Christ. In the next two years I put down some roots to fortify this trust. The next major step taken on trust was ordination. This was accompanied by fear and trepidation. The last twenty-eight years of ministry have been lived in a background of trust, but what crevasses, hurricanes and minefields.

The quotation I most clearly identify with in this section comes from *Mister God, This is Anna*: 'And what a word it is! Define it how you like and I bet you'll miss the main point! It's more than confidence, more than security; it doesn't belong to ignorance or, for that matter, to knowledge either. It is simply the ability to move out of the, "I'm the centre of all things" and to let something or someone take over.'

This fits in well with my underlying vision of faith. I have consistently pointed out that God in the first instance is a 'presence' to be found in the depths of ourselves. Somehow we have to let go of the insistent claims of the ego for predominance and let this 'something or someone' take over. To this end, *Visions of Glory* acts as a skeleton or framework of faith, designed to undergird trust. The practice of reflection can be used as an aid to let Anna's 'something or someone' take over, and to foster a spirit of trust.

The Lord will provide.
Genesis 22:14

Trust in the Lord, and do good; so you will dwell in the land, and enjoy security. Take delight in the Lord, and he will give you the desires of your heart.

Psalm 37:3–4

I send you out as sheep in the midst of wolves; so be wise as serpents and innocent as doves.

Matthew 10:16

I will never fail you nor forsake you.

Hebrews 13:5

Let this be my last word, that I trust in thy love.

Rabindranath Tagore, 'Stray Birds', cccxxv, in *Collected Poems and Plays of Rabindranath Tagore,*
Macmillan and Co., 1936, page 329

The whole of God's being cannot be understood, but enough of it can be understood to trust it.

Henry Ward Beecher, *Proverbs from Plymouth Pulpit,* Charles Burnet & Co., 1887, page 145

You can trust and rest in God simply because He has said, you may and you must.

Henry Ward Beecher, *Proverbs from Plymouth Pulpit,* Charles Burnet & Co., 1887, page 173

When we trust as far as we can, we often find ourselves able to trust at least a little further.

Mark Gibbard, *Jesus, Liberation and Love,* A.R. Mowbray & Co., 1982, page 55

The recurrent needs of every day are all known to God. A full reliance can be put upon all His promises.

W.E. Sangster, *He is Able,* Hodder and Stoughton, 1936, page 42

We have reached that stage in human development when we are able to ask the questions, but are not always able to understand the answers. God expects us to trust His love.

W.E. Sangster, *He is Able,* Hodder and Stoughton, 1936, page 23

In such a world as this, with such ugly possibilities hanging over us all, there is but one anchor which will hold, and that is utter trust in God; let us keep that, and we may yet get to our graves without *misery* though not without *sorrow.*

Charles Kingsley, *Daily Thoughts,* Macmillan and Co., 1884, page 239

In simple trust like theirs who heard
Beside the Syrian sea
The gracious calling of the Lord,
Let us, like them, without a word,
Rise up and follow thee.

John Greenleaf Whittier, 'The Brewing of Soma', 13, in *The Poetical Works of John Greenleaf Whittier,*
Macmillan and Co., 1874, page 457

And what a word that is! Define it how you like and I bet you'll miss the main point! Its more than confidence, more than security; it doesn't belong to ignorance or, for that matter, to knowledge either. It is simply the ability to move out of the, 'I'm the centre of all things' and to let something or someone take over.

Fynn, *Mister God, This is Anna,* William Collins Sons & Co., 1974, page 62

Trust in the good God who loves us, who cares for us, who sees all, knows all, can do all things for my good and the good of souls. One thing Jesus asks of me: that I lean upon him; that in him alone I put complete trust; that I surrender myself to him unreservedly. I need to give up my own desires in the work of perfection. Even when all goes wrong, and I feel as if I were a ship without a compass, I must give myself completely to him.

Mother Teresa, *Jesus, the Word to be Spoken*, compiled by Brother Angelo Devananda, William Collins Sons & Co., 1990, page 39

If you have doubts about the existence of God or misgivings as to the kind of God He is, I do not think your need will be met by argument. It will be met only by an act of trust on your part. You must be willing to be found by the pursuing love of God which will not let you go; to face the challenge which is relentless; to move out fearlessly from your narrow self-centred life into a new, wide, spacious life with Christ at the centre—trusting not in yourself but in the all-sufficient love and power of God.

Leslie J. Tizard, *Facing Life and Death*, George Allen & Unwin, 1959, page 73

The animals teach us to trust ourselves; what we are to trust is not the self-confident, self-directed part of ourselves, the 'plain man' who knows what is what and how to get on, but the whole of ourselves. And the greater part of this whole we can only become acquainted with after many years, and only then by the patient surrender of pride in a willingness to live with the shabby and unpredictable in ourselves, without trying to pretend it isn't there. It can destroy us if we ignore it, but if we acknowledge it it becomes our guide. It is itself changed, no longer hidden but a known part of ourselves.

Rosemary Haughton, *Tales from Eternity*, George Allen & Unwin, 1973, page 64

My Lord God, I have no idea where I am going. I do not see the road ahead of me. I cannot know for certain where it will end. Nor do I really know myself, and the fact that I think I am following your will does not mean that I am actually doing so. But I believe that the desire to please you does in fact please you. And I hope that I have that desire in all that I am doing. I hope that I will never do anything apart from that desire. And I know that if I do this you will lead me by the right road, though I may know nothing about it. Therefore I will trust you always though I may seem to be lost and in the shadow of death. I will not fear, for you are ever with me, and you will never leave me to face my perils alone.

Thomas Merton, *Thoughts in Solitude*, Burns & Oates, 1958, page 70

Over the greater part of the so-called civilised world is spreading a deep distrust, a deep irreverence of every man towards his neighbour, and a practical unbelief in every man whom you do see, atones for itself by a theoretical belief in an ideal human nature which you do not see. Such a temper of mind, unless it be checked by that which alone can check it, namely, the grace of God, must lead towards sheer anarchy. There is a deeper and uglier anarchy. There is a deeper and uglier anarchy than any mere political anarchy—which the abuse of the critical spirit leads to—the anarchy of society and of the family, the anarchy of the head and of the heart, which leaves poor human beings as orphans in the wilderness to cry in vain, 'What can I know? Whom can I love?'

Charles Kingsley, *Daily Thoughts*, Macmillan and Co., 1884, page 165

I am becoming more and more aware that the great difficulty of many of us who live in community is that we lack self-confidence. We can so quickly feel that we are not really lovable, that if others saw us as we really are, they would reject us. We are afraid of all that is darkness in ourselves; we are afraid to face our emotional or sexual problems; we are afraid that we are incapable of real love. We swing so quickly from exhilaration to depression, and neither expresses what we really are. How can we become convinced that we are loved in our poverty and weakness and that we too are capable of loving?

That is the secret of growth in community. It comes from a gift of God which may pass through others. As we gradually discover that God and the others trust us, it becomes a little easier for us to trust ourselves, and in turn to trust others.

Jean Vanier, *Community and Growth*, Darton, Longman & Todd, 1991, page 20

The mutual trust at the heart of community is born of each day's forgiveness and acceptance of our frailty and poverty. But this trust is not developed overnight. That is why it takes time to form a real community. When people join a community, they always present a certain image of themselves because they want to conform to what the others expect of them. Gradually, they discover that the others love them as they are and trust them. But this trust must stand the test and must always be growing.

Newly-married couples love each other a great deal. But there may be something superficial in this love, which has to do with the excitement of discovery. Love is even deeper between people who have been married for a long time, who have lived through difficulties together and who know that the other will be faithful until death. They know that nothing can break their union.

It is the same in our communities. It is often after suffering, after very great trials, tensions and the proof of fidelity that trust grows. A community in which there is truly mutual trust is a community which is indestructible.

Jean Vanier, *Community and Growth*, Darton, Longman & Todd, 1991, page 18

There is a time in every man's education when he arrives at the conviction that envy is ignorance; that imitation is suicide; that he must take himself for better, for worse, as his portion; that though the wide universe is full of good, no kernel of nourishing corn can come to him but through his toil bestowed on that plot of ground which is given to him to till. The power which resides in him is new in nature, and none but he knows what that is which he can do, nor does he know until he has tried. Not for nothing one face, one character, one fact, makes much impression on him, and another none. This sculpture in the memory is not without pre-established harmony. The eye was placed where one ray should fall, that it might testify of that particular ray. We but half express ourselves, and are ashamed of that divine idea which each of us represents. It may be safely trusted as proportionate and of good issues, so it be faithfully imparted, but God will not have his work made manifest by cowards. A man is relieved and gay when he has put his heart into his work and done his best; but what he has said or done otherwise, shall give him no peace. It is a deliverance which does not deliver. In the attempt his genius deserts him; no muse befriends; no invention, no hope.

Trust thyself: every heart vibrates to that iron string. Accept the place the divine providence has found for you, the society of your contemporaries, the connection of events. Great men have always done so, and confided themselves childlike to the genius of their age, betraying their perception that the absolutely trustworthy was seated at their heart, working through their hands, predominating in all their being. And we are now men, and must accept in the highest mind the same transcendent destiny; and not minors and invalids in a protected corner, not cowards fleeing before a revolution, but guides, redeemers, and benefactors, obeying the Almighty effort, and advancing on Chaos and the Dark.

Ralph Waldo Emerson, 'Self-Reliance', in *The Works of Ralph Waldo Emerson*, George Bell & Sons, 1906, volume 1, *Essays* and *Representative Men*, page 24

TRUTH

Truth—quality or state of being true or truthful

Having spent over twenty years in a university setting I have come across many different kinds of truth—both in the arts and sciences. Our definition above speaks of personal truth. F.W. Robertson, in his *Sermons*, wrote: 'Truth lies in character. Christ did not simply *speak* truth: He *was* truth: true through and through; for truth is a thing, not of words, but of Life and Being.'

The Psalmist thought of God desiring truth in the inward being and requested to be taught wisdom in his secret heart. According to the writer of St John's Gospel, truth came through Jesus Christ, and his promise was: 'You will know the truth, and the truth will set you free.' St Paul encouraged members of the early church: 'Stand therefore, having girded your loins with truth.'

Nicolas Berdyaev, the Russian religious philosopher, thought that truth was not the product of a rational quest but the result of 'a light which breaks through from the transcendent world of the spirit' into the beclouded environment. He believed that man's greatness was 'his share in this world of spirit and in his divine capacity to create'. This fits in well with the divine inbreathing in the Genesis story of the creation of man. We are born with a seed or a spark of truth in the depths of our being. The consequences of this were fully worked out in the life of our Lord, so much so that he became *Truth*, true through and through. In our baptism the seed or spark of truth is brought to life. Reflecting on the contents of this section enables us to grow in a truth, not of words, but of 'Life and Being'.

Behold, thou desirest truth in the inward being; therefore teach me wisdom in my secret heart.

Psalm 51:6

These are the things that you shall do: Speak the truth to one another, render in your gates judgments that are true and make for peace.

Zechariah 8:16

Grace and truth came through Jesus Christ. No one has ever seen God; the only Son, who is in the bosom of the Father, he has made him known.

John 1:17–18

Stand therefore, having girded your loins with truth.

Ephesians 6:14

All truth is precious, if not all divine.

William Cowper, 'Charity', line 331, in *The Poetical Works of William Cowper*, Oxford University Press, 1950

Truth . . . loves to be centrally located.

Herman Melville, *Typee*, Heron Books, 1968, page 203

Truth is the highest thing that men may keep.

Geoffrey Chaucer, *The Franklin's Tale*, G. Routledge & Co., 1838, page 319

. . . we are to answer for any truth we have understood.

Anthony Bloom, *The Essence of Prayer*, Darton, Longman & Todd, 1989, page 10

In the usefulness of truth lies the hope of humanity.

Norman Douglas, *An Almanac*, Chatto and Windus in association with Martin Secker & Warburg, 1945, page 37

Truth does not lie beyond humanity, but is one of the products of the human mind and feeling.

D.H. Lawrence, *The Rainbow*, Cambridge University Press, 1989, page 317

Ethical axioms are found and tested not very differently from the axioms of science. Truth is what stands the test of experience.

Albert Einstein, *Out of My Later Years*, Thames and Hudson, 1950, page 115

I think the most important quality in a person connected with religion is absolute devotion to the truth.

Albert Schweitzer, *Out of My Life and Thought*, translated by C.T. Campion, Henry Holt and Company, 1949, page 249

I thirst for truth,
But shall not drink it till I reach the source.

Robert Browning, 'The Ring and the Book', vi. 2038, in *The Complete Poetical Works of Robert Browning*, Ohio University Press, 1988, volume 8, page 156

Love of truth asserts itself in the ability to find and appreciate what is good wherever it be.

Johann Wolfgang von Goethe, *Wisdom and Experience*, selected by Ludwig Curtius, translated and edited by Hermann J. Weigand, Routledge & Kegan Paul, 1949, page 212

The arrogance of supposing that, what could not be clearly expressed could be cheerfully discarded, has impoverished religion and made lonely men of its mystics and seers.

W.E. Sangster, *The Pure in Heart*, Epworth Press, 1954, page 3

Truth, in a word, is whatever cleanses you. Truth is whatever delights the higher you in you. Truth is whatever summons your spirit to do battle in her service. Truth is whatever makes you or me one with the mind of God.

Alistair MacLean, *The Happy Finder*, Allenson & Co., 1949, page 71

The purpose of obedience to truth is not to graze in the flat lands of orthodoxy, but to climb the sharp, high, narrow ridges of faith in order that we may understand more and more the relevance of the revelation of God to our own age.

Reuel L. Howe, *The Miracle of Dialogue*, The Saint Andrew Press, 1969, page 125

There is truth that merely brightens and intrigues the mind for a while, and truth which we are able to take deeply into ourselves to help us make a more constructive response to our challenges and anxieties.

J. Neville Ward, *Friday Afternoon*, Epworth Press, 1989, page 118

To find Truth . . . we must break through the outward shell of words and phrases which house it, and by *experience and practice* discover the 'inward beauty, life and loveliness of Truth.'

Rufus M. Jones, *Spiritual Reformers in the 16th and 17th Centuries*, Macmillan and Co., 1914, page 317

You must fuse mind and wit with all the senses
before you can feel truth.
And if you can't feel truth you can't have any other satisfactory sensual experience.

D.H. Lawrence, 'Sense of Truth', in Vivian de Sola Pinto and Warren Roberts, editors, *The Complete Poems of D.H. Lawrence*, William Heinemann, 1967, volume 2, page 653

Truth is what safeguards the conscience, and nothing but truth. Truth is not a logical relation between reason and the world of phenomena. Reason is phenomenal, too. Truth is an intimate interpenetration between the substantial world and conscience, for conscience is substantial, too.

Miguel de Cervantes Saavedra, *The Life of Don Quixote and Sancho*, translated by Homer P. Earle, Alfred A. Knopf, 1927, page 141

It is not enough for a man to have an idea of truth—he needs to have a moral shock that shall electrify his being, and give to the truth instantaneous and over-whelming power. The enthusiasm comes from God. Like other gifts, it comes instrumentally.

Henry Ward Beecher, *Proverbs from Plymouth Pulpit*, Charles Burnet & Co., 1887, page 178

To speak the truth is to be more than a purveyor of pious information: it is to show the way to think and not to offer the results of thought; it is to sharpen a man's perception rather than to tell him what to see; it is to describe to him the love of God but not to define it.

R.E.C. Browne, *The Ministry of the Word*, SCM Press, 1958, page 59

God hath now sent his living Oracle
Into the World, to teach his final will,
And sends his Spirit of Truth henceforth to dwell
In pious Hearts, an inward Oracle
To all truth requisite for men to know.

John Milton, *Paradise Regained*, i .460, in Helen Darbishire, editor, *The Poetical Works of John Milton*, Oxford at the Clarendon Press, 1952, volume 2, page 14

Why should we neglect the mass of truth which tends to reconciliation with existence for the truth which breeds despair? We do not seem to understand that there is any duty in the selection of truths. It is not the duty of an ordinary person to investigate and dwell upon all truth. He should choose that which will help him. There is enough of it to occupy him. Much of the reflection which separates and depresses is uncertain, as, for example, that on the relationship of man with the infinite.

Mark Rutherford, *Last Pages From a Journal*, Oxford University Press, 1915, page 281

... the truth which Jesus brings to us shows us the real values of life. The fundamental question to which every man has consciously or unconsciously to give an answer is: 'To what am I to give my life?' 'Am I to give it to a career? Am I to give it to the amassing of material possessions? Am I to give it to pleasure? Am I to give it to the obedience and to the service of God?' The truth which Jesus brings enables us to get our scale of values right; it is in His truth that we see what things are really important and what things are not.

William Barclay, *The Gospel of John*, The Saint Andrew Press, 1965, volume 2, page 25

... the desire for truth is a spiritual activity just because truth is desired for its own sake and without even the further aim of communicating it to others. The communication is not the essence of the activity. A man writes really to make the truth more clear to himself. It is his means of discovering the truth more precisely than he can discover it otherwise. And, having discovered it thus precisely, he communicates it to others because of the social instinct that is in all of us. But he must satisfy himself that it is truth before he wishes to communicate it at all.

A. Clutton-Brock, *The Ultimate Belief*, Constable & Co., 1916, page 67

... in my opinion the two greatest utterances in the world are Pilate's question: 'What *is* Truth?' and Jesus' unscientific and super-personal saying: '*I* am the Truth.' These two remarks together cover the whole field. In fact there is in reality no such thing as scientific *truth*. There are scientific methods, scientific hypotheses, scientific guesses, and scientific inventions; but 'truth' is something that in its inherent nature—simply because it is alive—for ever must baffle science. Science can torture and kill the possessors of truth, but truth itself will always escape; and it will escape because it is never totally without free-will, never totally without the god-like power of destruction and creation.

John Cowper Powys, Autobiography, Macdonald & Co., 1967, page 428

Everything which concerns religion occurs in the realm of the soul and is the outcome of direct relations between the human spirit and the Divine Spirit. In every age, and in every land, the inner Word of God, the Voice of the Spirit speaking within, clarifying the mind and training the spiritual perceptions by a progressive experience, has made for itself a chosen people and has gathered out of the world a little inner circle of those who know the Truth because it is formed within themselves. This 'inner circle of those who know' is the true Church: 'The Church is a chosen, saved, purified, sanctified group in whom God dwells, upon whom the Holy Ghost has poured out His gifts and with whom Christ the Lord shares His offices and His mission.'

Rufus M. Jones, Spiritual Reformers in the 16th and 17th Centuries, Macmillan and Co., 1914, page 41

What [F.D.] Maurice feared most of all is the danger of anyone saying, 'I have got the truth. I have comprehended it; it is adequately and satisfactorily expressed in my teaching, and I have nothing more to learn'—not that people will say this openly, but it underlies the attitude. Maurice would have agreed with F.W. Robertson, with whom he was only very occasionally associated: 'God's truth must be boundless. Tractarians and Evangelicals suppose that it is a pond which you can walk round and say, "I hold the truth". What, all! Yes, all; there it is circumscribed, defined, proved, quite large enough to be the immeasurable Gospel of the Lord of the Universe!' Maurice's refuge is to say that the truth is in God and in Christ, that God is his own system, a system vaster than that of all thinkers, orthodox and heterodox; for God is his own system and by him all things subsist, and in him they live and move and have their being.

W. Merlin Davies, An Introduction to F.D. Maurice's Theology, SPCK, 1964, page 18

The Greek word for truth means: making manifest the hidden. Truth is hidden and must be discovered. It dwells in the depth, beneath the surface. The surface of our existence changes, moving continually like the waves in the ocean, and it is therefore delusive. The depth is eternal and therefore certain. In using the Greek word, the Fourth Gospel accepts the Greek concept, but at the same time it transforms it.

'Doing the truth', 'being the truth', 'the truth has become', 'I am the truth'—all these combinations of words indicate that truth in Christianity is something which *happens*, something which is bound to a special place, to a special time, to a special personality. Truth is something near, something which is *done* by God in history, and, because of this, something which is *done* in the individual life. Truth is hidden, truth in mystery—in Christianity as well as in Greek thought. But the mystery of truth in Christianity is an event which has taken place and which takes place again and again. It is life, personal life; revelation and decision. Truth is a stream of life centered in Christ, actualized in everybody who is connected with Him, organized in the assembly of God, the Church. In Greek thought truth only can be found. In Christianity truth is found if it is done, and done if it is found.

Paul Tillich, The Shaking of the Foundations, SCM Press, 1949, page 116

UNION

Union—uniting, being united, a whole resulting from a combination of parts or members

One of the features of modern life is busyness. Most people seem to be rushing here, there and everywhere, for no apparent reason. The result is fatigue, exhaustion and a feeling of being torn to pieces.

I first experienced this hectic pace of life in my final year at school. I had been appointed Captain of School, and was heavily involved in rugby, hockey and cricket, as well as studying for A levels and entrance to Oxbridge. The first few days of the new academic year were chaotic, but in them I did at least learn how to stand back and take stock. From time to time, when feeling stressed and strained, I would withdraw to my room and quietly think about decisions which needed to be made. In the seclusion of my room I would write out possible solutions in an old notebook. Often in these sessions, new insights would come flooding to the surface and help in the decision-making process. For me, this was the start of the practice of reflection.

The notebook gradually gave way to the keeping of a journal. Into this journal I fed all my thoughts, feelings and ideas. Before long I became conscious of a spiritual dimension at work, and discerned the presence of 'the God within'. Over the years I came to know something of the Father, Son and Holy Spirit in the depths of my being, as well as attributes such as life, light, truth, joy and love, etc. This has resulted in a few precious moments when I have felt a sense of union and oneness with the divine—a foretaste of heaven on earth.

Let us join ourselves to the Lord in an everlasting covenant which will never be forgotten.
Jeremiah 50:5

And I will betroth you to me for ever; I will betroth you to me in righteousness and in justice, in steadfast love, and in mercy.
Hosea 2:19

I do not pray for these only but also for those who believe in me through their word, that they may all be one; even as thou, Father, art in me, and I in thee, that they also may be in us.
John 17:20–21

He who is united to the Lord becomes one spirit with him.
1 Corinthians 6:17

Prayer unites the soul to God.
Julian of Norwich, *Revelations of Divine Love*, translated by Clifton Wolters, Penguin Books, 1976, page 128

When one comes into the mystic union with God, and feels the stimulating influence of the Divine nature, he is dead to the lower life.
Henry Ward Beecher, *Proverbs from Plymouth Pulpit*, Charles Burnet & Co., 1887, page 160

The ultimate spiritual union is probably as impossible to achieve as the perfect work of art or the unflawed human relationship.

Patrick White, *Flaws in the Glass*, Jonathan Cape, 1981, page 74

By the saint's faith, God not only works miracles *through* him but the greatest miracle *in* him. Faith issues in union of personalities—the one believing and the One believed in. The Lord lives again in His servant and the great longing of these servants is that He might live in us all.

W.E. Sangster, *The Pure in Heart*, The Epworth Press, 1954, page 223

The spiritual life is union with God in love, leading ultimately to reconciliation, wholeness, and unity. It is both a gift and a task; a gift, which keeps us utterly dependent upon God, and a task, which we must pursue with unremitting earnestness and resolution to the last days of our lives.

Olive Wyon, *On the Way*, SCM Press, 1958, page 31

The more united we are to God, the greater will be our love and readiness to serve the poor whole-heartedly. Much depends on this union of hearts. The love of God the Father for the Son, and of the Son for the Father, produces God the Holy Spirit. So also the love of God for us and our love for God should produce this whole-hearted free service for the poor.

Mother Teresa, *Jesus, the Word to be Spoken*, compiled by Brother Angelo Devananda, William Collins Sons & Co., 1990, page 84

Wherever thou goest, whatever thou dost, at Home, or Abroad, in the Field, or at Church, do all in a Desire of Union with Christ, in Imitation of his Tempers and Inclinations, and look upon all as Nothing, but that which exercises, and increases the Spirit and Life of Christ in thy Soul. From Morning to Night keep Jesus in thy Heart, long for Nothing, desire Nothing, hope for Nothing, but to have all that is within Thee changed into the Spirit and Temper of the Holy Jesus.

William Law, in Sidney Spencer, editor, *The Spirit of Prayer and the Spirit of Love*, James Clarke & Co., 1969, page 39

… there is happiness only where there is co-ordination with the Truth, the Reality, the Act that underlies and directs all things to their essential and accidental perfections: and that is the will of God. There is only one happiness: to please Him. Only one sorrow: to be displeasing to Him, to refuse Him something, to turn away from Him, even in the slightest thing, even in thought, in a half-willed movement of appetite; in these things, and these alone, is sorrow, in so far as they imply separation, or the beginning, the possible separation, from Him who is our life and all our joy. And since God is a Spirit, and infinitely above all matter and all creation, the only complete union possible, between ourselves and Him, is in the order of intention: a union of wills and intellects, in love, in charity.

Thomas Merton, *Elected Silence*, Hollis and Carter, 1949, page 323

All self-seeking and self-love do but imprison the soul, and confine it to its own home: the mind of a good man is too noble, too big for such a particular life; he hath learned to despise his own being, in comparison of that uncreated beauty and goodness, which is so infinitely transcendent to himself or any created thing; he reckons upon his choice and best affections and designs, as too choice and precious a treasure to be spent upon such a poor sorry thing as himself, or upon anything else but God Himself.

This was the life of Christ, and is, in some degree, the life of every one that partakes of the Spirit of Christ. Such Christians seek not their own glory, but the glory of Him that sent them into this world: they know they were brought forth into this world, not to set up or drive a trade for themselves, but to serve the will and pleasure of Him that made them, and to finish that work He hath appointed them. It were not worth the while to have been born or to live, had it been only for such a penurious end as ourselves are: it is most godlike, and best suits with the spirit of religion, for a Christian to live wholly to God, to live the life of God, 'having his own life hid with Christ in God;' and thus, in a sober sense, he becomes deified. This indeed is such a 'deification' as is not transacted merely upon the stage of fancy, by arrogance and presumption, but in the highest powers of the soul by a living and quickening spirit of true religion there, uniting God and the soul together in unity of affections, will, and end.

John Smith, Select Discourses, Cambridge at the University Press, 1859, page 415

Those who are interested in that special attitude towards the universe which is now loosely called 'mystical' find themselves beset by a multitude of persons who are constantly asking—some with real fervour, some with curiosity, and some with disdain 'What *is* mysticism?' When referred to the writings of the mystics themselves, and to other works in which this question appears to be answered, these people reply that such books are wholly incomprehensible to them.

Here is the definition:—*Mysticism is the art of union with Reality. The mystic is a person who has attained that union in greater or less degree; or who aims at and believes in such attainment.*

It is not expected that the inquirer will find great comfort in this sentence when first it meets his eye. The ultimate question, 'What is Reality?'—a question, perhaps, which never occurred to him before—is already forming in his mind; and he knows that it will cause him infinite distress. Only a mystic can answer it; and he, in terms which other mystics alone will understand. Therefore, for the time being, the practical man may put it on one side. All that he is asked to consider now is this: that the word 'union' represents not so much a rare and unimaginable operation, as something which he is doing, in a vague, imperfect fashion, at every moment of his conscious life; and doing with intensity and thoroughness in all the more valid moments of that life. We know a thing only by uniting with it; by assimilating it; by an interpenetration of it and ourselves.

It gives itself to us, just in so far as we give ourselves to it; and it is because our outflow towards things is usually so perfunctory and so languid, that our comprehension of things is so perfunctory and languid too. The great Sufi who said that 'Pilgrimage to the place of the wise, is to escape the flame of separation' spoke the literal truth. Wisdom is the fruit of communion; ignorance the inevitable portion of those who 'keep themselves to themselves,' and stand apart, judging, analysing the things which they have never truly known...

Because mystery is horrible to us, we have agreed for the most part to live in a world of labels; to make of them the current coin of experience, and ignore their merely symbolic character, the infinite gradation of values which they misrepresent. We simply do not attempt to unite with Reality. But now and then that symbolic character is suddenly brought home to us. Some great emotion, some devastating visitation of beauty, love, or pain, lifts us to another level of consciousness; and we are aware for a moment of the difference between the neat collection of discrete objects and experiences which we call the world, and the height, the depth, the breadth of that living, growing, changing Fact, of which thought, life, and energy are parts, and in which we 'live and move and have our being.' Then we realise that our whole life is enmeshed in great and living forces; terrible because unknown. Even the power which lurks in every coal scuttle, shines in the electric lamp, pants in the motor omnibus, declares itself in the ineffable wonders of reproduction and growth, is supersensual. We do but perceive its results. The more sacred plane of life and energy which seems to be manifested in the forces we call 'spiritual' and 'emotional'—in love, anguish, ecstasy, adoration—is hidden from us too. Symptoms, appearances, are all that our intellects can discern: sudden irresistible inroads from it, all that our hearts can apprehend. The material for an intenser life, a wider, sharper consciousness, a more profound understanding of our own existence, lies at our gates. But we are separated from it, we cannot assimilate it; except in abnormal moments, we hardly know that it is there…

The old story of Eyes and No-Eyes is really the story of the mystical and unmystical types. 'No-Eyes' has fixed his attention on the fact that he is obliged to take a walk. For him the chief factor of existence is his own movement along the road; a movement which he intends to accomplish as efficiently and comfortably as he can. He asks not to know what may be on either side of the hedges. He ignores the caress of the wind until it threatens to remove his hat. He trudges along, steadily, diligently; avoiding the muddy pools, but oblivious of the light which they reflect. 'Eyes' takes the walk too; and for him it is a perpetual revelation of beauty and wonder. The sunlight inebriates him, the winds delight him, the very effort of the journey is a joy. Magic presences throng the roadside, or cry salutations to him from the hidden fields. The rich world through which he moves lies in the foreground of his consciousness; and it gives up new secrets to him at every step. 'No-Eyes,' when told of his adventures, usually refuses to believe that both have gone by the same road. He fancies that his companion has been floating about in the air, or beset by agreeable hallucinations. We shall never persuade him to the contrary unless we persuade him to look for himself.

Therefore it is to a practical mysticism that the practical man is here invited: to a training of his latent faculties, a bracing and brightening of his languid consciousness, an emancipation from the fetters of appearance, a turning of his attention to new levels of the world. Thus he may become aware of the universe which the spiritual artist is always trying to disclose to the race. This amount of mystical perception—this 'ordinary contemplation' as the specialists call it—is possible to all men: without it, they are not wholly conscious, nor wholly alive. It is a natural human activity, no more involving the great powers and sublime experiences of the mystical saints and philosophers than the ordinary enjoyment of music involves the special creative powers of the great musician.

Evelyn Underhill, *Practical Mysticism*, J.M. Dent & Sons, 1914, page 1

VOCATION

*Vocation—divine call to, or sense of fitness for a career or
occupation; employment, trade, profession*

Occasionally people ask me—why did I become ordained? My answer is usually as
follows. In my early twenties, I took a step of faith and became a committed
Christian. Two years later, I went on a long train journey and read a book entitled
Margaret by James Davidson Ross. 'Margaret' was a fifteen-year-old schoolgirl, the life
and soul of a party, and a keen Christian. She came home one day not feeling very well
and spent a few days in bed. At first she was thought to be suffering from flu, but
eventually the news was broken to her that she had cancer, and not long to live. I was very
moved by the way Margaret faced up to her ordeal. She accepted it all in faith. Visitors
who came to cheer her up found the roles reversed and she was cheering them up. As I
read through the pages of this book I became convinced the Holy Spirit was at work in
her life, and that she was 'living in the power of the resurrection'. By the time the train
reached Paddington I had already resolved to live my life in like manner.

After a week or so, I became aware of a little voice inside me asking, 'If this is so
important to you, shouldn't you be actively engaged in spreading this, rather than just
living it?' I was unable to sidestep this searching challenge, and shortly afterwards offered
myself for ordination.

In this section I like the words of Henry Ward Beecher: 'There is a specialty of work
in the world for each man. But man must search for it, for it will not hunt for the man.'
Reflecting on this section might well reveal our specialty of work and lead to the discovery
of our vocation.

... I have called and you refused to listen, have stretched out my hand and no one has
heeded.

Proverbs 1:24

Before I formed you in the womb I knew you, and before you were born I consecrated you;
I appointed you a prophet to the nations.

Jeremiah 1:5

You did not choose me, but I chose you and appointed you that you should go and bear
fruit and that your fruit should abide.

John 15:16

Forgetting what lies behind and straining forward to what lies ahead, I press on toward the
goal for the prize of the upward call of God in Christ Jesus.

Philippians 3:13–14

God has a task for every one of us, which is made to measure for us.

William Barclay, *The Gospel of Matthew*, The Saint Andrew Press, 1965, volume 2, page 19

The test of a vocation is the love of the drudgery it involves.

Logan Pearsall Smith, *Afterthoughts*, Constable & Company, 1931, page 54

There is a specialty of work in the world for each man. But man must search for it, for it will not hunt for the man.

Henry Ward Beecher, *Proverbs from Plymouth Pulpit*, Charles Burnet & Co., 1887, page 48

If a man could take his choice of all the lives that are possible on earth, there is none so much to be desired for its joy-producing quality as a truly self-denying, consecrated Christian life.

Henry Ward Beecher, *Proverbs from Plymouth Pulpit*, Charles Burnet & Co., 1887, page 165

Looking at the masses of humanity, driven this way and that way, the Christian teaching is apt to be forgotten that for each individual soul there is a vocation as real as if that soul were alone upon this planet.

Mark Rutherford, *Mark Rutherford's Deliverance*, Hodder and Stoughton, 1913, page 79

God's principal job is *to make man*: 'Let us make man in our image.' So, to work at 'making man'—developing, helping and protecting him—is to join God in his essential plan, working to realise his project.

Michel Quoist, *With Open Heart*, translated by Colette Copeland, Gill and Macmillan, 1983, page 49

Vocation today means also to understand the hard but stupendous mission of the church, now more than ever engaged in teaching man his true nature, his end, his fate, and in revealing to the faithful the immense riches of the charity of Christ.

Mother Teresa, *Jesus, the Word to be Spoken*, compiled by Brother Angelo Devananda, William Collins Sons & Co., 1990, page 89

Our vocation is to belong to Jesus. The easiest way and the simplest way of belonging is this: the Holy Spirit makes us do that giving of self, that total surrender to God, without any reflection, without any counting the cost. We call that 'blind surrender.' It is like Our Lady: when she knew that the Lord was calling, she said yes. And she never withdrew that yes. It was a blind, continual yes in her life. It is the same thing for us. The whole of our life must come to that one word yes. Yes to God: that is holiness. We allow God to take from us whatever he wants and we accept whatever he gives with joy. That is yes in action.

Mother Teresa, *Jesus, the Word to be Spoken*, compiled by Brother Angelo Devananda, William Collins Sons & Co., 1990, page 26

His vocation is to become fully human himself by helping others to achieve a deeper, fuller humanity by all means available. This is what Christians are for, and at this time perhaps we are able to see our vocation as part of the universal striving towards a more complete understanding and living of human life. If the Christian's part in this is a special one, this 'specialness' does not lie in any exclusive claim on the God whom we know only by the love and the need we encounter in others and the craving we know in ourselves. It is 'special' in that each Christian is called to attempt, however feebly, to do the work that Christ did: to serve without tiring, to give without limit, and to witness by word and act to the hope that makes sense of the apparently ridiculous aspirations of a race of fear-ridden, security-craving, suspicious, ambitious and doggedly alive animals.

Rosemary Haughton, *On Trying To Be Human*, Geoffrey Chapman, 1966, page 33

The doctrine of vocation has been corrupted in the Christian tradition to refer especially to the work of the ordained ministry (not more than 1 per cent of the church) or paid church work; and to spill over from that to work with a high personal content, such as nursing, teaching, or social work, but not to manufacture; so that a Christian in industry is more likely to regard personnel management as a vocation and not the job of works manager. In particular semiskilled or unskilled work has not been thought of within a doctrine of work. There has also been a bias to think of work in agriculture as more of a vocation than work in industry, an indication of the slowness with which Christians have come to terms with the new kind of society produced by industrialism. However, agriculture is so mechanized in Western countries that it makes this attitude increasingly absurd.

Ronald Preston, in James F. Childress and John Macquarrie, editors, *A New Dictionary of Christian Ethics,* SCM Press, 1986, page 666

I was at a stand in my mind whether I should practise physic [medicine] for the good of mankind, seeing the nature and virtues of the creatures were so opened to me by the Lord. But I was immediately taken up in spirit, to see into another or more steadfast state than Adam's in innocency, even into a state in Christ Jesus that should never fall. And the Lord shewed me that such as were faithful to Him, in the power and light of Christ, should come up into that state in which Adam was before he fell; in which the admirable works of the creation, and the virtues thereof, may be known through the openings of that divine Word of wisdom and power by which they were made. Great things did the Lord lead me into, and wonderful depths were opened unto me beyond what can by words be declared; but as people came into subjection to the Spirit of God, and grow up in the image and power of the Almighty, they may receive the Word of wisdom, that opens all things, and come to know the hidden unity in the Eternal Being.

George Fox, *The Journal of George Fox,* J.M. Dent & Sons, 1924, page 17

Our vocation is not simply to *be,* but to work together with God in the creation of our own life, our own identity, our own destiny. We are free beings and sons of God. This means to say that we should not passively exist, but actively participate in His creative freedom, in our own lives, and in the lives of others by choosing the truth. To put it better, we are even called to share with God the work of *creating* the truth of our identity. We can evade this responsibility by playing with masks, and this pleases us because it can appear at times to be a free and creative way of living. It is quite easy, it seems to please everyone. But in the long run the cost and the sorrow come very high. To work out our own identity in God, which the Bible calls 'working out our salvation,' is a labour that requires sacrifice and anguish, risk and many tears. It demands close attention to reality at every moment, and great fidelity to God as He reveals Himself obscurely, in the mystery of each new situation. We do not know clearly beforehand what the result of this work will be. The secret of my full identity is hidden in Him. He alone can make me who I am, or rather who I will be when at last I fully begin to be. But unless I desire this identity and work to find it with Him and in Him, the work will never be done. The way of doing it is a secret I can learn from no one else but Him. There is no way of attaining to the secret without guilt—But contemplation is the greater and more precious gift, for it enables me to see and understand the work that He wants done.

Thomas Merton, *New Seeds of Contemplation,* Burns & Oates, 1962, page 25

The word *vocation* comes from the Latin *vocare,* which means 'to call.' God calls us together into one people fashioned in the image of Christ. It is by Christ's vocation that we are gathered. Here we need to distinguish carefully between vocation and career. In a world that puts such emphasis on success, our concern for a career constantly tends to make us deaf to our vocation. When we are seduced into believing that our career is what counts, we can no longer hear the voice that calls us together; we become so preoccupied with our own plans, projects, or promotions that we push everyone away who prevents us from achieving our goals.

Career and vocation are not mutually exclusive. In fact, our vocation might require us to pursue a certain career. Many people have become excellent doctors, lawyers, technicians, or scientists in response to God's call heard in the community. Quite often, our vocation becomes visible in a specific job, task, or endeavour. But our vocation can never be reduced to these activities. As soon as we think that our careers *are* our vocation, we are in danger of returning to the ordinary and proper places governed by human competition and of using our talents more to separate ourselves from others than to unite ourselves with them in a common life.

A career disconnected from a vocation divides; a career that expresses obedience to our vocation is the concrete way of making our unique talents available to the community. Therefore, it is not our careers, but our vocation, that should guide our lives.

Henri J.M. Nouwen, *Seeds of Hope*, edited by Robert Durback, Darton, Longman & Todd, 1989, page 94

I went to All Souls as usual for the week-end and on the Sunday walked over to Cuddesdon with Henry Wakeman... It was a beautiful early summer day. I said nothing of what was in my mind... and watched the young men with a critical scrutiny. I liked the look of them, but plainly they were not 'my sort.' I went to the Parish Church for evensong. The whole scene is indelibly impressed on my memory. I sat in the second pew from the pulpit, then on the north side. I paid little attention to the service and less to the sermon, preached, I don't know about what, by the curate. But I had a strong sense that something was about to happen. I was not in the least excited; there was no sort of nervous tension; I had only prayed in a rather weary way during the service in some such manner as this—'I can't go on with this strange struggle. End it, O God, one way or another. If there *is* anything real, anything of Thy will, in this question, help me to answer it.' Then suddenly, while the unheeded sermon went on, I was gripped by a clear conviction. It had all the strength of a masterful inward voice. 'You are wanted. You are called. You must obey.'

I knew at once that the thing was settled. The burden of the long struggle dropped. My mind was free. I don't want to write emotionally, but it is only recording fact to say that a wave of such peace and indeed joy as I had never known before filled my whole being. In the Chapel later, at Compline, it seemed to flow out in happy worship. I said nothing to anyone. But when, having missed the train at Wheatley, Wakeman and I... set out to walk back to Oxford over Shotover Hill in the moonlight, I felt like a man who had been suddenly set free from chains; and I really could have shouted for joy. Little did my companions realise what was passing in my mind as we ran down the hill with the lights of Oxford twinkling beneath us. That night in my rooms at All Souls I prayed as I had never prayed in my life before. But all my prayers had the one refrain: 'I obey and I am free.' Later the words came to my mind: 'I will run the way of Thy commandments when Thou hast set my heart at liberty.'

J.G. Lockhart, *Cosmo Gordon Lang*, Hodder and Stoughton, 1949, page 64

THE WAY

*The way—way of life, principles or habits governing one's actions,
a way of faith, a journey of faith—pilgrimage*

W. R. Inge once wrote that every man and woman has two journeys to make through life. There is the outer journey, with its various incidents, and milestones of youth, marriage, middle age and senility. There is also an inner journey, a spiritual odyssey, with a secret history of its own.

I was thoroughly absorbed with the outer journey until my early twenties. I enjoyed my schooldays, and the various phases of National Service, especially with the Gurkhas in the Far East. On being demobbed I studied law at university with a view to joining the family firm and becoming a solicitor. The way was set fair for marriage and a family.

I went to listen to a sermon by the then Bishop of Coventry, Cuthbert Bardsley. He confronted me with the challenge of an inner journey, the way of Christ. Before I left the church that morning I had already taken the first faltering steps.

I began to read the Bible and discovered more steps on 'the way'. I read other books—about prayer and the Holy Spirit—and progressed slowly on *the way*. At the end of three years, ordination beckoned. My spiritual odyssey continued with two years at theological college and four years on the staff of Bradford Cathedral. I then came across *The Choice is Always Ours*, by Dorothy Berkley Phillips, an anthology specializing on 'the way'. This book enabled me to discover the riches of 'the God within' and the practice of reflection. I then decided to compile *Visions of Faith, Hope, Love* and *Glory* as an aid to help people on 'the way'.

This God—his way is perfect; the promise of the Lord proves true; he is a shield for all those who take refuge in him.

2 Samuel 22:31

Seek the Lord while he may be found, call upon him while he is near; let the wicked forsake his way, and the unrighteous man his thoughts; let him return to the Lord, that he may have mercy on him, and to our God, for he will abundantly pardon. For my thoughts are not your thoughts, neither are your ways my ways, says the Lord. For as the heavens are higher than the earth, so are my ways higher than your ways and my thoughts than your thoughts.

Isaiah 55:6–9

I am the way.

John 14:6

But earnestly desire the higher gifts. And I will show you a still more excellent way.

1 Corinthians 12:31

The way to God is through the heart.

Henri J.M. Nouwen, *The Way of the Heart*, Darton, Longman & Todd, 1981, page 78

He is the Way.
Follow Him through the Land of Unlikeness;
You will see rare beasts, and have unique adventures.

W.H. Auden, For the Time Being, Faber and Faber, 1945, page 124

When the dimensions of faith, hope, love, forgiveness become real to us, we are given at the same time a freedom, an openness towards a way of living which is quite new.

John Bowden, Voices in the Wilderness, SCM Press, 1978, page 76

However distasteful some folk may find it, there is no way to the mastery of life and to radiant personality which leaves out God. He made us and He made us for Himself.

W.E. Sangster, The Secret of Radiant Life, Hodder and Stoughton, 1957, page 20

We have to find our own way, I am sure of that; and I have a distrust of deflecting anyone from his own orbit. I believe in co-operation, not in influence.

A.C. Benson, Extracts from the Letters of Dr. A.C. Benson to M.E.A., Jarrold Publishing, 1927, page 58

'The way to spiritual life,' wrote George Meredith in one of his recently published letters, 'lies in the complete unfolding of the creature, not in the nipping of his passions... To the flourishing of the Spirit, then, through the healthy exercise of the senses!'

Havelock Ellis, Impressions and Comments, Constable & Co., 1914, page 38

And therefore, good Christian, come a little way with me, and I will teach thee about the way thou must go. Look before thee; dost thou see this narrow way? THAT is the way thou must go: it was cast up by the Patriarchs, Prophets, Christ, and his Apostles; and it is as straight as a rule can make it: This is the way thou must go.

John Bunyan, The Pilgrim's Progress, J.M. Dent & Sons, 1964, page 29

Jesus chose the Apostles to be with Him that they might observe the life lived and then live it themselves. It was the only way. His privacy must be sacrificed to it; His mind continually jarred by their inconsequential chatter concerning position and prestige. But there was no other method, because in its very essence this message was a way of life. The origin of all life is deep and mysterious, and deep and mysterious is the origin of this spiritual life as well. But its fine flower all may see. And its fine flower is a fragrant life.

W.E. Sangster, Why Jesus Never Wrote a Book, Epworth Press, 1932, page 17

'I am the way'—the words themselves are full of the silence of eternity and they impose this awful silence upon our concepts and upon discourse, warning us at once that analysis is not going to be enough. There is more in this than we can begin to analyse: for even a poor, familiar human personality in the end is beyond analysis. We can find out something about this character, but the *persona* that we see in him is the mask behind which the spiritual reality hides. And that reality can only be known by love. But here, we have more than a human person. We have a man who, mysteriously, is God. He does not expound to us a way. He Himself, eternal, divine, is 'the way.' And if He is the way, then, although He is the Truth and the Life, He is still not the end. He is the way to another. Who is this Other?

Thomas Merton, The New Man, Burns & Oates, 1961, page 122

In saying that He is the 'way' Jesus adds that He is the truth and the life. He is the truth, because the way is Truth, and in Himself He contains the Truth which is the beginning and the end. He is the life because, knowing Him, we live by Him as He lives by the Father. This communion in His truth and life immediately puts us on the 'way' to the Father. We are in contact with the stream of life and power that flows from the hidden source, and ascending the stream we are making our way to the Source of life. The contact and the ascent are made through faith—faith which sees that Jesus is the Son and that He comes forth from the Father. This faith sees that while Jesus comes forth from the Father, the Father remains in Him. And it sees that Jesus lives in us, and that the Father lives in us with Him. Christ is then the 'way' to the Father because He brings the Truth and the Life of the Father into direct contact with our souls by sending His Spirit into our spirit, to make us one with Him.

Thomas Merton, *The New Man*, Burns & Oates, 1961, page 125

To discover that there is a Way, and that life has meaning, is a great step forward. But although we may see this quite clearly with our minds, it is still no easy matter to adjust ourselves to the reality of which we have caught a fleeting glimpse. At the outset we cannot see the implications of this change in our direction. Quite literally, 'all things have become new', and in the midst of our new-found joy and freedom there is also a sense of bewilderment. It is at this point that so many newly-awakened souls find themselves without direction. The initial experience may have been very wonderful, or it may have taken place so quietly that sometimes we are tempted to wonder whether it has ever happened at all. Too often, at this critical stage, there is no one to answer the question: Where do we go from here?

Here again, the ancient symbol of the journey or the pilgrimage comes to our aid. We have entered on a new path. We do not know to what it will lead. We feel at a loss. We may even wonder whether there is a 'way' after all. Yet there is a Way: 'And a highway shall be there, and a way; and it shall be called the Way of Holiness: the unclean shall not pass over it; for He shall be with them: the wayfaring man, yea fools, shall not err therein.' (Isaiah 35:8) (R.V.). The poetical symbolism of this beautiful chapter suggests that this Way is plain for all to see; that those who walk along it will be secure, even in the midst of danger; and that at the end there will be a wonderful welcome.

Olive Wyon, *On the Way*, SCM Press, 1958, page 20

My hearer! If you imagine a youth who stands at his life's beginning, where many ways open before him, asking himself which course he might wish to enter upon: is it not true that he then inquires carefully where the individual ways lead, or, what amounts to the same thing, he seeks to learn who has earlier walked this way. Then we mention to him the celebrated, the acclaimed, the glorious names of those whose memory is preserved among men. At first we perhaps mention several, so that the choice may have some relation to the youth's potentialities, so the wealth of advice proffered may be excessive. But even if he, impelled by an inward urge, makes a lesser choice, at last there comes to be for him only one. The only one, the one which in his eyes and according to his belief is the most advantageous of all. Then his heart beats violently, when he enthusiastically mentions this name, to him the only name, and says: 'This is the way I will go, for this is the way He walked!'

We shall not divert our attention or waste time by mentioning such names; for there is indeed only one name in heaven and on earth, one alone, and consequently but one way to choose—if a man is to choose earnestly and choose rightly. There may indeed be several ways, since a man is given a choice; but there must be only one way to choose if the earnestness of eternity is to rest upon the choice...

There is only one name in heaven and on earth, only one way, only one pattern. He who chooses to follow Christ, chooses the name which is above all names, the pattern which is highly exalted above all heavens, but at the same time human that it can be a pattern for a human being, so that it is named and will be named in heaven and on earth, in both places as the highest. For there are examples whose names are only mentioned on earth, but the highest, the only one, must precisely have this exclusive quality whereby it is indeed recognizable as the only one: that it is named both in heaven and on earth. This name is the name of our Lord Jesus Christ...

Is it so glorious a thing to eat on silver when others go hungry; to dwell in palaces when so many are homeless; to be the scholar which no simple man can become; to have a name that in a sense excludes thousands and thousands: is that so glorious? And if this, the *envious distinction of the earthly life*, were the highest, would it not be inhuman and life unendurable for the fortunate! How different, on the contrary, when the only joy consists in following Christ. Greater joy cannot be vouchsafed than this: to be able to become the highest; and this exalted joy cannot be made freer, more blessed, more secure than it is through the glad thought of a *merciful heaven*: that every man can do this.

Søren Kierkegaard, *The Gospel of Suffering*, Augsburg Publishing House, 1948, page 14

'Enter ye in by the narrow gate: for wide is the gate, and broad is the way, that leadeth to destruction, and many be they that enter in thereby. For narrow is the gate, and straitened the way, that leadeth unto life, and few be they that find it.'

This is the 'doctrine of the two ways'. Human instinct has seized on the metaphor in many parts of the world; the easy way of self-pleasing, the difficult way of duty. It speaks home to every heart, to every intelligence, and nothing needs to be said about it. But I would ask your attention to one question which in our time arises instantly as we read these words—Are we to suppose that our Lord is here saying that at the last issue many will be 'lost' and few 'saved'? Is this the meaning of 'Few be they that find it'?

To this question we may reply thus: On one occasion the disciples categorically asked our Lord, 'Are there few that are being saved?' and our Lord replied, 'Strive to enter in by the narrow door.' And on another occasion Peter asked the question about John, 'What shall this man do?' and was answered, 'What is that to thee? Follow thou Me.' Beyond all question, our Lord does not intend us to know the answer to the questions which our curiosity raises as to the ultimate destinies of men. He fixes our attention, we may say, on three great principles: the character of God our Father, and His impartial, individual, disciplinary love; the final and universal victory of His Kingdom over all resisting forces within and without; the critical character of our present life with its capacities for good and for evil, and the limitless consequences for good or evil which flow from the present attitude of each individual towards his personal responsibilities.

It is not unfair to translate our Lord's words here, 'Many there be that *are entering* the broad way; few there be that *are finding* the narrow way.' Thus they embody what is always found to be true in the experience of men. Always to one who wants to do his duty, it will become plain in the long run that he has to be prepared to stand alone, or at any rate to go against the majority. He cannot tell the opportunities and responsibilities that others may have. He knows that God is infinitely considerate, and will do the best possible for every soul that He has created; but he can, he does, know his own responsibility and his own duty, and in following that he will have to bear the burden of going with the few and watching the spectacle, so depressing or staggering to the imagination, of the multitude running to do evil.

Charles Gore, *The Sermon on the Mount*, John Murray, 1897, page 174

WILL

Will—faculty by which a person decides or conceives himself as deciding upon and initiating action; power of determining one's choice of action independently of causation; doing the will of God, God's will

I wonder if most of us are born with strong wills, bent on doing what we want to do. I certainly received a rude shock on going into the army and clashing with the powers that be. After my first lot of 'jankers' (army slang for some form of punishment, i.e. peeling potatoes) I thought twice about doing my own thing.

When I was demobbed and went to university I began to explore 'the will' in the context of the Christian life. I chanced to come across some words of William Temple which influenced the future course of my life. In his book *The Hope of a New World* he wrote that the one complete cure for the sense of frustration and futility is to know and do the will of God. He added that everyone to whom this becomes a reality is at once supplied with a purpose in life and one which covers the whole of life. I found these words thought-provoking. They raised at least one important question: How does one know and do the will of God? For me there was no black-and-white answer. I probed forward, a step at a time. In *The Reasons of the Heart*, John Dunne provides us with some guidance. He wrote, 'The will of God cannot be simply read off from facts or events but must be discerned, must be found through insight, through the kindling of the heart and the illumining of the mind that occur on the spiritual adventure.' This is one reason for the existence of *Visions of Glory*, and the practice of reflection—to help discern the will of God.

I delight to do thy will, O my God; thy law is within my heart.
Psalm 40:8

Teach me to do thy will, for thou art my God! Let thy good spirit lead me on a level path!
Psalm 143:10

Thy kingdom come, Thy will be done, On earth as it is in heaven.
Matthew 6:10

Not every one who says to me, 'Lord, Lord,' shall enter the kingdom of heaven, but he who does the will of my Father who is in heaven.
Matthew 7:21

Today, more than ever, we need to pray for the light to know the will of God, for the love to accept the will of God, for the way to do the will of God.
Mother Teresa, *Jesus, the Word to be Spoken*, compiled by Brother Angelo Devananda, William Collins Sons & Co., 1990, page 98

The one great principle was that in all things a man must seek God's will and that, when he knows it, he must dedicate his whole life to the obeying it.
William Barclay, *The Gospel of Matthew*, The Saint Andrew Press, 1965, volume 1, page 127

... the will of God cannot be simply read off from facts or events but must be discerned, must be found through insight, through the kindling of the heart and the illumining of the mind that occur on the spiritual adventure.
John S. Dunne, *The Reasons of the Heart*, SCM Press, 1978, page 21

God's will does not waver. Nor can it be manipulated. From all that we have said hitherto, from the concrete requirements of Jesus himself, it should already have become clear that God wills nothing for himself, nothing for his own advantage, for his greater glory. God wills nothing but man's advantage, man's true greatness and his ultimate dignity. This then is God's will: *man's well-being.*

Hans Küng, *On Being a Christian*, translated by Edward Quinn, William Collins Sons & Co., 1977, page 251

The highest perfection consists not in interior favours or in great raptures or in visions, or in the spirit of prophecy, but in the bringing of our wills so closely into conformity with the will of God that, as soon as we realize that He wills anything, we desire it ourselves with all our might, and take the bitter with the sweet, knowing that to be His Majesty's will.

St Teresa of Avila, *Complete Works*, translated and edited by E. Allison Peers, Sheed and Ward, 1963, volume 3, page 23

The spiritual life, the Christian life does not consist in developing a strong will capable of compelling us to do what we do not want. In a sense, of course, it is an achievement to do the right things when we really wish to do the wrong ones, but it remains a small achievement. A mature spiritual life implies that our conscious will is in accordance with the words of God and has remoulded, transformed our nature so deeply, with the help of God's grace, that the totality of our human person is only one will.

Anthony Bloom, *The Essence of Prayer*, Darton, Longman & Todd, 1989, page 61

This transforming of the will in love, this simplifying and supernaturalizing of the whole drive and intention of our life, by its immersion in the great movement of the Infinite Life, is itself the work of the Creative Spirit. It is only possible because that Spirit already indwells the soul's ground, and there pursues the secret alchemy of love; more and more possessing and transmuting us, with every small movement of acceptance or renunciation in which we yield ourselves to the quiet action of God.

Evelyn Underhill, *The Golden Sequence*, Methuen & Co., 1932, page 137

There is a clue in the Gospel of John in the saying of Jesus, 'I have food to eat which you do not know' ... 'My food is to do the will of him who sent me, and to accomplish his work.' There is a sense here of relating to other human beings out of a fullness rather than an emptiness ... As one passes from the languishing to the love it becomes possible to relate to others out of a fullness. The will of God is no longer what happens to one but is something to be done, as is this saying of Jesus, something to be accomplished.

John S. Dunne, *The Reasons of the Heart*, SCM Press, 1978, page 13

It is important to be aware of the multiple nature of God's will. At any given moment God's will is a complex of many considerations, such as the maintenance of that reliable order of cause and effect which is the condition of scientific and moral progress, the preservation of human freedom, our need to learn our dependence on him and on each other, our need to learn how to pray, and a host of other factors, some of which in our cleverness we think we know, but always we come to the far rim of knowledge and can go no further, can only return to this mixture of ignorance and faith in which humanity has lived all the time.

J. Neville Ward, *The Use of Praying*, Epworth Press, 1967, page 93

Not only does he, in a general way, thus make the will the decisive element in a human destiny, he also implies that the creative 'flash' of spiritual insight, 'the innermost birth' which brings the soul into living union with its source is due, on the human side, to 'resolution,' to 'earnestness,' to 'valiant wrestling,' to a brave venture of faith that risks everything. It requires 'mighty endurance,' 'hard labour,' 'stoutness of spirit,' and 'a great storm, assault, and onset' to open the Gate. In a word, the key to any important spiritual experience is *intention*, inward pre-perception, that holds the mind intently focussed in expectation, without which the 'flash' of spiritual vision is not likely to come.

Rufus M. Jones, *Spiritual Reformers in the 16th and 17th Centuries*, Macmillan and Co., 1914, page 204

In his Passion our Lord says, 'Thy will be done. Do with me what you want.' And that was the hardest thing for our Lord even at the last moment. They say that the Passion in Gethsemene was much greater than even the crucifixion. Because it was his heart, his soul that was being crucified, while on the cross he never said, 'Thy will be done.' He accepted in silence, and he gave his mother, and he said, 'I thirst' and 'It is finished.' But nowhere, not once did he say, 'Thy will be done' because he had already totally accepted the Father's will during that terrible struggle of the isolation and the loneliness. And the only way that we know that it was so difficult for him at that hour is that he asked, 'Why could you not spend one hour with me?'—we know he needed consolation. This is total surrender: not to be loved by anybody, not to be wanted by anybody, just to be a nobody because we have given all to Christ.

Mother Teresa, *Jesus, the Word to be Spoken*, compiled by Brother Angelo Devananda, William Collins Sons & Co., 1990, page 24

'Not to do Mine own will, but the will of Him who sent me.' Only let a man—whatsoever his work may be—renew each day that purpose in his heart, and seek God's grace to keep it, and then, be sure of it, two things will come about. First, that for him even the most ordinary tasks, the mere routine of life, will be ennobled; the very drudgery will shine with some reflection of the obedience of heaven; it will seem like those most attractive of all faces, in which there may be no natural beauty, in the usual sense of the word, which may be even plain, but in which there certainly is a supernatural charm of moral beauty that we may learn a little to understand as life goes on. And secondly, in that routine he will be bringing his inner life into a habit of attention and allegiance to the voice of duty; by constant drilling and discipline he will be training his heart almost to take it for granted that at all times duty is the one thing to be thought about, and that whatever clashes with duty must give way; and so, whenever the time comes, he will be ready.

Francis Paget, *The Spirit of Discipline*, Longmans, Green, and Co., 1891, page 125

St Paul did not want to be an apostle to the Gentiles. He wanted to be a clever and appreciated young Jewish scholar, and kicked against the pricks. St Ambrose and St Augustine did not want to be overworked and worried bishops. Nothing was farther from their intention. St Cuthbert wanted the solitude and freedom of his hermitage on the Farne; but he did not often get there. St Francis Xavier's preference was for an ordered life close to his beloved master, St Ignatius. At a few hours' notice he was sent out to be the Apostle of the Indies and never returned to Europe again. Henry Martyn, the fragile and exquisite scholar, was compelled to sacrifice the intellectual life to which he was so perfectly fitted for the missionary life to which he felt he was decisively called. In all these, a power beyond themselves decided the direction of life. Yet in all we recognise not frustration, but the highest of all types of achievement. Things like this—and they are constantly happening—gradually convince us that the over-ruling reality of life is the Will and Choice of a Spirit acting not in a mechanical but in a living and personal way; and that the spiritual life of man does not consist in mere individual betterment, or assiduous attention to his own soul, but in a free and unconditional response to that Spirit's pressure and call, whatever the cost may be.

Evelyn Underhill, *The Spiritual Life*, Harper & Row, 1936, page 33

WISDOM

*Wisdom—being wise, (possession of) experience and knowledge
together with the power of applying them critically or practically,
sagacity, prudence, common sense*

In introducing 'wisdom' I want to go back to the Genesis story of the creation of man
and the divine inbreathing. I wonder if a seed or spark of wisdom was implanted in the
depths of our being at the birth of mankind? If we want to see this worked out in a life, we
go to the life of our Lord, as revealed in the Gospels. Here we notice those who heard him
were astonished, saying, 'Where did this man get all this? What is the wisdom given to
him?' Perhaps he found wisdom in the depths of himself, and drew on this source in the
wilderness and nights spent in prayer. Certainly when difficult decisions were to be made
we read of him: 'And in the morning, a great while before day, he rose and went out to a
lonely place, and there he prayed.'

The sacrament of baptism is about cleansing and spiritual rebirth. In this sacrament
(and confirmation) a seed or spark of wisdom is brought to life. The teaching of the
Church is that we increase daily in wisdom—through prayer and sacrament. In *Spiritual
Reformers in the 16th and 17th Centuries* Rufus Jones writes: 'By "a new nativity,"
initiated by obedient response to the inward Light... of God the indwelling Spirit—he
may put on the new man, created after the likeness of God, and become the recipient of
heavenly Wisdom springing up within him from the Life of the Spirit.'

This is the ultimate source of wisdom. *Visions of Glory* is a repository of wisdom and
provides a means of furthering 'the daily increase'.

My mouth shall speak wisdom; the meditation of my heart shall be understanding.

Psalm 49:3

The Lord by wisdom founded the earth.

Proverbs 3:19

And on the sabbath he began to teach in the synagogue; and many who heard him were
astonished, saying, 'Where did this man get all this? What is the wisdom given to him?

Mark 6:2

But the wisdom from above is first pure, then peaceable, gentle, open to reason, full of
mercy and good fruits, without uncertainty or insincerity.

James 3:17

God waits for man to regain his childhood in wisdom.

Rabindranath Tagore, 'Stray Birds', ccxciv, in *Collected Poems and Plays of Rabindranath Tagore*,
Macmillan and Co., 1936, page 325

There is a deep wisdom inaccessible to the wise and prudent but disclosed to babes.

Christopher Bryant, S.S.J.E., *The Heart in Pilgrimage*, Darton, Longman & Todd, 1980, page 98

'You have the wisdom of Love... and it was the highest wisdom ever known upon this
earth, remember.'

Charles Dickens, *The Mystery of Edwin Drood*, J.M. Ouseley & Son, 1914, page 113

Wisdom lies more in—affection and sincerity—than people are apt to imagine.

George Eliot, *Middlemarch*, J.M. Dent & Sons, 1959, volume 2, page 77

Common sense mellowed and experienced is wisdom; and wisdom in its ripeness is beauty.

A.R. Orage, *On Love*, The Janus Press, 1957, page 60

With these celestial wisdom calms the mind,
And makes the happiness she does not find.

Samuel Johnson, 'The Vanity of Human Wishes', line 367, in *The Yale Edition of the Works of Samuel Johnson*, Yale University Press, 1964, volume 6, *Poems*, page 109

Accumulated knowledge does not make a wise man. Knowledgeable people are found everywhere, but we are cruelly short of wise people.

Michel Quoist, *With Open Heart*, translated by Colette Copeland, Gill and Macmillan, 1983, page 50

Wisdom requires no form; her beauty must vary, as varies the beauty of flame. She is no motionless goddess, for ever couched on her throne.

Maurice Maeterlinck, *Wisdom and Destiny*, translated by A. Sutro, George Allen, 1898, page 69

Wisdom is the knowledge of truth in its inmost reality, expression of truth, arrived at through the rectitudes of our own soul. Wisdom knows God in ourselves and ourselves in God.

Thomas Merton, *Thoughts in Solitude*, Burns & Oates, 1958, page 64

The clouds may drop down titles and estates;
Wealth may seek us; but Wisdom must be sought;
Sought before all; but (how unlike all else
We seek on earth!) 'tis never sought in vain.

Edward Young, *Night Thoughts*, viii. 620, in *The Complete Works of Edward Young*, William Tegg and Co., 1854, volume 1, page 166

It is part of the Christian spiritual tradition that God dwells in the centre of every man, an unseen, largely unknown Strength and Wisdom, moving him to be human, to grow and to expand his humanity to the utmost of its capacity.

Christopher Bryant, S.S.J.E., *The Heart in Pilgrimage*, Darton, Longman & Todd, 1980, page 6

As people come into subjection to the Spirit of God and grow up in the Image and Power of the Almighty, they may receive the *Word of Wisdom that opens all things, and come to know the hidden Unity in the Eternal Being.*

Rufus M. Jones, *Spiritual Reformers in the 16th and 17th Centuries*, Macmillan and Co., 1914, page 224

But the wisdom that is human, that feeds constantly on the desires, the feelings, the hopes and the fears of man, must needs have love ever by its side; and these two, marching together, must inevitably find themselves, sooner or later, on the ways that lead to goodness.

Maurice Maeterlinck, *Wisdom and Destiny*, translated by A. Sutro, George Allen, 1898, page xii

Aristotle defined *sophia*, wisdom, as knowledge of the most precious things. Cicero defined it as knowledge of things both human and divine. *Sophia* was a thing of the searching intellect, of the questing mind, of the reaches of the thoughts of men. *Sophia* is the answer to the eternal problems of life and death, and God and man, and time and eternity.

William Barclay, *The Epistles to the Galatians and Ephesians*, The Saint Andrew Press, 1958, page 95

Wisdom is not cheaply won. It is achieved through hard sacrifice and discipline, through the endurance of conflict and pain. It is the perfection of human living, the ceaseless straining of the human soul to pierce through the crushing body, the distracting intellect, the selfish will, and to apprehend the unsheathed spirit. It is intent living, the most fruitful act of man by which he tries to reach reality behind the restless stream of nature and his own feelings and desires. The destiny of the human soul is to realize its oneness with the supreme.

Sir Sarvepalli Radhakrishnan, *Eastern Religions and Western Thought*, Oxford University Press, 1940, page 96

The Wisdom which is incarnate in Jesus of Nazareth is not a different wisdom from that which underlies the laws of nature and the laws of human nature and the events of history. If we tried to learn only from some supernatural wisdom which was not available in the world of history and nature and other people, then it would not be the Wisdom to which we sing in Advent that would be teaching us. The Wisdom to which we sing reaches mightily from one end of the earth to the other, and the more we enlarge our sympathies to reach out like Wisdom—the more likely our chance of hearing the echoes of its voice and learning from it.

Geoffrey Preston, O.P., *Hallowing the Time*, Darton, Longman & Todd, 1980, page 19

By humanity we search into the powers and faculties of the Soul, enquire into the excellencies of human nature, consider its wants, survey its inclinations, propensities and desires, ponder its principles, proposals, and ends, examine the causes and fitness of all, the worth of all, the excellency of all. Whereby we come to know what man is in this world, what his sovereign end and happiness, and what is the best means by which he may attain it. And by this we come to see what wisdom is: which namely is a knowledge exercised in finding out the way to perfect happiness, by discerning man's real wants and sovereign desires. We come moreover to know God's goodness, in seeing into the causes wherefore He implanted such faculties and inclinations in us, and the objects and ends prepared for them. This leadeth us to Divinity. For God gave man an endless intellect, to see all things, and a proneness to covet them, because they are His treasures; and an infinite variety of apprehensions and affections, that he might have an all-sufficiency in himself to enjoy them; a curiosity profound and unsatiable to stir him up to look into them: an ambition great and everlasting to carry him to the highest honors, thrones, and dignities: an emulation whereby he might be animated and quickened by all examples, a tenderness and compassion whereby he may be united to all persons, a sympathy and love to virtue; a tenderness of his credit in every soul, that he might delight to be honoured in all persons; an eye to behold Eternity and the Omnipresence of God, that he might see Eternity, and dwell within it; a power of admiring, loving, and prizing, that seeing the beauty and goodness of God, he might be united to it for evermore.

Thomas Traherne, *Centuries*, The Faith Press, 1969, page 132

Let us see what the wisdom of God will do.

'Expect neither truth,' she says, 'nor consolation from men. I am she who formed you, and who alone can teach you what you are. But you are now no longer in the state in which I formed you. I created man holy, innocent, perfect. I filled him with light and intelligence. I communicated to him my glory and my wonders. The eye of man saw then the majesty of God. He was not then in the darkness which blinds him, nor subject to mortality and the woes which afflict him. But he has not been able to sustain so great glory without falling into pride. He wanted to make himself his own centre, and independent of my help. He withdrew himself from my rule; and, on his making himself equal to me by the desire of finding his happiness in himself, I abandoned him to himself. And setting in revolt the creatures that were subject to him, I made them his enemies; so that man is now become like the brutes, and so estranged from me that there scarce remains to him a dim vision of his Author. So far has all his knowledge been extinguished or disturbed! The senses, independent of reason, and often the masters of reason, have led him into pursuit of pleasure. All creatures either torment or tempt him, and domineer over him, either subduing him by their strength, or fascinating him by their charms, a tyranny more awful and more imperious.

'Such is the state in which men now are. There remains to them some feeble instinct of the happiness of their former state; and they are plunged in the evils of their blindness and their lust, which have become their second nature.

'From this principle which I disclose to you, you can recognise the cause of those contradictions which have astonished all men, and have divided them into parties holding so different views. Observe, now, all the feelings of greatness and glory which the experience of so many woes cannot stifle, and you see if the cause of them must not be in another nature.'

Blaise Pascal, *Pensées*, translated by W.F. Trotter, Random House, 1941, page 137

WORSHIP

Worship—reverent homage or service paid to God; acts, rites or ceremonies of honour and respect, adoration and devotion

One of my heroes is Archbishop Anthony Bloom. In the last twenty years I have been fortunate in being taught by him on a number of occasions. In his book *Living Prayer* he comes out with a crucial truth about institutional worship. He points out: 'One of the reasons why communal worship or private prayer seem to be so dead or so conventional, is that the act of worship, which takes place in the heart communing with God, is too often missing. Every expression, either verbal or in action, may help, but they are only expressions of what is essential, namely, a deep silence of communion... if we want to worship God, we must first of all learn to feel happy, being silent together with him.'

This is why I have spent the last few years compiling *Visions of Faith, Hope, Love* and *Glory*, and in developing the simple practice of reflection. In public worship, the emphasis is on God 'out there'—in the church building, on the altar, in a Bible on the lectern. In reflection the emphasis is on 'God within'—in the depths of our being, enabling that 'deep silence of communion' to take place, and providing a way in which we can 'learn to feel happy, being silent together with him'. Once direct contact is made with God, public worship naturally follows. Private devotion and public worship should complement and nurture each other. To the question—why worship?—Peter Shaffer responds: 'Without worship, you shrink; it's as brutal as that.'

... you shall worship no other God.
Exodus 34:14

O come, let us worship and bow down, let us kneel before the Lord, our Maker! For he is our God.

Psalm 95:6–7

You shall worship the Lord your God and him only shall you serve.
Matthew 4:10

The hour is coming, and now is, when the true worshippers will worship the Father in spirit and truth, for such the Father seeks to worship him. God is spirit, and those who worship him must worship in spirit and truth.

John 4:23–24

Without worship you shrink; it's as brutal as that...

Peter Shaffer, *Equus*, II. xxv, Longman, 1983, page 67

... my hope has been nourished in the warmth of liturgical gatherings.

Carlo Carretto, *The Desert in the City*, translated by Barbara Wall, William Collins Sons & Co., 1983, page 86

But the purpose of all worship is the same: to offer praise to God for his grace and glory.

Alan Richardson, in Alan Richardson and John Bowden, editors, *A New Dictionary of Christian Theology*, SCM Press, 1985, page 605

... worship is a communing, the opening of human life to God, the response to grace, the growing up into union with God, who has made us for himself.

John Macquarrie, *Paths in Spirituality*, SCM Press, 1972, page 21

... a spiritual discipline must be freely accepted and embraced if it is to be fully effective... worship must be a free response of love rather than a homage exacted.

John Macquarrie, *Paths in Spirituality*, SCM Press, 1972, page 20

Unless the members of a group are finding some encounter of their own with the Other, their act of joining together for religious services usually becomes one more meaningless activity, merely the ritual indulgence of a nice habit.

Morton T. Kelsey, *The Other Side of Silence*, SPCK, 1977, page 93

This alone is true worship—the giving to God of body, soul and spirit ('ourselves, our souls and bodies') with all that they need for their full development, so that He may take and use them for His purpose.

William Temple, *Citizen and Churchman*, Eyre & Spottiswoode, 1941, page 43

A man's life is great in proportion as his mind dwells on things precious for their own sake and not as means to ends. There is no end to be obtained by worship and love. But alas! how much of every day is taken up in labouring at something which is to bring something else! This something else is generally of no value.

Mark Rutherford, *Last Pages From a Journal*, Oxford University Press, 1915, page 297

Worship at its best is a social experience with people of all levels of life coming together to realize their oneness and unity under God. Whenever the church, consciously or unconsciously, caters to one class it loses the spiritual force of the 'whosoever will, let him come' doctrine and is in danger of becoming little more than a social club with a thin veneer of religiosity.

Martin Luther King, *The Words of Martin Luther King*, selected by Coretta Scott King, William Collins Sons & Co., 1986, page 65

The word 'worship' is an Anglo-Saxon word and means 'worthship' or 'worthiness'. The word commonly translated 'worship' in the New Testament—though there are several other Greek words—is *proskuneo*, to 'kiss the hand towards'. This is thought to be derived from the slave's manner of salutation and homage when he entered the presence of his master, the act being a mark of reverence and respect, and also implying affection. Hence, in ascriptions of worship, we have the expression, 'Thou art worthy.'

Anon.

The true worship, the really spiritual worship, is the offering of one's body, and all that one does every day with it, to God. Real worship is not the offering of elaborate prayers to God; it is not the offering to God of a liturgy, however noble, and a ritual, however magnificent. *Real worship is the offering of everyday life to God.* Real worship is not something which is transacted in a church; real worship is something which sees the whole world as the temple of the living God, and every common deed an act of worship.

William Barclay, The Letter to the Romans, The Saint Andrew Press, 1969, page 169

Abide in me, and I in you. The whole phrase has an imperative tone: let there be mutual indwelling. *Abide in me*, of which the consequence will be that I shall abide in you...
    All forms of Christian worship, all forms of Christian discipline, have this as their object. Whatever leads to this is good; whatever hinders this is bad; whatever does not bear on this is futile. This is the life of the Christian: *Abide in me and I in you.* All truth and depth of devotion, all effectiveness in service spring from this. It is not a theme for words but for the deeper apprehensions of silence.

William Temple, Readings in St. John's Gospel, First and Second Series, Macmillan and Co., 1947, page 258

Worship is not getting information about God; though learning from those who know more about Him than we do may help us to worship better. It is not telling Him our sins and asking for forgiveness—though once the human creature begins to grasp what worship is, it is driven to confess its rebellions, imperfections, and nothingness, and ask for that restoring energy we call grace. Nor is it recommending to His notice the persons and causes which happen to interest us. Exhortation, confession, intercession, all have their place in man's religious life; but they are something less than worship. Worship is the little human spirit's humble adoring acknowledgements of the measureless glory of God.

Evelyn Underhill, in John Stobbart, editor, The Wisdom of Evelyn Underhill, A.R. Mowbray & Co., 1951, page 26

... worship can be a continuously creative thing. It means coming from the world, from the squalor, the hunger, the misery, the heartbreak, for the act of acknowledging again the love and kingship of God. It means ascending the hill of the Lord to receive again His pardon, to receive again the bread and wine of life, to offer obedience again and find the strength for it, to bring all that has been learned and suffered at the crossroads of life to God for His dealing. But it does not mean a permanent lodging in the cathedrals and churches where worship in community is offered. It means going back from the hour of worship to the arena of the world's life and the place of man's need, only to discover that God to whom the worship was offered is the contemporary friend and partner to farmer and healer, teacher and preacher and all others who for the love of God and man seek to meet man's need.

Leonard Hurst, Hungry Men, The Livingstone Press, 1955, page 107

The worship of God is itself the inner core of Christian spirituality: the heart, the mind, and the will, directed towards the glory of God as man's goal. Every time that a Christian lifts up his soul to God in desire towards him he is, however faintly, realising that fellowship with the Creator for which he was created, and he is, in a tiny and yet significant way, anticipating the goal of heaven. Thus regarded, spirituality is no escape from the world. It is lived out in all the complexities of our social life, in family, city, country, industry, culture, joy, sorrow, for it is the spirituality of a man, and a man is involved in all these things. It is inseparable from service, love, duty, the moulding of the common life. Yet in deep-down essence it is the spirit of worship.

Allow me to quote some words of a former Archbishop of Canterbury, William Temple. He said, 'The proper relation between prayer and conduct is not that conduct is supremely important and prayer may help it, but that prayer is supremely important, and conduct tests it.'

Michael Ramsey, *Through the Year with Michael Ramsey*, edited by Margaret Duggan, Hodder and Stoughton, 1975, page 75

Churches, liturgies and private devotional habits spring probably and have their use from the soul's curious trick of playing truant. If we have a soul at all, it is fairly certain that we have it not always: it flits away sometimes, or shrinks down within us, exactly as the mind does; and as there are absent-minded moments, so there are men and moments absent-souled. The mind may be very active, working at full power, but we know that we are dead at this time: there is no movement where the soul once beat with its wings—bare ruined choirs where erst the sweet birds sang: something is certainly changed in us; we are lessened, lonely. I do not find that the soul in going or coming plays with the mind at all; sometimes when the brain is quickest, eagerest, there is most lift and radiance of the soul, the deep, warm sense of things above the mind; sometimes when the brain is sunk to a dull puddle, the man is comforted with the sun and knows that somewhere, in some way, in some shape or kind 'his Redeemer liveth,' and in his flesh he knows the eternal things. The spirit bloweth where it listeth and we can only wait and hope. But it is well to have one's litany or liturgy for a safeguard in the dull times: the soul—if it be, or as it must be if it is the best and highest in oneself—will come back the sooner if the place be swept and garnished and the arm-chair set for it pleasantly by the fire: the exercises which seem quite foolish when the soul is there become the only saving when the place is empty and cold: they invite or compel the return—and, as we can never foreknow the truancy of the soul, the disciplines are to be done always.

Stephen MacKenna, *Journal and Letters*, Constable & Co., 1936, page 123

Index

A

Abbott, Eric Symes 39, 103, 235
Amiel, Henri Frédéric 61, 136, 137, 168, 178, 250
Andrew, Father 44, 52, 57, 65, 77, 117, 132, 148, 149, 161, 166, 170, 173, 183, 185, 202, 209, 210, 231, 233, 242, 245, 258, 269
Andrews, C.F. 216
Anker-Larsen, Johannes 73
Appleton, George 148
Armstrong, John 250
Arndt, Johann 130
Arnold, Matthew 20, 137
Auden, W.H. 196, 242, 287
Augustine of Hippo 64, 93

B

Baillie, Joanna 156
Baillie, John 27
Ballantrae, Lord 107
Barclay, William 20, 23, 26, 49, 52, 56, 64, 68, 73, 75, 77, 91, 100, 102, 110, 111, 114, 118, 125, 144, 149, 157, 164, 169, 178, 184, 186, 191, 194, 197, 199, 223, 227, 232, 234, 246, 258, 265, 276, 282, 290, 294, 298
Barry, F.R. 19, 26, 38, 168
Barton, John 30, 31
Beecher, Henry Ward 26, 29, 34, 37, 60, 72, 75, 79, 101, 105, 109, 113, 122, 125, 137, 144, 148, 167, 168, 183, 194, 201, 205, 215, 246, 249, 264, 271, 276, 278, 283
Beeson, Trevor 152
Benson, A.C. 56, 57, 87, 110, 113, 137, 287
Benson, Robert 141
Bernhardt, Sarah 160
Betti, Ugo 133, 249
Blake, William 26, 94, 186
Blanton, Smiley 98
Bloom, Anthony 64, 109, 148, 152, 175, 200, 227, 274, 291

Bonhoeffer, Dietrich 85, 106, 107, 111, 252
Boreham, F.W. 201
Bowden, John 287
Brabant, Frank Herbert 73
Bragdon, Claude 194
Bridges, Robert 126, 144, 169
Brontë, Charlotte 106
Brooks, Phillips 86, 99, 222
Brown, David 35
Brown, Raymond E. 145
Brown, T.E. 138
Browne, R.E.C. 48, 276
Browne, Sir Thomas 118, 123, 131, 149
Browning, Robert 26, 41, 55, 64, 275
Bryant, Christopher 137, 206, 262, 293, 294
Buechner, Frederick 162
Bunyan, John 287
Burnaby, John 114
Burns, Robert 99, 258
Butterfield, Herbert 114

C

Cabasilas, Nicholas 22
Camus, Albert 148
Cargas, Harry James 53, 58, 132, 158, 203, 266
Carlyle, Thomas 144
Carpenter, Bishop Boyd 146
Carrel, Alexis 159
Carretto, Carlo 26, 85, 152, 197, 198, 225, 269, 297
Casteel, John L. 242
Caussade, Jean-Pierre de 85, 110, 127, 201
Cervantes 276
Challoner, Richard 172
Chambers, Arthur 192
Channing, William Ellery 247
Chapman, Rex 65
Chardin, Pierre Teilhard de 57, 134, 181, 194, 254

Chaucer, Geoffrey 274
Chesterton, G.K. 64, 179, 206, 261
Childress, James F. 130, 222
Clements, Keith 84
Cloud of Unknowing, The 80, 205
Clutton-Brock, A. 276
Coleridge, Samuel Taylor 30, 60, 72
Collis, John Stewart 165
Colton, Charles Caleb 65, 161, 205, 222
Conn, Walter E. 45
Cowper, William 19, 274
Cox, Harvey 242
Cupitt, Don 234

D

Dale, R.W. 89, 177, 213
D'Arcy, Charles F. 153
Darwin, Charles 48
Davies, W. Merlin 277
Dickens, Charles 293
Dickinson, Emily 56
Dillistone, F.W. 213
Dixon, W. Macneile 81, 160, 177
Dodd, C.H. 197
Dostoyevsky, Fyodor 27, 30, 123, 150, 191, 198
Douglas, Norman 40, 48, 95, 125, 137, 275
Dryden, John 250
Dunne, John S. 56, 67, 105, 160, 246, 268, 290, 291

E

Ecclestone, Alan 241
Eckhart, Meister 249
Einstein, Albert 275
Eliade, Mircea 230
Eliot, George 130, 252, 293, 294
Elizabeth of the Trinity 24, 130, 139
Ellis, Havelock 178, 287
Emerson, Ralph Waldo 60, 67, 161, 163, 168, 169, 251, 273

F

Fairbairn, A.M. 16
Faith in the City 39
Farmer, H.H. 84
Farrar, F.W. 259
Farrar, Austin 24, 49, 169, 225, 229
Ferre, Nels F.S. 157
Ford, Clay 43
Forster, E.M. 161
Forsyth, P.T. 183
Fosdick, Harry Emerson 16, 160, 187, 216, 254, 269
Fox, George 259, 284
Francis de Sales 172, 198, 238
Fromm, Erich 56
Froude, James A. 248
Fuller, Thomas 25, 182, 258
Furlong, Monica 39, 64
Fynn 271
Fénelon, François de la M. 68, 202, 230

G

Galbraith, J.K. 30
Gandhi, Mohandas K. 215, 216
Garvie, Alfred E. 176
Gibbard, Mark 271
Gibran, Kahlil 58, 194, 218
Gide, André 64, 178
Gill, Eric 206
Goethe, Johann Wolfgang von 30, 79, 125, 138, 156, 275
Goldsmith, Joel S. 99
Goodacre, Norman 234
Goodall, Norman 38, 56, 125
Goodman, Paul 98
Gore, Charles 289
Gossip, A.J. 99, 261
Greene, Graham 222
Greeves, Frederic 16
Gregory of Nazianzus 269
Gregory of Nyssa 134, 199
Griffiths, Bede 91
Guyon, Madame 172

H

Hammarskjöld, Dag 78, 243
Happold, F.C. 106, 179, 188
Harcourt, Giles 83, 210

Harcourt, Melville 83
Hare, Augustus William 269
Haughton, Rosemary 231, 272, 283
Heard, Gerald 234
Helme, Elizabeth 261
Herbert, George 183, 191, 198, 261
Hesse, Hermann 100
Hick, John 39, 68, 192
Hillesum, Etty 76, 99
Hobhouse, Professor 139
Hoffer, Eric 242
Holland, Henry Scott 57
Hollings, Michael 142
Hopkins, Gerard Manley 105, 229
Howe, Reuel L. 275
Hume, Basil 113, 130, 184
Hurst, Leonard 298
Huxley, Aldous 122
Hügel, Baron Friedrich von 161

I

Inge, W.R. 203
Irenaeus 102
Israel, Martin 127, 128

J

Jackman, Stuart B. 194
Jacks, L.P. 80
James, William 44, 99, 197, 202, 209, 258
Jefferies, Richard 249, 251
Jenkins, Daniel 37
Jeremias, Joachim 109
John of the Cross 249
Johnson, F. Ernest 59
Johnson, Samuel 163, 294
Johnston, William 79, 83, 178, 264
Jones, E. Stanley 27, 33, 41, 152
Jones, Rufus M. 23, 31, 34, 35, 38, 46, 48, 51, 61, 69, 72, 73, 77, 79, 81, 85, 90, 91, 105, 106, 109, 110, 112, 114, 115, 119, 122, 125, 126, 127, 130, 131, 137, 138, 139, 146, 152, 157, 161, 164, 165, 169, 170, 172, 179, 180, 194, 195, 216, 217, 226, 231, 232, 234, 243, 246, 250, 275, 277, 291, 294
Julian of Norwich 48, 137, 230, 258, 278
Jung, C.G. 15, 23, 34, 44, 79, 80, 81, 130, 144, 176, 216, 234, 249

K

Kant, Immanuel 16
Kazantzakis, Nikos 170
Keats, John 41, 61, 238
Keller, Helen 80
Kelsey, Morton T. 99, 172, 173, 297
Kempis, Thomas à 67, 144, 258
Kennedy, G.A. Studdert 258
Kennedy, Gerald 230
Kierkegaard, Søren 68, 288
King, Edward 262
King, Martin Luther 76, 95, 211, 217, 239, 246, 252, 297
Kingsley, Charles 52, 67, 73, 75, 91, 111, 118, 122, 126, 130, 145, 156, 157, 164, 165, 169, 184, 212, 239, 268, 271, 272
Kroll, Una 51
Kushner, Rabbi H. 253
Küng, Hans 34, 38, 41, 42, 45, 46, 52, 84, 106, 118, 153, 169, 184, 187, 238, 253, 264, 265, 291

L

Lampe, G.W.H. 241
Lash, Symeon 61
Law, William 24, 51, 68, 123, 149, 195, 205, 212, 213, 220, 222, 236, 246, 262, 268, 279
Lawrence, Brother 26, 109, 182, 184, 201, 203
Lawrence, D.H. 67, 98, 100, 106, 131, 160, 239, 275
Leech, Kenneth 134, 264, 265
Leo, St 134
Lerner, Max 61
Leseur, Elizabeth 160
LeShan, Lawrence 172
Levi, Carlo 60
Lewis, C.S. 19, 42, 95, 123, 133, 175, 176
Lindbergh, Anne Morrow 98
Lockhart, J.G. 285
Longfellow, Henry Wadsworth 163
Lossky, Vladimir 22, 265

M

MacDonald, George 19
MacDonald, Murdo Ewen 19
McGinley, Phyllis 242
McKeating, Henry 34, 84, 234

MacKenna, Stephen 181, 251, 299
MacLean, Alistair 183, 275
Macleod, G.F. 243
Macquarrie, John 42, 84, 87, 102, 106, 110, 265, 297
Madeleine, Sister 183
Maeterlinck, Maurice 294
Main, John 173
Manners, Elizabeth 76
Manning, Cardinal 205
Marmion, D. Columba 23, 102, 134
Martin, W.B.J. 84, 243
Martineau, James 92
Matheson, George 93
Maurice, F.D. 123
May, Rollo 99, 110, 216
May, William F. 239
Medley, William 89
Melville, Herman 19, 71, 274
Merton, Thomas 30, 38, 41, 98, 104, 134, 173, 179, 191, 197, 235, 242, 246, 253, 262, 266, 268, 272, 279, 284, 287, 294
Millay, Edna St Vincent 20
Miller, Henry 249
Miller, Samuel H. 84
Milton, John 95, 109, 113, 118, 122, 156, 163, 164, 183, 276
Moltmann, Jürgen 226
Montefiore, Hugh 53, 77, 120, 195
Moore, George 19
Morris, Colin 38, 48, 151
Moss, C.B. 134
Moule, Handley C.G. 145
Muggeridge, Malcolm 28
Muller, F. Max 107, 187
Mumford, Lewis 76, 98, 119, 176, 178

N

Neil, Stephen 229
Newbigin, Lesslie 83
Newman, John Henry 16, 35, 217, 240
Nouwen, Henri J.M. 34, 102, 225, 284, 286

O

O'Donovan, Oliver 209
Oestreicher, Paul 37, 183
Oldham, J.H. 26, 28, 38

Oman, John 219
Orage, A.R. 63, 98, 156, 205, 211, 245, 294
Origen 103
Osborne, John 109

P

Paget, Francis 292
Panikkar, Raimundo 186
Pascal, Blaise 102, 109, 225, 295
Penn, William 71, 186, 207
Pittenger, Norman 86, 91, 106
Plotinus 60
Potter, Dennis 105
Powys, John Cowper 194, 277
Preston, Geoffrey 295
Preston, Ronald 283
Priestland, Gerald 20, 38
Priestley, J.B. 191
Pulsford, John 130, 139

Q

Quick, Oliver 195
Quoist, Michel 34, 43, 92, 118, 134, 138, 156, 168, 207, 211, 239, 283, 294

R

Radhakrishnan, Sir Sarvepalli 65, 152, 156, 180, 217, 239, 295
Rahner, Hugo 106
Rahner, Karl 31, 106
Raine, Kathleen 156
Rambo, Lewis R. 223
Ramsey, Michael 50, 88, 95, 103, 119, 141, 180, 191, 209, 225, 226, 253, 261, 264, 266, 298
Rashdall, Hastings 135
Redwood, Hugh 26, 175
Reeves, Donald 265
Renault, Mary 148
Rhoades, James 241
Rhymes, Douglas 145
Richardson, Alan 138, 297
Robertson, F.W. 144
Robinson, John 15, 141, 198
Rolland, Romain 168
Romanes, Professor 16
Root, H.E. 38
Rosa, Peter de 175

Rose, Pauline 194
Rupp, E.G. 238
Ruskin, John 21, 118
Russell, Bertrand 102
Rutherford, Mark 26, 34, 48, 76, 90, 102, 156, 222, 229, 276, 283, 297

S

Saavedra, Miguel de Cervantes 276
Sanford, Agnes 64
Sangster, W.E. 17, 20, 21, 27, 81, 87, 88, 102, 113, 184, 187, 201, 238, 261, 271, 275, 279, 287
Santayana, George 84
Schmidt, William 79
Schutz, Roger 39
Schweitzer, Albert 145, 212, 275
Scott, Sir Walter 102
Scougal, Henry 219
Seaver, George 84
Selden, John 29
Shaffer, Peter 297
Shakespeare, William 64, 75, 76, 79, 184, 197, 205, 222
Shaw, George Bernard 19, 176
Shelley, Percy Bysshe 72, 122, 168, 172
Sheppard, David 26, 208
Sheppard, H.R.L. 44
Simcox, Carroll E. 126
Singh, Sadhu Sundar 120, 240
Slater, Graham 80
Smail, Thomas A. 23, 88, 103, 152
Smiles, Samuel 195
Smith, John 62, 279
Smith, Logan Pearsall 283
Stanley, H.M. 216
Steuart, R.H.J. 157
Stevenson, Robert Louis 87
Stoppard, Tom 19
Stravinsky, Igor 48
Suenens, Leon Joseph, Cardinal 37
Swedenborg, Emanuel 215

T

'T Hooft, W.A. Visser 37
Tagore, Rabindranath 42, 56, 71, 98, 113, 193, 219, 230, 238, 249, 271, 293
Taylor, John V. 20, 41, 103, 114, 141, 179, 253

Temple, William 41, 88, 110, 114, 144, 148, 149, 186, 199, 205, 229, 230, 238, 297, 298
Tennyson, Alfred, Lord 60, 67, 90, 163, 205
Teresa of Avila 291
Teresa of Calcutta, Mother 65, 188, 198, 201, 205, 272, 279, 283, 290, 292
Tersteegen, Gerhard 35, 45, 114, 138, 179, 202, 250
Theologia Germanica 76, 219
Thielicke, Helmut 25, 51, 79, 96, 118, 176
Thomas, J. Heywood 66
Thornton, L.S. 268
Thornton, Martin 265
Tillich, Paul 30, 38, 64, 110, 264, 277
Tissot, Joseph 103
Tizard, Leslie J. 272
Tolstoy, Leo 72, 77, 186, 247
Tournier, Paul 42, 222
Traherne, Thomas 72, 129, 164, 295
Trench, Richard Chenevix 202

U

Unamuno, Miguel de 64

Underhill, Evelyn 46, 82, 84, 127, 137, 145, 166, 179, 198, 199, 212, 280, 291, 292, 298

V

van der Post, Laurens 95
van Zeller, Hubert 119
Vanier, Jean 57, 96, 115, 131, 146, 165, 199, 240, 272, 273
Vann, Gerald 45
Vatican Council II 16, 187
Vincent, John J. 183
Voillaume, René 92

W

Walton, Izaak 34
Ward, J. Neville 55, 56, 88, 95, 96, 115, 215, 222, 229, 242, 253, 261, 275, 291
Weatherhead, Leslie 80, 175
Webb, C.C.J. 126
Weil, Simone 19, 186
Weizsacker, Carl Friedrich von 265
Wells, H.G. 52, 144
West, Morris 91, 148
Whichcote, Benjamin 75, 102, 134, 148, 205, 215, 242

White, Patrick 279
Whitehead, Alfred North 193, 215
Whiting, Lilian 127, 153
Whitman, Walt 175
Whittier, John Greenleaf 271
Wilde, Oscar 117, 250
Wilder, Thornton 72
Williams, Charles 152
Williams, Daniel D. 110
Williams, H.A. 64, 69, 107, 212, 223, 231, 264
Williams, Rowan 61
Wilson, Edward 84, 107
Winter, David 118
Winter, Gibson 95
Wollstonecraft, Mary 76
Wordsworth, William 49, 160, 168, 209
Wright, Frank 29, 233
Wyon, Olive 30, 32, 161, 174, 206, 224, 244, 259, 262, 279, 288

Y

Yarnold, E.J. 110
Yeats, W.B. 25
Young, Edward 79, 198, 294